What People Are Sa[illegible]
Astrology in the Era of Uncertainty

Joe Landwehr is one of those rare individuals who, working independently and largely against the spirit of the times, has dedicated his life to the advancement of a field of study. *Astrology in the Era of Uncertainty* is a book of considerable breadth and careful reflection, illuminating astrology's theoretical premises and purposes in relation to science, and demonstrating the author's rich mythopoetic approach to astrological practice. What emerges from his work is a sense of intuitive wisdom, shaped by his own life experience and informed by a nuanced imaginative and intellectual engagement with the archetypal energies of the universe. – **Keiron Le Grice**, professor of depth psychology at Pacifica Graduate Institute, author of *The Archetypal Cosmos* and co-editor of *Jung on Astrology*.

Landwehr's *Astrology in the Era of Uncertainty* provides a thought-provoking historical narrative to the various spirits that have moved through the art of astrology through the centuries. Defining astrology as "an attempt to understand and more consciously occupy our place in a larger, living cosmos" his book aids us in the task of revivifying our sense of life embedded in conscious relationship to the *anima mundi*. – **Safron Rossi**, core faculty in the Jungian and Archetypal Studies program at Pacifica Graduate Institute, author of *The Kore Goddess* and co-editor of *Jung on Astrology*

Erudite, poetic and revelatory, *Astrology in the Era of Uncertainty* offers a rich and detailed map to help us navigate an ever-more confusing and challenging world. In a book which is destined to become a classic, Joe Landwehr provides a series of anchor-points for the evolution of self and psyche, and an astropoetic guidebook on the examined – and the fully lived – life. – **Sharon Blackie**, author of the best seller *If Women Rose Rooted* and *The Enchanted Life*.

Landwehr's astrological *tour de force* moves step by step from the earliest human cultures, up through ancient and classic civilizations, and into the scientific present to trace interwoven, ever-changing, and often competitive theoretical cosmological strands of "objective meaning" and the possibilities for "individual enlightenment." Meticulously researched, his triumph is bringing all of this together in his own practice with the convincing and multi-faceted argument that each human "self" is a unique dimension, not merely an observer, of the cosmos. – **Bethe Hagens**, retired faculty mentor for Goddard College; an editor for *Anthropology of Consciousness*; and a reviewer for the *Journal of Applied Hermeneutics*.

Astrology in the Era of Uncertainty provides a kaleidoscopic panorama of astrology and related fields, amplifying its relevance and indispensability for exploring the world now and in the future. In this book, author Joe Landwehr places astrological practices and our attitudes toward them into historical relief and examines other relevant psycho-spiritual traditions regarding their compatibility with an astrological worldview. The book skillfully and subtly operationalizes the Hermetic paradigm "as above, so below; as without, so within" for the reader, fulfilling Landwehr's initial promise to relate our personal truth with the cosmos. A wonderful read! – **Ken James**, Jungian analyst

Other Books by the Author

The Birth of the Shining One (1988)

The Seven Gates of Soul: Reclaiming the Poetry of Everyday Life (2004)

Tracking the Soul With an Astrology of Consciousness (2007)

Astrology and the Archetypal Power of Numbers, Part One: A Contemporary Reformulation of Pythagorean Number Theory (2011)

Astrology and the Archetypal Power of Numbers, Part Two: Arithmology in the Birthchart (2018)

The Table of Contents, Introduction and Reviews for all my previous books can be found on my website at joelandwehr.com/ancient-tower-press

Astrology in the Era of Uncertainty

An Astropoetic Exploration of Psyche and Cosmos

Joe Landwehr

Ancient Tower Press
Mountain View, Missouri

www.joelandwehr.com/ancient-tower-press

Cover Design by Anne Marie Forrester
Front Cover Image by Josef Tornick (with the aid of Midjourmey AI software)
Interior Design by Joe Landwehr
Copy-Editing by Deborah DeNicola

Publisher's Cataloging-in-Publication
(Provided by Cassidy Cataloguing Services, Inc.)

Names: Landwehr, Joe, author.

Title: Astrology in the era of uncertainty : an astropoetic exploration of psyche and cosmos / Joe Landwehr.

Description: Mountain View, Missouri : Ancient Tower Press, [2024] | Includes bibliographical references and index.

Identifiers: ISBN: 978-0-9747626-4-7 (paperback) | 978-0-9747626-5-4 (ebook) | LCCN: 2023912389

Subjects: LCSH: Astrology. | Astrology--History. | Science--History. | Civilization, Western--History. | Postmodernism. | Paradigm (Theory of knowledge) | Archetype (Psychology) | Archetypes in civilization. | Cosmology. | Astrology and psychology. | Psychology. | Spirituality. | Mysticism. | Mystagogy. | Spiritual intelligence. | Individuation (Psychology) | Identity (Philosophical concept) | Soul. | Spiritual biography. | BISAC: BODY, MIND & SPIRIT / Astrology / General. | BODY, MIND & SPIRIT / Mysticism. | HISTORY / Civilization.

Classification: LCC: BF1711 .L36 2023 | DDC: 133.5--dc23

Ancient Tower Press
210 W 1st Street #119
Mountain View, MO 65548

www.joelandwehr.com/ancient-tower-press.com

About the Author

Joe Landwehr is an astrologer of 52 years experience, seeking an eclectic integration of astrology, spiritual psychology and ancient wisdom teachings. Trained as a scientist in undergraduate school at Worcester Polytechnic Institute, Joe became increasingly disenchanted with the limitations of science, changing his major and turning to a study of philosophy, psychology, and world literature in his junior year.

After an initiatory reading in 1971 by an astrologer in Ashland, Oregon known only as Sunny Blue Boy, Joe began his own study of astrology in earnest. Moving to southern California in 1973, Joe became the resident astrologer at the Kundalini Research Institute, taught kundalini yoga and meditation in the surrounding colleges, and obtained a masters degree in Marriage, Family and Child Counseling. In graduate school, Joe encountered the same limitations of science and mathematics, in a different form as applied to the study of human psychology – and began to formulate the ideas that eventually led to the writing of this book.

Upon leaving the ashram in 1977, Joe moved to Florida, where he continued to study, write and teach. In 1978, he was introduced to the teachings of Swami Muktananda, and began to supplement his knowledge of yogic philosophy with the theory and practice of Siddha yoga – evolving a perspective that was shared in his previous book, *Tracking the Soul With an Astrology of Consciousness*.

Over the next 45 years, Joe developed an international astrology practice, combining a Rudhyarian approach to astrology with a foundation in spiritual psychology.

In 1993, Joe started an intimately personal correspondence course called The Eye of the Centaur, and for the next 8 years, worked intensively with a small number of dedicated students, willing to let the crucible of their own lives be their classroom. In 2001, Joe took a sabbatical from his course to research and write his first book. In 2005, Joe resumed teaching his correspondence course, now transformed into The Astropoetic School of Soul Discovery. Since then, the course has undergone a complete revision to incorporate new principles of astropoetics not taught elsewhere.

In 2004, Joe published *The Seven Gates of Soul: Reclaiming the Poetry of Everyday Life* – a 6,000 year history of ideas about the soul, drawn from religion, philosophy, science, psychology and an intuitive form of astrology called astropoetics. *Tracking the Soul* was the sequel to that book, published in 2007, followed by *Astrology and the Archetypal Power of Numbers , Part One* in 2011 and *Part Two* in 2018.

Additional information about astropoetics, The Astropoetic School, courses, worshops offered and the books mentioned above, as well as an archive of articles, blog posts and newsletters can be found at www.joelandwehr.com.

Acknowledgements

This book could only have been written because the cumulative collective efforts of thousands of astrologers - some known and many unknown - over the past four thousand years have contributed to a story worth telling. Before that, before astrrology had a name, there were countless others who looked up to the night sky and felt a powerful mystery to be explored and articulated. I stand on all their shoulders as I reach for the next chapter of our story in this book.

In particular, I am indebted to the scholars who have come before me, who have illuminated the history and philosophical theory of astrology from a somewhat different perspective than I am entertaining here, particularly Nicholas Campion, Chris Brennan, Geoffrey Cornelius and Rick Tarnas. I am likewise indebted to the many astrologers, past and present, who have more directly influenced me, especially Dane Rudhyar, Marc Edmund Jones, Michael Heleus, Stephen Arroyo, Donna Cunningham, Liz Greene, Karen Hamaker-Zondag, Ingrid Naiman, Steven Forest, Greg Bogart, Brad Kochunas and Rick Tarnas. There are, of course, many others outside the field of astrology, whose work has also shaped my own worldview, with special mention here going to Carl Jung, James Hillman, Thomas Moore, Joseph Campbell, Ram Dass, Carlos Castaneda, Yogi Bhajan, Swami Muktananda, Pema Chodron, Bill Plotkin, Barry Lopez and Steven Buhner.

I would like to honor an important mentor, Dick Prosapio, who passed away earlier this year. Dick believed in me at a time in my life when I did not really believe in myself, and gave me the space to discover what I was made of. For that I will be eternally grateful.

I wish to thank all those who read my manuscript, in whole or in part, and gave me their feedback, friendship, encouragement, and/or an endorsement, including Stephanie Austin, Sharon Blackie, Jennifer Browdy, Leslie Casler, Judith and Dennis Corvin-Blackburn, Sara Firman, Bethe Hagens, Jack Hebrank, Ken James, Paul Kelley, Dale Kushner, Fran Laakman, Keiron Le Grice, Lynda Leonard, John and Sandra Malluck, Anyaa McAndrew, Lin Reams, Safron Rossi, Linda Ryan and Louie Kistler, Larry Sweet, Sally Thomason, Josef and Cinta Tornick and Julie Yeaman, as well as all those who have contributed to the Go Fund Me campaign I started to underwrite the manifestation of this book - with special thanks to Jess Barreira and Irvin Torres, Patrick Curtin, Bethe Hagens, Charlene Mason, and Maryann Pehonsky.

I greatly appreciate the efforts of my editor Deborah DeNicola, who kept me from being too wordy or confusing in my wordiness. I thank Josef Tornick for a stunning cover image and Anne Marie Forrester for turning that image into another memorable cover design.

Lastly, I thank all of you, who hold this book in your hands, are willing to read it, let it enchant you, and entertain its invitation to the next step in your own astrological journey.

This book is dedicated
to all those in every walk of life
who choose not to be cynical or despairing
in the face of the world's painful unraveling
and agonizing uncertainty
but rather ask,
"How can I access what is most powerful
most beautiful, most vibrantly alive
within myself
and dedicate that
to the possibility of something
mysteriously wonderful emerging
through the ancient conversation
between myself and the gods
who have claimed me
as one of their own?"

Table of Contents

Part One: The Awkward Dance of Astrology, Science & Religion

Part Two: Astrology's New Landscape in the Era of Uncertainty

Part Three: An Astropoetic Exploration of Psyche and Cosmos

Preface

If you knew that a map existed, designed specifically for you, to show you the way not only into your own deepest truth, but into the very heart of the cosmos, the place where the gods and goddesses of old continue to live, wouldn't you want access to this map? If you could ask these numinous beings why your life, indeed why the world itself, is as it is, wouldn't you jump at the opportunity? If you yourself could become more godlike in the use of this map, wouldn't that possibility intrigue you?

If I told you that such a map existed, would you scoff at my delusional naiveté or would you want to know more?

Some of you may have already guessed I am talking about an astrological birthchart, but most of you probably didn't know astrology could do all that. Most of you probably think that astrology can give a fair description of your personality, or help you get more of a handle on what you are experiencing now or shed some light on a difficult issue or concern. But take you into the heart of the cosmos? Facilitate a conversation with gods and goddesses? Teach you how to become more godlike yourself? That is, no doubt, going too far.

Or is it?

What if I were to tell you that once upon a time, this was exactly what astrology was, but that over the course of thirty thousand years or more, we have been taught otherwise, to discount the very possibility?

Science has, of course, disparaged astrology as pseudoscience, the superstitious, albeit persistent vestige of a primitive culture. But science has also denied the possibility of a meaningful cosmos, mapped as well by story as by measurable fact. Science has taught us to eschew the imagination in favor of rational discourse. Science has taught us to doubt the validity of our own subjective experience in favor of consensus. Science has disenchanted the world and explained the gods and goddesses away.

Those of us who have grown up in a world dominated by science - which is all of us, astrologers included - have been conditioned to dismiss the very idea that a conversation with the deeper, sacred intelligence at the heart of this world, is possible. So, we lower our expectations and become more realistic.

Some of us, perhaps, attempt to take refuge in religion, which after all, is where one would expect to find the divine. And yet, religion has historically wound up being more about belief and conformity to a prescribed code of conduct than an invitation to commune with the sacred. Go back far enough, and we can see the mystical roots of all religion, but those roots have been severed long ago. Now religion teaches us to place more faith in the supposed experiences of the long dead, rather than our own, to pretend we don't hear the voice of the divine in our own heads and hearts, and to follow the dictates of authority instead of finding and cultivating our own connection to the Source.

Those of us who have grown up in a world in which religion claims a monopoly on access to the divine – which is all of us, astrologers included – have been conditioned to believe we can't possibly have our own unmediated relationship to a numinous cosmos. So, we lower our expectations, and become more passive and prosaic.

Religion and science aside, most of us also live in a culture that values achievement and material success more than spiritual maturity; that encourages endless progress and mindless consumption, rather than awareness of cycles and living in balance with oneself and the environment; that rewards outwardly focused busyness and rolls its eyes at those who seek a stillness in which life is felt to be sacred.

Those of us who live in such a world – which is all of us, astrologers included – not only fail to recognize the presence of gods and goddesses walking among us, and living within us, but fail to create a world in which the sanctity of life is respected and a quality of life is ensured for future generations.

Through our collective history, we have in fact created a world that is increasingly uncertain and out of balance. We have lost our way as a species, and it has become increasingly difficult for individuals living in such a world to truly thrive, to live lives of dignity, to feel themselves to be part of something meaningful that encompasses but also transcends the tired melodramas of their own fractured lives.

The answers to this universal dilemma do not lie out there in the world. Neither science, nor religion, nor culture at large can help us make sense of the mess we have created. While proposing astrology as an alternative way of knowing that can take us closer to the truth of who we are, and how we fit into the larger cosmic scheme of things might seem preposterous to some, what if it is really just a measure of the cynicism that our conditioning by science, religion and culture has instilled in us?

Is it so far-fetched to consider the idea that a language based on a map of the cosmos, populated by celestial bodies named after gods and goddesses, timed to coincide with our entry into this world, could possibly facilitate an intimately personal conversation with the sacred intelligence at the heart of the world?

If you are intrigued by this possibility, then I invite you to read on, to see how this might be so.

Astrology in the Era of Uncertainty

An Astropoetic Exploration of Psyche and Cosmos

Introduction

What we say we know for sure changes every day, but no one can miss now the alarm in the air. Our question is, 'What is out there, just beyond the end of the road, out beyond language and fervent belief, beyond whatever gods we've chosen to give our allegiance to? Are we waiting for travelers to return, to tell us what they saw beyond that line? Or are we now to turn our heads, in order to better hear that call coming to us from that other country?

Barry Lopez[1]

For those of us who have heard the call, and been blessed to discover astrology's unlikely and sometimes seemingly magical ability to shed intuitive light on some inscrutable aspect of our lives, we take it as a given that astrology "works," although it has not been easy to say exactly how. Trying to explain astrology to a skeptic, to someone whose only exposure has been the daily horoscope, to an intelligent, open-minded agnostic, or even to a true believer, is not easy.

Is astrology a science? An art? A language? A belief system? A religion? A philosophy? A kind of proto-psychology? A branch of metaphysics? A spiritual practice? A socio-cultural phenomenon? Is it some combination of these possibilities? Or is it something else entirely? Is astrology "the most persistent hallucination which has ever haunted the human brain," as Belgian archeologist and historian Franz Cumont once declared it in disgust?[2] Or is it "the algebra of life," as seminal astrologer Dane Rudhyar once proudly proclaimed it?[3] Those of us who are convinced of astrology's value, because we have experienced it for ourselves, know we are not hallucinating. But what are we doing when we glean information from a birthchart? Can we actually say?

Astrology's Sad Scientific Track Record

Those who have been most serious about attempting to answer this question have generally approached astrology with the intent to prove it scientifically. This is understandable, since achieving scientific validation has been the gold standard in a world that is dominated by science. But such efforts have failed miserably and may have done more harm to astrology's credibility than good.

In the 1950s, when Michel Gauquelin, John Addey and a tiny handful of others were beginning their research, there were few studies available that had put astrology to a scientific test. By the turn of the twenty-first century, there were at least 100 studies published in psychological journals and 400 in astrological journals, "equivalent to about 200 man-years of scientific research."[4] Some of these studies were conducted by scientists; some by astrologers; some were obviously biased; some were not. In nearly every single case, astrology has either failed the test to which it was put, or its studies have been dismissed by critics for any one of a number of possible errors in research design or implementation.

Although many astrologers might disagree with this assessment, and would, in any case, probably be justified in dismissing the biased claims of skeptics like Geoffrey Dean and company, the mainstream consensus remains that, in the face of existing evidence, "astrology is . . . diametrically opposed to the findings and theories of modern Western science."[5] Or, alternately, as summed up by astrologer Sirman A. Celâyir:

> *. . . astrology is too elusive and complex to be tested on the spot. However, even when all tools (e.g., sample data and astrological software) are readily available and no time constraints are set, astrology is still not able to provide the type of evidence, pattern, and proof which specialists in other fields present at technical conferences; nor the type of meticulous derivation and empirical support which appear in technical journals.*[6]

Meanwhile, astrology's detractors continue to nitpick those few studies that have shown promise, finding sampling errors or other "artifacts" that negate statistically significant results, or if all else fails, negating positive results because "it is important not to confuse significance with utility."[7]

At the same time, scientifically-minded astrologers continue to press their case, pick apart existing studies,[8,9] rework the statistical analyses to reinforce their arguments,[10] and/or insist that with better, more sophisticated, less biased research models, we can still prove the validity of astrology scientifically.[11,12,13] I, for one, do not believe this is ever going to happen, not because I don't believe astrology has value, but because I don't believe astrology is a science. This is an admission that I will argue in this book gives astrology an advantage over science where a study of the human soul (or psyche) and the possibility of an ensouled universe is concerned.

Meanwhile, as the debate rages, scientifically-minded astrologers and skeptics often cite the same studies as evidence, while drawing entirely different conclusions. Where critics see no credible evidence that astrology is factually true, astrological researchers see cumulative confirmation.

According to Geoffrey Dean in Tests of Astrology, published in 2016:

> *. . . the outcomes from these hundreds of tests are quite consistent – they deny that astrology is a source of factual truth . . .* [14]

According to Patrick Curry:

> *Over the past fifty years, scientists and astrological researchers are discovering a growing body of objective evidence of correlations between celestial positions and terrestrial life. These statistically significant results have been published in peer reviewed journals (including Correlation, a specialist astrological journal). Ironically, some of the strongest evidence has come from experiments backed by skeptical groups including CSICOP.*[15]

Both sides are presumably looking at the same studies, but apparently not seeing the same thing. Some of this back-and-forth is simply the nature of scientific research, in which the results of any experiment are considered to be tentative until they are replicated or refuted by other researchers – and in this vein, debate can continue nearly indefinitely without final or definitive conclusion.

On the other hand, despite protestations of neutrality on both sides, one would have to be rather naive not to assume that each side has an agenda that biases their approach to research. Astrologers who care about establishing astrology's credibility on scientific grounds are obviously trying to prove something they already believe to be true. Those who have taken it upon themselves to "debunk" what they consider to be a pseudoscience have already decided that astrology will fail before they design their experiments, and lo and behold, it does.

While there may be a few sincere researchers out there, in some remote corner of the universe or in some alternate reality, who have not yet made up their minds about astrology, and can genuinely claim to be neutral, this is a contest that is largely predetermined in a realm beyond the exercise of science, where pre-established opinions determine what can possibly be true and what cannot. This is a contest that astrologers cannot win, no matter how much research we do, because in the end, it is really not about the research at all. Ultimately, it can be argued that the history of astrological research on both sides is a battle of confirmation biases, in which prior beliefs and prejudices predetermine outcomes. Astrologers who are determined to prove that astrology is a *bona fide* science will never concede their point; those who believe astrology is a pseudoscience will reject all research that suggests otherwise, regardless of how scientifically impeccable it might be.

Gauquelin's Legacy

The one piece of research that has broken through this impasse and stood the statistical test against an unrelenting half-century onslaught of critique and analysis is the celebrated Mars effect, first documented extensively by Michel and Francoise Gauquelin in 1955.[16] These results have subsequently been replicated and confirmed by additional experiments, conducted by the Gauquelins themselves,[17] as well as by other researchers.[18,19] Twenty years after Michel's death in 1991, however, Gauquelin's legacy remains shrouded in controversy, sadly fading into indifference, despite a lifetime of prodigious effort. As one of his more respectful critics, German-born British psychologist Hans Eysenck observed in his gently laudatory obituary:

> *There can no longer be any doubt that Michel Gauquelin did discover something; questions remain about its importance. The effect, while real, is modest in size; it certainly has no practical importance.*[20]

To this day, skeptics continue to peck away at even this "modest effect," looking with earnest resolve for non-astrological explanations, social or astronomical artifacts, hidden persuaders, sampling errors, unconscious biases in the collection and/or recording of data, or anything within science's bag of statistical parlor tricks to discredit this minor triumph in the otherwise overwhelming failure of astrology in general to measure up to the rigorous standards that science demands.

The Astrological Community's Ambivalent Embrace of Science

Meanwhile as Dean and company have noted:

> *Astrologers reacted to the Gauquelin work in two main ways. The first was to overstate the significance of Gauquelin's positive results for astrology . . . The second was to relentlessly ignore Gauquelin's important negative results.*[21]

Leaving aside for the moment Dean's extreme bias against astrology, this particular assertion appears to be true. Despite the fact that the astrological community has long claimed Gauquelin as its premier scientific champion, staunchly defending his cherished Mars effect against all attacks, few practicing astrologers have paid much real attention to the body of his work, within which the Mars effect was an anomaly, nor for that matter, have they embraced the Mars effect itself in their practice of astrology.

In general, Gauquelin was quite critical of astrology, dismissing signs, houses and aspects,[22] for example, as having no scientific validity, and at the end of a long, illustrious career, finding little to encourage future generations of astrological researchers. After nearly 35 years of investigation, he eventually came to the following dismal conclusion:

> *Having collected half a million dates of birth from the most diverse people, I have been able to observe that the majority of the elements in a horoscope seem not to possess any of the influences which have been attributed to them.*[23]

Elsewhere, he notes:

> *The casting of horoscopes provides a living to thousands of individuals and provides dreams to an infinitely larger number of consumers . . . [But] since the most painstaking studies have shown the inanity of horoscopes, there should be a strong rising up against this exploitation of public credulity.*[24]

Ignoring for the moment this withering general indictment, as most astrologers have, few astrologers have taken seriously the one specific discovery Gauquelin did make that can claim to have legitimately withstood the rigorous tests of scientific scrutiny. To prove this to yourself, you need only ask how many practicing astrologers you know, perhaps yourself included, who still consider planets in the angular 10th house as most relevant to career, ignoring Gauquelin's conclusion that planets just past the Midheaven (moving clockwise) in the cadent 9th house were the more reliable significators? This was a *bona fide* scientifically validated discovery, one of the very few to which astrologers can unabashedly point. Yet, it has been both trumpeted as scientific validation of astrology in theory and ignored in practice. If, as a community, we are not going to take our own science seriously, what little of it there is, then how can we complain when critics call us pseudo-scientific?

If we were going to stake our credibility as a professional discipline on science, would we not, as Gauquelin did, throw out signs, houses and aspects? Would we not, as Gauquelin did, focus solely on planets in the relevant sectors, on the clockwise side of the Midheaven, as possible indicators of career – and even then, primarily for those who rise to a certain level of eminence in their profession,[25] not necessarily those who pursue merely ordinary careers?

I think most of us would have to agree that this leaves us with a mighty thin and wobbly peg on which to hang our scientific hat, despite the gargantuan amount of effort it has taken to attach it, however tentatively, to the wall; and in practice, most of us go about our work as astrologers as though it wasn't there at all.

The fact that we, who would presumably benefit most, have not embraced Gauquelin's science as a foundation for our work, and yet continue to practice an astrology with little other scientific confirmation, suggests that the conceptual basis of our field probably rests on something other than scientific grounds. Indeed, over 30 years ago now, feedback from members of NCGR (the National Council for Geocosmic Research) indicated that scientific research, as proposed by Francoise Gauquelin in the wake of her separation from Michel, "does not serve the needs of the majority."[26]

The Real Issue Underlying Scientific Research of Astrology

There is a reason why this is so that bears further scrutiny. First, while scientific validation of a particular astrological assertion might lend some small bit of credibility to astrology's general utility as a predictive tool, any specific conclusion that might be drawn through scientific research would be of limited use to a working astrologer. This is so for the same reasons that the statistical results in general are of limited use for shedding light on individual experience; they speak only to the aggregate and not to any specific case (more about statistics in Chapter Six).

Beyond this practical consideration for actual astrologers, there are widely divergent metaphysical assumptions governing the practice of astrology and science that make them awkward bedfellows at best, and representative of antithetical worldviews at the most extreme. In my more idealistic moments, I would like to believe that there might one day in the distant future, be some kind of opening for the resumption of a complimentary dialogue between astrology and science, such as existed up until the middle of the seventeenth century. All hubris aside, that will depend upon science evolving to the point where it can encompass an astrological worldview that transcends its current capacity.

In the meantime, until these metaphysical distinctions are taken into account, the assumption made by both critics of astrology and serious astrological researchers – that astrology ought to be able to prove itself scientifically – will never be examined or questioned. However much additional research is done, astrology will fail to measure up to criteria rooted in a fundamental misunderstanding of what astrology is, or ought to be.

I have written about these metaphysical distinctions at some length elsewhere,[27] and won't repeat all that here, except by way of the briefest of summaries:

> Science is interested in objective truth. Astrology – at least psychological astrology – is interested in subjective truth that may only be meaningful to the person who receives it. While certain astrological statements may be true in a general way, it is the skilled application of those statements, within an individual context – both astrological and personal – that yields the most useful information, and such application may modify the general statement considerably.
>
> Science accepts as truth only what can be replicated by others and that to some extent represents a consensus. The best astrology is that which happens in the moment of exchange between astrologer and client, and that may never happen again in exactly the same way.
>
> Science can only really comment on aspects of reality that can be quantified. Astrologers speak to circumstances and processes that are far better understood in terms of their qualitative dimensions.
>
> Science understands reality to be a literal, rational affair with causal links between subject and object that can be explained. Astrology is an acausal symbolic language that speaks in poetic similes, metaphors and archetypal allegories as an intuitive and

imaginative point of entry into mysteries that do not always lend themselves easily to rational explanation.

Science considers time to be a linear, quantitative dimension of the physical world. Astrology considers time to be cyclical, meaningful in ways that speak to more to the actual subjective experience of what happens at a given time, rather than anything that can be quantified.

Science is concerned with the what and the how of reality, disavowing any possibility of meaning or purpose behind what it observes. The meaning and purpose within life experience *is* what astrology addresses, the metaphysical assumption being the anti-scientific notion that life is meaningful and guided by the unfolding of purpose.

Science requires its practitioners to be neutral witnesses to the object of their study. Astrology requires the full participation of an astrologer in dialogue with her clients, and beyond that with the symbolic field of information in which both astrologer and client are immersed. In any counseling situation, which is where most astrology is applied, one can simply not be neutral and do meaningful work.

These and other metaphysical distinctions make science and astrology two very distinct ways of understanding reality on radically different terms. Scientists do not generally acknowledge the metaphysical biases and assumptions inherent in the scientific method, but for that matter, beyond "as above, so below," neither do most astrologers consider the metaphysical biases and assumptions inherent in their practice of astrology. Unless we do, however, any attempt to assess astrology by scientific standards is doomed to failure – not because astrology is non-scientific, although I would argue it is, but because astrologers and scientists are not looking at the same thing, or at anything, for that matter, in the same way.

A particular astrological statement can be measured as statistically significant or not, but this tells us nothing about the relevance of a particular astrological statement made at a given time in relation to a specific birthchart in dialogue with an individual client. With this understanding of the difference between science and astrology, it can readily be seen that a statement which is astrologically true – true to the symbolism and to the specific situation in which it applies – may well be scientifically false, and vice versa: a scientifically true statement may be astrologically irrelevant, or false in a specific case.

Ultimately, it is a question of apples and oranges, or more precisely, of two entirely different epistemologies, each of which makes no sense in terms of the metaphysical worldview of the other, but each of which, in its own domain, can provide a point of entry into knowing something that the other cannot. Astrology cannot measure the temperature in Seattle on a given day, account for the mechanism inside a black hole, or tell you what percentage of children under the age of 16 will contract the coronavirus. But science cannot help you explore the deeper meaning and purpose of your childhood trauma, or suggest a viable pathway into an exploration of your spirituality or track the evolution of your anger toward authority figures over the course of a lifetime. Scientific research into astrology misses the mark because it assumes astrology ought to behave like a science and provide the same kind of information that science does. These are false assumptions.

As astrological historian Nicholas Campion more succinctly notes:

> *The problem (with) scientific research is obvious: if scientific method requires causal mechanisms and universally testable, replicable results, then any astrology which depends on the astrologer and cosmos engaging in a conscious, psychic relationship must fail.*[28]

Astrology as a Participatory Sport

The astrological observer is not a neutral witness seeking verifiable facts, but a co-creative participant in the extraction of meaning from the objective data that is science's limited preoccupation. This capacity to facilitate the discovery of meaning from an objective map of the cosmos at a given time and place is a gift that astrology is well-poised to keep on giving, despite the fact that it fails to register on the scientific Richter scale. Even Dean acknowledges this when he says (to finish the quote shared earlier):

> *. . . the outcomes from these hundreds of tests are quite consistent – they deny that astrology is a source of factual truth, which is not to say it cannot be meaningful.*[29]

Astrology *is* meaningful. Using it as a language, astrologers provide insight to their clients seeking to make sense of their lives, as part of a larger cosmos unfolding, in which they participate. This is something that science, which admits that the possibility of anything being meaningful is beyond its purview, can never do. To call ourselves a science then, or to try to be one, is to squeeze ourselves into a mold where we are inhibited from doing what we do best. Why would we want to do that, when we could instead be using all the tools at our disposal to bring meaning back into the world?

Multiple Astrologies Make for Superior Cloud Watching

Because it is participatory, astrology is, by nature, anything but a uniform discipline, measured by a science that expects it to be. Not only do we participate in a dialogue with our clients, but as Campion notes, we are also in a dialogue with the cosmos, a dialogue that can and does take any number of astro-logical forms. We ask different questions than science is prepared to answer, and we go about our quest for answers in a variety of different ways, all of which are ultimately astro-logical because they all assume the possibility of exploring meaningful symbolic correlations between the patterns in the sky and what happens here on earth.

This is an assumption that science disavows, but that forms the metaphysical bedrock on which astrology rests. Science dismisses the assumption, not because making meaningful symbolic correlations cannot be done, but because doing so takes the investigation beyond the scope of science. Science does not have the tools to investigate reality in this way, but astrology does.

Once you allow the idea that there could potentially be a symbolic correlation between celestial patterns and patterns here on earth, you also have to acknowledge, in a way science would never do, that there are many different possible ways to conceptualize this correlation. Astrologers of different persuasions see the patterns in the sky through different lenses, and they see different symbolic correlations when they look through these lenses. This is not scientific, but it is perfectly astro-logical.

Indeed, as we all know, there are and have been many astrologies, some serving for a time within a certain era or culture; others competing with each other within the same era or culture. Vedic astrology references an entirely different zodiac than Western tropical astrology, based on the precession of the equinoxes through the constellations, rather than fixed seasonal reference points. A multiplicity of house systems within Western astrology gives a shifting range of planetary placements within the houses. Traditional astrologers use only the Sun, Moon and five visible planets; most contemporary astrologers use the transpersonal planets; cutting edge astrologers use minor asteroids, centaurs, Trans-Neptunians and Kuiper Belt Objects; Uranian astrologers use hypothetical planets. Some astrologers use minor aspects; others don't. Some use wide orbs; some use narrow orbs. Some astrologers use declination, midpoints, harmonics, antiscia and other more esoteric techniques; others don't. Natal astrologers reference the birthchart and its derivatives; horary astrologers work with a chart calculated for the moment a question is posed. Evolutionary astrologers, shamanic astrologers, and archetypal astrologers all work with different techniques and come to different conclusions. Even astrologers working within the same basic approach do not always see the same thing in a given birthchart.

All of these discrepancies cause those who attempt to view astrology through a scientific lens to throw up their hands in despair. Indeed, critics have pounced on this inconsistency within our discipline as "evidence" that astrology is whatever its gullible practitioners think it is, but nothing that has any universal validity. Dean calls it "cloud-watching,"[30] apparently not aware that scientists who measure clouds, or anything else for that matter, are also investing their measurements with meaning that may or may not exist outside of a scientific framework.

Astrology's Kaleidoscopic Advantage

Astrologers operate within a different framework, one where meaning arises not out there in the objective cosmos, in any way that could ever be universally accepted, but rather out of what we see when we look through a particular lens – patterns in the sky, considered not literally, but symbolically. Ultimately the lens is less important than what it reveals. Astrology reveals an entirely different order of truth than science, which ultimately is just another lens.

Personally, I have always celebrated the fact that astrology is what I call a kaleidoscopic language, meaning that it allows for a turning of the lens this way or that, and within this "fudge factor" – taboo in scientific circles – it attains a liberating flexibility that will speak to different astrologers in different ways, or even to an ambidextrous astrologer in ways that yield different insights. If the quest is for meaning, rather than absolute, objective truth, then being able to look at any question from multiple perspectives enriches the journey far more deeply than having a definitive answer with universal validity.

When astrologers make specific statements, or predictions, as an expression of factual objective truth, then the accuracy of these statements can be measured statistically – and has been, most often to disastrous results. This does not obviate the value of astrology as a superior form of "cloud watching" through which to constellate truth as a subjective work in progress – an exploration of what is true for this person in this moment. It is here that astrology offers what science in its present form cannot.

When astrology is used as a point of entry to a deeper understanding of life – as it is in most astrological consultations, or better yet, in most applications to one's own life – it becomes a symbolic language, whose function as a catalyst to self-understanding cannot be measured by scientific standards. The quest for self-understanding itself, in fact, does not make sense at all in scientific terms. It does not matter in the least if a statistically significant portion of people with similar features in their birthchart experience such and such; nor even if a statistically significant portion of astrologers agree on what these features mean. What does matter is how the language, in the hands of an individual astrologer or anyone fluent in the language, can take an individual into the heart of their experience and allow them to extract a sense of meaning and purpose from those experiences. This is not a scientific venture.

Leaving Science Behind

Whether you believe that astrology is rightfully understood as a science or not, both stances presuppose that science is the best or only measure of truth and validity. Indeed, this has been presumed to be the case at least since the mid-nineteenth century, and as the debate has continued into the twenty-first century, we generally make the same assumption. We tacitly assume that astrology is an ancient discipline that either measures up to contemporary standards or not. I would argue it is more accurate to say that both science and astrology have evolved in ways that have caused them to diverge.

Until fairly recently, astrology would have measured up to the scientific standards of the day. In fact, for most of our history – as will be outlined in more detail in Part One of this book, astrology and astronomy have been inseparable. But science has changed and so has astrology, so the two are no longer in sync. It seems obvious to me – and hopefully will be to you as well after reading this book – that it is time to simply acknowledge this and move on. This is not the same as accepting defeat. Quite the contrary, it is release from bondage to an inappropriate idea of what we should be that has taken us to a dead end.

Critics insist that we measure up to scientific standards, and then castigate us when we don't. Some astrologers in turn insist that astrology ought to measure up to scientific standards, and then feel inferior, or become defensive, when it doesn't. At best, this is a self-defeating pattern that goes nowhere; at worst it is a slapstick comedy routine in which astrologers become the butt of a really old and really bad joke – not unlike the classic Abbott and Costello routine of "Who's on First?"[31]:

The confusion at the heart of the joke arises because the word "Who" is both a question and someone's name – just as astrology is understood as both a classic textbook example of pseudoscience by most scientists, and a serious discipline, quite capable of yielding powerful insights by astrologers who know how to use it. When the answer to any question is "astrology," a mainstream scientist will simply not hear it, and ask the same question again – *ad nauseum*. How long do we really want to get caught up in the spin cycle of this joke?

Why Astrology is Considered a Pseudoscience

So why do most educated people tend to take this joke seriously? In part because there is a small cadre of debunking pseudoscientists out there, beating the drum and calling the kettle black as they distort and manipulate their own science to prove a point. But also, in part, because some astrologers themselves continue to take the joke seriously and swallow the bait. If we want to move beyond this impasse, we have to see the joke for what it is, have a good laugh, and then get on with the more serious business of creating an inherently astrological approach to knowledge, one that makes sense within the metaphysical parameters of our discipline. Before we make a start in that direction, just to drive the point home, let's take a closer look at what we're up against, striving to be something we will never be.

According to a common current definition of pseudoscience,[32] a discipline has to satisfy the following two criteria to be declared one:

(1) it is not scientific, and

(2) its major proponents try to create the impression that it is scientific.

As far as the first criteria goes, there has been a great deal of debate about who gets to decide what is scientific and what is not, and what are the criteria by which the scientific community makes that determination. This is known as the issue of "demarcation," and it includes not just a consideration of where science ends and pseudoscience begins, but also which disciplines are non-scientific – that is to say, metaphysical or religious or simply various organized systems of non-scientific knowledge – or as they are sometimes called, "parasciences."[33] Demarcation also raises the question about what constitutes good science and bad science – an endless, often heated discussion that generally comes to no definitive conclusion, and in any case, is always changing as science itself evolves. This piece of the demarcation debate, for example, often marks the exchange between scientifically-minded astrologers and self-proclaimed skeptics, each of whom endlessly accuse the other of bad science.

Even outside of a fruitless exchange fueled by dueling confirmation biases, the question of whether or not a given statement, experiment, avenue of inquiry, or entire field is or is not pseudoscientific, is a tricky one to answer – particularly as will become abundantly clear in Part One of this book, because both science and astrology have been in constant flux throughout the ages. Science is a vastly different discipline than it was a thousand years ago, or even a hundred years ago – but so is astrology; and until relatively recently the demarcation between them was fairly non-existent. So, where the line is drawn now is not the absolute, definitive or final determination that fierce defenders of their particular understanding of demarcation might want it to be.

Swedish philosopher Sven Ove Hansson has suggested alternatively that instead of calling something a pseudoscience because it is not scientific, it might be more appropriate to call it that because "it is at variance with the most reliable knowledge about its subject matter that is currently available."[34]

While this revised definition might seem to favor astrologers, who are certainly the source of the most reliable knowledge about astrology, in all honesty, we would have to ask, "Which astrologers?" since as a community, we agree about so little. In any case, the source of the most reliable information that Hansson had in mind suggesting this alternate definition was "*scientists* specialized in the subject-matter that the statement or doctrine relates to." While some scientifically-minded astrologers might consider this an invitation to step up, fighting for the honor with debunking skeptics like Dean and company, at best, even the most legitimate among them face an uphill battle to prove that a "scientifically-minded astrologer" is not an oxymoron.

In the 1960s, Austrian-British philosopher Karl Popper suggested that "statements or systems of statements, in order to be ranked as scientific, must be capable of conflicting with possible, or conceivable observations"[35] - a stance commonly known as "falsifiability." By this criterion, a pseudoscience is contrasted to metaphysics in that it makes statements that are falsifiable - that is to say conceivably scientific, pending actual empirical investigation, whereas metaphysical statements are not falsifiable, but rather a matter of unprovable belief. In elaborating his ideas, Popper explicitly mentions astrology as a clear example of a pseudoscience - tellingly, along with psychoanalysis and individual psychology - because of its vagueness.[36] That is to say in his opinion, most astrological predictions are so general as to be easily confirmed - or verified - by almost anything that happens, and thus, are not falsifiable.

Why he did not consider astrology to be a form of metaphysics, or a useful "metaphysical research program," as he did the Darwinian theory of evolution, is probably a reflection of confirmation bias in the application of his own theory than anything else. In *Conjectures and Refutations*, written in 1962, when astrological research was still in its infancy, he used astrology as a classic example of pseudoscience, based on its "pseudo-empirical method - that is to say, a method which although it appeals to observation and experiment, nevertheless does not come up to scientific standards."[37] In Popper's view, astrology was a trivial example - obvious to everyone and hastily conjured - that would make his critique of what he considered other more serious pseudosciences like Freudian psychoanalysis, Adler's theory of individual psychology, Darwinian theory of evolution, and Marx's theory of history, more understandable.[38]

Others have considered astrology to be a pseudoscience for other reasons. In basic agreement with Popper's criterion, but at odds with his assessment of astrology, Hansson considers astrology to be quite falsifiable.[39] Citing Shawn Carlson's famous 1985 study[40] and the 1988 compilation of studies by astronomers Roger Culver and Phillip Ianna *Astrology: True or False? A Scientific Evaluation*,[41] he concludes that astrology - potentially a science - has been duly falsified. Dean and company (the authors of two volumes of studies that, in their view, prove astrology false) would agree; most scientifically-minded astrologers would not.

Thomas Kuhn considered science to be a puzzle-solving activity, with failed predictions providing puzzles to be solved. By contrast, the failure of astrological predictions, in his opinion, is that they "did not give rise to research puzzles, for no man, however skilled, could make use of them in a constructive attempt to revise the astrological tradition."[42] Here, I would tend to agree: most astrologers who make predictions do not re-examine those that fail, in order to refine their predictive capacity; they simply move on and make new predictions.

Canadian philosopher of science, Paul Thagard, who eschews Popper's idea of falsifiability altogether, instead rejected astrology, because its "community of practitioners makes little attempt to develop the theory towards solutions of the problems, shows no concern for attempts to evaluate the theory in relation to others, and is selective in considering confirmations and disconfirmations," which is, in his opinion, what a scientific community ought to do.[43]

A tiny minority of scientifically-minded astrologers are making a sincere attempt to address these concerns. Mostly failed research, vagueness, little interest in addressing ongoing theoretical or practical issues and problems, and a selective approach to confirmation and disconfirmation are all valid criticisms for any discipline intending to present itself as a science. Meanwhile, those astrologers that aren't actively debating scientists, and even some of those, tend to get defensive when scientists raise basic questions such as:

> *How does astrology actually work?*
>
> *How is it that two astrologers looking at the same chart come up with different interpretations?*
>
> *How can so many diverse approaches to astrology – using different zodiacs, different house systems, different planets and so forth – all be valid, when these diverse approaches often contradict each other?*
>
> *When our predictions fail, why do they fail?*
>
> *Why does astrology continue to fail scientific test after scientific test?*

While there are certainly scientists for whom these questions are merely intended to discredit or embarrass astrologers, they are not unreasonable questions for a scientist, or an astrologer, for that matter, to ask. If we don't ask them of ourselves, do we really have a right to complain when others, assuming astrology ought to be scientific, answer them for us, and then conclude that astrology is a pseudoscience?

The other criterion for declaring any discipline a pseudoscience is that after repeatedly failing to come up with a satisfactory answer to the first criterion – that is to say, failing to prove itself scientific – its major proponents continue to try to create the impression that it *is* scientific. If astrologers fail to understand the metaphysical distinctions between astrology and science and keep beating their heads against the same impenetrable wall, attempting to create the impression – through subsequent research – that astrology *is* scientific, astrology will perpetually be judged to be a pseudoscience by scientists who also fail to understand these same metaphysical distinctions.

Round and round we will go in a vicious cycle that reinforces astrology's dismal reputation in scientific circles and adds to our own confusion about who and what we really are. As Geoffrey Cornelius astutely notes, "The more research that is done, the less we discover astrology."[44]

Do we really need to keep this vicious cycle going? Must we prove ourselves scientific to feel OK about what we do? Or is it possible for us to go more deeply into what we do, and find our own validation according to criteria that arise more naturally from within our discipline itself, and discover - or rediscover - what astrology can become? When we plie our craft with technical skill, compassion, and a conscious intention to make a difference in our clients' lives, we generally do. The result cannot be measured in statistical significance, but it can be measured in our capacity to shed light on the otherwise inscrutable mysteries of life, proven over and over again collectively in countless sessions with no shortage of clients, and this is worth celebrating in its own right, as a value unto itself.

The fact that people have not stopped consulting astrologers, despite the prodigious efforts of many brilliant people to convince others that astrology is rubbish, attests to the fact that it is not. This should be enough to enable us to sleep at night, and go on doing our valuable work, without having to convince the scientifically-minded that we are something that we are not.

Science's Reluctance to Do Boundary Work

Having said that, we should all be prepared to continue to be called a pseudoscience by those who don't really know what they are talking about. I say this because in some quarters, a pseudoscience is any doctrine that "purport(s) to offer alternative accounts to those of science or claim(s) to explain what science cannot explain."[45] This assertion speaks to the arrogance of scientists, who want to defend their turf against all those who might infringe upon it, even when they are actually off their turf. It also exposes an important legitimate question on the scientific side of the line: how does science distinguish itself from other intellectual disciplines, other ways of knowing? Or does it? Does it instead, simply assume that all other non-scientific ways of knowing are illegitimate, or less than, or pseudoscientific?

The attempt to address this question - or avoid it - was termed "boundary work" by the sociologist Thomas Gieryn, who noted that the same scientists could at different times point to different and even contradictory aspects of their practice to promote it as science, depending on what they thought would successfully advance their professional interests to whom. This led Gieryn to conclude that science's boundaries were variable depending upon what a given scientist wanted to prove - or in his words, "ambiguous, flexible, historically changing, contextually variable, internally inconsistent, and sometimes disputed."[46]

It is interesting here to note that while a scientist might not be aware that she was rationalizing her opinion about where the boundary is between science and nonscience or pseudoscience, perhaps not even realizing it was nothing more than an "opinion," this becomes evident to a sociologist observing the behavior of scientists. The demarcation problem, in fact, is really only a problem for philosophers of science or other outsiders who stand apart and observe science itself; for most scientists working in the trenches, it is routinely taken for granted that what they do is science by definition, and that what others do, who are lacking in *bona fide* scientific credentials, or pushing too far past the boundaries of what is generally accepted as scientific consensus, is not. By the same token, it might not be apparent to scientifically-minded astrologers – most of whom are not philosophers of science or outsiders – that they perhaps also unwittingly move the boundary when attempting to show that astrology is on the scientific side of the line, as a reflection of their own biases.

Leaving aside for the moment the impossibility of ever reconciling the extremes on either side of this ongoing boundary war, in this book I am suggesting that science's hegemony in the debate belies a more fundamental possibility: that astrology and science are more accurately understood as alternative and potentially complementary epistemologies – or ways of knowing – neither adequately measured by the parameters of the other. Science is adept at exploring the external parameters of physical realities, and somewhat useful in exploring collective phenomena in the social sciences. It is embarrassingly clumsy in exploring the inner dimensions of the human psyche, and utterly inept at making sense of a human life. This is precisely where astrology shines on its own merits, and where trying to fit into a scientific mold would most severely neuter it.

It is also potentially where a natural boundary exists between astrology and science, one that allows astrology to function in its own domain, where not being scientific is actually an advantage. As a very wide smorgasbord of human endeavors attest daily, not being scientific is by no means the end of the road, but quite the contrary, a potential beginning for a more liberating set of opportunities for articulation and full actualization of astrology's value on more organic grounds, that is to say according to criteria that are appropriate to the metaphysics of our craft.

As I see it, astrology shares science's passion for observing patterns, but sees something entirely different when it does. At the same time, astrology makes room for metaphysical speculation in the way that many nonsciences do, but science doesn't, and in so doing, opens up a space for a deeper, richer, more multi-dimensional inquiry. This makes astrology a language potentially suitable for exploring an entire range of human experiences to which science has an awkward relationship at best – love, friendship, compassion, caring, creativity, wellbeing, beauty, integrity, wonder, imagination, pleasure, purpose, identity and meaning, to name just a few.

We are all observers of our own experiences, and the best among us learn from these observations. But what we learn – in this middle ground between the outer facts of our experience and the meaning we ascribe to them as we come to understand them more clearly – will generally fall more gracefully under the auspices of astrology, particularly psychological astrology, than of science. It is my contention that to advance our discipline, we have to be strong enough to shrug off accusations of pseudoscience and get on with our own work of occupying and delineating this middle ground.

Putting Our Quest into Historical Perspective

In order to talk at all about how astrology might rightfully do this, we must first recognize that both science and astrology have evolved and changed, in some cases, in ways that would have rendered them unrecognizable to preceding eras. Nor has the relationship between astrology and science been uniform throughout their shared history, but rather a parallel development of separate, but often interdependent epistemologies, both in perpetual transition. To even address the question, "Is astrology a science?" if in fact, you could address the question at all, you must not only know who is asking the question, but in what era they are asking it.

The debate about whether or not astrology can be considered a science has been going on for a very long time, although not as long as we might imagine without the perspective of history. Although astrology is still considered by its critics to be a superstitious and antiquated vestige of a pre-scientific age; and a *bona fide* science by those astrologers looking for the mantle of credibility they believe science would bestow; the truth about the relationship between astrology and science is more complex and more interesting than that. Astrology and science have, for most of their history, co-evolved together, along with religious thought, political developments and the ever-mutating cultural zeitgeist in which these various threads have intertwined and differentiated.

Before we validate astrology's contribution on different grounds, then, it will behoove us to look back to that forgotten time at the beginning of the story, when the question of whether or not astrology could be considered a science would not have made any sense to ask. Indeed, for most of our human history – that is to say, for all but the last three or four hundred years – this would have been the case.

> *The split between the two words, astronomy and astrology, is a feature of the modern West; in the classical world, their meanings overlapped . . . The separation between the words 'astronomy' and 'astrology' in any history which deals with the pre-modern West, earlier than the seventeenth century, therefore runs the risk of being anachronistic . . .*[47]

Living as we do post-seventeenth century we will also take some time to look at the part of the story where science established itself as the dominant epistemology and disowned its older sibling. Because science's hegemony has altered our entire culture and conditioned the collective mindset in which we consider what is truth and what is not, we will also necessarily take stock of the ways in which astrology has been shaped by science, as well as by religious, political and cultural agendas, and major philosophical schools of thought in each era. In particular, we will look at the ways in which astrology has reinvented itself in order to establish its credibility as an intellectual discipline, tried to fit into a world where it was marginalized, and has bent itself out of shape in doing so.

Lastly, we will peer into a time, one that might have actually arrived, where astrology can find its rightful place within a broader kaleidoscope of postmodern worldviews, each with a useful lens through which to understand a more complex truth that is not reducible to any one perspective, much less fundamentalist thinking, however convincingly it is presented, or dominant it might be. In reaching toward an astrology of the future, we will necessarily work toward retrieving what has been lost from the past in exchange for adaptation to the standards and conventional wisdom of preceding eras, as well as preserving what legitimate astrological advances we have made that we can truly call our own.

How Do We Know What We Know?

If we trace both astrology and science back to their roots, past the days when science was not The Lens, but just a lens, we come to a more fundamental question: "How do we know what we know?" This is ultimately a metaphysical question to which science only knows one answer, but astrology potentially has many, each one capable of leading the questioner on a quest for a multivalent truth that goes much deeper than what can be measured by the rigorous (and sometimes rigid) tools of science.

It is this possibility that we will explore in this book. We will begin at a time when neither science nor astrology existed, but both were beginning to evolve out of a human need to get some kind of a handle on this deeper question – on how we humans can know ourselves and our place within the cosmos. This is an important question that has more than one answer. Science has tried to answer it in a definitive, objective way by outside observation of causal relationships among those things that can be quantified. Astrology tries to answer it in a more subjective, personal way that serves each of us individually, as the basis for a meaningful life, filled with purpose, a sense of belonging to something larger than ourselves, and an elevated chance to participate and contribute to the greater good.

"How do we know what we know?" is a question worth asking both in general, and more specifically as astrologers – for it is here that we will get at astrology's unique contribution to our place within a cosmos built not just of matter, but also of the meaning we ascribe to our perceptions of it and the stories we tell ourselves about it, whether those stories are factually true or not. If we can do that, we won't have to teeter awkwardly on science's ill-fitting scale. We can instead weigh in confidently on our own:

> *Is modern science – objective, socially neutral science – really the only acceptable road to truth? Would any wise extraterrestrial come upon the same logical system we have to explain the structure of the universe? Yes, argues Nobel physicist Sheldon*

Glasgow. At the other extreme, perhaps there are as many roads to perceived truth as there are species that could have evolved to think them up. Philosopher Mary Hesse retorts that scientific theory is just one way humans have tried to make sense of our world, one among manifold sets of myths, models and metaphors. There is nothing special about it.[48]

Notes

1. Lopez, Barry. *Horizon*. Vintage, 2019, 512.
2. Cumont, Franz. "Astrology and Religion Among the Greeks and Romans." Sacred Texts. Accessed April 28, 2023. https://www.sacred-texts.com/astro/argr03.htm, xiii.
3. Rudhyar, Dane. *The Astrology of Personality: A Re-Formulation of Astrological Concepts and Ideals, in Terms of Contemporary Psychology and Philosophy*, Doubleday, 1970, 18.
4. Smit, Rudolph. "Grand Summary (Abstract + Article)," Accessed April 28, 2023. https://www.astrology-and-science.com/u-gran2.htm.
5. Gilbert, Robert Andrew, and David E. Pingree. "Astrology | Definition, History, Symbols, Signs, & Facts." Encyclopedia Britannica. Accessed April 28, 2023. https://www.britannica.com/topic/astrology.
6. Celâyir, Sirman A. "Astrology, Reality & Common Sense by Sirman A. Celâyir," Accessed April 28, 2023. http://cura.free.fr/xx/17sirman.html.
7. Dean, Geoffrey, and Arthur Mather. *Recent Advances in Natal Astrology: A Critical Review 1900-1976*, Bromley, England: The Astrological Association, 1977, 547.
8. Currey, Robert. "Why It Is Unacceptable to Dismiss Astrology as Rubbish.," Accessed April 28, 2023. https://www.astrology.co.uk/tests/basisofastrology.htm.
9. McRitchie, Kenneth. "Commentary of Geoffrey Dean and Ivan Kelly's Article, 'Is Astrology Relevant to Consciousness and Psi?" Astrological Reviews and Essays. Accessed April 28, 2023. https://www.astrologicalreviewletters.org/.
10. Ertel, Suitbert. "Appraisal of Shawn Carlson's Renowned Astrology Tests." *Journal of Scientific Exploration* 23, no. 2 (January 1, 2009): 125–37. https://journalofscientificexploration.org/index.php/jse/article/download/99/37.
11. Perry, Glenn. "Astrological Research: From Paradigm To Method." Accessed April 28, 2023. https://aaperry.com/astrological-research/.
12. Aurata, Aquila. "Welcome to the Network for Objective Research in Astrology (NORA)." Objective Astrology.net - Home. Accessed April 28, 2023. http://www.objectiveastrology.net/.

13. Westran, Paul. "Replicated Study Enhances Astrological Claims." Astrology News Service, June 11, 2021. https://astrologynewsservice.com/research/replicated-study-enhances-astrological-claims/.

14. Dean, Geoffrey, David Nias, and Rudolf Smit. *Tests of Astrology: A Critical Review of Hundreds of Studies*. Amsterdam, Netherlands: AinO Pubns, 2016, 3.

15. Curry, Robert. "Why It Is Unacceptable to Dismiss Astrology as Rubbish." Accessed May 6, 2023. http://www.astrology.co.uk/tests/basisofastrology.htm.

16. Gauquelin, Michel. *L'influence des astres. Etude critique et experimentale. Edition du Dauphin*, 1955.

17. Gauquelin, Michel. *Les Hommes et Les Astres*, FeniXX, 1959.

18. Snow, Edward. "New Study Confirms Gauquelin 'Plus Zones.'" The Friends of Astrology Inc. Accessed May 6, 2023. http://www.friendsofastrology.org/featured-articles/new-study-confirms-gauquelin-plus-zones-may-2016.

19. West, Anthony. "The Gauquelin Controversy April, 2016." The Friends of Astrology Inc. Accessed May 6, 2023. http://www.friendsofastrology.org/featured-articles/the-gauquelin-controversy-april-2016.

20. Eysenck, Hans. "Michel Gauquelin. [1928-1991] Obituary. *The Independent*. 20 June 1991." Accessed May 6, 2023. http://www.astrology.co.uk/bio/gauquelin.htm.

21. Dean, Mather, Nias and Smit, *Tests of Astrology*, 89.

22. Gauquelin, Michel. *Birthtimes: A Scientific Investigation of the Secrets of the as Astrology*, Hll & Wang, 1983, 131.

23. Gauquelin, Michel. *Neo-Astrology: A Copernican Revolution*. Penguin, 1991, 20.

24. Gauquelin, Michel. *Dreams and Illusions of Astrology*, Amherst, NY: Prometheus Books, 1979, 158.

25. Dean, Mather, Nias and Smit, *Tests of Astrology*, 76-77.

26. *NCGR Journal*, Winter 1989, 5, quoted in Dean, Mather, Nias and Smit. *Tests of Astrology*, 90.

27. See Landwehr, Joe. *The Seven Gates of Soul: Reclaiming the Poetry of Everyday Life*, 2004, 91 – 316, and Landwehr, Joe. "Why Astrology Is Not a Science." Accessed May 6, 2023. https://www.joelandwehr.com/blog-posts-2/why-astrology-is-not-a-science.

28. Campion, Nicholas. *A History of Western Astrology Volume II: The Medieval and Modern Worlds*. Bloomsbury Publishing, 2009, 271.

29. Dean, Mather, Nias and Smit, *Tests of Astrology*, 3.

30. Dean, Mather, Nias and Smit, *Tests of Astrology*, 173.

31. Abbott & Costello Fan Club. "Abbott and Costello's Classic 'Who's on First?' Routine | Abbott & Costello Fan Club," July 16, 2021. https://www.abbottandcostellofanclub.com/whos-on-first/.
32. Hansson, Sven Ove. "Science and Pseudo-Science." Stanford Encyclopedia of Philosophy, Summer 2021 Edition. May 20, 2021. https://plato.stanford.edu/archives/sum2021/entries/pseudo-science/.
33. Mahner, Martin. "Demarcating Science from Non-Science." In Elsevier EBooks, 548, 2007. https://doi.org/10.1016/b978-044451548-3/50011-2.
34. Hansson, Sven Ove. "Defining Pseudoscience and Science." In University of Chicago Press EBooks, 61–78, 2015. https://doi.org/10.7208/chicago/9780226051826.003.0005.
35. Popper, Karl Raimund. *Conjectures and Refutations: The Growth of Scientific Knowledge*, 1963, 39.
36. Popper, Karl Raimund, *Conjectures and Refutations*, 2.
37. Popper, Karl Raimund, *Conjectures and Refutations*, 44.
38. McDonough, Richard. "Karl Popper's Critical Rationalism and The Notion of an 'Open Society.'" The Postil Magazine, March 1, 2021. https://www.thepostil.com/karl-poppers-critical-rationalism-and-the-notion-of-an-open-society/.
39. Hansson, "Science and Pseudo-Science," 4.2.
40. Carlson, Shawn. "A Double-Blind Test of Astrology." Nature 318, no. 6045 (December 5, 1985): 419–25. https://doi.org/10.1038/318419a0.
41. Culver, Roger B., and Philip A. Ianna. *Astrology: True Or False? A Scientific Evaluation*. Prometheus, 1988.
42. Kuhn, Thomas. "Logic of Discovery or Psychology of Research?" In *The Philosophy of Karl Popper*, edited by Paul Arthur Schilpp. La Salle, IL: Open Court, 1974, 804.
43. Thagard, Paul. "Why Astrology Is a Pseudoscience." *PSA*, 1978, no. 1 (January 1, 1978): 228. https://doi.org/10.1086/psaprocbienmeetp.1978.1.192639.
44. Cornelius, Geoffrey. *The Moment of Astrology: Origins in Divination*. Wessex Astrologer Limited, 2002, 66.
45. Grove, J. W. "Rationality at Risk: Science against Pseudoscience." *Minerva* 23, no. 2 (January 1, 1985): 219. https://doi.org/10.1007/bf01099943.
46. Gieryn, Thomas F. "Boundary-Work and the Demarcation of Science from Non-Science: Strains and Interests in Professional Ideologies of Scientists." *American Sociological Review* 48, no. 6 (December 1, 1983): 792. https://doi.org/10.2307/2095325.

47. Campion, Nicholas. A *History of Western Astrology Volume I: The Ancient and Classical Worlds*. Bloomsbury, 2009, x.

48. Aveni, Anthony. *Conversing with the Planets: How Science and Myth Invented the Cosmos*. Times Books, 1992, 18.

Part One

The Awkward Dance of Astrology, Science & Religion

Although each society's cosmology is unique, nevertheless there are broad structures that derive from the brain. At the same time, in many societies there are people, we can all them 'seers', who believe that they can actually see and travel through the cosmos to capture insights hidden from ordinary people. For the former, the cosmos is not just a concept; it is a lived, explored reality.

David Lewis-Williams and David Pearce, Inside the Neolithic Mind, 2018

If we listen, we can know – all we need to do is give up being in charge. Knowing inside is not something unusual; it is how we are (meant to know). All humans can have that connection with All-That-Is. The connection is within us.

Robert Wolff, Original Wisdom, 2001

Chapter One

The Direct Experience of Truth in the Mythopoetic Era[1] Thirty Thousand B.C.E (or earlier) – Second Millennium B.C.E.

Astrology per se would not likely have been recognized as a coherent system – at least in the way we recognize it today in the West – until about 1,800 B.C.E.[2] Eastern forms of astrology, originating in India and China likely go back much farther, possibly to the fourteenth century B.C.E.[3] Even before this, however, it is clear that the same widespread fascination among the earliest humans with the nighttime sky had practical, mythological and religious application, and by implication, also expressed both proto-scientific and proto-astrological sensibilities:

> *As soon as human beings realized that sunrise, the most dramatic event of the day, was necessarily connected to the experience of heat and light, they were doing astronomy, in the modern sense of the word. And the moment they attached meaning to this phenomenon, they were well on the way to becoming astrologers.*[4]

Neolithic peoples throughout Europe routinely aligned their stone circles, passage cairns, and ceremonial sites – such as Stonehenge (circa 3,000 – 2,000 B.C.E.) and New Grange (circa 3,200 B.C.E.) – with solstices, equinoxes, and the midpoints between these cardinal stations of the Earth's annual revolution around the Sun. There is some evidence to suggest these structures were imported from north-western France, where they originated several millennia earlier.[5] In Dordogne, France, carved bone plates dated from the Aurignacian period (circa 25,000 B.C.E.) depicting waxing and waning lunar cycles have been found, suggesting that an awareness of celestial rhythms was already present within the earliest human cultures on the planet.[6]

Within such cultures, the interface between astronomical observations, religious rites and daily life was fairly seamless. Although the phenomenon of the personal horoscope – which is the most commonly known expression of astrology today – was a more recent invention of the Hellenistic Era (roughly from the third century B.C.E to the third century C.E.),[7] the confluence of these streams in earlier times nonetheless constitutes the fertile mix out of which astrology arose. This astrology was both practical and metaphysical, rooted in a sense of reverence for the Earth that was inextricably intertwined with an awe of the cosmos:

> *Human beings cannot function without meaning, and this is actually the primary level at which social cohesion is created . . . One respects the earth because it is one's mother, an animal because it may be a reborn ancestor, and the stars because they*

are messengers, guardians and protectors. The prevailing myth was what we would call ecological.[8]

Animism

Ecology today is understood as a scientific study of the interactions between living organisms and their biophysical environment. While many passionate ecologists feel an intimate connection to the natural world, there is still a perceptual distance – endemic to science – that turns passion into a coherent statement of objective truth, stripped of personal considerations. This is quite a different way of knowing than the ecological myth of which Campion speaks.

In Neolithic times, there was no such thing as ecology. There was instead a web of intimate relationships within the environment in which humans participated, largely out of necessity. Within such a web, to call the Earth one's mother was not just a sentimental metaphor; it was an intimately felt experience of the living reality of the Earth as Mother – the source of sustenance for all of Life. From the mythopoetic perspective, the Earth is alive, as are all of its sentient creatures, including not just plants and animals, but mountains, rivers, and stars. Each has a spiritual presence that can be felt, as well as a practical function within the whole, and each is a being with whom one can commune and interact, just as humans can with each other.

Such a perspective is generally understood by contemporary scholars as animism, although as with all such anthropological designations, to call it anything at all, suggests a capacity to observe and comment on one's own perceptions, which probably didn't exist then, certainly not with anything resembling scientific objectivity. To the extent that animistic peoples were in relationship to the Sun, Moon, planets, stars, and other celestial objects visible in the night sky, they would have not likely known them in any other way than as living beings who had their place within the overall circle of Life. In this way, the astrology of the Mythopoetic Era, though it would not be named as astrology, would necessarily be ecological and animistic.

Participation Mystique

The epistemology that gave rise to this prevailing mythos can be understood in terms of what French philosopher Lucien Lévy-Bruhl once called *participation mystique* – a way of being (and knowing) that he attributed to "the primitive mind."[9] Within the perceptual field in which *participation mystique* operates, the barrier between subject and object is essentially erased, and one becomes partially identified with whatever it is one encounters, whether that be a bear in the wild, a dream, or a celestial event. Here direct experience of the object of one's perception – through the registration of sensory input, emotional and imaginal response, symbolic thinking and relational interchange – becomes the basis for knowledge instead of the artificially manufactured neutrality of the observer in relation to the observed, which is the current mythos on which scientific knowledge is predicated.

On the one hand, *participation mystique* can be understood as the projection of human attributes, motives, and understanding into the natural world, at best resulting in the evolution of mythology, folk tales, and essentially the entire zeitgeist of the Mythopoetic Era; at worst in superstition and delusional thinking. On the other hand, this is a mindset in which a more intimate way of knowing was the norm, one in which – despite our sophisticated protestations to the contrary – forms the evolutionary bedrock of our own culture.

Well before Lévy Bruhl coined the term *participation mystique*, French physician and embryologist Étienne Serres, building on the work of German anatomist Johann Friedrich Meckel, developed Meckel-Serres law, otherwise known as the "theory of recapitulation," in which the embryo of an animal revisits successive stages in the evolution of its ancestors as it matures. This discovery is commonly summed up in the maxim, "*ontogeny* (the development of an individual animal from embryo to birth) recapitulates *phylogeny* (the evolutionary history of the species)."[10]

These ideas were rooted in a study of evolutionary biology, but were later adopted and adapted by sociologists and psychologists such as Herbert Spencer, G. Stanley Hall, Sigmund Freud and Jean Piaget to explain the cognitive development of humans. Carl Jung relied implicitly upon this concept to bolster his explication of the collective unconscious.[11] As summed up by twentieth century American anthropological linguist, Mary LeCron Foster, the central idea behind cognitive recapitulation is that "both biological evolution and the stages in the child's cognitive development follow much the same progression of evolutionary stages as that suggested in the archaeological record."[12]

If this is so, then the mythopoetic epistemology of an earlier age – informed by *participation mystique* – is hardwired into our psyches as part of the cognitive foundation upon which the more analytical faculties valued by science are based. The truth of recapitulation has been readily observed in the cognitive development of children by the above-mentioned psychologists and many others.

> *In the child the great images and archetypes of the collective unconscious are living reality . . . Hence, the child, whose life as a personal entity is largely determined by the collective unconscious, actually is the living carrier of this ancestral experience.*[13]

Participation Mystique and Archetypal Psychology

Jung and many psychologists since have tracked the process of cognitive recapitulation archetypally, that is to say, through reference to various mythological motifs, such as creation myths, the hero's journey and the *hieros gamos*, in which a sacred marriage of masculine (*animus*) and feminine (*anima*) principles takes place – itself an archetypal depiction of *participation mystique* as all polarity melds together in seamless integration. The same archetypal understanding has presented itself in less academic ways in the myths, folktales and teaching stories of civilizations around the planet since humans first gathered around communal fires for comfort and companionship, as well as subsequently in dreams, world literature, film and art. Other archetypal expressions prevail in situations of "abnormal" psychology, in which "the hitherto latent primitive mind suddenly bursts forth with contents that are too incomprehensible and too strange for assimilation to be possible."[14]

To be sure, Jung and others, including Lévy Bruhl, aspiring to scientific credibility, considered *participation mystique* to be a regressive state, inferior to that experienced by contemporary humans with a more differentiated consciousness. Nonetheless, the fact that psychoanalysts working in the field still encountered it in their patients, and educators still observed it in the children under their charge, meant that it was an important factor to be reckoned with in an understanding of human psychology.

In more recent years, psychotherapists, especially those within the Jungian tradition, have begun to acknowledge that *participation mystique* is more than just a regressive state; it actually contributes greatly to some of the most profound experiences a human being can have.[15] Aside from the well-documented phenomenon of transference in the psychotherapeutic relationship, through which therapy becomes possible, falling in love, feeling empathy or compassion for another person, communing with nature, immersing oneself in the creative process, and entering into a mystical state of union with the divine are all dependent, to some extent, on the capacity to relax the boundaries between self and other, and experience a deeper connection of identification with the object of one's attention. This is not something to be avoided, but rather a skill, intrinsic to the psyche, to be reclaimed and cultivated – particularly if the goal, as it is with astrology, is to understand one's rightful place within the cosmos.

Participation Mystique and Mythopoetic Astrology

An astrology capable of addressing human psychology at the deepest possible level, where the ancient repository of the collective unconscious still forms the bedrock of our experience, even now, tens of thousands of years after it was not just an "aberration," but the norm, must pay homage to this way of knowing that also lies at its primordial roots. Spanning the gamut of human experience, normal, "abnormal" and extraordinary, this more fundamental understanding speaks to the possibility of a psychological astrology in which cosmos and the psyche, soul and the sacred, human culture and the biosphere are in symbolic dialogue, tending toward symbiotic union. This is an astrology that is rarely practiced today, but was at one time the expression of a more general way of knowing much closer to the ontological roots of our species.

As conducted through the lens of *participation mystique* within the Mythopoetic Era, astrology was not just a dispassionate observation of the night sky – as it is today in the hands of astronomers. Nor was it a mere extraction of meaning from abstract symbols on a piece of paper or a computer screen as it is for most contemporary astrologers. It was instead a *felt* participation in the celestial order of things, as revealed through a communion, across the subject-object barrier, with Sun and Moon, planets and stars. Jung, for whom the work of Lévy-Bruhl made a significant contribution to his own understanding of symbolism in general, wrote:

> *{Participation mystique} is an irrational, unconscious identity, arising from the fact that anything which comes into contact with me is not only itself, but also a symbol. This symbolization comes about firstly because every human being has unconscious contents, and secondly because every object has an unknown side.*[16]

If so, then pursued as an exercise in *participation mystique*, the same smorgasbord of celestial phenomena that is open to scientific observation, or intellectual abstraction, also potentially becomes a window into the workings of the unconscious psyche of human beings, as well as to the relationship between the individual and the cosmic order in which each individual and all human beings collectively participate. As we will explore in more detail later in the book, the possibilities encompassed by such a participatory approach to astrology restores what the science of our era is unprepared to offer.

Whether the night sky of the Mythopoetic Era was actually experienced this way must, of course, be a matter of speculation, but as Carl Jung wrote about *participation mystique*, it seems plausible that as early peoples encountered the night time sky, without the aid of astronomy, symbolic logic, or psychology, they learned about themselves and their relationship to the cosmos through just such an approach, and this way of knowing was the basis for the proto-astrology of the early Mythopoetic Era.

In many ways the opposite of analytical thinking, which was to rise in importance parallel to the development of science over the course of the next three to four thousand years, *participation mystique* precluded the categorization and dissection of experience. While we might consider that a disadvantage today, it also behooves us to consider the price to be paid for the cultural value we place on distancing ourselves from the object of our observation.

> *Children are introduced to the scientific method in middle school and informed that it is the only accurate process by which to gather knowledge and learn about the real world around us . . . (Yet) the scientific observer is never a participant in the reality he or she observes, but only a voyeur. As for the world he or she observes, it is a cold, uncaring place, devoid of awe, compassion, or sense of purpose. Even life itself is made lifeless to better dissect its component parts. We are left with a purely material world, which is quantifiable but without quality. . . The scientific method is at odds with virtually everything we know about our own nature and the nature of the world. It denies the relational aspect of reality, prohibits participation, and makes no room for empathic imagination. Students in effect are asked to become aliens in the world.*[17]

An astrology rooted in the mythopoetic mindset of *participation mystique* – which is inherently unscientific, at least as science is practiced now – might just possibly help restore a more integrated approach to understanding the world, one in which we are no longer aliens, but rather conscious participants with an integral though not dominant part to play in a larger story that includes us all, humans, creatures of the wild, deities of upperworld and underworld, mountains, rivers and stars. At the very least, it would help restore what was lost when astrology – and our culture at large – entered the age of scientific dominance, and so much of that story was repressed and denied.

Mythopoetic Astrology and the Evolution of Consciousness

Recent psychedelic research has corroborated the idea that beneath the ego-dominated mind is this more primordial layer, where cognition is not so easily bound by the usual limitations of time and space, past and future, self and other, inner and outer.[18] These limitations make our brains more functional, though less comprehensive in our capacity to fully know reality. They also incidentally make possible the objective measures upon which science depends, which in turn, provide a limited, but functional perspective.

At the deeper, more primordial level, we essentially return to our perceptual roots, where *participation mystique* is the norm. In this state, which consciousness researcher Stanislav Grof calls "holotropic," we potentially gain access to a much broader and deeper reservoir of knowledge than a focus on mere objective facts can ever hope to provide.

> *Holotropic consciousness has the potential to reach all aspects of existence. This includes the postnatal biography of the individual, events in the future, biological birth, embryonal and fetal development, the moment of conception as well as the ancestral, racial, karmic, and phylogenetic history.*[19]

Holotropic states include transpersonal experiences, reflecting "levels of reality denied by Western mechanistic science, but recognized and acknowledged by many ancient and non-Western cultures and by the great mystical traditions of the world."[20] In a holotropic state, which is essentially an intentionally induced state of *participation mystique*, the usual barriers between knower and known are dissolved. Empirical science is not possible in such a state, but direct experiential knowledge of an immense range of phenomena is.

To the extent that *participation mystique* played a role in the discovery of knowledge about the cosmos, the confluence of proto-science and proto-astrology of the Mythopoetic Era would point toward a way of knowing largely absent from the world today. But as psychedelic and consciousness research is revealing, this may be a way of knowing much closer, not just to the way our earliest ancestors saw the world, but to the root of the very possibility of knowing anything through a human brain. If so, then we might further postulate that an astrology that was rooted in such an approach to knowledge could be, in some ways, more relevant to the future evolution of human consciousness and the possibility of knowing, than abstract, rational, objective science.

Mythopoetic Astrology and the Roots of Language

American ethnobotanist Terrence McKenna has postulated that the use of psilocybin mushrooms was largely responsible for an unprecedented expansion of brain size some 100,000 years ago among Homo sapiens in Africa, giving rise to the kind of community bonding that would ensure survival for early tribes, as well as the development of human language and early religious ritual.[21] In addition, psilocybin promotes the kind of visual acuity, coupled with heightened imagination that would have clearly seen patterns in the sky, and perhaps articulated an understanding of our relationship to the cosmos that was inseparable from the evolution of consciousness and the development of language. If so, then the development of proto-astrology in the Mythopoetic Era would have been an exercise in *participation mystique* that paralleled and no doubt influenced the development of the human psyche itself.

> *. . . in the presence of hallucinogens, a culture is quickly introduced to ever more novel information, sensory input, and behavior and thus is bootstrapped to higher and higher states of self-reflection. I call this the encounter with the Transcendent Other . . . The Transcendent Other . . . is the crucible of the Mystery of our being, both as a species and as individuals. The Transcendent Other is Nature without her cheerfully reassuring mask of ordinary space, time, and causality.*
>
> *Of course, imagining these higher states of self-reflection is not easy. For when we seek to do this we are acting as if we expect language to somehow encompass that*

> *which is, at present, beyond language, or trans-linguistic . . . Psilocybin's main synergistic effect seems to be in the domain of language. It excites vocalization; it empowers articulation; it transmutes language into something that is visibly beheld.*[22]

While astrology is not commonly thought of in this way, for reasons that will become clear as we proceed with this narrative, it is not unlikely to assume that during the Mythopoetic Era, it was a visual, trans-linguistic language that allowed one to commune with the Transcendent Other, "the crucible of the Mystery of our being," out of which our relationship to the cosmos evolved as an essential component of the development of the human psyche itself.

This would have been a profound experience of *participation mystique* through which psyche and cosmos merged as an inseparable Whole. Out of this experience could potentially come knowledge, not just of the Transcendent Other, but of anything one wished to know.

In *Original Wisdom: Stories of an Ancient Way of Knowing*, psychologist Robert Wolff tells the story of a Sng'oi shaman of Malaysia, who, standing on the edge of the ocean (actually, the Strait of Malacca between the Indian and Pacific Oceans), without touching, tasting or otherwise entering into the water, was able to know that the water was salty, that below the surface of the ocean were mountains and valleys, that within the ocean were currents, that the water was home to many creatures, some "bigger than elephants" and many other facts about the ocean "that he could not possibly have known" in any way obvious to a contemporary Westerner.[23]

While this possibility might seem preposterous to those who are conditioned by modern science to view *participation mystique* as an antiquated vestige of human evolution, we might consider that for many of these so-called primitive cultures, one did not need a Ph.D. in some arcane specialization, obtained in isolated labor from the rest of humanity, to have a meaningful relationship to knowledge of self or universe. In fact, while the vocabulary necessary to discuss this distinction did not exist in the Mythopoetic Era, it would have been taken for granted that such a rarified and removed approach to knowledge of the sky – or anything else for that matter – would not lead to knowledge of anything worth knowing.

Shamanism

While the mythopoetic world did not produce Ph. Ds, there were in most indigenous cultures, shamans with the capacity to commune, not just with the beings of the visible world, but also with spirit beings in other dimensions not readily accessible to most people, armed only with the usual physiological senses. While the derivation of the word shaman is subject to some debate among scholars,[24] at least one possible meaning appears related to the Tungus word *saa*, meaning "to know."[25] suggesting that the practice of shamanism was a way of knowing endemic to many indigenous cultures from the Mythopoetic Era onward to the present day, although the actual practice of shamanism, not unlike astrology, has necessarily changed over the millennia of its practice.

What distinguishes shamanism from other ways of knowing, including the more inclusive practice of *participation mystique* is the derivation of information through the intentional cultivation of altered - or what Stanislav Grof would call holotropic - states of consciousness. Whether induced by drumming, ceremonial trance dance, psychedelic substances or some combination of these and other techniques, shamans are able to directly access the invisible realms and enter into relationship with benevolent and malevolent spirit beings, denizens of a realm beyond the pale of the experiences available to most of us in ordinary consensus reality, much less any kind of scientific inquiry into the nature of truth.

Although few anthropologists would dispute the existence of shamanism as a widespread cultural phenomenon, a strictly scientific anthropology has a harder time understanding or validating the reality of the shamanic experience itself, since to do so would take it into realms where measurement is impossible and largely irrelevant. When anthropologist Jeremy Narby, for example, set out to study the *ayahuascaros* - shamans of the Peruvian Amazon - he soon found himself boxed in by a tightly prescribed scientific paradigm that did not admit the existence of that which fell beyond its purview:

> *So, here are people without electron microscopes who choose, among some 80,000 Amazonian plant species, the leaves of a bush containing a hallucinogenic brain hormone, which they combine with a vine containing substances that inactivate an enzyme of the digestive tract, which would otherwise block the hallucinogenic effect. And they do this to modify their consciousness.*[26]

Anthropologists are at a loss to explain how this is possible, nor could they, using modern research tools, hope to duplicate it with a small army of scientists working around the clock for decades, even with the aid of computers and artificial intelligence, given the 40,000 estimated plant species in the Amazon - many of which remain unknown to science to this day.[27] Yet, when the *ayahuascaros* shrug and say, "The plants told us what to do" they are dismissed by scientists, who are ill-equipped to consider the possibility that there are other, more direct ways of knowing than empirical analysis, as well as other dimensions of reality beyond the reach of rational, methodical objective inquiry.

While there are no written records of astrologers from the Mythopoetic Era, and what has been written about the shamanism of preliterate cultures is necessarily educated speculation long after the fact at best, it seems likely that as shamans of the era encountered the night sky, they found it filled not just with stars but with spirit beings with whom they may or may not have been entirely synonymous.

In their exploration of mythopoetic consciousness, *Inside the Neolithic Mind*, anthropologists David Lewis-Williams and David Pearce argue that the evolution of cosmology, culture and neurological development were inseparable:

> *Although each society's cosmology is unique, nevertheless there are broad structures that derive from the brain. At the same time, in many societies there are people, we can all them 'seers', who believe that they can actually see and travel through the cosmos to capture insights hidden from ordinary people. For the former, the cosmos is not just a concept; it is a lived, explored reality.*[28]

While Lewis-Williams and Pearce are scientists, and do not discuss astrology in their book, is it really that big a stretch to imagine that the essence of astrology in the Mythopoetic Era was just that: a matter of "travel(ing) through the cosmos to capture insights hidden from ordinary people?" Or perhaps, it was hidden only from those who have lost abilities we all once had, which have become extraordinary only because most of us have failed to maintain or cultivate these faculties.

At the very least, it is clear to anyone who has ever looked up at night in a place of relatively low light pollution and allowed themselves to wonder and marvel at the sparkling panorama of stars, that a Great Mystery lives in the sky, that speaks to the hungry part of us that wants direct knowledge that is awesome in its intensity and immensity. Terrence McKenna might have called this Great Mystery the Transcendent Other; we might call it by other names, all of which take us not only more deeply into the unknown reaches of the Cosmos, but also more deeply into ourselves. If that hunger still exists in us, then how much more did it exist in those that were not conditioned to dismiss it as the vestige of a primitive age or squeeze it down to something comprehensible by reason? To the extent that mythopoetic shamans opened themselves to the night sky and all it had to teach, traveling through and immersing themselves in the "live, explored reality" of the cosmos, then they were indeed, the first astrologers, even if there was no word to call them that.

A Matrilineal Embrace of the Archetypal Feminine

There is perhaps one other dimension of the overarching philosophical worldview that informed the general mindset of the Mythopoetic Era, recognizing again that it is only in retrospect that we can discuss it this way. This dimension – which encompasses animism, *participation mystique* and shamanism – can be understood as an embrace of the archetypal Feminine.

The archetypal Feminine is emotional, rooted in the body and its sensory experiences, imaginal, and intuitive. It informs a worldview that is built on relationship – to family, to community, to the entire web of life, and to the unseen realms traversed by shamans, populated by invisible spirit beings, plant devas, animal totems and the living essence of many beings that we would consider to be inanimate objects today – mountains, rivers, clouds, storms and stars. This relational aspect of the Feminine worldview relies upon animistic sensibilities but goes beyond that to the possibility of merging with the Other to whom one is in relationship. This is essentially what happens in a more general sense through *participation mystique*, and in a more particular way through shamanism. Within the overarching context of the archetypal Feminine, what is implied is that we can know anything at all only to the extent that we have entered deeply into an intimate relationship with it.

This, of course, is the antithesis of what has become the scientific worldview, where one knows something because one has been able to stand apart from it and observe it as a neutral witness – a stance that we might recognize as a dimension of the archetypal Masculine. If the archetypal Feminine is oriented around relationship, the archetypal Masculine is oriented around the cultivation of independent individuality. The archetypal Masculine is rational, rooted in abstract thought, literal, linear and analytical because it allows one to remain separate from the world that it observes.

The archetypal Masculine tends to think in terms of hierarchies, a mindset within which, for example, it tended to assume a position of superiority with respect to the so-called "primitive" peoples, many of whom lived according to Feminine principles that are much more egalitarian by nature. This same preoccupation with hierarchies also gives rise to the whole demarcation issue discussed in the introduction, in which some disciplines are admitted to the exclusive club and others are not, while from a Feminine perspective, the more cross-pollination between disciplines, the more complete an understanding can be derived.

The archetypal Masculine thinks of time in linear, chronological terms, with the implication that as history moves through time, it progresses from what is less developed toward a more fully realized state. This is a view that necessarily fosters a dismissal of the past as regressive, antiquated and superstitious – that is to say, replaced through the progression of time by superior knowledge.

The archetypal Feminine, by contrast, thinks of time in cyclical, seasonal terms, through which a recurrent familiarity with repeating patterns breeds a more intimate depth of knowing, and a gradual mastery of those patterns. This, of course, is a worldview that supports an astrology based on planetary cycles, as well as the more secular observation that history repeats itself – a point it is always wise to remember.

The Integration of Masculine and Feminine In the Mythopoetic Era

Hopefully, it goes without saying that both the archetypal Feminine and the archetypal Masculine are psychological concepts with broader implications than can be encompassed by gender, and that both women and men must integrate their inner Masculine and Feminine in order to become whole beings. This is a perspective that was introduced to modern sensibilities by Carl Jung, who understood the synergy of the opposites to be a requisite for, as well as an attribute of the Self that embodied Wholeness.

In Mythopoetic times, distinctions between the archetypal Masculine and Feminine would not have been made, although as a way of life, tribal members were valued both for their individual gifts and attainments as well as for their participation in and contribution to the wellbeing of the whole community. Shamanic seers who had access to other realms and what Jungians might today call distinctly Feminine ways of knowing were no less valued for these skills as they were for their practical application in matters of healing and psychic protection. Hunters were valued not only for their practical skills, stalking and killing prey and feeding the community, as they were for their intuitive capacities in becoming one with the animal spirits they tracked. Women often served as priestesses and at the same time, worked the fields.

Such seamless intermingling of Masculine and Feminine, as well as the practical and spiritual dimensions of life, were widely practiced in cultures around the planet through at least the fourth millennia B.C.E. From about 4,000 B.C.E. to about 1,450 B.C.E, these more egalitarian cultures were routinely supplanted by invading Indo-Europeans, who brought patriarchal attitudes of hierarchical superiority, domination of the weak by the strong, up to and including slavery, genocide, ecocide, the suppression of women and the archetypal Feminine in general, the worship of male warrior gods, and the idea of "might by right."[29]

There is some controversy in anthropological circles about the meaning of the word "matriarchy," which has historically been used to refer to any early, generally prehistoric society that was not patriarchal. The word, in this broader sense, is sometimes construed as the mirror image of patriarchy, with women, instead of men, in roles of political leadership, moral authority, social privilege and control of property. Such cultures may be more accurately understood as matrilineal, matrilocal and matrifocal societies, where women held certain advantages but not exclusive power, while some doubt that a pure matriarchy, where women reigned supreme and men were marginalized, ever actually existed.[30]

What is most likely is that within the earliest cultures on the planet, men and women cooperated, largely out of necessity, in order to survive. There was a natural division of labor, with men more likely to be hunters and women more likely to raise children, gather and/or cultivate plants for food. Such cultures likely had a matrilineal structure, in which women held positions of leadership and spiritual authority, but men were not relegated to secondary status, as women are in patriarchy

Gylany

In *The Chalice and the Blade*, cultural historian Riane Eisler proposes the word "gylany" to describe this arrangement, (with "gy" referring to women; "an" to men; and the "l" in between to the egalitarian link between the sexes).[31] In celebrating this conceptual shift, renown feminist anthropologist Marija Gimbutas notes:

> *Old Europe and Anatolia (western Asia), as well as Minoan Crete, were a gylany. A balanced, nonpatriarchal and nonmatriarchal social system is reflected by religion, mythologies, and folklore, by studies of social structure of Old European and Minoan cultures, and is supported by the community of the elements of a matrilineal system in ancient Greece, Etruria (southern Italy), Rome, the Basque, and other countries of Europe.*[32]

In these, and probably other, parts of the world, gylany represented a much more egalitarian system in which men and women both had their place as equal co-participants in a larger web of life that included plants, animals, the ecological habitat in which all participated, and the larger cosmos in which all had their roots in a larger, undefined but palpable sense of Mystery. The archetypal Masculine and Feminine were valued equally, complemented each other, and formed a cultural foundation upon which both women and men thrived into the third millennium BCE.[33]

Within the Mythopoetic Era, animistic, shamanic, and gylanic sensibilities converged to fuel a form of proto-astrology very different than the astrology we practice today, but nonetheless based in an intimate relationship between psyche and cosmos. This relationship, perceptually rooted in *participation mystique*, was emotional, imaginal and intuitive, and although lacking in the conceptual sophistication that was to follow, it was in some ways perhaps a more direct and immediate way of knowing the cosmos than what we have inherited through later developments.

As Robert Wolff concludes his investigation into ancient ways of knowing:

> *If we listen, we can know – all we need to do is give up being in charge. Knowing inside is not something unusual; it is how we are (meant to know). All humans can have that connection with All-That-Is. The connection is within us.*[34]

Notes

1. My delineation of eras in this book departs somewhat from that in common usage. I take ahistorical liberties with these dates to emphasize a different sort of development particularly pertinent to the co-evolution of astrology and science. What I call the Mythopoetic Era, for example, begins in antiquity in what is generally referred to as the Neolithic period, or possibly as far back as the Paleolithic, otherwise known as the Stone Age, so named because during this period, wood and stone were the most common building materials.

2. Koch-Westenholz, Ulla. *Mesopotamian Astrology: An Introduction to Babylonian and Assyrian Celestial Divination*, Copenhagen: Museum Tusculanum Press, 1994, 11.

3. Needham, Joseph. *Science and Civilisation in China: Volume 3, Mathematics and the Sciences of the Heavens and the Earth*. Cambridge University Press, 1959. Without denying the development and complex interweaving of the astrologies developed by prehistoric Eastern cultures, this present work will focus primarily on the evolution of Western astrology, arising through ancient Greece and partially adopted and adapted from Mesopotamian sources.

4. Campion, Nicholas. *A History of Western Astrology Volume I: The Ancient and Classical Worlds*. Bloomsbury, 2009, 2-3.

5. Paulsson, B. Schulz. "Radiocarbon Dates and Bayesian Modeling Support Maritime Diffusion Model for Megaliths in Europe." Proceedings of the National Academy of Sciences of the United States of America 116, no. 9 (February 26, 2019): 3460–65. https://doi.org/10.1073/pnas.1813268116.

6. Cashford, Jules. *The Moon: Myth and Image*, New York: Four Walls Eight Windows, 2003, 16-18.

7. Ferguson, John. "Hellenistic Age | History, Characteristics, Art, Philosophy, Religion, & Facts." Encyclopedia Britannica, March 17, 2023. https://www.britannica.com/event/Hellenistic-Age.

8. Campion, *A History of Western Astrology, Volume I*, 4-5.

9. Levy-Bruhl, Lucien. *How Natives Think*, translated by Lillian A. Claire. Martino Fine Books, 2015, 13.

10. Haeckel, Ernst. *The Riddle of the Universe at the Close of the Nineteenth Century*. Harper & Brothers EBooks, 1900. https://doi.org/10.1037/13290-000. Twentieth century morphologists and biologists have since discovered that Haeckel's pithy phrase is an oversimplification. The complex intertwining of ontogeny and phylogeny is nonetheless valid as

a general principle, even if the particulars of how this works, and where it doesn't work, are still being sorted out.

11. Jung, Carl G. *Collected Works of C.G. Jung, Volume 9 (Part 1): Archetypes and the Collective Unconscious*. Princeton University Press, 1980, 162.
12. LeCron Foster, Mary. "Symbolism: The Foundation of Culture." In *Companion Encyclopaedia of Anthropology*, edited by Tim Ingold. Routledge, 1994, 386-7.
13. Neumann, Erich. *The Origins and History of Consciousness*. Bollingen Series. Vol. XLII. Princeton University Press, 1970, 24.
14. Jung, Carl G. *Collected Works of C.G. Jung, Volume 3: Psychogenesis of Mental Disease*. Princeton University Press, 1960, 244.
15. Winborn, Mark, ed. *Shared Realities: Participation Mystique and Beyond*. Skiatook, OK: Fisher King Press, 2014, 1.
16. Jung, Carl G. "Transformation Symbolism in the Mass." In *The Mysteries: Papers from the Eranos Yearbooks*. Princeton University Press, 1955, 320.
17. Rifkin, Jeremy. *The Empathic Civilization: The Race to Global Consciousness in a World in Crisis*. Penguin, 2009, 608.
18. Pollan, Michael. *How to Change Your Mind: What the New Science of Psychedelics Teaches Us About Consciousness, Dying, Addiction, Depression, and Transcendence*. Penguin, 2018, 314.
19. Grof, Stanislav. *The Adventure of Self-Discovery: Dimensions of Consciousness and New Perspectives in Psychotherapy and Inner Exploration*. SUNY Press, 1988, 41.
20. Grof, *The Adventure of Self-Discovery*, 42.
21. McKenna, Terence. *Food of the Gods: The Search for the Original Tree of Knowledge - A Radical History of Plants, Drugs, and Human Evolution*. Bantam, 1992, 20-26.
22. McKenna, *Food of the Gods*, 42.
23. Wolff, Robert. *Original Wisdom: Stories of an Ancient Way of Knowing*. Inner Traditions, 2001, 155.
24. Laufer, Berthold. "Origin of the Word Shaman." *American Anthropologist*, July 9, 1917. https://doi.org/10.1525/aa.1917.19.3.02a00020.
25. Hutton, Ronald. *Shamans: Siberian Spirituality and the Western Imagination*. A&C Black, 2007, vii.
26. Narby, Jeremy. *The Cosmic Serpent: DNA and the Origins of Knowledge*. Tarcher, 1998, 11.
27. World Wildlife Fund. "Amazon | Places | WWF." Accessed May 11, 2023. https://www.worldwildlife.org/places/amazon.

28. Lewis-Williams, David, and David Pearce. *Inside the Neolithic Mind: Consciousness, Cosmos and the Realm of the Gods*. Thames and Hudson, 2018, 11.
29. Metzner, Ralph. *Well of Remembrance: Rediscovering the Earth Wisdom Myths of Northern Europe*. Shambala, 1994, 38.
30. Prine Pauls, Elizabeth. "Matriarchy | Social System." Encyclopedia Britannica, July 20, 1998. https://www.britannica.com/topic/matriarchy.
31. Eisler, Riane. *The Chalice and the Blade*, 1987. https://openlibrary.org/books/OL2740056M/The_chalice_and_the_blade.
32. Gimbutas, Marija. *The Language of the Goddess*. Thames and Hudson, 1989, xx.
33. Gimbutas, *The Language of the Goddess*, xx.
34. Wolff, *Original Wisdom*, 197.

Chapter Two

The Intertwining of Astrology and Science In the Mystical Era: Second Millennium B.C.E. – Seventh Century B.C.E.[1]

The practice of a more recognizable form of Western astrology has been dated to the second millennium B.C.E,[2] when early cultures like those in Babylonia and Assyria developed calendrical systems, largely for agrarian purposes of predicting seasonal shifts and as a source of omen-based guidance for political leaders, while at the same time subscribing to a worldview in which celestial movements were observed as a form of communication with the gods. Shifting patterns in the visible sky were primarily used as a timing device for propitiation of appropriate deities through various ceremonies and rituals of religious significance. Religion in turn was not separate from astronomical/astrological observations, nor from cultural or political activity.[3]

Babylonian texts began making explicit references to celestial phenomena in relation to political developments during the reign of King Hammurabi (1,792 – 1,750 B.C.E.) and his successors. Sometime between 1,595 – 1,157 B.C.E., the *Enuma Anu Enlil* codified the astrological knowledge of the era in a series of about 70 tablets – which included observations of the phases of the Moon, solar and lunar eclipses, and the movement of the visible planets.[4] The Venus tablet of Ammisaduqa (Tablet 68), for example, documented the heliacal rising and setting of the planet Venus during the reign of the king of the same name, the fourth ruler after Hammurabi. By the seventh century B.C.E., the heliacal risings and settings of about 70 fixed stars had been catalogued along with 18 constellations that were designated as lying "in the path of the Moon" – which at the time was used, rather than the ecliptic (the Earth's orbit around the Sun) as the basic system of reference for planetary positions.[5]

Although at this point, astronomical information was not arranged in any pattern recognizable as a modern birthchart, it was still used to make predictions and for guidance, particularly of the ruling elite. About 6,500 – 7,000 astronomical observations were rendered as omens of interest to the rulers of the day and information from the *Enuma Anu Enlil* were extracted and summarized in regular astrological reports to the king, compiled by scholars. Over 500 such reports were published in Volume Eight of the *State Archives of Assyria*.[6] Others were gathered by Ashurbanipal and placed in the royal library at Nineveh between 660 – 630 B.C.E.[7]

In other parts of the world, such as India, China, and Mesoamerica, independent systems of astrology arose that were rooted in these cultures, and were very different from those practiced in the ancient Middle East.[8] Yet, within each culture, the central idea that celestial movement could form the basis for more participatory communication and interaction with the divine, as well as for the conduct of human affairs in alignment with divine intent as written in the sky, was essentially the same.

It should be noted here that this approach to astrology represents a step away from the *participation mystique* of the Mythopoetic Era. In the Mystical Era, the divine was separate from human affairs, and the gods, were to be communicated with, propitiated and appeased. Here we are no longer communing directly with the Transcendent Other through an automatic, involuntary union with it, but rather seeking to reach across a psychic divide to make contact with it, to understand it, and to align oneself with it. The alignment is not a given arising from a shared ground of being; it is now something to be sought and attained.

Divination

Geoffrey Cornelius calls this approach to astrology "divination" (the parenthetical expression is mine):

> *Divination was understood to reside in the sacred. Although in developed systems (such as divinatory systems of astrology) the omens might bear at many points on details of the mundane world, the effect of divination was to bring the matters enquired about, the vital concerns of man, within the guidance of the sacred. Seen in this light, a prediction through divination was none other than the revelation of what the gods willed to come to pass.*[9]

Cornelius is speaking here primarily about the astrological practice of *katarche*, which considers the moment in which an astrological inquiry is made to be the timing for an appropriate astrological chart from which guidance can be derived, rather than the natal chart or one of its permutations, which became more common practice later. *Katarche* survives in modern convention as horary astrology, and also in a different way, as electional astrology, which seeks the optimal moment for the beginning of something significant. This also became the basis of an approach to astrology that was rooted in magical sensibilities and aspirations.

These more modern adaptations continue to occupy their respective niches within the broader umbrella of our contemporary craft. Yet, as Cornelius points out, the fundamental attitude behind *katarche* - which was an intent to align human action with the will of the divine - was predominant throughout what I am calling the Mystical Era, and an important sensibility in astrological practice as well as to the general zeitgeist of the age. Eventually transported to the West through Greek culture, this was an attitude that first arose within Mesopotamia, as part of a diverse omen-based tradition, and developed within that tradition as a divinatory approach to astrology.[10]

Although not a direct immediate experience of the intimate oneness of psyche and cosmos, like the astrology of the Mythopoetic Era, divinatory astrology was participatory in nature – that is to say, not a matter of analyzing abstract symbols on a piece of paper, but rather of observing the sky, the divine intelligence written across the sky, and through that sacred act, as well as through attendant rituals and ceremonies, communing directly with the deities who wrote it.

> *Divination is here to be understood as the interpretation of the will of the divine beings, as the Latin root of this word 'divinus' suggests. These divine beings include the daemones ('demons'), intelligences between mortals and gods. The gods and daemones communicate their will in various ways. They might work directly through inspiration. They might appear in dreams and visions, directly or in disguise, or show themselves in the symbolism of signs and omens, the remarkable occurrences of the natural world.*[11]

While some would seek their omens through dream incubation, the reading of entrails, or the flight of birds, divinatory astrologers would observe the ever-changing visible patterns in the sky and attempt to glean from those patterns, the sacred intent behind them. Then at another level of participation, through ceremony and ritual, astrologer/priests would attempt to work with deities and daemons to steer divine will toward an outcome favorable to humans. Within the sacred space in which ceremony was conducted, working with an omen was very much a co-creative endeavor between humans and the divine.

Divination, Intent and Receptivity

It should be noted here that although divinatory astrology has become associated with the prediction of the future, for which it was in fact frequently used during the Mystical Era, this was not its original or deepest intent. At its heart, divinatory astrology stemmed from a desire to understand and align with the will of the gods, or what we might call divine intelligence – the innate sacred dimension permeating all of life and the entire manifest creation – which also informed the relationship between humans and the cosmic order on the deepest possible level that could be known.

In order to rise to this level of intent, one had to work toward a certain purity of consciousness – ultimately derived from optimum physical health; emotional clarity in the resolution of psychological issues with the potential to cloud perception; the mental balance of the meditative mind; and heartfelt devotion to the deities one hoped to align with and supplicate. Divinatory astrology was, in other words, not just a way of knowing, but a deep spiritual practice of preparation to receive divine guidance, and it is reasonable to assume that the best divinatory astrologers were deeply committed to this practice. Divinatory astrologers were, in fact, priests, and although the priesthood was to some extent subservient to political rulers, and at times corrupted by that relationship, there was a sacred dimension to the practice that, when it became primary, brought out the best in its practitioners.

The spiritual practice was in its own way, a profound exercise in *participation mystique*, since in order to work with an omen, the diviner had to enter into an "identity of substance" with the divine intelligence being accessed, which in turn, was not separate from the message being divined, nor from any predicted outcome conveyed in the message.

> *The omen and the spirit-agency intending it become identified, or "consubstantial." Further, the omen is seen as fully implicated in the event that it portends; indeed, it is also the event it portends.*[12]

As in the Mythopoetic Era, this form of divination was also essentially shamanic, as it involved a kind of communion with unseen spirits as well as an entry into the spiritual essence of things in order to know something through mystical identification with the source of knowledge. In the Mystical Era, priests effectively replaced shamans. But like shamanic practice, which was dependent on the broader prevalence of *participation mystique* as a general way of knowing, the divinatory priesthood was also the natural expression of a cultural mindset that allowed omens to reveal themselves and be understood as a matter of course, provided that a clear intention and adequate preparation rendered a practitioner ready to receive them.

> *In a culture that accepts omens, their pre-visionary potential, and a faith that they shall show themselves when needed, is granted to them in advance of any particular showing. This presentiment is therefore the prerequisite basis for taking up any omen as meaningful even where its specific meaning remains obscure. The particular forms of divination, the mechanics and methods, are of a secondary status to this presentiment. Individuals are likely to recognize it and therefore recognize the intentionality of divination, even if this intention is articulated in a form of practice they have never before encountered.*[13]

In the Mystical Era, divination was a deliberate matter of intention, presentiment and balanced receptivity. Evoking an omen, like shamanic practice, was something that required adequate training and preparation, even if the cultural acceptance of omens made them readily accessible. It was, in fact, not just something that happened, but a calling that one actively pursued.

Omens could come unbidden as a spontaneous act of revelation, but increasingly they were sought out as deliberate requests for divine guidance. Those seeking divine guidance would begin by putting themselves in the proper state of mind, evoking the appropriate deity, and then paying attention to what was happening around them – and more specifically in the case of divinatory astrologers, what was happening in the sky – and to worldly events to which the patterns seemed intuitively or by imaginal association to be correlated.

Such awareness of correlation was not, initially at least, a matter of hard and fast rule, although as these correlations were written down and codified into astrological reports, they assumed the mantle of authority, along with the astrologer/priests who made them. The basis for such authority was rooted in a willingness to open oneself to divine instruction within a ritual space (and in a ceremonial state of mind) conjured specifically for that purpose:

> *On what grounds does the diviner refer omen to event? He does so within the templum, the sacred space created in ritual. The sacred space is that wherein a god may be present. Within the ritual is brought forward man's concern, the worldly matters past, present, or future, in which will be discerned the working of the sacred. The god's response occurs within the sacred space of ritual, spontaneous blessing or touching that which has been ritually presented.*[14]

Divination and Mysticism

Just as the mythopoetic worldview arose as a natural outgrowth and expression of the more fundamental way of knowing understood in retrospect as *participation mystique*, so too did the divinatory worldview arise out of a way of knowing that can be broadly understood as mystical. Mystical traditions have long been associated with the formalized religions with which they generally co-existed awkwardly, as an attempt to seek direct knowledge of the divine, rather than rest content to merely know of the divine through canonized experience of religious forebearers like Moses, Jesus, Mohammed, Zoroaster, Mahavira or Gautama Buddha. But as Jungian psychologist Erich Neumann points out:

> *The experience of God as a sacred adventure represents only one specific, experimental, form of mysticism; it is by no means the most common and perhaps not even the most significant. But all mystical forms have in common the intensity of experience, the revolutionary, dynamic impetus of a psychological event which takes the ego out of the structure of its consciousness; and in all of them the numinous appears as the antithesis of consciousness.*[15]

In this broader sense, mysticism is the intentional quest for that which lies beyond what the conscious mind can know, often a quest for a direct encounter with the sacred – the hidden dimension of things, the living intelligence that operates beneath appearances – but in any case, a quest that "calls for an act of attention and devotion on the part of the ego, an aptitude for being 'moved,' a willingness to see what wants to appear."[16] It is through their aptitude for being moved and the willingness to "see" that astrologers in the Mystical Era were guided to read the will of the divine in the movement of the cosmos. To some extent, this orientation still guides all skilled astrologers today, who are moved beyond a strictly rational interpretation of the symbolism to "see what wants to appear" in a birthchart under consideration.

As Neumann and others are quick to note, the *participation mystique* of the Mythopoetic Era was itself a kind of early mysticism, perhaps largely involuntary, except among shamans, who intentionally courted the numinous through the deliberate induction of altered states of consciousness. This attitude - of intentional opening to whatever revelation might lie at the heart of direct experience was also at the root of religious experience, which back in the days before written scripture, was oriented around various practices - shamanic, yogic, contemplative, ritual, magical and mystical - designed to create such an opening. Within a mystical approach to knowledge, it was the clarity of intent behind a given practice, as well as the diligence with which one pursued it, that generated a sacred space in which divination became possible.

The Mystical Roots of Eastern Religion

Within the Mystical Era, this general approach to knowing evolved along a number of different pathways, cloaked in various cultural guises. In northern India, beginning about 1,500 B.C.E., the hymns of the *Rigveda*, considered some of the oldest sacred texts on the planet, became available as a written account of an earlier oral tradition. These hymns describe the use of *soma* (a hallucinogenic plant associated with the god Soma, believed to have possibly been the fly agaric mushroom, *Amanita muscaria*) to induce a mystical communion with Parusha, a cosmic being both immanent within the manifest world and transcendent of it. Other rites within the *Rigveda* employed other plant medicines and rituals to connect with other deities such as Rudra or Shiva.

In this approach, the *Vedas* were very much in line with the earlier shamanic tradition of the Mythopoetic Era, which employed altered states as a pathway to an experience of *participation mystique* in pursuit of sacred knowledge. It also entailed a distinctly divinatory element in its emphasis on ritual, ceremony, sacrifice and symbolic sacrifice, all designed to allow the priests, or *brahmans*, of the Vedic tradition to enter into a direct relationship of supplication to the deities with which they sought to commune.

It was out of these rituals that the *brahmans* sought and exercised knowledge as intermediaries between humans and the realm of the sacred. Later, as the teachings of the *Vedas* were reinterpreted and elaborated in the *Upanishads* somewhere during the first millennia C.E., they became less a prescriptive experiential practice and more a philosophical canon, providing a foundation for the religious tradition broadly known today as Hinduism.

Before Hinduism existed, however, the Vedic tradition entailed a more deeply mystical element in its emphasis on receptivity to the divine. The authorship of the *Vedas* was generally considered to be *apauruseya*, alternately translated as "not of a man, superhuman, impersonal, or authorless," the implication being that the *Vedas* were not a written construction, but perhaps instead a revelation received directly from the divine. The original *Vedas* were also often described as *sruti* (what is heard) as opposed to *smrti* (what is remembered), with reference to the idea that these texts were not composed so much as transmitted in deep meditation.

Some scholars reject this idea using logical arguments, yet are at a loss to adequately explain the origin of the earlier oral tradition out of which the written *Vedas* sprang.[17] It is true, as these scholars argue, that these oral teachings were both heard (*sruti*) and remembered (*smrti*), and eventually written down, but where did these oral teachings come from? A truism within the study of these mysteries holds that the *Vedas* were without a beginning, which is where scholarship moves into the fog of conjecture. It is within this fog, where there is no written record, and yet something without a clear origin comes into being as a practice, a set of beliefs, and eventually a written scripture, that the Mystical Era – and the traditions out of which it takes shape – are rooted.

Other major religions in the East – including Buddhism, Taoism, Confucianism, Shinto, Jainism and Sikhism – all evolved from oral teachings that were only written down toward the end of the Mystical Era. Some of these written teachings – such as those of the *Tao Te Ching* are attributed to an original author – Lao Tzu (meaning "Old Master") – who may or may not have actually existed as an historical figure. Other religions, like Shinto, seem to have emerged directly from an oral tradition – polytheistic *kami* (god or spirit) worship – without a central figure.

Even among those Eastern religions with an identifiable oral teacher of a clear historical record – Buddhism (Gautama Buddha), Confucianism (Confucius), Jainism (Mahavira) and Sikhism (Guru Nanak) – the oral teachings themselves generally stemmed back to an earlier mystical tradition or confluence of traditions, in which the object of spiritual practice was a direct experience of the divine. Gautama Buddha, Mahavira and Guru Nanak were outright mystics, obtaining their knowledge of the divine and their teachings through meditation, ascetic austerities that induced altered states of consciousness, and cultivated receptivity to divine revelation.

Confucius is sometimes considered more of a political philosopher than a religious figure in this same sense, although in the *Analects* – a collation of Confucius' oral teachings, written down by his disciples somewhere between the fifth century B.C.E. and the third century C.E. – Confucius refers to himself as a "transmitter" of earlier teachings from the Zhou Dynasty (circa 1,000 to 800 B.C.E.), rather than the source of the teachings attributed to him. The Zhou Dynasty in turn was said to have begun with the semi-historical, quasi-mythical Emperor Ku and his consort Jiang Yuan, who – in an echo of the Christian myth – gave virgin birth to a miracle child after stepping into a footprint left by the supreme deity Shangdi. As with the Vedic Tradition, the farther one goes back into Chinese religious history, the more blurred the line becomes between official religion and a precursor to that religion that is steeped in mythology, mysticism and shamanic practice, where direct contact with the source of knowledge becomes the object of the quest.

The Mystical Roots of Western Religion

By a similar process in the West, the Judeo-Christian tradition that now revolves around the written word of the *Bible* and the slightly more recent Muslim tradition that revolves around the written word of the *Koran* have both largely forgotten their mystical origins. These religions actually began in a much earlier era where there was no written word, just an oral tradition in which stories were told and passed down to successive generations. Within this culture, circa the fourth millennium B.C.E., before the existence of Judaism, Christianity or Islam, there was actually no word for "religion" as such, since everyday life was as much a matter of communion with spiritual and primal forces as it was a mundane matter of physical survival and socio-cultural activity.[18]

The oldest surviving manuscript of the Babylonian *Talmud*, out of which the Hebrew *Bible* gradually evolved through a rather complex history is dated to 1,342 B.C.E.[19] From the eighth through the sixth centuries B.C.E. - near the end of the Mystical Era - the ancient Judeans of the Assyrian Empire began collecting the stories and oral teachings of their predecessors into written manuscripts that gradually coalesced into scripture that eventually found its way into the Hebrew *Bible*, emerging in its present form sometime during the first century C.E. As is well documented throughout the *Bible*, these oral teachers, known as prophets, were those who routinely saw visions and heard God speaking to them, as was the norm for all religious figures during the Mystical Era. It was during the first century C.E., as well, that the gospels of the *New Testament* were written down and collated, and that Christianity began to emerge as a distinct religion of its own, in the wake of Christ's brief career as an oral teacher.

The *Koran* - the other major religious scripture in the West - was said to have been revealed to the prophet Muhammad over the course of 23 years before his death in 632 C.E. Muhammad could neither read nor write, but heard the word of God directly - very much in the spirit of the Mystical Era - and then told it to scribes who wrote it down.[20] Like the founders of nearly every other major religion on the planet, Muhammad was an oral teacher, whose teachings were divinely inspired.

The Gradual Transition to Written Language in the Mystical Era

Toward the end of the Mystical Era, these newly emerging religions gradually constellated around various written scriptures, but for most of the era, this would not have been the case. Archeological discoveries at Wadi-el Hol in Egypt currently date the invention of the first alphabetic language to around 2,000 B.C.E.[21] - at the beginning of the Mystical Era, but it would take the entire period for written language to evolve to the point where it could provide the basis for a coherent and comprehensive scripture. The Phoenician alphabet was widely in use throughout the Mediterranean by the ninth century B.C.E. The Paleo-Hebrew alphabet had been in use since the twelfth century B.C.E., but it was in the Aramaic alphabet, derived from the Phoenician, sometime around the sixth century B.C.E., that the first Hebrew *Bible* was written - only toward the very end of the Mystical Era.

Before this, there had been a number of ideographic languages - a precursor to modern Chinese found on tortoise shells dated back to the seventh millennium B.C.E.;[22] a set of Vinca symbols, otherwise known as Old European script found on Neolithic artifacts in Serbia, dating to the fifth and sixth millennium B.C.E.; the Kish tablet found at Tell al-Uhaymir in Iraq, a precursor to the cuneiform script of Sumeria, dated to the end of the fourth millennium B.C.E.; and probably the most famous, Egyptian hieroglyphs, a relatively sophisticated system slightly more recent than the Sumerian. None of these ideographic languages, however, were capable of articulating the kind of complex thought that we normally associate with written languages today. Despite a universal need and desire to communicate in writing that characterized these early cultures of the Mythopoetic Era, it wasn't until the beginning of the Mystical Era, circa 2,000 B.C.E. that the oral teachings of the world's religions could potentially be expressed in writing, and only toward the end of the era that this potential was actualized.

After the Mystical Era, a struggle ensued between proponents of the new written scriptures and the oral tradition that proceeded it. Christianity was relatively quick to adopt its Bible, while the more mystical oral tradition persisted primarily among various Celtic, Druidic, gnostic and pagan cultures who resisted the authority of the Church and kept alive the old ways, based on a continuing hunger for direct experience. The oral tradition persisted a bit longer in Judaism, where prophets and sages (known as the *hakhamim* in Hebrew) had been transmitting kabalistic knowledge since at least the tenth millennium B.C.E. In Islamic cultures, the mystical approach to direct experience of Allah in his myriad forms was kept alive by the Sufis, who relied less on the literal meaning of the words in the *Koran* and more upon its invitation to ecstatic experience.

Spoken Language and Whole-Brain Intuition

Within the transitional culture of the Mystical Era, the oral traditions of the Middle East and Europe eventually gave rise to more codified forms of religion, oriented around written scripture. Within the oral tradition itself, however, divination was a natural extension of the use of spoken language, and its distinct differences from written language.

While modern neuroscience generally associates both spoken and written language with various functions in the left hemisphere of the brain, when you are speaking and/or listening to someone else speaking, you are more likely to be fully engaged with your environment than you will be when you have your nose buried in a book or words on a computer screen. With full engagement comes an awareness of visual, spatial and emotional cues, as well as simple processing of language, information that engages the right hemisphere as well as the left. In addition, the more imaginative and intuitive right brain is necessary "to comprehend metaphors as well as patterns of intonation and poetic meters" – the more auditory, rhythmical, and musical qualities of the spoken word.[23]

As noted by cultural historian Leonard Shlain, the use of metaphorical language to process inner experience in particular is an especially complex use of language that engages both hemispheres of the brain:

> *When people find it necessary to express in words an inner experience such as a dream, an emotion, or a complex feeling-state, they resort to a special form of speech called metaphor that is the right brain's unique contribution to the left brain's language capacity. The word "metaphor" combines two Greek words – "meta," which means "over and above," and "pherein: to bear across." Metaphors allow one to leap across a chasm from one thought to the next. Metaphors have multiple levels of meaning that are perceived simultaneously. They supply a plasticity to language without which communication would be less interesting, sometimes difficult, and occasionally impossible . . . Metaphors beget poetry and myth, and are essential to the parables of religion and the wisdom of folktales.*[24]

They are also essential to a whole brain practice of astrology, where information is infused not just with identifiable facts, but also emotion, subjective memories and associations, archetypal and mythological references, intuitive flights of non-linear association and awareness of poetic synchronicities emerging in the moment. In the Mystical Era, and the practice of divinatory astrology in any era, this is even more critical, as it is simply impossible to hear what the gods are saying with half a brain.

In addition, the inclusion of the right brain in spoken language allows for an integration of what we hear with what we see. The most obvious level on which this synthesis occurs is in normal face-to-face conversation, where the whole brain not only interprets what it hears, but also takes into account facial expressions and other non-verbal cues. While skeptical scientists evaluating astrology sometimes consider the use of visual cues – called "cold reading" in their language – to be a kind of cheating,[25] the fact is, to be at our best as astrologers, we need both halves of our brain, reading both the visual and auditory cues presented by our clients, as well as a general awareness of everything happening in the moment, all in relation to the written birthchart before us, informed by the movement of heavenly bodies above, in order to discern the relevant metaphors that bring meaning to the astrological experience.

If we extend this everyday experience into a context where one is in conversation with the gods and goddesses and the heavens on which they write their messages for humans to decipher, then it was a whole-brain spoken language that allowed astrologers of the Mystical Era to both see and hear the messages they received as they observed the nighttime sky – perhaps a language directly descendant from that described by Terrence McKenna as one rooted in visual acuity as well as the capacity to interpret sound. It is my contention that this was – and is – the essence of divinatory astrology, born of a much more holistic and broader definition of language that encompasses not just the written word, but a capacity to see, hear, and clearly intuit "what is written in the stars."

Spoken Language and Magic

There was also likely a more inherently magical component to spoken language in which words spoken with intention had transformative power – alluded to in the *Bible*, but increasingly de-emphasized as widespread mythopoetic sensibilities gave way to formalized religions, and a more formal codified practice of astrology. As it says, at the very beginning of Genesis:

> *God said, "Let there be light," and there was light.*
>
> *God said, "Let there be a vault in the waters to divide the waters in two." And, so it was.*[26]

And so it went, through the seven days of creation, culminating with the creation of man in the image of the gods. This was Yahweh demonstrating the magical power of speech to create something out of nothing.

In yogic tradition, on the other side of the world, this power is called *vach siddhi* – a by-product of serious yogic practice, which endowed those who attained it with the capacity to render something true just by saying it out loud. This is the same power that was preserved in the magical incantations of Druid priests, witches, and hermetic occultists, as well as kabbalists of the mystical Jewish traditions, and perhaps in a somewhat different way, by the Sufis chanting the 99 names of God. Although we know little of these powers today, during the Mystical Era, they were the basis not just for a capacity to hear the will of the deities being supplicated, but to speak out loud what one heard with a certain innate authority, resonating with metaphorical truth and aligned with the creative capacity of divine intelligence.

The Socio-Political Impact of Written Language

The oral traditions out of which these mystical, divinatory and magical approaches to knowledge arose persisted well beyond the Mystical Era, because written language was slow to catch on and become widespread in the lives of ordinary people. Throughout the entire era, written languages were largely the closely guarded province of the power elite, political and religious leaders, gradually extending to scholars and academics. It wasn't until the middle of the second millennium C.E. – well past the end of the Mystical Era – that Gutenberg's printing press forever changed the cultural landscape – and unleashed the power of the written word into the mainstream. Because of this relatively slow evolution in our use of written language, the process by which religion in the West began to coalesce around sacred scripture, and supplant the oral culture of the Mystical Era, was a transition that took the better part of four millennia.

This is not to say, however, that the changes wrought during the Mystical Era were not profound. As written scripture replaced oral tradition as a basis for the relationship between humans and the realm of the sacred, it began to erode the dominance of the archetypally Feminine worldview that allowed the receptivity necessary for divination to take place. As noted in Chapter One, the archetypal Feminine is emotionally intuitive, image-based and relational; while a scripture-based approach to religion is more archetypally Masculine, and typically oriented around a literal interpretation of words, a strict adherence to "the letter of the law," and a hierarchical social order based on status, privilege, education, and often gender.

In the West, the appearance of the written *Bible* was the primary catalyst for this transition, although as Leonard Shlain points out, the transition began (the parenthetical phrase is mine):

> *. . . in the Sinai approximately thirty-eight hundred years ago (at the beginning of the Mystical Era) when desert people revolted against the florid icon worship of Egyptian polytheism . . . The defining event of the Israelite's reformation was the appearance of the first sacred alphabet book. Coincident with its appearance, men sharply circumscribed women's rights, denounced the worship of goddesses as an abomination, and declared that images were profane.*[27]

The Origins of Astrology in the Mystical Era

The evolution of the written languages that eventually coalesced as scripture began, not coincidentally, around the same time as the first written record of astrological knowledge appeared on the tablets of the *Enuma Anu Enlil* that served the Babylonian rulers of that era. As Hellenistic astrologer Chris Brennan notes, "for many Mesopotamian cultures, (astrology) became one of the languages through which the gods communicated their intentions to humankind,"[28] that is to say, essentially a language of divination, destined to change rather dramatically when astrological knowledge was written down, and began to be codified in what essentially became astrological scripture.

Later, when the early Hellenistic astrologers began reinventing astrology for a new era (see Chapter Three), they often paid homage to the traditions inherited from Mesopotamia and Egypt, even as they radically altered those traditions as to be virtually unrecognizable. At the same time, many of the earliest astrological texts were also attributed to a legendary, mythical or religious figure from the past. As Brennan notes:

> *This was a common practice in the ancient world, especially for texts dealing with what we might classify today as "occult" matters, such as astrology, alchemy, or magic, although it also happened with philosophical, religious, and medical texts as well. The genre of falsely ascribed texts is generally referred to as "pseudepigrapha."*[29]

It is noteworthy that the authors to which these pseudepigraphic texts were ascribed were often oral teachers such as Abraham, born Abram ben Terah (circa 2,150 B.C.E.), considered the Hebrew patriarch of the Abrahamic religions, including Judaism, Christianity, and Islam; or Zoroaster, an Iranian prophet who lived sometime during the Mystical Era (historians disagree wildly about actual dates), who founded the religion that bears his name. Some scholars question whether or not Zoroaster was a real person, along with others like Lao Tzu, whose work may have been amalgams of a number of oral teachers – part of a trend prior to the tenth century C.E. of rendering legend and myth as history.[30]

Other astrological texts were associated with figures such as Nechepso and Petosiris, who, if they actually existed, left no written record themselves, even though they were often quoted by subsequent astrologers. Taking another step back into the mystical fog of the oral tradition, some early astrological texts were attributed to mythological or divine figures such as Orpheus, Asclepius, Hermes or Hermes Trismegistus.

Although there may be other possible reasons for this attribution, Brennan also alludes to "the apparent existence of mystery traditions, within the astrological community, and the possibility that many of the ancient doctrines were kept secret, with some of the astrological schools being kept private or underground."[31] If so, then it is not unlikely to assume that like the more organized religions, astrology also harkens back to an oral tradition, designed to facilitate direct experiential knowledge, rather than a simple transmission of knowledge previously obtained. This practice, like the early religions with which it co-evolved, was likely divinatory and mystical in nature.

Divinatory astrology was the practice of reading the omens written in the sky within a ritual space, created through clear intention, adequate preparation of mind, heart, body and spirit, and consummated by an open psyche receptive to intuitive association, imaginal experiences of divine presence, and direct observation of correlation between celestial phenomena and worldly events. Though a more mystical union between a diviner and the specific deity being supplicated was always possible – and probably common among the best divinatory astrologers – to some extent, one could obtain useful information through skilled adherence to the divinatory protocol. The protocol in turn would have been a spiritual practice designed to prepare the astrologer to receive a direct transmission of knowledge, rather than interpret the astrological patterns in play as an analytical exercise.

The oral tradition, in general, also likely had a secular component, which was used in the case of the scriptures that later evolved to preserve a certain historical account of events, but also other mundane bits of knowledge of a practical nature, used to secure food, shelter, health and other necessities of life. In relation to astrology, this dimension of oral tradition would encompass various techniques, some of which were passed on to or rediscovered by early Hellenistic authors. These, however, were likely secondary to the cultivation of the necessary mystical sensibilities through which an understanding of divine intent was discerned by whatever techniques were employed.

The Confluence of Astrology, Science, Religion And Culture in the Mystical Era

Returning to the central theme of our historical overview, we can lastly note that within the mystical worldview, science – as it is known today – did not technically exist. Yet, the reading of astrological omens required the calculation and attempted prediction of astronomical events such as equinoxes and solstices, the monthly lunar cycle, the nodal cycle of the Moon, eclipses, planetary stations, heliacal risings and settings of planets and fixed stars, and other celestial phenomena. Throughout both the Mythopoetic and the Mystical Eras, these phenomena were observed and measured with an astonishing level of sophistication to an unexpected degree of accuracy in a way that can be considered pre-scientific and are certainly well within the spirit of modern science's current scope.

Likewise, the interpretation of astronomical events as a series of messages from the gods that could be interpreted – although at this point in history, without an actual birthchart – can be understood to be essentially pre-astrological, if by astrological we mean what is generally considered astrology today. As noted throughout this chapter, divinatory interpretation was not a practice of reading symbolism, as astrology has since become, but rather one involving a cultivation of intuitive, imaginal and experiential receptivity in service to a specific question for which one sought an answer directly from the heavens.

Special care was taken in the formulation of the question itself, as poorly formed questions would generally be expected to provide ambiguous answers. Poorly formed questions with either a lack of clear intent, frivolous intent, or no intent at all, could not expect to provide reliable guidance. These considerations are still entertained within the contemporary practice of horary astrology, but are generally not considered central to the practice of astrology in general, as they would have been throughout the Mystical Era.

Strictly speaking, divinatory practice was neither scientific nor astrological, although in the Mystical Era, this would have largely been a moot point, since there was no separation between these fields of human endeavor. In addition, the use of astronomical timing and astrological interpretation as a basis for ceremony and ritual adds an inherent spiritual dimension to this early melding of science and astrology that is entirely missing from science now and not as clearly or universally taken for granted in the contemporary practice of astrology.

From the Neolithic Era through at least the height of Mesopotamian culture (a period of more than 15,000 years), it is not unlikely to assume that we could take this idea of confluence one step further. Those who had sacred knowledge of astronomy, could accurately interpret the heavenly signs, and perform the appropriate rituals, also held enormous influence over those in political power. Throughout this period, as in the preceding Mythopoetic Era, not only were astrology and science inseparable from each other, but also from religion, politics, and the sociocultural fabric of everyday life. The various streams within this confluence were more easily discerned during the Mystical Era than the Mythopoetic, but the integral nature of knowledge – which to some extent relied on this confluence – was taken for granted as the cultural foundation of human endeavor.

Notes

1. The year in which a recognizable form of Western astrology has been noted (circa the second millennium B.C.E.) would have taken place at the beginning of the Middle Bronze Age, while the ending of the Mythopoetic Era would have coincided with what is generally referred to as the Classical Era of Ancient Greece and the beginning of the Roman Empire.
2. Ulla Koch-Westenholz, *Mesopotamian Astrology: An Introduction to Babylonian and Assyrian Celestial Divination*, Copenhagen: Museum Tusculanum Press, 1994, 11.
3. Nicholas Campion, *A History of Western Astrology Volume I: The Ancient and Classical Worlds*, Bloomsbury, 2009, 6.

4. Brown, David. *Mesopotamian Planetary Astronomy-Astrology*. Vol. 18 of Cuneform monographs. University of Virginia Press, 2000, 254-55.

5. Whitfield, Peter. *Astrology: A History*. New York: Harry N. Abrams, 2001, 19.

6. Hunger, Hermann. *Astrological Reports to Assyrian Kings. Vol. 8*. Helsinki University Press, 1992.

7. Whitfield, *Astrology: A History*, 10.

8. On page 67 of *A History of Western Astrology Volume I*, Campion notes a likely intermingling of the Vedic astrology of India and Mesopotamian astrology in the third millennium B.C.E., as well as some potential influence of Chinese astrology on the Vedic system.

9. Cornelius, Geoffrey. *The Moment of Astrology: Origins in Divination*, Wessex Astrologer Limited, 2002, 130.

10. Cornelius, *The Moment of Astrology*, 126.

11. Cornelius, *The Moment of Astrology*, 129.

12. Cornelius, Geoffrey. "Divination, Participation and the Cognitive Continuum." Field of Omens | Astrodivination. Accessed May 12, 2023. https://www.astrodivination.com/field-of-omens/.

13. Cornelius, "Divination, Participation and the Cognitive Continuum."

14. Cornelius, *The Moment of Astrology*, 132.

15. Neumann, Erich. "Mystical Man." In *The Mystic Vision: Papers from the Eranos Yearbooks*, Bolligen Series XXX 6. Princeton University Press, 1968, 381.

16. Neumann, "Mystical Man," 382.

17. Pollock, Sheldon. "The Revelation of Tradition: Sruti, Smriti, and the Sanskrit Discourse of Power." In *Boundaries, Dynamics and Construction of Traditions in South Asia*, edited by Federico Squarcini. London: Anthem Press, 2011, 41-58.

18. Shlain, Leonard. *The Alphabet Versus the Goddess: The Conflict Between Word and Image*. Penguin, 1999, 77.

19. Golb, Norman. *The Jews in Medieval Normandy: A Social and Intellectual History*. Cambridge University Press, 1998, 530.

20. Donner, Fred. "The Historical Context." In *The Cambridge Companion to the Qur'an*, edited by Jane Dammen McAuliffe. Cambridge University Press, 2006, 31-33.

21. Schniedewind, William. "Origins of the Written Bible." NOVA | PBS, November 18, 2008. https://www.pbs.org/wgbh/nova/article/origins-written-bible/.

22. Rincon, Paul. "BBC NEWS | Science/Nature | 'Earliest Writing' Found in China." Accessed May 12, 2023. http://news.bbc.co.uk/2/hi/science/nature/2956925.stm.
23. Harte, Erin. "How Your Brain Processes Language." *Brain World*, September 13, 2021. https://brainworldmagazine.com/how-your-brain-processes-language/.
24. Shlain, *The Alphabet Versus the Goddess*, 20.
25. Dean, Geoffrey, Arthur Mather, David Nias, and Rudolf Smit. *Tests of Astrology: A Critical Review of Hundreds of Studies*. Amsterdam: AinO Publications, 2016, 438.
26. *The Jerusalem Bible*, edited by Alexander Jones. Doubleday, 1968, 1:3-7.
27. Shlain, *The Alphabet Versus the Goddess*, 323.
28. Brennan, Chris. *Hellenistic Astrology: The Study of Fate and Fortune*. Denver: Amor Fati Publications, 2017, 2.
29. Brennan, *Hellenistic Astrology*, 28.
30. Stausberg, Michael, Yuhan Sohrab-Dinshaw Vevaina, and Anna Tessmann. "The Wiley Blackwell Companion to Zoroastrianism." Wiley EBooks, 2015, 60-61. https://doi.org/10.1002/9781118785539.
31. Brennan, *Hellenistic Astrology*, 46.

Thomas Kuhn argued that competing paradigms are "incommensurable": that is to say, there exists no objective way of assessing their relative merits. There's no way, for example, that one could make a checklist comparing the merits of Newtonian mechanics (which applies to snooker balls and planets but not to anything that goes on inside the atom) and quantum mechanics (which deals with what happens at the sub-atomic level). But if rival paradigms are really incommensurable, then doesn't that imply that scientific revolutions must be based – at least in part – on irrational grounds? In which case, are not the paradigm shifts that we celebrate as great intellectual breakthroughs merely the result of outbreaks of mob psychology?

Naughton, John, "Thomas Kuhn: The Man Who Changed the Way the World Looked at Science," The Guardian, March 22, 2018

Chapter Three

The Divergence of Astrology and Science In the Philosophical Era: 7th Century B.C.E – 4th Century C.E.[1]

There is ample evidence to suggest that an integrated paradigm in which early astronomical measurement, astrological interpretation of celestial phenomena, and the astrological timing of spiritual, social and political activities were pursued as a seamless, participatory way of knowing that persisted at least until around the seventh century B.C.E. This cultural integration – which also provided the foundation on which astrology evolved for the first thirty millennia or so of its existence – began to unravel during what I am calling the Philosophical Era, in which various approaches to knowledge, including astrology, began to revolve around a more rational footing, and compete with each other for dominance. As noted in the previous chapter, written language was an important factor in this cultural shift, as was the rise of mathematics as the ultimate language of reason and logic.

As noted by astrological historian Jim Tester, "from the seventh century (B.C.E.) on, exact observation becomes increasingly important, and still later arithmetical computation plays a part in this sort of proto-astrology," thus precipitating the increasing separation of what would eventually become scientific astronomy from what was then an astrological/astronomical hybrid, rooted in spiritual practice, and pervasive as a cultural influence throughout the civilized world.[2]

The Milesian Evolution

As noted in my previous book *The Seven Gates of Soul*, this was a gradual evolution that took place over the better part of about two or three millennia.[3] The evolution started in earnest with Thales of Miletus – a pre-Socratic philosopher, mathematician, and astronomer, regarded by Aristotle as the first philosopher in the Greek tradition,[4] and by others as the first scientific philosopher in Western civilization.[5]

Thales and the other Milesians – primarily Anaximander and Anaximenes – became the first philosophers to ascribe observable phenomenon to natural causes, with no reference to gods or goddesses. While no twenty-first-century astronomer would risk his or her career by referencing anything remotely metaphysical, this was not the case at the dawning of the Philosophical Era. At this juncture in our collective evolution, the thought that local deities of choice might *not* be responsible for what happened in this world was a revolutionary idea and a radical departure from the dominant paradigm, which was still largely mythopoetic in nature. Within both the Mythopoetic and the Mystical Eras, gods and goddesses were taken to be as real as you or me, responsible for natural phenomena as well as the rise and fall of human fortunes and approached by humans in correlation with their celestial movements, which mirrored mundane reality as well as divine intent.

The Milesians were operating at a philosophical crossroads in our intellectual history – one at which the dominant worldview of a universe alive with divine intelligence met a desire to penetrate beneath the veils of this intelligence into the natural workings of the world itself. This desire would eventually evolve into a science in which mythopoetic sensibilities no longer played a part, and in which the observer had to remove himself from the world in which he would have previously been a participant, in order to comment credibly upon it – a comment that would in turn de-mystify the world.

Pythagoras

Born into this era and, in many ways, setting this emerging dichotomy in motion was the seminal philosopher and oral teacher Pythagoras. On the one hand, Pythagoras studied and absorbed the participatory worldview as presented in Babylonian, Egyptian and Celtic mystery teachings, among many other sources. His teachings reflected these sensibilities, in part, by presenting numbers as archetypal dimensions of divine intelligence at work within the manifest world.[6] Numbers were, in other words, like astrology in the Mystical Era, essentially a language through which the will of the divine could be known.

On the other hand, Pythagoras taught that aside from their metaphysical implications, number could also be used to measure the natural world objectively, that is to say, as a reality that existed in its own right, apart from human or divine participation. As passed on through his students Plato and Aristotle, this notion became the subsequent bedrock of Western philosophical history – later to be articulated by generations of mathematicians and scientists, who began stripping Pythagorean teachings about number of their essential mythopoetic, mystical and metaphysical underpinnings.

Having said that, it should be noted here that back in their day, Pythagoras and the Milesians were still primarily speculative philosophers and not actual mathematicians or scientists in the way we understand these disciplines today. As such, they often had to resort to fantastical explanations of the nature of things, with no way to test them, or adequately measure them or prove their validity. What Pythagoras said about numbers, or anything else for that matter, was also speculative philosophy – perhaps informed by previous oral teachings and infused with a certain spiritual authority – but by no means, a product of rigorous scientific or mathematical proof in the way that we understand these processes today.

Milesian theories about the origin of the universe were another case in point. Thales suggested that in the beginning, there was only water, and all else evolved from moisture. Anaximander proposed a boundless chaos, out of which the universe grew as from a seed. Anaximenes suggested that originally there was only air and that liquids and solids were formed by condensation. These assertions were taken not as metaphors but as literal truth. Rival speculations vied for popularity on a level playing field, with nothing more to measure their credibility than the conviction of their authors and their capacity to convince others.

Ironically, despite the considerable advances in scientific sophistication since the Philosophical Era, the advent of complex scientific endeavors such as string theory, contemporary macroeconomics, or consciousness studies – where the absence of clearly established methodologies for testing or validation blurs the line between science and philosophical speculation – brings us full circle. Some would say that this particular conundrum is in fact characteristic of science itself:

> *[Thomas Kuhn] argued that competing paradigms are "incommensurable": that is to say, there exists no objective way of assessing their relative merits. There's no way, for example, that one could make a checklist comparing the merits of Newtonian mechanics (which applies to snooker balls and planets but not to anything that goes on inside the atom) and quantum mechanics (which deals with what happens at the sub-atomic level). But if rival paradigms are really incommensurable, then doesn't that imply that scientific revolutions must be based – at least in part – on irrational grounds? In which case, are not the paradigm shifts that we celebrate as great intellectual breakthroughs merely the result of outbreaks of mob psychology?*[7]

Strictly speaking, in the Philosophical Era, outbreaks of mob psychology were constellated around philosophical theories, and not anything yet identified as a scientific paradigm, much less one that was derived through rigorous experimental methodology. As such, emerging proto-scientific explanations were no more credible than the stories told by the earlier mythopoetic writers Homer and Hesiod,[8] the folk tales and myths of indigenous cultures,[9] the truth revealed by omens and oracles, or, for that matter, astrological interpretations of celestial phenomena. In fact, within this heady mix of worldviews, astrology became popular – not just among the common people, but with the most intelligent thinkers of the day – because it presented as plausible an explanation for reality as any of its rivals.

Many of these worldviews held much in common with sensibilities from previous eras. They were rooted as much in imaginal truth derived through a widespread cultural exercise in *participation mystique* and openness to mystical communication with the divine, as in literal fact. Emerging proto-scientific theories of the era followed this model, waxing every bit as lyrical as the more overtly mythopoetic sources they were competing against. Listening to

Thales proclaim that everything began with water, one could easily be forgiven for assuming him to be a mystical poet, rather than the Father of Science.[10]

The Rising Importance of Rational Argument In the Discernment of Truth

What the Milesians introduced into the equation that was new was a gradually increasing emphasis on reason and rational argument. The importance of reason was also shared by early Christian thinkers such as Augustine, arguing that God made himself known to humans through the faculty of reason.[11] Within this newly emerging emphasis, astrology continued to hold its own, but also underwent a slow transformation from a participatory attempt to intuit and align with divine intelligence, into a secular system based on logically derived rules, underscored by increasing mathematical precision.

As Tester notes, "astrology appealed to the educated Greeks precisely because [astrologers] were rational, and because . . . [astrology] was a rational system, or could be made to look like one."[12] Certainly, in the Philosophical Era, astrology and proto-scientific theory were operating on a level playing field and were often considered side by side as equally credible and by no means mutually exclusive explanations for the nature of reality. This is true in part, however, because the astrology of the day began to mold itself in the emerging paradigm of rational discourse, losing in its transition, both its mythopoetic sensibilities and its divinatory attitude.

In actuality, the rational methodology of logical argument for which the Greeks have become known did not truly begin to emerge as a counterforce to the theoretical chaos of the Milesian philosophers until Socrates introduced his method of intellectual inquiry into philosophical discourse; and his student Plato applied the Socratic method to the rampant cosmological speculation of the day – several centuries into the Philosophical Era.

Before and for some time after that, the Greeks borrowed heavily from Babylonian notions of cosmological order,[13] which as noted in Chapter Two, were largely based on proto-astrological observations and an omen-based astral culture rooted in mythopoetic and mystical sensibilities. It is not unlikely to assume that Thales and his followers were well versed in Babylonian astrology, even as they sought to develop a more naturalistic approach to the understanding of celestial phenomena, increasingly devoid of metaphysical implications.[14] Thales' ability to predict an eclipse, in fact, likely lent credibility to astrologers in general in an era in which astrology and astronomy were essentially still one and the same.

Nonetheless, the Milesians did launch a slow-moving revolution that would eventually culminate in a widening philosophical gap between astrology and science. Before the Milesians, the validity of the astrological premise – namely that there was a knowable relationship between the movement of the heavens and what was happening on earth - was an *a priori* assumption of the mythopoetic worldview on into the Mystical Era and would not have been questioned or measured by scientific standards (which in any case, did not exist). Astrology would have stood on its own and been taken largely for granted - as science is now - as an essential voice of the dominant epistemological paradigm of its day, and a legitimate pathway to speculation about the nature of reality. Even in the Philosophical Era, where science began its slow ascent into dominance, and astrology its gradual descent into ignominy, all knowledge was speculative by definition, and any approach to knowledge that made rational sense - which astrology did - had a legitimate place at the table.

Xenophon

One of the Milesians - Xenophon of Athens - a student of Socrates and a contemporary of Plato, argued that the true nature of reality was ultimately unknowable, subject as it was to the clouding influence of imagination and perceptual illusion. Paradoxically, this train of thought led on one hand to the kind of compensatory scientific rigor later demanded by Francis Bacon (see Chapter 5) and on the other, to doubts about the capacity of astrologers like many of Xenophon's peers to predict the future with certainty.

> *Two competing approaches to knowledge were opened by Xenophon's thought, to which all Western philosophy is indebted; either the entire universe is one, and therefore knowable, or its essential truth is concealed and is therefore unknowable. And, from these arguments, all future arguments about the scope of astrology, and the extent to which we can understand and analyze the sky, were to flow. For these philosophers, from the first century B.C.E. onwards, for whom astrology was a topic of concern, the boundary they trod between faith and skepticism allowed them to assume a basic logic in which they accepted astrology's assumption of cosmic unity, but doubted its ability to make prognostications about the world.*[15]

As this wedge entered the emerging debate between astrology and science, certainty was gradually claimed as the prerogative of Philosophical Era scientists, seeking not just a plausible cosmological worldview, but a practical one that would explain and accurately predict the inner workings of divine intelligence in secular terms. To this point, the supremacy of astrological cosmology, taken as a worldview, was generally accepted, often respected, and sometimes borrowed by scientists who dabbled in both worlds, but the particulars of its use as a system of prediction were increasingly called into question. This was true, even as a desire for greater accuracy of astrological prediction often provided the impetus for advances in more precise astronomical measurements throughout the Philosophical Era and beyond.

It is worth noting here, that in the spirit of the shifting definition of science, as practiced in the Philosophical Era, Xenophon considers imagination a "clouding influence," whereas in the preceding eras, and in fact, at the beginning of the Philosophical Era itself, it would have been a primary faculty through which one could enter into a direct relationship with the object of one's scrutiny and learn something about it.

On the one hand, it could be argued that the mob psychology through which various philosophical theories rose to the fore in the Philosophical Era was itself the product of an overactive imagination. On the other hand, that very imagination gave rise to a prolific fertility of ideas, the cross pollination of which allowed reality to be approached from multiple perspectives at once. In this spirit, whether one thought about the origin of the world in water as did Thales, through a big bang, or as an expression of the *Thema Mundi*,[16] one could discover something new. How one discovers something new or knows what one knows, proceeding from a philosophical premise, was often the subject of lively debate, but in the spirit of the Philosophical Age, there was a far more open-minded atmosphere in which an exploration of ideas could take any number of irrational twists and turns, as long as their author could make a convincing case.

Such liberties are strictly forbidden today in scientific circles, while even among astrologers, there is a sense of embarrassment about the fact that different astrologers will interpret the same symbolism differently, and not necessarily draw the same conclusion about the same birthchart.[17] Perhaps there is room in a more liberated astrology for *both* a certain coherence to principles of symbolic logic *and* the exercise of projected imagination in a more meandering or open-ended exploration. At least, this will be part of the argument I present later in this book, as we seek to reclaim what was lost when reason began its ascendancy in the Philosophical Era.

Meanwhile, back to our story, in the fourth century B.C.E., the work of Plato and his student Aristotle started bringing some semblance of order to the speculative mob psychology of the era, by providing useful guidelines for separating logical truth from merely imaginative thinking.

Plato

Plato was, by all accounts, the predominant philosophical influence, from which Western civilization – as we have known it for the past 2,500 years – flows. His school in Athens – The Academy – survived over 800 years past his death, and really only shut down because the Emperor Justin was rabidly determined to put an end to all pagan teachings, of which he considered Plato to be a primary provocateur. Meanwhile, Platonic thought had already thoroughly infiltrated the seminal doctrines of the Christian Church Justin thought he was protecting.

In addition, Plato greatly influenced the ongoing cosmological debate begun by the Milesians, particularly through his publication of *Timaeus*; rekindled interest in a cosmological state predicated on alignment with cosmic rhythms - prevalent during the Mystical Era - through the Republic; and laid the foundation for a theory of knowledge in which astrology might play an integral role in *Symposium*, *Phaedo* and *Phaedrus*.

For Plato, as for those of a previous age, the cosmos was a mirror of divine order and intent, which could be read through a mapping of celestial movements. Unlike his purely mythopoetic and mystical predecessors, however, for Plato, such mapping would require increasing mathematical sophistication and rational interpretation of sensory information - criteria that would not be out of line with the development of modern science over the course of the next two thousand years.

On the other hand, Plato might also be understood to be blatantly unscientific by today's standards, for if actual observations of the sky failed to measure up to mathematical ideals, Plato chose the latter as being closer to the truth. Such priorities, for example, led him to postulate that the planets moved in perfect circles, or orbits defined by precise numerical and geometric ratios, when actual observation showed this not to be the case.[18] So influential was Plato's worldview that this idea of perfect circular orbits persisted for the next two millennia, while a more empirical science found its footing.

Meanwhile, as noted by Richard Tarnas, astrology was given a strong philosophical boost by Platonic thought, even as it contributed to the evolution of the empirical science that would eventually refute Plato's ideal cosmos:

> *. . . a large part of the impetus for the development of astronomy derived directly from its ties to astrology, which employed those technical advances to improve its own predictive power . . . Platonists elaborated on the means by which specific planetary alignments could bring about an assimilation of the planet's character with the individual, an archetypal unity between agent and receiver . . . In the course of the Hellenistic era, astrology became the one belief system that cut across the boundaries of science, philosophy, and religion, forming a peculiarly unifying element in the otherwise fragmented outlook of the age.*[19]

This is not to say that the astrological theories of the day were any more coherent than the proto-scientific theories with which they mingled. As Tester notes, "the mixture of different 'sciences' with astrology, took place in a confused and confusing way, with no general consensus of opinion, in (the) third and second centuries B.C.E."[20] The Hellenistic era was nothing if not a fertile confluence of ideas from diverse sources - Babylonian cosmology, emerging Milesian, Platonic and Stoic philosophies, Aristotelian science, vestiges from the mythopoetic pagan cultures still very much alive, and later, the advent of Christianity, which was itself in turbulent flux. It is natural to assume that the development of astrology throughout this period would be subject to the same confusing stirring of the cultural pot – an experimental work in progress rather than a monolithic source of absolute authority.

Within this flux, nonetheless, Plato's ideas were primary shaping influences:

> *Plato's effective provision of a comprehensive cosmological and philosophical manifesto for astrology provided the gateway for its wholesale introduction into the Greek world. So great was his impact on both astronomy and astrology that we should talk of a Platonic revolution to rival the Copernican revolution.*[21]

In the end, Plato was an idealist, for whom the actual practice of astrology – primarily as influenced by the Babylonians – was problematic. He was also a speculative philosophical theorist, very much in the tradition of the Milesians, and contributed very little to a practical approach to epistemological methodology – either for astronomy or astrology. In fact, his philosophical speculation, as noted above, "that the cosmos was regulated by divinely determined perfect mathematical and geometrical ratios" – although empirically simplistic and in many cases, untenable – "dictated the course of European astronomy until Newton."[22] It also dictated an astrology focused on the delineation of some imagined ideal of cosmic order, rather than the observed correlation of earthly phenomena with celestial movements – an attitude that prevails among many astrologers weaned on New Age thinking (heavily influenced by Platonic ideals) to this day.

Aristotle

Plato's student Aristotle, meanwhile, pursued a multi-faceted inquiry into the nature of reality that was at least based upon some semblance of a method, including observation of natural phenomena, systematic gathering of data, identification of patterns, and inference of causal explanations from the data. Although Aristotelian science could not be said to be truly scientific in an empirical sense, nor did it meet the rigors of scientific methodology as it is currently understood and practiced, it was nonetheless a critical first step in the scientific revolution that would follow.

It is important to note, however, that what Aristotle considered to be science was actually more akin to what we might call logical deduction today. The Greek word *epistêmê* – the subject of Aristotle's *Posterior Analytics* (his masterwork on scientific knowledge) – is often translated to mean science, when "Aristotle clearly thinks that . . . knowledge of the premises is what brings about knowledge of the conclusion."[23] Scientific knowledge according to Aristotle, is in other words, logically, and not empirically deduced. Aristotle was generally considered to be the pre-eminent logician of his day, and his science was an extension of this orientation.

Ultimately the practice of astrology in this era was also understood and refashioned to become more logical, that is to say – like the logical form of science derived from the Aristotelian worldview – a rational way of understanding the order inherent in the manifest universe. Astrology is logical in a very different way than Aristotelian science is, but in the Philosophical Era, both were using the mind to analyze the relationships between what could be observed and what could be deduced from observation.

Aristotelian science seeks to understand causal relationships based on logical reasoning, whereas astrology seeks to understand the logic of symbolism in which poetic similes and metaphors hint at relationships of resonance that are more imaginative, intuitive, and suggestive. This is a different way of knowing than that of science, with a different goal in sight. We might nonetheless suspect that as astrology was influenced by the logical science of the day, it lost some of its mythopoetic sensibilities, becoming more analytical and less experiential; more rational and less imaginative; more deterministic and less poetic; more predictive and less suggestive. If so, then its inclusion in the scientific and religious discourse of the day came at a price. When we return to explore the epistemology of astrology in Part Two of this book, we will return to this idea with the intent of reclaiming the imaginative, poetic, suggestive ways of knowing that informed the astrology of an earlier era, without ignoring the importance of a distinctly astrological form of logic, what I like to call "astro-logic."

Meanwhile, if we understand astrology to be a symbolic language in which knowledge of the "premises" – in this case, the mythopoetic correlations between symbol and experience – leads to knowledge, then we can call astrology a science in the Aristotelian sense. Having said this, however, we must acknowledge that this definition of science has not been the standard for nearly four hundred years, so this is a specious and hopelessly antiquated syllogism.

Aristotle's Philosophical Support of Astrology

Be that as it may, in the Philosophical Era, as eminent astrologer and classical scholar Robert Hand points out, Aristotle's philosophy at least provided a conceptual foundation for the subsequent development of astrology. It did so by asserting the existence of a living cosmos, evolving through "*telos*," suggesting "that there is will and intention, to say nothing of something like 'foresight' in the universe, not merely in our individual minds, but in the trans-personal universe that transcends all of our individual minds."[24] This is one way, as we shall see in more detail later, that astrology provides what is missing in the scientific worldview and thus, potentially complements it.

Furthermore, Aristotle suggested that the end or purpose of all change is contained in the movements of the heavenly bodies, and that the soul is the final cause of the embodied human life – that is to say, the life of the soul constitutes the ultimate purpose for human existence. Although Aristotle did not explicitly endorse astrology, within the context of his worldview, the meaning and ultimate purpose of a human life could theoretically be seen reflected within a map of the sky – as it is routinely for astrologers of all stripes and persuasions.

Finally, although not the first to discuss the four elements foundational to astrology, Aristotle developed the doctrine of elements as a then-scientific explanation for the mechanism by which the movement of the heavens influences what happens on Earth.[25] Aristotle understood the elements to be composed of various combinations of essential attributes: fire = hot and dry; air = hot and wet; water = cold and wet; and earth = cold and dry. Aristotle's worldview was one that – like astrology – was best illuminated by a poetic language of quality, rather than quantity, as would increasingly become the norm as science evolved – presenting another dimension in which astrology can restore what has been stripped from the scientific worldview.

It should be noted here that these Aristotelian principles were not only supportive of astrology, but they were also the philosophical basis for a science very different than that practiced today – one that was not separate from metaphysical speculations about the meaning and purpose of human existence. In fact, it could be argued that Aristotelian science was antithetical to what is now understood as science in its embrace of metaphysical principles. In this regard, what science has lost or banished from its lexicon in moving away from Aristotelian principles, astrology potentially retains.

It was during the latter part of the Philosophical Era that Hellenistic Astrology arose in the Mediterranean region as a bridge between ancient Egyptian and Mesopotamian astrology, rooted in a mystical relationship to the cosmos, and the then newly emerging Aristotelian science, based on the rules of logic. According to Chris Brennan, the earliest known Mesopotamian birth charts date to 410 B.C.E.,[26] at which time Greek natal astrology began to distinguish itself from the prior predominantly omen-based astrology of the *Enuma Anu Enlil.*

In the early third century B.C.E., Berossus established an astrological school on the Greek isle of Kos. Foundational texts attributed to Hermes Trismegistus, Asclepius, Nechepso and Petosiris were believed to have done their work, not written down, but quoted by others, around the first century B.C.E. Subsequent astrologers like Manilius, Thrasyllus, and Dorothea of Sidon in the first century C.E.; Claudius Ptolemy and Vettius Valens in the second century; Porphyry of Tyre in the third century; and Firmicus Maternus, Paulus Alexandrinus, and Anonymous of 379 in the fourth century all made their contributions, along with others, to an astrology that mirrored the emerging rational ordering of metaphysical speculation in the Philosophical Era.

Stoicism

A major influence on the development of astrology in the Philosophical Era was a branch of Hellenistic philosophy called Stoicism, developed by Zeno of Citium. The Stoics were known for their promotion of wellbeing through acceptance of what is, and their attempt to align themselves with the order of the natural world. They stressed control of the emotions and moral self-discipline so that a clear rational mind could provide direct understanding of natural order – a goal they shared with the early Milesians, both Plato and Aristotle, and other rationalists of the age. Theirs was a deterministic model of reality, over which the individual had little control, and within which virtuous adaptation to fate was the highest good. Chrysippus, a student of Zeno, also developed his own approach to logic to rival that of Aristotle's, based on the truth or falsity of simple and compound statements.

Stoicism became popular among the educated elite in the Hellenistic world and especially in the Roman Empire, where it influenced such important thinkers as Seneca, advisor to Nero, Epictetus and Marcus Aurelius. So widespread was the popularity of Stoicism during this era, that it prompted classical historian Gilbert Murray to quip that "nearly all the successors of Alexander . . . professed themselves Stoics".[27] Marcus Aurelius in particular, aside from being a Roman Emperor, was also the author of *Meditations* – an important philosophical work through which the modern sense of Stoicism is largely derived. Stoicism also influenced Christianity and was an integral part of the ongoing cosmological debate, which had its roots in religion, philosophy and the emerging science of the Philosophical Era.

Although not all Stoics were proponents of astrology, the Stoic idea that life was predestined predisposed itself to an astrology that could articulate this point of view – a need that was fulfilled by the Hellenistic astrologers, who essentially translated Stoic philosophy into a codified system of rules mapped to the heavens:

> *. . . astrological correspondences were interpreted by the Greek and Roman Stoics as signifying the fundamental determinism of human life by the celestial bodies. Hence, astrology was regarded as the best method for interpreting the cosmic will and aligning one's life with the divine reason. With their conviction that a cosmic fate ruled all things, and with their belief in a universal sympathy of law unifying all parts of the cosmos, the Stoics found astrology highly congenial to their world view.*[28]

Although the Greek idea of fate was somewhat more complex and less incontrovertible than the Stoic influence on the astrology of the era might otherwise dictate, it is not unreasonable to make the connection between fate and prediction. This is necessarily so for what is not fated is subject to mediation in ways that can have any number of possible outcomes. To the extent that astrologers of the Philosophical Era were influenced by Stoicism, however, they would be more likely to adopt rule-bound systems that promised success at prediction.

It can be argued, in fact, that it is the Stoic influence on astrology, more than any other, that was responsible for the astrological impetus toward prediction in the Philosophical Era, since Stoicism was the primary tradition of the day in which prediction became both possible and a worthy goal – a goal incidentally also central to the emerging science of the era. Prediction, of course, was also part of the divinatory approach to the astrology of an earlier age, but in the Philosophical Era, it was no longer an incidental by-product of alignment with divine intelligence, but rather a primary outcome of rational inquiry for which the gods were no longer necessary, except as symbolic reference points.

Ptolemy

The most important astrological voice of the Philosophical Era was the seminal Alexandrian scholar, mathematician, astronomer and astrologer Claudius Ptolemy. Although influenced by Stoicism, Ptolemy built his cosmological model of the astronomical universe and his astrology primarily on Aristotelian principles. In so doing, he – arguably more than any single astrologer prior to that time – helped secure astrology's place within academic circles as a respectable and useful line of inquiry, and as part of his legacy, slowed the gradually widening schism between science and astrology. In particular, Ptolemy's masterworks on astronomy (*Almagest*) and astrology (*Tetrabiblos*) laid a philosophical foundation for a meaningful dialogue between science and astrology not just during the Philosophical Era, but throughout the Logical Era that followed – a period of well over two thousand years.

Ptolemy essentially collated and summarized the astrological practices of his predecessors and sought to explain astrology as a logical extension of the philosophical and scientific principles of his day – namely the doctrine of the four elements as espoused and elaborated by Aristotle, and the geocentric astronomical worldview. Such principles of course are no longer particularly relevant to what we consider science; in fact, to contemporary scientists they would be derided as antiquated, laughable and erroneous vestiges of a pre-scientific past. In the second century C.E., however, they were sufficient to secure astrology's place wherever knowledge was pursued and discussed. Because of Ptolemy's reputation as a pre-eminent scientist, Ptolemaic astrology continued to be central to the curriculum at European universities on into the seventeenth century.[29]

Ptolemy's gift of credibility to the astrological community, however, came at a price. Astrology had in previous eras been understood primarily as a mirroring of mundane reality by the celestial pattern in the sky at a given moment. By contrast, it was defended by Ptolemy, and became understood in his wake, as a mechanism of celestial causation[30] – a position that became increasingly indefensible as science continued to evolve and began to study the actual empirical basis for causality. It is essentially because of Ptolemy that scientists today assume that astrology should have a causal basis, explaining, for example, how planets at a distance can influence life on Earth. Although some have tried (see Chapter Five), astrologers are unable to produce such an explanation, because Ptolemy's notion of celestial causation is radically different than the current empirical understanding.

In addition, through the influence of Ptolemy, the technique and practice of astrology began to depend less on sensory observations of the sky and more on idealized logical assumptions that had no basis in experiential fact. In the Mystical Era, for example, and on into the first couple centuries of the Philosophical Era, the signs of the zodiac were associated with the uneven constellations that lay along the ecliptic, which were routinely observed in the sky. By the fifth century B.C.E., Mesopotamian astrologers had adopted a stylized version of the constellational zodiac, in which each sign was assigned a 30° range, regardless of the actual range of the constellation after which it was named. As Hellenistic astrology was developed a few centuries later, most astrologers were using this stylized sidereal zodiac, despite the fact that in the second century B.C.E., the Greek astronomer Hipparchus had discovered the precession of the equinoxes, which shifted the reference system from the constellations (a sidereal orientation) to an alignment with the seasons (a tropical orientation).

Ptolemy was one of the first astrologers to break with his peers, embrace the concept of precession, and whole-heartedly adopt the tropical zodiac, which except for a few contemporary Western siderealists such as Cyril Fagan and Kenneth Bowser, has been standard practice ever since. Of course, we can also easily identify Plato's influence here, as the assignment of equal arcs to each of the twelve signs was a mathematically elegant model that made rational and mathematical sense, but had no real basis in experiential reality.

As the tropical zodiac became increasingly popular, the astrology that revolved around it became divorced from the actual visible scenario that had informed previous astrological ages. Brennan notes:

> *. . . the existence, in the century after Ptolemy, of astrologers who defended the tropical zodiac on the grounds that it had some sort of intrinsic value that could be grasped with the mind, even if it could not be observed with the senses.*[31]

This distinction would become increasingly important in the succeeding Logical Era, but even at this juncture, there was the beginning of a divergence between the rational constructs of Hellenistic astrology in the Philosophical Era, and the more intuitive reading of divine intelligence in the sky, based on actual observation, that had informed the astrology of the Mystical and the Mythopoetic Eras.[32]

Hermeticism

Rising in parallel with early Christianity, Aristotelian science, Hellenistic astrology and Stoicism, Hermeticism presented another important stream of thought in the Philosophical

Era. Hermetic philosophy was attributed to the teachings of Hermes Trismegistus, as were a number of the earliest pseudepigraphic astrological texts, as noted in Chapter Two.

Hermes Trismegistus was a mysterious being who was thought by some to be a divine amalgamation of the Greek god Hermes with the Egyptian god Thoth; seen by Christian writers such as Augustine, Giordano Bruno and Marsilio Ficino, as a wise pagan prophet who foresaw the coming of Christ; and believed by still others, to be an Egyptian priest-king who was a contemporary of Moses, or perhaps Abraham.

In the spirit of many oral teachers of the Divinatory Era, his origins are obscure, and the question of whether or not he even existed in human form remains a mystery. Hermes Trismegistus is nonetheless credited with a hallowed canon of work collectively known as the *Hermetica*, the most important works of which were the *Asclepius*, the *Emerald Tablet of Hermes Trismegistus* and the *Corpus Hermeticum* (all thought to have been written in the second or third century C.E.). The most plausible explanation for these works is that they were written by various unknown authors, probably Greek[33] or Egyptian.[34]

Whatever their authorship, the *Hermetica* has greatly influenced the Western esoteric tradition, including the astrologers of the Hellenistic Era and the Renaissance; and had a role to play in the development of Aristotelian science, as well as in the evolution of Christianity. The *Hermetica* was also popular within the Islamic tradition, where Hermes Trismegistus is identified as Irdis, believed by some to be an infallible prophet who traveled from outer space to Egypt and from whom Muhammad was believed to have descended.[35]

Within the Hermetic texts, astrology merges with philosophy, alchemy, magic and medicine to provide something for everyone. Christians liked the hermetic notion of the *prisca theologia*, which postulated a single, true theology present in all traditions and given to humans in antiquity – a theory which they quickly co-opted for their own political ambitions in promotion of the One True Faith. Hermetic texts also emphasize the basic goodness of a monotheistic God (sometimes called the All or the One). They provide a pathway for purification of the soul and lend support to the veneration of images and iconography especially dear to the Catholic Church. Scientists liked the idea of influencing or controlling nature that was central not just to science, but to magic and its allied arts. Meanwhile, those inclined toward the esoteric, found (and continue to find) in the *Hermetica*, a philosophical basis for a more deliberate form of magical practice.

From Hermeticism or more specifically *The Emerald Tablet of Hermes Trismegistus*, comes one of its central axioms of astrology: "as above, so below." The actual text reads:

> *That which is Below corresponds to that which is Above, and that which is Above corresponds to that which is Below, to accomplish the miracle of the One Thing.*[36]

Although, there are many levels on which this enigmatic maxim can be understood, as commonly used by most astrologers, it means that everyday life on planet Earth (the microcosm) is reflected in patterning of the cosmos (the macrocosm), specifically as it is rendered as a map of the sky at any given moment. Within the Hermetic tradition, astrological symbols – and the planetary dynamics to which they refer – are conceived as thoughts (or today we might say archetypes) within the mind of God, or alternately at a deeper level of practice, as embodiments of the gods, all of whom exist as aspects of the One. As in Aristotelian science, the four elements central to astrological understanding are also central to the Hermetic cosmology. As an extension of astrological practice within the Hermetic tradition, theurgy is the magical art of working intentionally and ritually with these elements and the archetypes, summoning the spirit of the deities to which they refer, in an attempt to align the individual soul with divine intent – a practice that harkens back to the Mystical Era.

Hermetic philosophy itself did not encompass technical rules for the practice of astrology, but like Aristotelian science and Stoicism, provided a philosophical rationale for its practice, which became adapted to specific techniques in the hands of Hellenistic astrologer/magicians. In general, the lineage through which Hermetic philosophy was said to have entered into astrological practice as an oral tradition extending from Hermes to Asclepius to Nechepso and Petosiris. This oral tradition was then incorporated into the written works of Hellenistic astrologers like Manilius, Ptolemy, Porphyry and Vettius Valens.[37]

Vettius Valens

While Claudius Ptolemy is probably the most famous astrologer of this period – known primarily for his philosophical contributions, as well as his outline of specific techniques – the practice of astrology in this era was also significantly influenced by Ptolemy's younger contemporary Vettius Valens. Valens' major work was the ten-volume *Anthology*, written somewhere during the period 150 – 175 C.E., more or less around the same time as Ptolemy's astrological masterwork *Tetrabiblos*.

Valens' astrology was thoroughly infused with Hermetic teachings, magic and alchemy as well as Platonic philosophy and Stoicism. He is credited with preserving the major portion of extant oral teachings of Nechepso and Petosirus, the acknowledged torchbearers of the Hermetic tradition,[38] and as such can be considered an important link in the chain by which astrological practice of the Philosophical Era was influenced by Hermeticism. Valens' language was sometimes confused and obscure, perhaps purposely so to keep dabblers and dilettantes out of what was becoming a more elite esoteric club,[39] or perhaps because the source material from which he was working was itself somewhat impenetrable.[40] Despite its dense language, many of the general principles presented in the *Anthology* are nonetheless still recognized and in use today – particularly among contemporary Hellenistic astrologers.[41]

The *Anthology* was essentially a rulebook for the practicing astrologer, which included characteristics of each sign derived through multiple classifications (by element, gender, modality, season, rulership, etc.) in which the emerging logic of astrology was evident, as it was in somewhat different ways throughout the writing of most Hellenistic astrologers.

In keeping with the emerging emphasis on rational explanations among the Milesians, there was, however, little mention of the Olympian gods or goddesses in either Valens or Ptolemy – which would not have been the case in the previous era. There was also a subtle message – probably absorbed through the influence of the Church – a warning to those who eschewed the rational in favor of the emotional, imaginative and instinctual dimensions of human psyche. These were, of course, precisely those faculties that would have been most intimately engaged in the astrology of the Mythopoetic and Mystical Eras, but that were now associated with the temptation of sinners within the philosophical orientation of the Church.

Neoplatonism

From the third to the sixth centuries C.E., the original teachings of Pythagoras and Plato began to morph in more useful directions that were less theoretical and more pragmatic. The Neoplatonic school of thought began with the Greek philosopher from Alexandria, Ammonius Saccas and his student Plotinus and extended to later teachers such as Porphyry, Iamblichus and Proclus.

The Neoplatonists were by no means uniform in their beliefs, and for each, astrology occupied a somewhat different place within the larger lexicon of ideas in circulation at the time. In general, however, the Neoplatonists were practical mystics who combined in various ways the spiritual idealism of Pythagoras and Plato with the Aristotelian focus on epistemological method. Within this overall context, astrology increasingly became a practical means for spiritual awakening, conceived within Neoplatonism as a matter of returning through this earthly life to the spiritual Source of being, or what they, following in the footsteps of Pythagoras, called the One. In particular, the soul was thought to descend through the planetary spheres into embodiment, and then back in the opposite direction toward spiritual release from embodiment – thus presenting a theoretical model for an astrological approach to the soul's evolution.

Unlike the empiricists that came after, early Neoplatonists like Plotinus and Porphyry mistrusted information coming from the senses, while like the Milesians, they strove to develop a rational understanding of signs and omens as presented by the heavens, believing that reason was the best psychic tool for approaching divine intent.

As pointed out in my previous book *The Seven Gates of Soul*, this is a somewhat constrictive strategy, since the soul's attempt to make sense of divine intelligence is every bit as irrational as rational, weaving together emotion, imagination and yes, the sensory information shunned by the Neoplatonists into a potent brew that defies strictly logical analysis.[42] This was, in fact, the way that astrologers of the previous eras approached their craft, which was essentially an imaginal projection of soulful yearnings into a visible sky that mirrored back practical as well as metaphysical truths.

Unfortunately, this was no longer a viable strategy for astrology to maintain its presence within the intellectual climate of the Philosophical Era, where the more rational and logical approach to knowledge being developed in different ways by Plato and Aristotle, as well as by astrologers such as Ptolemy and Vettius Valens, provided new, more current theoretical foundations on which astrology could lay claim to intellectual credibility. It became even more unfortunate, as Neoplatonists among others drove a deeper wedge between the soul and its less rational dimensions.

Iamblichus

The exception to this trend was the Syrian Neoplatonist Iamblichus, who argued that one could approach a deeper understanding of the divine through ritual magic, especially when correlated with an astrological sense of timing. This approach – known as "theurgy" within the Hermetic tradition, by which Iamblichus was also influenced – was both practical and mystical, and represented the most truly useful integration of Platonic and Aristotelian thought, at least in terms that preserved the sensibilities of earlier eras. Theurgy was a synthesis of ideas and visceral experiences through which astrology became less theoretical, less oriented toward predication and more useful as an intentional spiritual practice, rooted in pagan ceremony and ritual, not unlike the astrology of the Mystical Era.

Iamblichus' theurgic masterwork was *On the Mysteries of the Egyptians, Chaldeans and Assyrians*[43] (sometimes called the *Theurgia*) – giving direct reference to the earlier divinatory astrology of Mesopotamia. The basic principle of the *Theurgia* was that the various gods and goddesses, all of which were diverse manifestations of the One and its divine intelligence, could be summoned through the ritual use of objects, images, invocation of spirits, plants, animals, stones and other embodied talismans that shared the nature of the deity being supplicated. In an Aristotelian sense, theurgy can be considered a science, as well as a magical practice, in that through it, empirical understanding gained through experience becomes the basis for a body of practical knowledge.

Theurgy can also be understood as an approach to knowledge steeped in the *participation mystique* of the Mythopoetic Era, through which one enters into a direct relationship of union with the divine in its myriad guises, not just symbolized – but embodied – by the planets and stars, as well as by all the earthly talismans with which the various gods and goddesses were resonant. As already noted, it is also an epistemology aligned in spirit with the more intentional use of ceremony and ritual to evoke sacred space and divine discourse, as practiced in the Mystical Era. As Iamblichus says:

> *Divine divination, therefore, which is conjoined with the Gods, alone truly imparts to us a divine life, since it participates of [divine] fore-knowledge, and divine intellections, and renders us in reality divine.*[44]

The Roman Era

Because of the profound influence of the Church, especially during the years of the Roman Empire (marked in time from the crowning of Octavian as the first Emperor Augustus in 27 B.C.E. to the fall of Rome and the resignation of the last Emperor Romulus Augustus in 476 C.E.), astrology was not without its challenges and detractors. Often its greatest private adherents were publicly opposed. The first Roman Emperor Augustus, for example, "used and abused astrology to the utmost, proudly promoting it to legitimize his own ambitions and proclaim himself savior of Rome, and then legislating against astrology to prevent others from using it against him."[45] The evolution of Hellenistic astrology during this same period bore testimony to astrology's vitality, even in the face of such hypocritical institutionalized opposition.

In the Roman era, astrology was very much a part of the fabric of everyday life (Augustus named the days of the week after the astrological gods) and used routinely by the elite. It was, in fact, as integral to the political machinations of the Roman state as it had been during Mesopotamian culture seven centuries earlier, essential to Augustus and his successors throughout the Roman Empire, most of whom sought to control its use by political rivals. Its central function within the Roman political system echoed the earlier omen-based astrology of the *Enuma Anu Enlil.*

As assistant professor in the Department of Classical Languages and Literatures at the University of Chicago David Wray notes, for example, after the assassination of Julius Caesar in 44 B.C.E., a comet streaking across the sky was taken as a sign that he was ascending into heaven to become a god.

> *Divination or prophecy through reading the signs and portents of the sky was not merely a folk belief in the ancient Mediterranean; it was also part of the state religion at Rome. There was a group of official priests known as augurs whose functions included reading omens in the sky.*[46]

Within the Roman Empire, astrology was one of many systems competing for oracular authority, increasingly dependent upon mathematical certainty and practical political utility for its underground acceptance, while increasingly being castigated publicly, largely for political reasons having little to do with its efficacy. Because the omen-based traditions of the Roman era were rooted in a form of divination, astrology also ironically maintained more of its original mythopoetic/mystical nature under the Romans, despite their official promotion of the Christian agenda, bent on eradicating pagan cultures that shared these sensibilities.

For a fleeting revolutionary moment, the Emperor Julian (332-363), who favored Iamblichus' teachings, made an ultimately failed attempt during his brief two-year reign (361-363) to replace Christianity with a form of Neoplatonic paganism. This attempt was an anomaly within the march of Roman emperors toward an official embrace of Christianity and was immediately repealed after Julian's reign by the Council of Laodicea (a regional synod of approximately thirty clerics from Asia Minor that assembled about 363–364 C.E.), which banned astrologers and magicians from the priesthood. As Campion notes, however, "the Empire may have become officially Christian (in the fourth century C.E.), but classical paganism took about 200 years or more to die out."[47]

In retrospect, it appears that the root system upon which the magical approach to astrology bloomed in the compost of the Roman Christian Era has proven a hardier perennial than even its staunchest advocates could have foreseen, since various forms of neopaganism remain alive and well alongside Christianity in today's world.[48] More specifically, the theurgic practices of Iamblichus have survived through esoteric Christian groups such as the Theosophists, the Rosicrucians, the Freemasons, and the Hermetic Order of the Golden Dawn.[49] The various offshoots of these seminal groups have many local variations in theory and practice, but all are essentially of the same spirit - harkening back to the teachings of Hermes Trismegistus and beyond that to the cultural worldview of the Mythopoetic era - in which the lines between science, magic, astrology and spirituality are blurred or nonexistent, as the practitioner becomes one with the practice.

Notes

1. What I am calling the Philosophical Era encompasses the Classical Era of Ancient Greece and the duration of the western Roman Empire with its strong official alliance with Christianity. This period also encompasses the rise of Islam in the East and the Hellenistic period, during which there was a fertile intermingling of Judaic, Christian and Islamic cultures in the Mediterranean.
2. Tester, Jim. A *History of Western Astrology*. Ballentine Books, 1987, 14.
3. Landwehr, Joe. *The Seven Gates of Soul: Reclaiming the Poetry of Everyday Life*. Abilene, TX: Ancient Tower Press, 2004, 95.
4. "Thales of Miletus | Internet Encyclopedia of Philosophy." Accessed May 12, 2023. https://iep.utm.edu/thales/.

5. Fowler, Michael. "Early Greek Science." Accessed May 12, 2023. http://galileoandeinstein.physics.virginia.edu/lectures/thales.html.

6. In my previous book *Astrology and the Archetypal Power of Numbers, Part One*, I talk about this aspect of Pythagorean teachings in relation to numbers, which have important implications for the kind of participatory astrology practiced in previous eras. Taken as a whole, numbers as understood by Pythagoras can also be seen to reveal how the divine intelligence inherent within the world permeates the psyche revealed by a birthchart – a premise I explored in some detail in *Astrology and the Archetypal Power of Numbers, Part Two*.

7. Naughton, John. "Thomas Kuhn: The Man Who Changed the Way the World Looked at Science." *The Guardian*, March 22, 2018. https://www.theguardian.com/science/2012/aug/19/thomas-kuhn-structure-scientific-revolutions.

8. Nicholas Campion (in *A History of Western Astrology Volume 1*, 129, Note 20) cites several sources (Florence Wood and Kenneth Wood, *Homer's Secret Iliad: The Epic of the Night Skies Decoded*, London: John Murray, 1999; Emmeline Mary Plunkett, *The Judgment of Paris and Some Other Legends Astronomically Considered*, London: John Murray, 1908; and Laurin R. Johnson, *Shining at the Ancient Sea; The Astronomical Ancestry of Homer's Odyssey*, Portland, Oregon: Multnomah House Press, 1999) that suggest parts of Homer's poem the *Iliad*, dating to the eighth century B.C.E., can be traced further back to the ninth millennium B.C.E., making Homer a Milesian torchbearer for the mythopoetic sensibilities of the Neolithic Era.

9. Thales assertion that in the beginning, all was water is identical to the Cherokee creation myth. The only real difference is that Thales version of the creation story is rooted in natural phenomena, while the Cherokee speak of Dâyuni'sï, "Beaver's Grandchild," the little Water-beetle, who dives to the bottom of the water for soft mud, which he brings to the surface to form the Earth. Whether or not this can be understood to be literally true, neither story can be proven or disproven by any technique considered scientific today and are therefore equally plausible.

10. Singer, Charles. *A Short History of Science to the Nineteenth Century*. Oxford: Clarendon Press, 2007, 35.

11. Mendelson, Michael. "Saint Augustine," November 12, 2010. https://plato.stanford.edu/archives/win2012/entries/augustine/.

12. Tester, *A History of Western Astrology*, 18.

13. Campion, Nicholas. *A History of Western Astrology Volume I: The Ancient and Classical Worlds*. Bloomsbury, 2009, 127.

14. Campion, *A History of Western Astrology Volume I*, 138.

15. Campion, *A History of Western Astrology Volume I*, 141.
16. The *Thema Mundi* was a central construct of the Hellenistic tradition (as noted in Chris Brennan's *Hellenistic Astrology: The Study of Fate and Fortune*, 228), a hypothetical birth-chart in which each of the seven visible planets is in its domicile, or a sign that it rules. Aside from its role as a teaching device, various versions of the *Thema Mundi* were considered to be the chart for the birth of the world. Alternately, other Hellenistic astrologers and some late Mesopotamian astrologers believed that the periodic alignment of all planets in Cancer and Capricorn signaled the cyclical creation and destruction of the world (Brennan, *Hellenistic Astrology*, 230).
17. Nasser, Rafael, Steven Forrest, and Robert Hand. *Under One Sky*. Borrego Springs, CA: Seven Paws Press, 2004, 103.
18. Although the notion of elliptical orbits would not become firmly established until Kepler formulated his three laws of planetary motion in the early seventeenth century, observers as early as the third century B.C.E. observed that there were irregularities in planetary motion that belied the concept of the circular orbit. In the third century B.C.E. Apollonius of Perga proposed the mechanism of epicycles (cycles within cycles), which was subsequently adopted by Hipparchus and then extensively used by Ptolemy, at which point (by the publication of *Almagest* in the second century C.E.) it became the workaround explanation of choice when defending circular orbits that did not exist, but that conformed to a Platonic ideal.
19. Tarnas, Richard. *The Passion of the Western Mind: Understanding the Ideas That Have Shaped Our World View*. Ballantine Books, 1991, 82-83.
20. Tester, *A History of Western Astrology*, 25.
21. Campion, *A History of Western Astrology Volume I*, 153.
22. Campion, *A History of Western Astrology Volume I*, 193.
23. Smith, Robin. "Aristotle's Logic." Stanford Encyclopedia of Philosophy. November 22, 2022. https://plato.stanford.edu/entries/aristotle-logic/#AriLogWorOrg.
24. Hand, Robert. "Arhat Media | Books, Articles and Information on the History of Astrology." Accessed May 15, 2023. https://www.arhatmedia.com/Matter&FormArticle.htm.
25. The doctrine of the four elements is generally credited to Empedocles, born about a century before Aristotle, and was nearly universally accepted without question, becoming a fundamental principle of the Western worldview for the next 2,000 years. Even into the twentieth century, seminal thinkers like Carl Jung, Ken Wilbur and Bill Plotkin have created theories modeled on these four-fold divisions – which are generally understood not just as primitive theories of physical chemistry, but as psychological analogues. Hippocrates – traditionally regarded as the father of medicine – was probably the first to

apply the doctrine of four elements to the concept of temperament, which by the time of Aristotle, had become a cornerstone, not just of medical astrology (with medicine being inseparable from the practice of astrology), but of astrological theory and practice in general during the Hellenistic era.

26. Brennan, Chris. *Hellenistic Astrology: The Study of Fate and Fortune*. Denver: Amor Fati Publications, 2017, 4.
27. Murray, Gilbert. "The Stoic Philosophy; Conway Memorial Lecture Delivered at South Place Institute on March 16, 1915: Internet Archive. https://archive.org/details/thestoicphilosop00murruoft.
28. Tarnas, *The Passion of the Western Mind*, 83.
29. Rutkin, H. Darrel. "The Use and Abuse of Ptolemy's Tetrabiblos in Renaissance and Early Modern Europe." In *Ptolemy in Perspective : Use and Criticism of His Work from Antiquity to the Nineteenth Century*, edited by Alexander Jones. Springer, 2010, 135-47. http://ci.nii.ac.jp/ncid/BB00470708.
30. Cornelius, Geoffrey. *The Moment of Astrology: Origins in Divination*. Wessex Astrologer Limited, 2002, 81.
31. Brennan, *Hellenistic Astrology*, 217
32. An argument can be made that Mythopoetic cultures especially built their proto-astrology, in part, around an awareness of equinoxes and solstices. This was, however, a practice distinct from the division of the ecliptic into signs, which was a later development of the Mystical Era. During this earlier period, signs were a matter of observation; during the Philosophical Era and beyond, they increasingly became a logical abstraction.
33. Yates, Frances. *Giordano Bruno and the Hermetic Tradition*. Routledge, 2014, 2-3.
34. Campion, *A History of Western Astrology Volume I*, 188.
35. Wheeler, Brannon M. *Prophets in the Quran: An Introduction to the Quran and Muslim Exegesis*. A&C Black, 2002, 46.
36. Trismegistus, Hermes. *The Emerald Tablet of Hermes*. Createspace, 2017, 28.
37. Brennan, *Hellenistic Astrology*, 68-73.
38. Brennan, *Hellenistic Astrology*, 73.
39. See Tester, *A History of Western Astrology*, 48-49 and Campion, *A History of Western Astrology Volume I*, 216. Campion suggests that Valens may have been involved with a mystery school in the Egyptian temple tradition that required secrecy.
40. Brennan, *Hellenistic Astrology*, 90.
41. Whitfield, Peter. *Astrology: A History*. Harry N. Abrams, 2001, 39.

42. Landwehr, Joe. *The Seven Gates of Soul: Reclaiming the Poetry of Everyday Life*. Abilene, TX: Ancient Tower Press, 2004, 121-32.

43. Authorship of *On the Mysteries of the Egyptians, Chaldeans and Assyrians* was ascribed to Iamblichus by his successor Proclus. Given differences in style between this work and other fragments written by Iamblichus, however, some scholars dispute his authorship, although most attribute it to a member of his school and believe it to be reliably characteristic of the theurgic practices of his day.

44. Iamblichus. *On the Mysteries of the Egyptians, Chaldeans, and Assyrians: The Complete Text*, translated by Thomas Taylor. Columbia, SC: Adansonia, 2019, 154.

45. Roberts, Courtney. "Christian Astrology, the Dark Ages, and the Celtic Church." Accessed May 16, 2023. http://cura.free.fr/xxx/29robts.html.

46. Wray, David. "Astrology in Ancient Rome: Poetry, Prophecy and Power." Accessed May 16, 2023. http://fathom.lib.uchicago.edu/1/777777122543/.

47. Campion, *A History of Western Astrology Volume I*, 266.

48. From the neopagan website Metal Gaia: "Between 1990 and 2000, the number of Wiccans in the United States increased from 8,000 to 134,000 according to the United States Census Bureau. That's an increase of 1600%! Between 2001 and 2008, the number of Pagans over all (Wiccans included) doubled, so that's a growth rate of 200%. That's an increase greater than almost anything seen among the other religions! The number of Christians overall, in comparison, only experienced an 8% growth rate between 2001 and 2008, which is actually a decrease when you account for population growth."

49. See, for example, *Astrological Magic: Basic Rituals & Meditations*, published in 2012 by Dr. Benjamin N. Dykes and Jayne B. Gibson, who are both astrologers and practitioners of ceremonial magic, trained in Golden Dawn teachings.

Astrology is a form of imagination, a way of organizing human reality that we should take seriously but not literally . . . The natal or birth chart is . . . imagined as a map of our inner landscape, the typography of our psychic life. It is an image first and foremost of psyche as soul . . . As a map of our inner landscape, an image of soul, it is fathomless. The natal chart is labyrinthine in complexity allowing us to draw deeply on imagination . . . The cycling of planets imagined as movements of soul suggests the survival of sacred order in secular times. They provide a touchstone for the poetic imagination to reach out and elaborate an intimacy between our selves and our world.

Kochunas, Brad Hiljanen, The Astrological Imagination, 2008

Chapter Four

The Ascendancy of Science in the Logical Era Circa Fourth Century – Seventeenth Century C.E.[1]

Until roughly the seventeenth century C.E. - science continued to be largely a matter of rational argument, perhaps less wildly speculative than during the Philosophical Era, but with nothing remotely resembling the empirical rigor that marked science past this point. Observations were made, and data was recorded, but interpretations were logical deductions, rather than proven hypotheses. These deductions were increasingly devoid of metaphysical implications, but the science of the Logical Era was often practiced side by side with sensibilities not antithetical to a metaphysical worldview.

Within this prolonged state of peaceful co-existence, astrology continued to flourish, albeit with periods of relative underground dormancy.[2] Earlier astronomers like Hipparchus and Ptolemy were astrologers, who saw no conflict of interest between science and astrology, and this relatively seamless confluence of the two parallel disciplines continued through the seventeenth century with later astrologer/astronomers like Nicholas Copernicus and Johannes Kepler. Indeed, as Tester notes, educated scholars throughout the Western world . . .

> *. . . accepted astrology. Its acceptance as a learned and scientific study was common, if not the normal, attitude to it down to the eighteenth century, and it is impossible to understand men like Kepler and Newton unless astrology is seen for what the Greeks made it, a rational attempt to map the state of the heavens and to interpret that map in the context of that 'cosmic sympathy' which makes man an integral part of the universe.*[3]

During the Logical Era, the science of the day largely derived from the approach to knowledge developed and practiced by Aristotle, which while increasingly rooted in observation, was mostly a matter of logic, with only rudimentary means of measuring or testing theories. Throughout the Logical Era, Aristotle went in and out of fashion, but after a revival of interest in the eleventh and twelfth centuries, his teachings became the *de facto* philosophical underpinning for science up to the empirical revolution. As long as science was based on logic, astrology held its own, because at its core - at least as it was developed by the Hellenistic Greeks - it was a logical system.

It was only when science became more empirical, that astrology started losing ground as a credible source of information, at least as measured by the new tools that science began developing in the seventeenth century. Meanwhile, this was a slow-moving evolution that took the better part of fourteen millennia, during which the Logical Era provided a bridge between philosophical speculation and empirical science. During this transitional phase, astrology was by no means banished as a legitimate form of inquiry into the nature of reality, including the conduct of human affairs. Quite the contrary, it was at the heart of the debate.

This was so, in part, as pointed out in Chapter Three, because for Aristotle, scientific knowledge was founded on metaphysical principles. In his day, metaphysics in turn was still thoroughly permeated by mythopoetic and Platonic ideas that supported astrology's further evolution. All scientific theories about the nature of reality prior to and through the Philosophical Era, in fact, would have had astrology at their core, because up through at least the fourth century C.E., astrology was a common language among all the various philosophical threads that were weaving together to form the science of the day – as discussed in Chapter Three.

During the Logical Era, there was increasing debate about the rightful scope of astrology; the *a priori* assumption about the astro-logical nature of reality that marked the Philosophical Era was increasingly called into question; and astrology and science started to diverge.

The Role of the Church In the Split Between Astrology and Science

Although Hellenistic astrology, Neoplatonism and the Babylonian omen-based astrology of the Roman augurs remained popular after the fall of the Roman Empire, during the years of what is known as the Byzantine or Eastern Roman Empire (roughly from the fifth century C.E. through the fall of Constantinople to the Ottoman Turks in 1453), the Church became an increasingly powerful voice. More importantly in the context of this current discussion, it also inserted a philosophical wedge between astrology and astronomy. Science was often compelled to at least pay lip service to the power of the Church, which at that time, emerged as the newly dominant metaphysical context in which all truth – secular and spiritual – was measured.

In the fourth century C.E., the Emperor Constantine (reigning from 324 – 337) reorganized the empire, made Constantinople the new capital, and legalized Christianity. Two generations later, Theodosius (reigning from 379 – 395) made Christianity the official state religion and banned other religious practices, namely those of the pagan religions, which along with astrology formed the nexus of mythopoetic culture as it had survived into the Christian era. Theodosius also issued a specific decree banning the practice of astrology after the Council of Laodicea had previously issued the first explicit official condemnation of astrology by the Church.

What is interesting here, however, and important to note was the distinction made by Church Fathers between the use of judicial astrology to make predictions and the practice of natural astrology, which was, at the time, considered to be the study of celestial movements *per se*, more in line with scientific astronomy.

> *Because of the intensity of the clash between the bishops and the astrologers, the impression is often created that all bishops were opposed to the cultivation of Science and to the research of the celestial phenomena rather than to that apocryphal art. However, the reality was different; the leaders of the Church with their writings and other actions were condemning not the science of Astronomy but the quackery, the omens and all those who claimed that they could predict the future from the relative positions of the celestial bodies . . . In other words, the attack of (the) Church Fathers is not directed against the scientific research of the celestial bodies and events, but rather against all those who proceed beyond the information gained through the observation and the experience, and want to infer conclusions from the stars.*[4]

It is telling that the Church Fathers – people like Basil of Caesarea and Gregory of Nazianzus – use the word "astronomy" for astrology, with distinctions made only through study of the context of their remarks, while others routinely called astrologers "mathematicians."[5] It appears from the writings of these men that what concerned them was the attribution of the cause of events to the movement of the stars, rather than to God, while at the same time, they considered the harmony and order of celestial mechanics – as today would be studied by scientists and mathematicians – to be testimony to the genius of God's handiwork.[6]

We can note here that in an earlier era, there would have been no distinction made between the movement of the stars and the deities that lent their name to the stars, nor any argument about the testimony of celestial mechanics – which was routinely interpreted not just as evidence of divine intelligence, but as an actual communication from God (or the gods). It was only when Ptolemy began reframing astrology in causal terms that it began competing with science on its own ground.[7] This is ironic, given that Ptolemy was also largely responsible for shoring up astrology's credibility through this reframe, which only upon closer examination over the course of the next 1,500 years, began to unravel.

In any case, Ptolemy's causal framework also ironically brought astrology into more direct confrontation with Church dogma, which like his, in sympathy with Aristotle's views, held God to be the ultimate cause of all things. Within this worldview, as understood by the Church, astrology's claim to be able to predict the future, because the stars presumably asserted their own level of causal influence on human affairs, became perceived as a challenge to God's authority.

At the beginning of the Logical Era, science did not yet have the language or methodology to challenge astrology's causal claims on empirical grounds, while the Church, coming at the issue from a metaphysical perspective, had no such limitations. It was thus the splitting of these philosophical hairs around the question of astrological causality, within a Christian context, that began driving a wedge between the science of astronomy and the presumed predictive capacity of astrology. Previously astronomy, astrology and mathematics had been part of the same study of celestial signs. Reframed by Ptolemy, predictive astrology became increasingly viewed as a rival religious practice, pitting the ultimate authority of God against the supposed causal powers of the planetary gods. To squelch this perceived competition, predictive (otherwise known as judicial) astrology was banned by the Church, while the mathematical study of celestial phenomena for its own sake (what was then natural astrology, and what would eventually become the independent science of astronomy) was embraced by the Church as a way to understand God's intelligent ordering of the cosmos.

The Church Fathers attacked astrology not just on religious grounds, but also for the perceived political implications of taking astrological influences seriously. Again, what was really at issue here, however, was not astrology *per se*, but astrological determinism (as derived primarily from Stoic influences, as well as Ptolemaic assertions of causality). As noted by Nemesius of Emesa:

> *Those who attribute the cause for all events to the revolution of the stars do not only combat common sense, but also they render useless all state justice. For the laws are out of place and the courts are unnecessary when they punish those who are responsible for nothing. But the stars, too, are unjust in cleansing the fornicators and the murderers...*[8]

Despite the immense influence of the Church, the practice of astrology continued, not just among the educated, including political figures of the era, but also among the clergy, who became tempted by astrology's appeal, even as they were charged with the task of warning their parishioners against it. As noted by Courtney Roberts:

> *Many contemporary Christians would hotly dispute the idea that their religion has any connection with astrology at all, but that is an entirely modern delusion. Among the earliest Christian writers, there was considerable argument over astrology, but not about whether the heavenly bodies exercised any influence. That they did was common knowledge.*
>
> *While wanting to differentiate themselves from the gullibility and excesses of their pagan neighbors, who were generally quite fond of horoscopes, these early Christians coveted the cosmological implications of astrology's overarching worldview, and not only sought to attribute that orderliness to the hand of God, but to read the preordained sanctification of their own faith into the cosmic order.*[9]

As was the case among the Roman Emperors, the issue was not the value and usefulness of astrology, but who would get to harness astrology's power and for what purpose, and who would not. The Church – which was as much a political force as a religious body – did not want astrologers usurping the authority of their own priests, much less suggesting that, armed with an astrological birthchart, a lay person could commune directly with God. So, to serve their own desire for expansion and control, they had no choice but to ban astrology, and because astrology had appeal not just to common people, but to the intelligent educated elite of the era, they had to underscore their hidden political agenda with sound, rational philosophical arguments.

Gnosticism

In counterbalance to the Church's insistence on serving as an intermediary between seekers of truth and their God, a Gnostic movement arose in the late first century C.E., among various Jewish and early Christian sects, that emphasized the possibility of direct knowing – such as was more commonly practiced in the days of oral teachings in the Mystical Era, before the advent of organized religions. By the second century C.E., Gnosticism was labeled heresy by the Church, even though most Gnostics considered themselves to be Christian. What was heretical about their approach was that it bypassed a politically ordained priesthood, suggesting that the Christian God could only be truly known directly through a mystical encounter.

Gnostics did not deny the power of reason that was gaining hegemony in their day; in fact, among others of the era, they championed it. But they were also aware that reason could be used to arrive at multiple interpretations of reality, and so they were aiming for something deeper, something more akin to direct mystical knowledge of self, Spirit, and the true nature of the world. In an era when written scripture provided the basis for religious truth, the Gnostics often railed against a literal interpretation of scripture, preferring instead to use the power of the imagination to explore the more symbolic and mythopoetic meanings of sacred texts.

Although there were many Gnostic sects, with varied teachings, Gnosticism in general entailed a highly dualistic understanding of reality, in which the manifest material universe was seen as a mistake propagated by the Demiurge, while the truth was only to be found within, where one could gain access to congress with a divine hierarchy called the Pleroma. The dogma promulgated by the Church, which was meant to be taken on faith as a matter of belief, was considered by the Gnostics to be the work of the Demiurge, attempting to lead the clueless astray.

The Gnostics were engaged in a conscious and deliberate effort to address the perennial questions: "Who am I?" "What is my purpose?" and "How can I participate in the world, flawed as it is, in a meaningful way?" – not through a blind acceptance of conventional answers provided by the Church or other cultural institutions, but through an inner process of deep self-reflection and penetration to a level of truth beyond appearances.

Within this process of self-reflection, astrology was considered useful as a way of navigating the false world of the Demiurge, conditioned by fate, through which the individual soul must make its way to a more reliable truth.

> *The world he (the Demiurge) creates, along with the autonomous rule of fate that governs it, is the product of the image-making power of his irrational soul – a labyrinth of deceptive semblances organized according to the structural principles of Hellenistic astrology.*[10]

Although scholars have yet to find pre-Christian Gnostic texts, the texts at the Nag Hammadi library, a collection of early Christian and Gnostic writings discovered in Egypt in 1945, were found alongside treatises from the *Corpus Hermeticum.*[11] Given the intermingling of cultures throughout the Mediterranean during the birth of the Gnostic movement, it is not unlikely to assume that they were influenced by Hermetic lore, as well as by the Jewish Kabalah and Platonic and Neoplatonic ideas. Within this mix astrology played its part,[12] although within the political maneuvering of the Church, this association with astrology became another wedge between the Gnostics and mainstream Christianity.

While Gnosticism was effectively banned from orthodox Christian circles by the second century C.E., it continued to flourish in as an influence throughout the Logical Era – among the Cathars in northern Italy and southern France between the twelfth and fourteenth centuries; among Jewish Kabbalists in the thirteenth century; and among the Sufis from the seventh century onward.[13]

Gnosticism also asserted a great deal of influence in more modern times on seminal nineteenth and twentieth century thinkers such as Carl Jung, Madame Blavatsky, and Aleister Crowley, all of whom contributed to the philosophical climate in which a postmodern astrology had taken root (see Chapters Eight and Nine). The harsh dualism at the heart of the Gnostic worldview has lost its appeal, but the idea that knowledge was something to be sought within, rather than simply through blind acceptance of some external authority has become one of the cornerstone canons of the postmodern era. There will be more said about this later in the book.

The Role of Islam in Preserving Astrology During the Reign of the Church

Meanwhile returning to our story, from the fourth through the tenth century, as the Church rose in dominance, stamping out competing worldviews such as Gnosticism and various strains of pagan culture, astrology also went underground. Campion attributes the decline of astrology in Western Europe during this period not just to the influence of the Church, but to the deterioration of European intellectual life in general.[14] This period is generally referred to as the "Dark Ages," although scholars tend to quibble about the exact dates during which Europe went "dark," with some preferring to avoid the term altogether.[15] In general, those who still consider the Early Middle Ages (from the late fifth or early sixth centuries to the tenth century) dark, do so either because they believed that intellectual life and cultural development languished between the glory days of Rome and the intellectual pinnacle of the Enlightenment; or because they believed the Church, the dominant institution of the day, was based in faith rather than what they felt to be the superior faculty of reason; or because there was a relative paucity of records kept during this period; or because many of the classical Greek texts had been apparently lost. In any case, this was a period in general when throughout most of Europe, astrology itself appeared to disappear.

> *The decline of the Roman Empire coincided with a decline in the practice of Hellenistic astrology, both due to a loss of learning and literacy in the wake of the decay of the state, and also due to changing intellectual, social, and religious trends that resulted from the rise in popularity of Christianity.*[16]

Around the eighth century, as a counterforce to the decay of the intellectual milieu in Europe in which astrology previously flourished, imperial patronage in the Byzantine Empire brought scholars together from Egypt, Persia and India to continue the cosmological debate that had been squashed in the West. While astrology was being suppressed by the Christian Church throughout most of Europe - not without lively debate, controversy, and ambivalence among the clergy - it found a new home in the Islamic world.

Within this creative ferment, Plato and Aristotle were rediscovered, along with the Neoplatonists, translated from Greek into the Arabic languages and given new life by Islamic scholars such as Jabir ibn Hayyan, Masha'allah, Abu Ma'shar, Al-Kindi, Ahmet Abu Ja'far, Avicenna and Ibn-Khaldun.

In particular, these Islamic scholars preserved the notion that astrology was a magical art - that is to say, not just a diagnostic tool, but a source of guidance for intentionally influencing and mitigating one's fate. These ideas - similar in principle, though somewhat different in practice than Iamblichus' theurgy, or the various threads of Hermeticism woven into Hellenistic astrology - were codified in a work called the *Ghayat al-Hakim* around the year 1,000, later translated into Latin two-and-a-half centuries later by Alfonso the Wise, and eventually reborn in medieval Europe as *The Picatrix*, the Bible of magical astrology through the seventeenth century, and in some quarters, to this day.[17]

As the Islamic revival slowly filtered back into Europe through the intermingling of cultures across the Mediterranean roughly between 800 – 1200, the stigma that the Church sought to impose upon all things astrological began to erode. Astrology was within this new context, no longer just about predicting the future, but also about managing the present with greater awareness – an approach that could be conceived, even by Christian scholars, as a way to live a good life in harmony with God's law. At the same time, within an Aristotelian context – also revived by Islamic scholars – astrology began to assume a new legitimacy as a form of natural philosophy, quite in line with the science of the day – that is to say, a way of entering into rational dialogue about the natural order of things.

> *There is absolutely no question that, in the hands of astrology's leading practitioners and theoreticians, it was not deterministic. Quite the opposite. Above all, it was participatory, a matter of the astrologer's active engagement with the cosmos.*[18]

This idea had broad appeal as Western European intellectual life began to re-emerge from religious suppression. It was also a retroactive nod to the sensibilities of the earlier Mythopoetic and Mystical Eras at the same time that it was a step forward.

The Islamic Revival and the Primacy of the Imagination

As documented by twentieth century Islamic scholar Henry Corbin, the Islamic revival was not just a rediscovery and embrace of the best rational scholarship of the Philosophical Era. It was also a recognition of the primacy of the imagination as a way of knowing, integral not just to Islamic mysticism, but also to the mystical foundations of all Western monotheistic religions, as discussed in Chapter Two.

What Islamic scholars like Ibn 'Arbi – the subject of Corbin's masterwork *Alone with the Alone: Creative Imagination in the Sufism Of Ibn 'Arabi* – were remembering and reminding the rest of the world about was that rational thought would only take us so far, that in order to know God, or for that matter, the nature of reality, one had to use the faculty of imagination to pierce the veils. Despite his prodigious scholarship (with 800 works attributed to him, at least 100 of which survived), Ibn 'Arabi was at heart a mystic, very much in the tradition of Muhammad and his forebearers of the Mystical Era – for whom the imagination was a better portal through which God could speak to those with clear intent than the more constrictive faculty of reason.

In the opening paragraph to *Alone with the Alone*, Corbin assures the scholar that:

> *Here we shall not be dealing with imagination in the usual sense of the word: neither with fantasy, profane or otherwise, nor with the organ which produces imaginings identified with the unreal; nor shall we even be dealing exactly with what we look upon as the organ of esthetic creation. We shall be speaking of an absolutely basic function, correlated with a universe peculiar to it, a universe endowed with a perfectly "objective' existence and perceived precisely through the Imagination.*[19]

Corbin called this peculiar universe the *Mundus Imaginalis*, coining the term to sidestep the pejorative connotations that had evolved around the word, "imagination" (or "imaginary") and its association with delusion. For Corbin, informed by his careful study of the way the Islamic mystics saw the world, the *Mundus Imaginalis* was where one arrived when one ventured inward rather than outward through the material world. This inward journey does not take place in a physical or geographic place in the same way that an outer journey seems to, but this does not mean that the landscape of the journey, nor the destination – if that word even applies – is unreal, or not to be taken seriously. Quite the contrary.

> *. . . strange as it may seem, once the journey is completed, the reality which has hitherto been an inner and hidden one turns out to envelop, surround, or contain that which at first was outer and visible. As a result of internalization, one has moved out of external reality. Henceforth, spiritual reality envelops, surrounds, contains so-called material reality. Spiritual reality can therefore not be found "in the where". The "where" is in it. In other words, spiritual reality itself is the "where" of all things.*[20]

The *Mundus Imaginalis* was, according to Corbin and the Islamic mystics, as ontologically real as the world of the senses and the world of the intellect, occupying a middle ground between them, reachable through the faculty of imagination. Again, however, Corbin is careful to insist that we think of imagination, not as a way of knowing inferior to reason or sensory perception, but as a vital, and absolutely necessary faculty for experiencing what neither reason nor sensory perception can access.

In Islamic thought, the physical universe is thought to encompass seven climes, while the imagination is the point of entry to the eighth clime, "a clime outside all climes, a place outside all places . . ." The eighth clime, as Corbin understood it, was where mystical experience occurred, and where we might postulate any experience capable of providing a spiritual context of meaning to the soul. Science, to the extent that it was wedded to the faculty of reason, as it was developing throughout the Logical Era, could reach seven climes, but not the eighth.

Such a distinction would not have been necessary in the preceding eras, up to and including the Philosophical Era, where imagination was both rampant and a fertile source of mythopoetic theory. But now it was. In an age that had forgotten, Corbin was simply reminding his peers (in the twentieth century) what was lost in the Logical Era but preserved in the mysticism of Islamic seers like Ibn 'Arabi.

> *This approach to imagination, which had always been of prime importance for our mystical theosophers, provided them with a basis for demonstrating the validity of dreams and of the visionary reports describing and relating "events in Heaven" as well as the validity of symbolic rites. It offered proof of the reality of the places that occur during intense meditation, the validity of inspired imaginative visions, of cosmogonies and theogonies and above all of the veracity of the spiritual meaning perceived in the imaginative information supplied by prophetic revelations.*[21]

Astrology and the Mundus Imaginalis

It is also worth considering that astrology itself – at least as it was practiced in the Mythopoetic and Mystical Eras – was an excursion into the eighth clime, one whose validity could better be established with reference to Corbin's *Mundus Imaginalis*, than as an appeal to reason. To the list of experiences for which imagination offers proof, in the quote above, we might add astrology's capacity to illuminate the human experience, and to help us derive spiritual meaning from the mundane reality of our lives. As astrology became more rational and wedded to a language of (symbolic) logic during the Logical Era, we forgot our roots in a more imaginative way of knowing – one in which a mystical receptivity combined with an intentional curiosity to allow us to see patterns in movement of the living cosmos.

As contemporary astrologer Brad Kochunas reminds us:

> *Astrology is a form of imagination, a way of organizing human reality that we should take seriously but not literally . . . The natal or birth chart is . . . imagined as a map of our inner landscape, the typography of our psychic life. It is an image first and foremost of psyche as soul . . . As a map of our inner landscape, an image of soul, it is fathomless. The natal chart is labyrinthine in complexity allowing us to draw deeply on imagination . . . The cycling of planets imagined as movements of soul suggests the survival of sacred order in secular times. They provide a touchstone for the poetic imagination to reach out and elaborate an intimacy between our selves and our world.*[22]

Of course, it can be argued that the evolution of both Aristotelian science and Hellenistic astrology as rational disciplines during the Logical Era were also attempts to articulate the sacred order. As Corbin spelled out, however, the sacred does not exist in the seven climes to which reason has access, but only in the eighth to which imagination is key, and for which an astrology approached through an imaginal contemplation of symbols can provide a map.

Be that as it may, in the Logical Era, imagination and the mystical approach to knowledge that naturally renders knowledge sacred became marginalized – by science as inferior to reason, by the Church as obviated by written scripture, and by astrologers as bound by logical rules. Within the Logical Era, all three of these streams converged to form the perfect wave in which reason increasingly carried acceptable knowledge to the world, while the mystical imagination of a bygone era languished only in eddies at the periphery of this all-consuming paradigm shift.

Scholasticism

With the twelfth century, in what is sometimes referred to as the third medieval renaissance, intellectual life returned to Europe, along with renewed interest in Greek and Latin classics, and the influence of the Islamic mystics began to fade, at least in the West. With the translation of *Tetrabiblos* into Latin in the twelfth century, the work of Ptolemy became the basis for an integration of Aristotelian science and astrology into the rational religious teaching of the Scholastics – through the work of Christian scholars such as Peter Abelard, Albertus Magnus, Thomas Aquinas and John Buriden.

Aristotle – or perhaps his first century C.E. editor – had coined the word "metaphysics;" postulated "*telos*" or purpose as the final cause; and was not shy in using the four-letter word "soul" in his writings.[23] These are liberties foreign to the modern practice of science, but of great appeal to the Scholastics, who wanted their Christian god to be at the center of everything that could be studied by the rising discipline of science, while at the same time, adding to the credibility of their religion by attempting to underscore it with an approach to science that was not at odds with Christian thought. Aristotle gave them a philosophical foundation for this goal, while Ptolemy's reinterpretation of astrological principles in terms of Aristotelian science – rediscovered by Islamic scholars and re-introduced to the West – now brought greater acceptance of astrology within religious circles.

The Scholastics trod a middle ground between science and Christian metaphysics, in which astrology was no longer always dismissed out of hand, and these very different worldviews could all have their place. The Dominican theologian Thomas Aquinas, for example, proposed that the stars ruled the imperfect "sublunary" body – or what we might understand as the embodied soul in its sojourn through this mortal life – while God ruled the eternal soul that the Christians believed survived bodily death. It should be noted here that Aquinas was still working within the overall context of an assumption of celestial causation passed on through Ptolemy's reinterpretation of astrology in Aristotelian terms, but now reframed in a way that provided an opening through which astrology could be re-included in the conversation about what a spiritually conscious life might look like.

Aquinas' distinctions are useful as a delineation of what became to be considered astrology's legitimate function, since it is the moment of birth - at which point a soul becomes embodied - that the natal birthchart depicts.[24] As astrologers, we can perhaps speculate about past lives - or, in Christian language, about the eternal soul that survives bodily death - but the substance of most astrologers' work with living clients is about how best to navigate this life, that is to say, the life of the embodied soul in the here and now. This is not to say, as hinted earlier, that we can't employ the imagination to take such an exploration into the spiritual dimensions of the eighth clime. But within the rational conversation about astrology that was raging in the Logical Era, it was astrology's contribution to life within the seven climes that was being parsed.

To be sure, the Church of the thirteenth century in general continued to have an ambivalent attitude toward astrology, ranging from qualified acceptance to outright rejection. Within the context of the Scholastics' distinction between the embodied and the eternal soul, however, what we see on closer examination is that the ambivalence of the Church can be more accurately understood, not as a condemnation of astrology *per se*, but again - as it was before - rather a question about astrology's rightful scope. As Tester notes:

> *It is important to remember that no one questioned the validity of astrology. It could be criticized as too complicated and too difficult to be possible, and parts of it . . . might be rejected as wrong. But that it was all possible, everyone accepted . . . Since the changes of the sublunary world were caused by heavenly movements, physical changes like chemical reactions and bodily diseases, and the weather (like the tides, always accepted as caused by the moon's movements) were clearly linked to the movements of the stars and planets, and no one could expect to alter the nature of metals (with their ancient links with the planets) or to cure diseases or to understand and forecast the weather and related phenomena, storm and flood and earthquakes and so on, without a knowledge of astrology. This was not superstition; it was good science.*[25]

Marsilio Ficino

Similarly, at a slightly later juncture during the Logical Era, the Italian Christian philosopher, Marsilio Ficino saw no contradiction between Christian faith and the classical worldview, which was thoroughly marinated in astrological perspectives. Ficino was a student, not just of astrology, but of Aristotle's teachings, Hermeticism, Neoplatonism and Scholasticism. Ficino founded the Platonic Academy at Florence in the mid fifteenth century, where astrology found its hallowed place in an attempted integration of contemporary scientific perspectives and Christian theology.

In his work, Ficino describes a kind of natural magic that draws down the intellectual and moral virtues of the heavens to the terrestrial world – and throughout his writings, he recognized astrology as its language. This sensibility, it can easily be recognized, comes from Ficino's immersion in Hermeticism and Neoplatonism, translated as it was by educated Christians in general, into a context of religious faith and a faith-based integration of philosophical principles.

To be sure, Ficino continued at times to rail against a more fatalistic form of astrology – which in his view obviated the supreme authority of God and the free will of men – for the same reasons that the Council of Laodicea had, more than a millennium ago. But he also viewed astrology as a way to understand the divine order of things. Within this more liberal context, again what we see within the work of Ficino is an educated attempt to delineate astrology's rightful scope.

In Ficino's case – as in the case of many of his peers toward the latter end of the Logical Era – the line was drawn between a deterministic form of astrology in which prediction of the future was possible, and a more liberating use of astrology, in which awareness and intention are focused through the symbolism toward the end of making informed choices in the here and now, in harmony with the divine intelligence that permeated the natural order of the cosmos.

In the third book of *De vita libri tres* (*Three Books on Life*), Ficino outlines a system in which human beings can observe, participate in and influence the divine order, which was essentially a system of astrological magic. It is said that Ficino borrowed heavily from *The Picatrix* in composing his treatise.[26] But what we see in practice throughout the Logical Era – within which, Ficino can be understood as a penultimate ambassador – was an evolutionary trend away from using astrology as a static language with which to articulate fate and toward its proactive use as a dynamic catalyst of creative possibility. Leaving aside the self-serving misuses of what was at times feared as a dark art, this proactive use of astrology to intentionally shape our fate was essentially what Ficino, as well as Alfonso the Wise and Iamblichus before him, meant by magic. Within this trend, we see a positive counterforce to the dominance of reason in astrology, religion and science, in which the role of imagination was preserved.

One could argue that this goal of facilitating creative, even magical possibility is also shared by science, which in its application has broken or transcended many of the "rules" governing God's creation – defying the limitations of gravity in aviation and space travel; eliminating distance in global communications; and altering the genetic structure of living things. Indeed, from the perspective of a scientist of the Logical Era, many of these achievements would be viewed as magic. Certainly, within the Logical Era, in which both Hermeticism and Neoplatonism continued to flourish as influential schools of thought – pervasive throughout the intellectual culture of the age, the boundaries between religion, science and magic were quite blurred.

> *We cannot hope to grasp Ficino's position unless we attempt to enter it and ask fundamental questions about the nature of astrology. Do we define it as a magical art, or a natural science? What exactly do we mean by magic and science? It would seem to us that these are two very different modes of perceiving reality, modes which could generally be defined as 'mystical' and 'rational'. One would seem to depend on subjective experience, the other on objective observation. Contemporary astrology is claimed by both camps, yet struggles to find its natural authority in either. But if we look at the various traditions that informed the Renaissance's claim of magic to be the highest form of natural science, we begin to see that such a distinction is superficial.*[27]

At the cutting edge of the Logical Era, then, as epitomized by the work of Ficino, is an imaginal form of astrology, practiced as a magical capacity to bend or break the rules by which reason is bound, and Corbin's eighth clime is entered. In this sacred space, the mythopoetic and mystical sensibilities of previous eras are carried forward, despite the dominant trend toward a rational monopoly on knowledge.

Notes

1. The Logical Era encompasses the period from the end of the western Roman Empire through the Middle Ages and the Renaissance into the very beginning of the so-called Age of Enlightenment. This period also encompasses an Islamic Golden Age, which saw a flourishing of science and mathematics within the Islamic World, a preservation of classical writings, such as those of Aristotle, and a cultural integration of intellectual traditions. This was, in addition, an era of colonial expansion, encompassing the global spread of Christianity and the Protestant Reformation.
2. This is not to imply that astrology's evolution during this period was linear or continuous. As Tester notes in *A History of Western Astrology*, on page 200, "there was no astrology in Western Europe from the early sixth to the late twelfth century." It disappeared partly due to its disapproval by the Church, but also because in general during the Middle Ages, there was a general collapse of academic scholarship and higher education of which astrology would otherwise have been an integral part.
3. Tester, Jim. *A History of Western Astrology*. Ballentine Books, 1987, 18.
4. Theodosiou, Efstratios, Vassilios N. Manimanis, and Milan S. Dimitrijevic. "Astrology in the Early Byzantine Empire and the Anti-Astrology Stance of the Church Fathers." Re-

searchGate, June 1, 2012, 18. https://www.researchgate.net/publication/248386545_Astrology_in_the_early_byzantine_empire_and_the_anti-astrology_stance_of_the_church_fathers.

5. Theodosiou, et al. "Astrology in the Early Byzantine Empire and the Anti-Astrology Stance of the Church Fathers," 19.
6. It is interesting to note here than many of the architects of the scientific revolution – particularly during the Empirical Era – were also staunch Christians. Men like Galileo Gallilei, Johannes Kepler, Francis Bacon and Isaac Newton all sought to develop their science within the confines of their faith, to varying degrees of success, or in Gallileo's case, failure.
7. Brennan, Chris. *Hellenistic Astrology: The Study of Fate and Fortune*. Denver: Amor Fati Publications, 2017, 102-103.
8. Quoted by Theodossiou, et al. in "Astrology in the Early Byzantine Empire and the Anti-Astrology Stance of the Church Fathers," 21.
9. Roberts, Courtney. "Christian Astrology, the Dark Ages, and the Celtic Church." Accessed May 16, 2023. http://cura.free.fr/xxx/29robts.html.
10. Plese, Zlatko. "Fate, Providence and Astrology in Gnosticism (1): The Apocryphon of John." Unc, June 3, 2014, 243. https://www.academia.edu/3063711/Fate_Providence_and_Astrology_in_Gnosticism_1_The_Apocryphon_of_John.
11. Meyer, Marvin W., and James M. Robinson. *The Nag Hammadi Scriptures: The International Edition*. HarperOne, 2007, 2-3.
12. Brennan, *Hellenistic Astrology*, 124.
13. Barnstone, Willis, and Marvin Meyer. *The Gnostic Bible: Revised and Expanded Edition*. Shambhala Publications, 2009, 603.
14. Campion, Nicholas. *A History of Western Astrology Volume II: The Medieval and Modern Worlds*. Bloomsbury, 2009, 19.
15. Halsall, Guy. "The Sources and Their Interpretation." In *The New Cambridge Medieval History: Volume 1, c.500-c.700*, edited by Paul Fouracre. Cambridge University Press, 2015, 90.
16. Brennan, *Hellenistic Astrology*, 123.
17. In their translation of *The Picatrix*, John Michael Greer & Christopher Warnock attribute authorship of the original *Ghayat al-Hakim* to "an anonymous wizard in North Africa or Spain, and credited in the fashion of the time to the notable Sufi and scholar al-Majriti" (on page 11). This fits the pattern of the oral tradition in which mysterious,

mythical and/or legendary teachers, who may or may not have existed, are the source of the teachings that later got written down.

18. Campion, *A History of Western Astrology Volume II*, 61.
19. Corbin, Henry. *Alone with the Alone: Creative Imagination in the Sufism of Ibn 'Arabi*. Princeton University Press, 1998, 3.
20. Corbin, Henry. "Mundus Imaginalis or the Imaginary and the Imaginal." *Cahiers Internationaux De Symbolisme* 6 (1964): 4. http://www.bahaistudies.net/asma/mundus_imaginalis.pdf.
21. Corbin, "Mundus Imaginalis or the Imaginary and the Imaginal," 6.
22. Kochunas, Brad Hiljanen. *The Astrological Imagination: Where Psyche and Cosmos Meet*. iUniverse, 2008, xvi-xvii.
23. Cohen, S. Marc. "Aristotle's Metaphysics." Stanford Encyclopedia of Philosophy. November 21, 2020. https://plato.stanford.edu/entries/aristotle-metaphysics/.
24. Geoffrey Cornelius argues persuasively in *The Moment of Astrology* (on pages 84-88) that it was the influence of Ptolemy through which the natal chart became the primary reference point for nearly all contemporary astrological practice – a now mostly unconscious *a priori* assumption that he called the "doctrine of origins." Before that, and to some extent as still practiced by horary or electional astrologers, any moment at which an astrologer applied his attention to a particular issue could yield relevant information. Within the revival of interest in Aristotelian philosophy and science, the real debate was not about whether astrology was a legitimate form of inquiry, but rather what was its proper scope – a debate that revolved around the then-dominant Ptolemaic formulation of astrology, which was based on the doctrine of origin.
25. Tester, *A History of Western Astrology*, 178.
26. Greer, John Michael, and Christopher Warnock, trans. *The Complete Picatrix: The Occult Classic of Astrological Magic Liber Atratus Edition: The Classic Medieval Handbook of Astrological Magic*. Adocentyn Press, 2011, 11.
27. Voss, Angela. "Astrology: The Astrology of Marsilio Ficino: Divination or Science?" Accessed May 17, 2023. http://cura.free.fr/decem/10voss.html.

Chapter Five

The Dominance of Science in the Empirical Era Seventeenth – Nineteenth Century[1]

The evolution of science took a significant leap in the late seventeenth century with the birth of empiricism. Empiricism is essentially the idea that knowledge comes primarily through sensory experience, that is to say in practice, the collection of data derived through careful observation. Empiricism emphasizes evidence gathered through experimentation over logic, reason, philosophical speculation, metaphysics or tradition in determining what is true. Over the course of a couple centuries, this epistemological approach culminated in what is currently understood as the scientific method. The emphasis of empirical evidence represents a departure from the Logical Era, in which rational arguments determined superiority among a crowded field of competing philosophical positions, whether imbued with metaphysical implications or not.

It should be noted here that empiricism was not necessarily antithetical to the rationalist worldview of philosophers like René Descartes, Baruch Spinoza and Gottfried Leibniz. Many rationalists - people like Robert Boyle and John Locke - were also advocates of the emerging empirical methodology. The difference in approach was that for empiricists, reason was a secondary faculty useful for analyzing raw data, while the data itself was primary.

As I have noted in my previous books– and will elaborate later in this book – this way of approaching knowledge is not necessarily at odds with astrology, which is largely built upon a great deal of empirical evidence gathered over centuries by a small army of practitioners generating data from their work with clients. Although empirical science has evolved to reject what it now calls "anecdotal" evidence, as information from direct experience is gathered, sorted and sifted by a community of practitioners, there was - even in the Empirical Era - some common ground between astrologers and scientists, both of whom were questing, albeit in different ways, to make sense of empirical data.

With the strictures that came to characterize the scientific method over time - which included the *a priori* assumption that all knowledge must be objective, replicable by others, and essentially a matter of widespread professional consensus - astrology became increasingly subject to criticism and rejection by the scientific establishment. When the anecdotal evidence for astrology's efficacy no longer met the rigorous standards set for empirical truth, the question, "Is astrology a science?" left astrology in the dust, despite a dedicated cadre of scientifically-minded astrologers that have worked feverishly to keep the question open.

That effort aside, what is important in the actual practice of astrology is the unique interaction between astrologer and client, where the raw data of the birthchart itself - derived mathematically in similar fashion to the raw data of science - must be interpreted according to rules of symbolic logic within the specific context of a human life experienced subjectively by the client. There are, of course, other forms and branches of astrology where this is less important, or not relevant at all. But for the majority of astrologers working with clients, astrology - as inherited from its reworking in the Logical Era - is a living language of symbolic logic and an art requiring fresh application in each instance of its use. Astrology is far less useful as a set of hard and fast rules codified by objective empirical laws. As Geoffrey Cornelius notes (parenthetical phrases are mine):

> *The only universal factors (in an astrological interpretation) are the theoretically constant meaning of the planets and signs, but these meanings which we share in our tradition have no meaning at all until they are brought into symbolic relation with actual situations and people, against whom they are interpreted . . . Whatever significance is involved, it is not amenable to scientific verification, and it is completely unreplicable. The significance of the unique case exists once and once only in the context in which it is interpreted.*[2]

We will return to this point later, but first let us look more closely at empiricism itself.

Empiricism

Many scientists contributed to the paradigm shift toward empiricism and to the gradual development of the scientific method that came to epitomize it. The seeds of the empirical attitude - the idea that sensory information, derived through observation, experience, and experimentation is primary, more important than reason in determining truth - were planted centuries before empiricism became the dominant paradigm. Indeed, in a rudimentary way, Aristotle himself could be considered to be an early practitioner of empiricism, although within the context of Aristotelian science, empirical inquiry is more accurately understood as an aid to reason and a possible confirmation of logical reasoning. It was only thirteen centuries after Aristotle that the roles of reason and empirical inquiry were reversed.

Galileo Galilei

One of the primary architects of this paradigm shift was Galileo Galilei, an Italian polymath well versed in astronomy, physics, philosophy, and mathematics, among other disciplines, as well as an inventor of scientific instrumentation. Galileo has been called the father of observational astronomy,[3] the father of modern physics,[4] the father of the scientific method,[5] and the father of science – that is to say, empirical science.[6] He was also by some accounts a practicing astrologer.[7,8,9]

Galileo is best known for his use of the telescope, previously invented by a Dutch eye-glass maker named Hans Lippershey in the Netherlands at the beginning of the seventeenth century, for empirical observation of celestial objects and phenomena, including the phases of Venus, the largest moons of Jupiter, the planet Saturn, and an analysis of sunspots. He was also a champion of the heliocentric theories of Copernicus at a time when the theory of a geocentric universe was widely accepted as a rational proposition by both the scientific establishment of his day and the Church. Eventually, he was tried by the Inquisition for his views, found "vehemently suspect of heresy," and placed under house arrest for the remainder of his life.[10] As concluded by his inquisitors:

> *Heliocentrism was 'foolish and absurd in philosophy, and formally heretical since it explicitly contradicts in many places the sense of Holy Scripture.'*[11]

Galileo's support of heliocentrism was condemned as heretical because it contradicted the philosophical view of the Church, which was considered rationally sound as well as scripturally correct. This fact alone illustrated the power of the dominant logical worldview, built on Aristotelian principles, at the dawn of the seventeenth century.

Ironically, Galileo's views (and heliocentrism in general) were also rejected by his fellow astronomers, because they lacked empirical evidence. For the heliocentric theory to be demonstrable on a scientific basis, it would require an observation of stellar parallax (the apparent shift of position of a nearby star or other celestial object against the background of more distant bodies). This was an observation that eluded astronomers until 1838, nearly two centuries after Galileo's death.

Thus, it can be seen that poor Galileo was castigated not just by the Church, but also by both the old order of Aristotelian logical science and the newly emerging paradigm of empiricism, even as he served a pivotal role in shepherding the transition between them. Despite all that, and beyond his readily acknowledged scientific achievements, Galileo was instrumental in changing the definition of science itself.

> *What Galileo accomplished by the end of his life in 1642 was a reasonably articulated replacement for the traditional set of analytical concepts connected with the Aristotelian tradition of natural philosophy. He offered, in place of the Aristotelian categories, a set of mechanical concepts that were accepted by most everyone who afterwards developed the 'new sciences', and which, in some form or another, became the hallmark of the new philosophy. His way of thinking became the way of the scientific revolution.*[12]

In his experimentation, Galileo began to rely on inductive reasoning rather than the deductive reasoning upon which Aristotelian science and indeed most of philosophy prior to the empirical revolution depended. Deductive reasoning asserts that if the premises of an argument are logically sound, the conclusion is certain. Inductive reasoning only accepts the conclusion if the premises are verified by experimental confirmation; they are, in other words, far more tentative. In fact, experimental confirmation itself is uncertain, which is why replication is a hallmark of the scientific method.

As a philosopher, weaned on deductive reasoning, Galileo was disturbed by the uncertainty that his experimentation seemed to entail, and so he presented his results mathematically.[13] He also preferred to quantify the objects of his study, rather than describe them as a simple matter of observation. This was also the approach taken by his friend and colleague, the German astronomer Johannes Kepler, and through the work of these men and others, mathematical rendition became a hallmark of the new science, according to which if it could not be measured and/or described by a mathematical equation, it could not be proven true.

In addition, Galileo dismantled the old Aristotelian doctrine of four elements, replacing them with the simple notion of corporeal matter, whose properties and dynamics could be quantified. Aristotle's qualitative consideration of various combinations of hot and cold, wet and dry was replaced by parameters such as weight and temperature, speed and time, that could and needed only to be measured mathematically.

Galileo called all those qualities that could not be measured, "secondary," meaning that they were essentially unverifiable subjective perceptions, carrying less credibility than those that could be measured mathematically and thus objectively verified to be certain. Appearances could be deceptive – as Copernicus had proven – and thus all observations would have to quantified to be reliable.

The significance of this development cannot be underestimated for most practicing astrologers today, who by and large give voice to a symbolic language designed to shed light on the qualitative dimensions of human psychology and the affairs of humans within the world:

> *Till the time of Galileo, it had always been taken for granted that man and nature were both integral parts of a larger whole, in which man's place was the more fundamental . . . Now, in the course of translating this distinction of primary and secondary into terms suited to the new mathematical interpretation of nature, we have the first stage in the reading of man quite out of the real and primary realm. Obviously, man was not a subject suited to mathematical study. His performances could not be treated by the quantitative method, except in the most meager fashion. His was a life of colors and sounds, of pleasures, of griefs, of passionate loves, of ambitions, and strivings. Hence the real world must be the world outside of man; the world of astronomy and the world of resting and moving terrestrial objects.*[14]

It was at this juncture that astronomy and astrology began to separate in a significant way, since within Galileo's insistence on quantitative measurement, and in the worldview of his contemporaries and successors, the qualitative astrological commentary on human psychology was clearly no longer within the scope of astronomy. Of course, there have been subsequent attempts to bring human psychology and other so-called "soft sciences" (involving measurement of secondary qualities) back into the fold, and some astrologers today still insist this is possible. It becomes less possible, however, within the scientific paradigm ushered in by Galileo and the other empiricists, where the subjective experience of quality is considered an unreliable source of knowledge. In seeking to redefine science in terms that were measurable, Galileo made it far less amenable to astrology, which at its heart is a qualitative language, despite its reliance on mathematical calculations.

In his studies of motion, Galileo considered time itself a measurable quantity – that is to say, a primary quality that could be measured. While we take this for granted today, it is important to understand that before Galileo and the empiricists, time was largely understood in more philosophical terms as a movement from potentiality to actuality – essentially as something to be lived and experienced. Although astrologers do measure time in cycles, for the most part, they also assume this earlier understanding, always with the hope that human beings can evolve through the various astrological cycles that challenge them and provide a temporal structure to their lived experiences. Time that is strictly a measurement of motion does not speak at all to this possibility.

Francis Bacon

While Galileo laid much of the philosophical foundation for the empirical worldview, the importance of its emerging experimental methodology was more vigorously emphasized by one of his contemporaries, the English philosopher Francis Bacon. Bacon argued that scientific accuracy could best be achieved by use of a skeptical approach that would allow experimental researchers to avoid misleading themselves. In 1620, Bacon published a book entitled *Novum Organum* (*New Method*), written to replace the scientific methods of the Aristotelian Era, as presented previously in Aristotle's *Organon*. The earlier book contained Aristotle's teachings on logic and syllogism – which formed the basis for science in the Logical Era – collated and published by Andronicus of Rhodes around 40 B.C.E, nearly 300 years after Aristotle's death.

Although the details of Bacon's specific methodology were never widely adopted by the scientific community, his fundamental premise that a systematic methodology was necessary to counterbalance the fallibility of the human mind (echoing the sentiments of Xenophon two millennia earlier) became the underlying rationale for the scientific method. Among the pitfalls that Bacon outlined in the *Novum Organum* were:

The Idols of the Tribe: Though it is human nature to want to measure reality according to human expectations and desires, Bacon argued that the universe has its own truth, which must be discovered and elucidated apart from human projections. Thus, for example, while it is satisfying to want to assume that planets move in circular orbits, as did Plato, because circles are a meaningful human symbol for wholeness, regularity, and divine perfection, this is not the actual case, but merely an idol of the tribe.

The Idols of the Cave: Each individual has certain prejudices based on temperament, education, conditioning and life experience, which can cloud or distort a clear perception of the truth. Bacon argued, for example, that Aristotle's preference for and skill at logic led him to assume that the truth itself was logical, while to an empiricist – for whom experimentation and inductive reasoning were more natural – this would not necessarily be the case.

The Idols of the Market: Because we speak in words, which are interpreted differently by different people, and because we converse with each other, false ideas get propagated throughout the "marketplace" of ideas. Among these idols, Bacon considered the use of Aristotle's doctrine of four elements to be a prime example, since the words for the elements – earth, air, fire and water – were used in imprecise ways as a kind of shorthand code for ideas to which they were not literally related.

The Idols of the Theatre: Here Bacon rejected the stories, which formed the heart of mythopoetic culture, as well as philosophy in general, all of which he believed replaced truth with hazy, speculative metaphysical suppositions, which compound the confusion posed by the imprecision of words (the Idols of the Market).

Given that astrology is rooted in mythological tradition; subject to interpretation not just by words but of symbols that must first be translated into words; filtered through the particular background, orientation and training of an individual astrologer; and is very much a human endeavor, aiming to understand human experience in terms that are meaningful to humans; it is essentially dependent on all four of Bacon's Idols. To the extent that the newly emerging scientific method that Bacon inspired depends upon counterbalancing these Idols, then astrology starts to become unscientific.

Furthermore, in his attempt to replace Aristotelian science with something, in his opinion, more precisely articulated, Bacon rejects Aristotle's notion of *telos* or final cause as being important to an understanding of scientific truth. In this rejection is an implied dismissal of all metaphysical explanations for reality, but more than that, the very idea of meaning and purpose – essential to the practice of any form of astrology that purports to illuminate the meaning and purpose of a human life. In place of this fundamental and – according to Aristotelian science – most important of causes, Bacon proposes the primacy of formal cause: an understanding of form and function, which is mostly what occupies empirical science today – how something works, rather than why it exists, what purpose it serves, or what it means.

Extending the work of Galileo, Bacon approached his understanding of form and function through a process of eliminative inductive reasoning, in an attempt to gradually get to what was essential about the object of his study. If both fire and steam emit heat, for example, then neither light (a characteristic of fire, but not steam) nor moisture (a characteristic of steam, but not fire) are part of the form and function of heat. Over the evolution of the scientific method that began evolving under Bacon's influence, this approach became integrated into the testing of hypotheses through manipulating independent variables. Independent variables are generally manipulated to measure how change affects the dependent variables that are being studied, usually in relation to a control in which nothing changes.

The Incompatibility of Inductive Reasoning and Astro-Logic

Such an approach does not generally work in relation to astrology, which is a symbolic system in which the intermingling of independent variables – considered through a process of intuitive synthesis – is of primary interest. Mars in Pisces will express itself quite differently than Mars in Leo or Mars in Taurus; Mars in Leo in the 5th house will express itself differently than Mars in Leo in the 8th or 12th houses. Mars in Leo in the 8th house square Neptune will express itself very differently than Mars in Leo in the 8th house conjunct Saturn. And so on.

Unlike empirical science, which depends upon stripping away independent variables, within an astrological context, independent variables ultimately only derive their nuanced meaning through interaction with each other. The form and function of Mars takes definite shape only when placed in an astrological context, in which Mars' placement by sign and house; its aspects to other planets in the birthchart; its rulership of various houses and its disposition of other planets in the signs it rules – at a bare minimum – are all taken into account. Beyond the purely astrological context, Mars must also be understood in a living context, where the particulars of a life, an event, or a question shape it and every other factor in the birthchart.

This is not to say, we cannot arrive at a core meaning of form and function for Mars, in the abstract. The meaning of Mars – or any other "word" in the astrological language – derives not from a systematic isolation of everything peripheral to Mars, but from a symbolic synthesis of suggestions from mythology, astronomical facts considered metaphorically, symbolic logic as developed by Hellenistic astrologers and others since, and the anecdotal observations of generations of practicing astrologers.

The Roman god Mars and his Greek counterpart Ares were warrior gods. The astronomical Mars appears to be red in color. Hellenistic logicians considered Mars a malefic masculine planet of the night sect. Gauquelin observed a prominent Mars in the charts of star athletes. These factors, and others too numerous and nuanced to be listed here, have over time led us as a professional community to associate the astrological Mars with anger, competition, conflict, action, passion, impulsive behavior, and inflammation, among other attributes that are projected imaginatively onto the layered multi-faceted symbolic logic encountered by practicing astrologers in their experience of Mars in the birthchart of their clients.

This is a different exercise in logic than that implied in the inductive reasoning of Bacon. Here the goal is not eliminating everything nonessential to the form and function of Mars, but rather extending the creative imagination to encompass all possibilities within the field of Mars' symbolic domain, as they reveal themselves in the specific life or situation under scrutiny by the individual astrologer. In this way, astrology operates more like a symbolic language in which words derive their meaning in the context of sentences and paragraphs, than a science, in which variables (the scientific equivalent of words) are studied in isolation. There is a logic inherent within the astrological language, but it is not the logic of science.

While the tendency does unfortunately exist in astrology to boil interpretations down to codified bits and pieces, uniformly interpreted as one size fits all, the actual art of astrology does not strive toward eliminative inductive conclusions, as does empirical science, but toward holistic intuitive impressions that take into account as extensive an inclusion of independent variables within a birthchart as possible. Even where two people have virtually identical charts, the consciousness of the person whose chart it is will forever be an independent variable not measurable outside of the context of the individual life in which it takes its meaning.

All of this makes the scientific method, as developed by Bacon and his successors of limited use in understanding astrology. What matters in astrological practice is not compensating for the fallibility of the human mind, as Bacon advised the scientists of his day, but broadening the human mind to consider relevant associations beyond the measurable parameters of material form and function. The meaning of a birthchart does not derive from a systematic decoding of astrological symbolism, but from the perceptive flexibility to understand how the symbolism expresses itself anew within each context in which it is considered, within what Cornelius has called "the moment of astrology."

Isaac Newton

To continue our story, ultimately, no scientist was more important to the empirical revolution that undid astrology's claim to scientific credibility than English mathematician, astronomer, physicist and theologian Sir Isaac Newton, born after Bacon was dead. In his *Principia Mathematica*, Newton formulated the laws of motion and gravitation of classic mechanics, mathematically proving Kepler's laws of planetary motion and Copernicus' heliocentric model of the solar system. In addition to his work as an astronomer, he made significant contributions in the fields of optics, thermodynamics, and mathematics. He was also a student of alchemy and biblical prophecies, though probably not astrology.[15]

Like Galileo, Newton presented his findings mathematically. Unlike Galileo, however, Newton insisted that mathematical proofs were secondary to physical evidence derived from experimentation; going so far as to suggest in *Universal Arithmetic* that some scientific problems could not immediately be translated into mathematical language.[16]

Along with merely mathematical statements, Newton held most hypotheses tentatively until they could be proven empirically. Like Bacon, Newton developed a set of guidelines for a more empirically sound methodology, laid down in his *Principia*. Unlike Bacon, who was really more of a philosopher and a theorist than a scientist, Newton took his ideas into the laboratory and demonstrated their usefulness as a viable foundation for scientific truth – which is no doubt why *Principia*, and not *Novum Organum* became the bible of the empirical revolution. The essence of that revolution, as summed up by science historian E. A. Burtt was this:

> *Careful experimentation must occur at the beginning and end of every important scientific step, because it is always the sensible facts that we are seeking to comprehend; but the comprehension, so far as it is exact, must be expressed in the mathematical language. Hence by experiments, we must discover those characteristics which can be handled in that language, and by experiments our conclusions must be verified.*[17]

With Newton, controlled experimentation became the primary avenue to direct knowledge, which was then ideally expressed mathematically. This was a continuation and a consolidation of developments initiated by earlier empiricists like Galileo and Bacon, and a distinct break from Aristotelian science in which rational consideration of empirical facts provided a more logical, less experimental measure of truth. It was also a move away from hypothesis and inductive reasoning – favored by the early empiricists – toward more rigorous methods rooted in perpetual experimentation – that is to say, largely what is known as the scientific method today, with perhaps a few modifications to come later, after the quantum theorists again changed the definition of science (see Chapter Six).

What is perhaps equally important is that despite his interest in alchemy and biblical prophecy, Newton's science was another giant step toward the disavowal of all metaphysical premises on which disciplines like astrology might have been considered scientific in the previous Logical Era. For his insistence on empirical rigor in the quest for knowledge, Newton has been called the first great positivist.[18]

Positivism would later become more fully developed as a theory when French philosopher August Comte wrote *The Course in Positive Philosophy* – a series of texts published between 1830 and 1842. But the basic tenet of positivism – namely that certain knowledge was only that derived through experimental observation of nature's laws – was also written into the scientific code as a cornerstone of empiricism by Newton.

Within this view, there was no longer any room for information derived from introspective, imaginal and intuitive knowledge, metaphysical or theological sources, since such information could not be validated by evidence available to precise observation, quantified and rendered mathematically, nor replicated as objective truth.

All of these scientist/philosophers, and many others, largely working independently of each other during the Empirical Era, gradually revolutionized the practice of science to be a matter of measuring what could be observed, and using the data alone to draw conclusions about reality that were previously a matter of logical argument, often buffered by metaphysical speculation. At the hands of Hellenistic astrologers working in the Logical Era, astrology had become a logical system of symbolic correspondences between observable celestial phenomena and the realm of human affairs. As empirical methods became more defined and established, the logical approach to truth, previously shared by science of the Logical Era and astrology, fell increasingly into disfavor. Within this brave new world, when the question was asked, "Is astrology an empirical science?" astrology suddenly found itself with no demonstrable foundation.

Astrology rests on an unprovable metaphysical speculation – primarily a central tenet of the Hermetic tradition – "as above, so below." While practicing astrologers give personal anecdotal testimony to the evidence for this assertion through their daily practice, in ways that endlessly fascinate and that have given rise to a very rich anecdotal tradition, it is not a proposition that lends itself to empirical validation, since the myriad ways in which above and below reflect each other are nearly always surprising to the disciplined mind seeking formulaic empirical laws.

The Misguided Quest for Scientific Proof

This, of course, does not stop a certain subculture within the astrological community from trying to prove astrology's validity on scientific grounds. Acknowledging astrology's failure to meet scientific standards within the empirical paradigm, such astrologers find new hope in the re-invention of postmodern science in the quantum era. Foremost among those presenting plausible arguments for this approach is psychotherapist and astrologer Glenn Perry:

> *Empirical science is based on certain metaphysical assumptions that prevent one from seeing any truths except those that fall within the purview of its method. But astrology does not conform to this way of knowing. Thus, its truths are either invisible, or appear to be disconfirmed. So long as astrologers believe that the only way to vindicate their model is via the experimental method of mechanistic science, they are caught in a Catch-22: astrology must conform to the experimental method to be accepted, but the experimental method is intrinsically incompatible with astrology.*[19]

Perry goes on to assert that the answer to this dilemma lies in the compatibility of "postmodern science" and the "magical, organic world view of pre-scientific cultures that astrology grew and flourished" – by which I presume he means the proto-science of the Mythopoetic Era that was not artificially divided from an emerging proto-astrology, nor from religion, magic, politics, or the everyday lives of ordinary people. Perry sees in the emerging science of quantum physics a new scientific methodology that will not only validate astrology on scientific terms, but also broaden and deepen astrology's knowledge base.

> *This new, emerging paradigm is not only capable of providing a climate of understanding that is hospitable to astrology, but of providing alternative methods of inquiry that are in accord with the type of knowledge that astrology professes.*[20]

I agree with Perry that the old scientific methodology of the Empirical Era is ill suited to an understanding or measurement of the validity of astrological truth. But I'm afraid I do not share his optimism that the emerging methodologies of quantum science will validate astrology on scientific grounds, for reasons I will elaborate on in Chapter Six.

Meanwhile, Perry has stated quite eloquently the limitations of the empirical paradigm as a suitable framework in which to study, much less validate, astrology, as I have also done in a different way in my previous book *The Seven Gates of Soul*, and before we move on, it is worth exploring a bit further why astrology is not an empirical science, and likely never will be. According to Perry, the four pillars of the empirical method are:

> **objectivism**: only that which can be objectively verified is real.
>
> **reductionism**: only by breaking any complex system down to its component parts can we understand it.

positivism: only that which can be experienced by the senses or their extension through technological enhancement (e.g. seeing planets invisible to the naked eye through a telescope) can be considered to exist.

determinism: only when we understand the cause of something, have we explained it scientifically.

As noted in the Introduction, astrology operates according to a different set of *a priori* assumptions about the nature of reality, and in so doing, fails to fit the empirical paradigm on metaphysical grounds. It also fails to fit the empirical paradigm, because these different metaphysical grounds lead to very different ways of assessing what is true. Let's look in more detail, how this is so.

Objectivism Versus Eclectic Fertility

There are two primary reasons why astrology fails to provide an objective measure of truth. First, as noted in the Introduction, the practice of astrology is not uniform or monolithic. It leads to a multiplicity of approaches, each of which parses the correlation between macrocosm and microcosm differently, using different techniques and coming to different conclusions, all of which can still be considered astro-logically valid within the appropriate context.

Most astrologers I know greatly value the eclecticism within our field. In practice, we all pick and choose our techniques subjectively and pragmatically – that is to say, according to what makes theoretical sense to each of us, given our background, training, and experience, and according to what we personally find useful in working with clients. Even those astrologers I know who are fairly entrenched within a particular astrological framework, still value the fact that other astrologers work with different methodologies that can be equally as effective for them, and don't deny the value of those alternative methodologies. Some astrologers see no problem whatsoever with switching from system to system, even when planets change signs (as they do from Western Tropical to Vedic), or rulerships (as they do from Hellenistic to modern psychological), or when the focus shifts from planetary placements to midpoints between planets (as it does from most systems to Cosmobiology). For those astrologers that are ambidextrous in this way, having access to multiple perspectives enhances their ability to provide useful insight and perspective to their clients, even though they appear to be all over the map and horribly inconsistent in a way that would make a scientist cringe.

Even if we limit ourselves to a particular approach, variations in house systems, orbs, and other minutiae of technological subtlety lead to a profusion of techniques, methodologies and interpretive conclusions. To the extent that empirical science depends upon objective truth – that is to say, a truth that rests not upon eclectic variety, but upon consensus – this profusion of techniques, methodologies and astrological schools of thought makes consensus virtually impossible. It also puts the practice of astrology distinctly out of sync with the scientific method, as established in the Empirical Era, not just in terms of methodology, but in terms of epistemology, which is how we understand what knowledge is, as well as how we pursue it.

Even if we felt objective consensus was important, would we really want to sacrifice the rich fertility and cross-pollination of ideas that currently makes our community at its best, a smorgasbord of possibilities? Astrology is what I call a "kaleidoscopic language," meaning it is capable of revealing fresh insight when we look at the birthchart in different ways, through a variety of lenses provided by a multiplicity of techniques. Would astrology become more valuable could astrologers all agree on which systems, techniques and methodologies work, and which do not? Or would such an objectivist approach impoverish our art, and diminish our knowledge of the relationship between cosmos and psyche?

Reductionism Versus Synthesis Within a Context

A second reason why an objectivist approach to astrological knowledge is limiting at best, stifling at worst is the fact experienced by any working astrologer in the field, that the most essential truth at the heart of any astrological consultation is most decidedly not a matter of breaking the complexity of a chart down to its component parts in order to understand it. Even though it can be argued that most of us set out to learn the basic vocabulary of astrology in this way, the art of astrology itself requires a facility in speaking the language that integrates and synthesizes the various bits and pieces of the chart, rather than analyzes them in isolation, as a scientist would do. This more holistic approach goes beyond the synthesis of independent variables, as discussed earlier, to a place in practice, where it becomes impossible to derive knowledge of any astrological factor taken out of context.

We inevitably start with certain general statements of understanding about what we are seeing, but then as we explore the various interconnections between the various components of the chart, and how they fit together, while dialoguing with the living client whose chart we are exploring, these general statements almost always morph into a more truly subjective understanding that is fairly unique, and at times, that renders the general statements we start with to be fairly unrecognizable.

To someone who has Sun in Cancer, for example, we can begin with a general statement like, "You are an emotionally sensitive person." Most astrologers would accept the relatively "objective" truth of that statement as an accurate reflection of Sun in Cancer in the abstract. A scientist would want this to be, not just our starting place, but also our testable hypothesis, and ultimately our conclusion, after extensive statistical validation and replication by others. Yet, in order for this statement to be astrologically accurate in the specific situation in which it is applied, astrologers must instead place the general statement within a larger context - one that will invariably modify, or even in some cases, nullify it.

Astrological Context

In part, this larger context comes from attendant astrological factors, as discussed briefly earlier, when speaking about Bacon's insistence on isolating independent variables. Here we can perhaps appreciate the way in which astrology's dependence upon a synthesis of independent variables also precludes the possibility of objective consensus, even around something as basic as the meaning of a Sun sign placement. This emphasis on synthesizing information is the antithesis of reductionist thinking. Just to drive the point home, let's take a more detailed look at Sun in Cancer, realizing the same argument can be made about anything astro-logical.

The meaning we ascribe to Sun in Cancer, and every other piece of the astrological puzzle we might want to "interpret," must shift as we consider its placement by house, its aspects to other planets, the placement of its dispositor - in this case, the Moon - current transits and progressions to the Sun, and other factors that will play a greater or lesser role depending on which particular astrological methodology we practice. So, even if we wanted to say to someone with Sun in Cancer, "You are an emotionally sensitive person," the truth of that statement would depend, at the very least, upon these attendant factors.

If, for example, Sun in Cancer were conjunct Saturn and square the Moon, perhaps the simple equation of Sun in Cancer with emotional sensitivity becomes a bit compromised. Think of George W. Bush (who has this configuration in his chart) proceeding calmly with a photo-op at a Florida grade school after being informed that the Twin Towers were being bombed. Or - with the aid of his "compassionate" conservatives - trying to justify the use of torture, or preemptive strikes, or the suspension of *habeas corpus*. Emotionally sensitive? Perhaps not so much. Or at least not in the simplistic way that the general statement implies.

Here's another astrological truism that within an empirical scientific context might be expected to pass for an objective truth: Sun in Cancer "likes to take care of other people."

What happens to this statement when Sun in Cancer is also conjunct Pluto and square Uranus? Think of Imelda Marcos, known as the Steel Butterfly for her selfish indulgence of the perks of political status, without much regard at all for the needs of her people. When asked to justify her extravagance in a country wracked by widespread poverty, she claimed it was her "duty" to be "some kind of light, a star to give [the poor] guidelines." Is this a Sun in Cancer who likes to take care of people? It doesn't appear to be.

What about the statement Sun in Cancer "is a homebody, who stays close to home?"

My ex-partner, who has Sun in Cancer trine Jupiter in the 4th house, moved from London to Kenya when she was two weeks old. By the time she was 20, she had lived in seven different countries on five different continents. Is this what we would think of as a typical Sun in Cancer homebody?

What exactly is a typical Sun in Cancer? According to the requirement that scientific truth be objective, astrologers at the very least must submit a rational hypothesis that can then be tested empirically. Can we give them one? Can we reduce Sun in Cancer - or anything astrological - to a simple formula that will be universally valid, regardless of where or how it appears in a birthchart?

Or is Sun in Cancer more like a word, whose meaning depends upon the linguistic context - or the sentence - in which it is used - say like the word, "piece." Would you like a "piece" of cake? When you lost the game of chess, how many "pieces" were left on the board? Was Lefty packing a "piece" when he broke into your house? It's the same word, but its meaning changes with context. I believe the same is true of astrological symbols, which renders them elusive when tested for reductive, objective meaning.

Living Context

Even more important than astrological context is the living context in which a mere set of symbols on a piece of paper correlate with an actual life, or a particular situation, or a specific moment in history - each of which has a back story, a unique nexus of associations, and an inherent level of expression that is not obvious given the birthchart alone.

In this sense, an astrological birthchart is more like an algebraic equation than a scientific statement of fact, in that it can be applied to any number of realities. The difference is that while an algebraic equation describes the quantitative dimensions of the reality to which it refers, astrology describes the qualitative dimensions. In any case, it is necessary to know what that reality is before we can make an intelligent astrological statement at all.

Consider, for example, the birthchart on the following page.

In order to interpret this chart, we would have to know something about its subject. Is it a person? Is it the chart for a country, the launching of a business venture, or the birth of a polar bear at the zoo? Is it the chart for an event, or a horary question? What exactly is the question?

Unless we know who or what a chart refers to, and we have a specific question in mind, then we cannot offer a meaningful interpretation. At the very least, we would look rather foolish interpreting the chart of a polar bear as though it were the chart for a horary question about a lost set of keys.

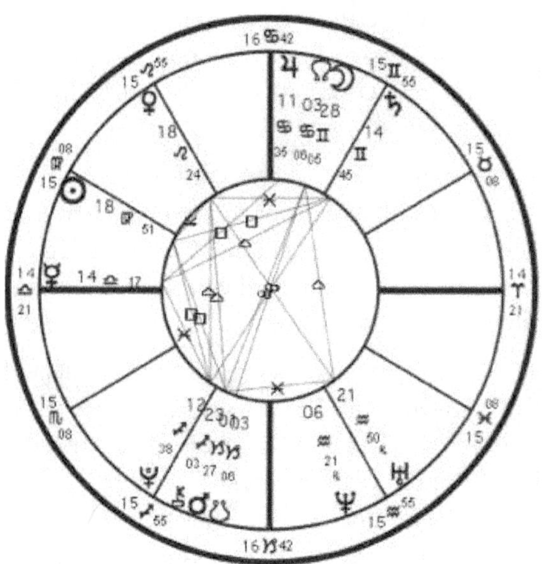

Supposing I told you – if you have not already recognized it – that this is the chart for the bombing of the Twin Towers on September 11, 2001, and that we are looking at this chart now in order to gain insight into how such a thing could have happened. Now that we know the subject of this chart, and have a context for our inquiry into its meaning, an interpretation of the chart becomes possible.

Most practicing astrologers know the subject of a birthchart and the context in which it is being approached for information, before we even enter the raw birth data into our computers. Thus, it is easy to take this preliminary knowledge of subject and context for granted. Yet without it, any interpretation of a birthchart at all is impossible.

Consider the possibility that this exact same chart could also describe the birth of a child, the beginning of a baseball game, a wedding ceremony, or a hospital admission. In each case, you would interpret the chart differently, even though the raw data – the chart itself – is exactly the same.

How can we explain this to an empirical scientist? We can't, because for a scientist, the same set of facts must refer consistently to the same conclusion. From the scientific perspective, the birthchart represents a set of facts, derived mathematically, and the expectation is that it ought to yield consistent information no matter who is reading it, and no matter what the circumstances of the reading.

Astrologers do not read the same chart in the same way, and we can't read a chart at all if we don't know something about the subject of the chart.

If we must know something about the subject of the chart before we can draw relevant conclusions about the chart, then the chart – and the astrology practiced interpreting it – yield a subjective truth. Science demands objective facts; astrology – especially psychological astrology – yields subjective truth. This is a fundamental principle on which astrology and science are not just a metaphysical mismatch, but by which they become unverifiable by the same criteria.

Replicability Versus Interpretive Flexibility

Because of its requirement that all truth be objective, empirical science demands replicable experiments as validation of its hypotheses. It is not enough for one scientist to conduct an experiment and find something to be true. Other scientists must be able to conduct the same experiment and come to the same conclusion. In this way, after rigorous testing, science becomes reasonably sure that its conclusions are objective and a matter of consensus. If we translate this requirement to a scientific approach to astrology, then the expectation is that two astrologers looking at the same birthchart will draw the same conclusions, using fairly standardized methodology. Does this ever happen?

At least 28 scientific studies so far have shown that astrologers given the same birthchart fail to come to any kind of meaningful consensus of interpretation. In fact, an aggregate analysis of these studies showed that agreement among astrologers was only 54.9% versus 50% by chance.[21]

Science's own studies, in the quantum era, have shown that the observer affects what is observed. But rather than take this into account, science continues to insist on objectivity, by attempting to negate the impact of the observer through double-blind studies, and other techniques that cancel out observer bias. Most practicing astrologers would go into cardiac arrest if they were told that as observers of the birthchart, they should not bring their own subjective experience, philosophy of life, or personal wisdom to the consultation.

If we value the role of the individual astrologer in the reading of a birthchart, and we value our eclecticism as a strength rather than a weakness, then we fail the empirical test of objectivity, because science demands consensus and uniformity of results that we simply cannot provide without rendering what we do unrecognizable as astrology, or surrendering the unique voice that each of brings to the astrology that we do.

Positivism Versus Metaphorical Possibility

The third pillar of empirical science – the idea that only that which can be experienced by the senses can be considered to exist – also neuters astrology, because what astrology measures – the symbolic correlation between celestial phenomena and what happens on earth – is a phenomenon that happens mostly within the psyche of the individual astrologer.

This is not to say that the astrologer does not make observations, nor that some of these observations are not sensory in nature. Some astrological schools of thought – such as the experiential astrology of Barbara Schermer[22] and Turning of the Ages astrology as taught by Daniel Giamario[23] – emphasize the sensory dimensions of astrological symbolism, that is to say, what can be known about a birthchart directly through direct experience, without an unnecessary or excessive overlay of intellectual ideas. My own practice of astropoetics considers the sensory dimensions of astrological symbolism to be as important, if not more important than any intellectual understanding to be obtained simply by thinking about the symbolism. All practicing astrologers learn and evolve their craft by observing the real-life stories of their clients in relation to astrological phenomena, and in this sense, can be understood to be operating within an observational, experiential framework, in which knowledge is rooted in the gathering of data.

Certainly, the origins of astrology in the Mythopoetic and Mystical Eras were primarily rooted in sensory experience – simple observations of the rising and setting of the Sun, the phases of the Moon, the wheeling of certain identifiable constellations overhead, the heliacal rising and setting of planets, and their periodic return to the same place in the sky. Astrologers today rely mostly on computers and abstract renderings of sky maps, rather than a direct observation of the sky, but this does not mean that empirical observations of celestial phenomena do not factor into the symbolic logic by which we make sense of astrological information.

These observations of celestial phenomena are not necessarily different than what might be known by an astronomer observing the same phenomena, but then, we take another step that would not be taken within a strictly empirical framework. We ascribe meaning to these experiences that derives not from the "raw data" itself, but from various metaphorical associations that can be made with the sensory facts of astronomical events.

Thus, for example, both astronomers and astrologers might observe that the orbit of Uranus is unique among planets in our solar system, in that its axis of rotation is tilted sideways, nearly into the plane of its solar orbit, with its north and south poles positioned where other planets have their equators. An astronomer would evoke this observed fact to explain further facts – why each pole receives 42 years of light, followed by 42 years of darkness; or why the polar regions in general receive greater solar radiation than the equator; and then seek causal explanations for this anomaly, the most commonly accepted one being that during the formation of the solar system, an Earth-sized proto-planet collided with Uranus, throwing it askew.[24]

An astrologer would draw an entirely different set of conclusions – for example, the idea that an eccentric orbit equates with a character trait of eccentricity. This is no longer something that can be understood from within a positivist framework, since it cannot be directly observed.

A scientist or a scientifically minded astrologer might argue that this is a testable hypothesis, perhaps further speculating, for example, that Uranus near an angle of a chart would correlate astrologically with the character trait of eccentricity. She would then proceed to gather birth data from a large enough collection of certifiably eccentric people (assuming a universally accepted standard for measurement of eccentricity could be found) and determine through rigorous comparison against a randomly chosen control group of normal people, whoever they might be, whether the occurrence of eccentricity with those who had an angular Uranus displayed statistical significance higher than what might be expected by chance.

This is not likely to be something, however, than will actually show a correlation, since the hypothesis itself is not a product of observation. It is a metaphorical association between an observable phenomenon - the eccentricity of Uranus' orbit - and personality. Science would not even be able to accept the possibility that such a correlation - any such correlation - could be meaningful, according to the positivist pillar of science, without direct observation. Given that metaphorical associations are made, not out there in the observable universe, but in the interior poetic imagination of an astrologer, who intuitively feels that in the moment of an actual consultation, it might apply. In another moment, it might not. It is, within the astrological lexicon, merely one possible resource in making sense of Uranus on the angle of a chart, or conjunct the Sun, or at the apex of a T-Square, or in any number of other possible astrological scenarios. To try to squeeze a metaphorical association into an empirical mold is to assume it should always be correlated with something in a literal way, which it isn't, or might not be in any given case, and the effort to do that will fail, every single time.

Determinism Versus Poetic Exploration

Lastly, we come to the question about how astrology works. Some astrologers, following philosophically in Ptolemy's shoes, have attempted to find some mechanism of celestial causation by which astrology can be explained. Countless studies have noted the apparent correlation of lunar cycles with menstruation, birth rates, loss of blood, sleep patterns, epilepsy, homicides, suicides, incidents of domestic violence, accidents and many other terrestrial and human phenomena.[25] In 1928, an associated of Rudolf Steiner, Lili Kolisko, did a series of experiments correlating the metals classically associated with each planet and pictures left by their absorption over a filter paper, noticing consistent differences of the patterns according to the position of the planets in relation to sun and earth.[26] In 1951, RCA engineer John Nelson published an article in *RCA Review* describing a theory for predicting shortwave radio propagation through reference to planetary positions relative to the sun.[27] In 1989, English astrophysicist Percy Seymour published a book *Astrology: The Evidence of Science*, in which he proposed that the planets telegraph electromagnetic signals that establish an intricate field of resonances, influencing sunspot activity and human behavior.[28]

These and other such attempts at establishing an actual mechanism for celestial causation have largely been met by scorn within the scientific establishment, although some continue to have their proponents within and outside the astrological community. While it is possible to find theoretical alignment between astrology and some emerging scientific models about how the universe is constructed (chaos theory, string theory, Bohm's theory of the implicate and explicate order, to name a few), experimental verification is lacking – not just for an astrology that fits these paradigms, but for the paradigms themselves.[29]

Meanwhile, since Jung, some astrologers have proposed an acausal mechanism like synchronicity to be at least a partial explanation, a proposal that seems plausible or even self-evident to many astrologers, but nonetheless fails to register on empirical science's scale, because such a mechanism is not testable or quantifiable. As with causal theories, Jung's ideas have found resonance with emerging theoretical constructs of quantum physics or even molecular biology,[30] but the actual empirical testability of these various hypotheses has proven elusive.

As Jung himself noted the results of an experiment he conducted investigating astrology, they were:

> *. . . nothing but a chance result from the statistical point of view, yet it is meaningful on account of the fact that it looks as if it validated this (astrological) expectation. It is just what I call a synchronistic phenomenon.*[31]

To the extent then that astrology can be considered a synchronistic phenomenon, this still fails to demonstrate a scientifically plausible mechanism by which astrology works, because synchronicity itself is not empirically measurable.

Meanwhile, if we understand astrology to essentially be a poetic language through which a sense of meaning and purpose is reflected back to us, as we bring intuitive, imaginative, and exploratory curiosity to the living symbolism in a birthchart, then it is not likely that there is anything causal or acausal for that matter, for science to explore. It can be exciting to think about cutting edge scientific theories lending credence to the possibility of astrology playing a more central role in our understanding of how the universe itself is constructed, perhaps as an intricate expression of innate intelligence, communicating itself in recognizable patterns that can actually correlate with the celestial order. Until and unless science finds a way to test these theories, however, neither they nor astrology will fit the empirical mold.

We can take it as some consolation that in the current scientific era, empiricism itself is in danger of becoming obsolete or at the very least, passé, while cutting edge scientists are finding it increasingly difficult to discuss complex phenomena without leaning into theories that defy empirical validation, and flirt at the edge of metaphysical speculation.

> *How are we to determine whether a theory is true if it cannot be validated experimentally? Should we abandon it just because, at a given level of technological capacity, empirical support might be impossible? If not, how long should we wait for such experimental machinery before moving on: ten years? Fifty years? Centuries?*[32]

In discussing the current state of particle physics, over a hundred years into the quantum era, scientists are fretting over what appears to be the looming dead-end of the empirical road, as they prepare to restart investigations of the elusive Higgs particle with the Large Hadron Collider, the world's largest particle collider, built near Geneva, Switzerland over the course of 10 years, at a cost of €7.5 billion through the cooperation of over 10,000 scientists from more than 100 countries:

> *If the upgraded collider does discover supersymmetric particles, it will be an astonishing triumph of modern physics. But if nothing is found, our next steps may prove to be difficult and controversial, challenging not just how we do science but what it means to do science at all.*[33]

Notes

1. The Empirical Era begins toward the end of what is often called the Early Modern Period and encompasses most of Modern History. The early part of this period includes the Age of Revolutions in Europe and the birth of the United States as an independent state. The Empirical Era also encompasses the Industrial Revolution, a time in which empirical science reached a pinnacle of application and an institutionalized entrenchment as a cornerstone of human culture.
2. Cornelius, Geoffrey. *The Moment of Astrology: Origins in Divination*. Wessex Astrologer Limited, 2002, 194-95.
3. Singer, Charles. *A Short History of Science to the Nineteenth Century*. Oxford: Clarendon Press, 1941, 217.
4. Whitehouse, David. *Renaissance Genius: Galileo Galilei & His Legacy to Modern Science*. New York: Sterling, 2009, 219.
5. King, Preston. *Thomas Hobbes: Critical Assessments*. Routledge EBooks, 1993. http://ci.nii.ac.jp/ncid/BA18891323, 59.
6. Finocchiaro, Maurice A. "Book Review – The Person of the Millennium: The Unique Impact of Galileo on World History." *The Historian* 69, no. 3 (2007), 601-02.

7. Kollerstrom, Nick. "Galileo's Astrology." Accessed May 18, 2023. http://www.skyscript.co.uk/galast.html.

8. Scofield, Bruce. "Were They Astrologers? – Big League Scientists and Astrology." *The Mountain Astrologer* 80: August/September (1998).

9. Williams, Matt. "Who Was Galileo Galilei?" Universe Today, October 8, 2019. https://www.universetoday.com/48756/galileo-facts/.

10. Hilliam, Rachel. *Galileo Galilei: Father of Modern Science*. New York: The Rosen Publishing Group, 2004, 96.

11. Hannam, James. *The Genesis of Science: How the Christian Middle Ages Launched the Scientific Revolution*. Simon and Schuster, 2011, 329-44.

12. Machamer, Peter. "Galileo Galilei." Stanford Encyclopedia of Philosophy. Summer 2017 Edition, May 10, 2017. https://plato.stanford.edu/archives/sum2017/entries/galileo/.

13. "History of Scientific Method." Wikipedia, May 8, 2023. https://en.wikipedia.org/wiki/History_of_scientific_method.

14. Burtt, E. A. *The Metaphysical Foundations of Modern Science*. Atlantic Heights, NJ: Humanities Press International, 1952, 89.

15. Van Gent, R.H. "Isaac Newton and Astrology." Accessed May 19, 2023. http://www.staff.science.uu.nl/~gent0113/astrology/newton.htm.

16. Burtt, *The Metaphysical Foundations of Modern Science*, 214.

17. Burtt, *The Metaphysical Foundations of Modern Science*, 222.

18. Brewster, David. *Memoirs of the Life, Writings, and Discoveries of Sir Isaac Newton, Vol. 1*. Cambridge University Press, 2010, 532.

19. Perry, Glenn. "How Do We Know What We Think We Know? From Paradigm to Method in Astrological Research." In *Astrological Research Methods: An ISAR Anthology*, edited by Mark Pottenger, Vol. 1. Los Angeles: International Society for Astrological Research, 1995, 13.

20. Perry, Glenn. "How Do We Know What We Think We Know," 13.

21. Smit, Rudolf. "Grand Summary." Accessed April 28, 2023. https://www.astrology-and-science.com/u-gran2.htm.

22. As stated by Barbara Schermer in "Experiential Astrology" at https://encyclopedia2.thefreedictionary.com/Experiential+Astrology:

> *Experiential astrology succinctly includes any technique that puts people into direct contact with their horoscopes. Its purpose is to place soul instead of prediction at the center of its inquiry. The horoscope need not remain a static, one-dimensional*

> *wheel of planetary glyphs and signs, but can become a field of planetary action that is interactive, imaginative, and vibrantly alive. Techniques include astrodrama (acting out the horoscope), group dynamics and process, in-depth therapeutic methods, artistic mandalas, contemplation of images, creating rituals and talismans, dramatic mythic storytelling, dreamwork, journaling, flower essences, and more. Many of these techniques are described in Barbara Schermer's Astrology Alive: Experiential Astrology and the Healing Arts.*

23. Although Giamario's astrology rests upon an important theoretical framework, a central tenet of the approach is summed up on the Turning of the Ages Mystery School website (https://turningoftheages.com/the-totams-astrology-paradigm/):

    > *The sky that can be directly experienced without telescopic or cybernetic enhancement has the greatest importance and power. Therefore, TOTAMS Astrology would be as effective in a non-technological age. This view can be termed Neo-Ptolemaic, an astrology for terrestrial humans experiencing the sky, perceivable with unaided vision without light pollution. The modern scientific reality of the heliocentric, Copernican worldview is essentially irrelevant to this approach. The practitioner of TOTAMS Astrology™ is trained in the unaided eye knowledge and experience of the night sky, and the sacred rhythms, cycles and motions of the cosmos.*

24. Bergstralh, Jay T., Ellis D. Miner, and Mildred Shapley Matthews. *Uranus*. University of Arizona Press, 1991, 485-86.
25. Zimecki, M. "The Lunar Cycle: Effects on Human and Animal Behavior and Physiology." PubMed, 2006. https://pubmed.ncbi.nlm.nih.gov/16407788/.
26. Kolisko, Lili. "Working With the Stars In Earthly Substance." Rex Research, 1928. http://rexresearch.com/kolisko2/koliskoworking.html.
27. Nelson, John. "Shortwave Radio Propagation Correlation with Planetary Positions." *RCA Review* XII, no. 1 (March 1951).
28. Seymour, Percy. *Astrology: The Evidence of Science*, 1991. https://openlibrary.org/books/OL15306678M/Astrology.
29. Frank, Adam, and Marcelo Gleiser. "Opinion | A Crisis at the Edge of Physics." *The New York Times*, June 5, 2015. https://www.nytimes.com/2015/06/07/opinion/a-crisis-at-the-edge-of-physics.html.
30. Limar, Igor V. "C. G. Jung's Synchronicity and Quantum Entanglement: Schrodinger's Cat 'Wanders' Between Chromosomes." *NeuroQuantology* 9, no. 2 (2011): 313–21.
31. Jung, Carl G. *Synchronicity: An Acausal Connecting Principle*. Princeton University Press, 1960, 61.

32. Frank and Gleiser, "Opinion | A Crisis at the Edge of Physics."
33. Frank and Gleiser, "Opinion | A Crisis at the Edge of Physics."

Chapter Six

The Deconstruction of Science in the Era of Uncertainty: Twentieth – Twenty First Century[1]

Stepping back 120 years or so from the current crossroads at the Large Hadron Collider, science began its current wave of transformation with a series of discoveries in physics that took place in the late nineteenth and early twentieth centuries, culminating with the formulation of quantum mechanics by Max Planck, Albert Einstein, Niels Bohr, Werner Heisenberg and others. As Richard Tarnas describes this revolution:

> *By the end of the third decade of the twentieth century, virtually every major postulate of the earlier scientific conception had been controverted: the atoms as solid, indestructible, and separate building blocks of nature; space and time as independent absolutes; the strict mechanistic causality of all phenomena; the possibility of objective observation of nature.*[2]

The Impossibility of Accurate Measurement

In the Empirical Era, Newtonian physics had been built upon the possibility of obtaining accurate measurement of material reality, which then extended to non-material reality, such as that measured by psychologists, social scientists, and other observers of human phenomena. In the Era of Uncertainty, however, the nature of material reality itself has been thrown into question, opening a much larger doubt about what can actually be measured.

In 1924, French physicist Louis de Broglie proposed and later demonstrated that matter had a dual nature, at times acting as a particle and at other times, acting like a wave – a discovery for which he won the Nobel Prize for Physics in 1929. With this discovery, also iterated in Einstein's famous equation: $E = MC^2$, we find ourselves in brave new territory, where we cannot even really be sure what we are measuring.

Building on the work of de Broglie, Austrian physicist Erwin Schrödinger proved mathematically that wave functions can only be related to the probable occurrence of physical events, not to their actuality. In 1927, German physicist Werner Heisenberg proposed his famous Uncertainty Principle, according to which either the position or the momentum of a particle can be known with certainty, but not both at the same time. Thus, within this new emerging quantum paradigm, science began to lose the sense of certainty that quantification gave it, and the empirically demonstrable and measurable causal laws that were the hallmark of the Empirical Era begin to give way to assessments of probability.

This aspect of quantum theory was not easy for many scientists to accept, since it put them – and science itself – in a rather precarious predicament. How can science legitimately claim to be an arbitrator of truth when it can no longer observe, measure, or make definitive statements about the nature of reality? The absurdity of this predicament was demonstrated by Schrödinger in his famous thought experiment conducted in 1935, later becoming known as the problem of Schrödinger's cat.

The Critical Role of the Observer in the Act of Observation

Suppose you lock a cat in a steel box with a small amount of a radioactive substance, measured so that there is an equal probability of an atom decaying or not decaying. If the atom decays, a device smashes a vial of poisonous gas, killing the cat. If the atom does not decay, the cat lives. Until the box is opened, and the outcome actually observed, the cat is equally likely to be alive or dead. It is clearly one or the other, and not both, but within this hypothetical case, dependent on the predictability of quantum behaviors, the fate of the cat is essentially suspended, unknown and unknowable. It is only an observation that turns probability into reality.

Schrödinger's work emphasized the role of the observer in affecting what is observed, as well as the idea that observation is always relative to the vantage point of the observer. According to the tenets of quantum mechanics, it is generally impossible to measure a system without disturbing it – or put another way, any observer will change what she observes through her perceptual interaction with it. This new understanding – which harkens back to the mythopoetic experience of *participation mystique* – further dismantles the foundation upon which empirical science rests, although the message has not apparently spread very far beyond the balkanized world of quantum physics.

For the most part, instead of acknowledging the primary role of the observer in a participatory universe in which what we call reality is a collaboration between observer and observed, scientists bend over backwards to negate the role – or "bias" – of the observer all together. Double-blind studies, control groups, and allocation concealment strategies essentially aim at producing objective truth without any participation at all of an actual observer. In *Introduction to the Study of Experimental Medicine*, French physiologist Claude Bernard – called by Bernard Cohen of Harvard in the introduction to that book, "one of the most intelligent of modern scientists"[3] – went so far as to suggest that a scientific researcher should not have any knowledge of the hypothesis being tested.[4]

It should be noted here that this represents a radically different kind of science than that practiced in the Empirical Era, where rigorous observation by a well-educated scientist was key. This understanding, in fact, turns empirical science on its head, just as empirical science previously turned the logical science of Aristotle on its head. For within the Era of Uncertainty, a pre-existent reality is not observed. It is brought into being by an act of observation. Subsequent experiments conducted by successors to Einstein, de Broglie and Schrödinger have, in fact, failed to find any pre-existent reality - certain to exist and ready to be measured - that was simply taken for granted by the empiricists.[5] The experiments prove instead that there is no underlying reality to the world, except what we imagine that we are observing.

Or at least, this was the conclusion drawn by some scientists. Others have not been so sure, while the debate itself has become one of the hallmarks of science in the Era of Uncertainty. The debate began in early 1927, on the heels of the earliest discoveries of the quantum physicists, when two giants of the revolution - Albert Einstein and Niels Bohr - squared off at a conference in Copenhagen, attended by seventeen attendees who either had or would eventually receive Nobel Prizes, including de Broglie and Schrödinger. In other words, anyone who was anybody in the quantum world was there.

Bohr was a Danish physicist who like Einstein, had made fundamental breakthroughs in the development and application of quantum theories, particularly the familiar model of the atom, in which layers of electrons circle an atomic nucleus. This theory has since been supplanted by more sophisticated models, but at the time of these debates, both Bohr and Einstein were respected contributors to the emerging field. In Copenhagen, they did not debate the validity of their new discoveries about the subatomic world, but how those discoveries might apply to the more familiar terrain of classic physics mapped by Newton and his contemporaries in the previous scientific era.

In what later became known as the Copenhagen interpretation, Bohr argued that wave equations only described where subatomic particles *could* be, not where they were; and that they only came into *actual* existence when they were observed. Einstein argued that whether or not a particle could be observed, it still existed independently of its observation.

Although history has generally come to accept Bohr's interpretation, the debate between these men, who were friends as well as colleagues, continued until Einstein's death three decades later, gradually morphing into a discussion about the nature and proper scope of science itself. Einstein argued that the purpose of science was to describe the nature of reality; Bohr disagreed, arguing this couldn't actually be done.

The debate continues to this day. What is the purpose and proper scope of science? In an era when the possibility of objective observation, the inexactitude of measurement, and the possibility of certainty are all in question, science has essentially become another voice in a postmodern cacophony of worldviews - ironically not unlike what prevailed in the Philosophical Era. In a very real sense, science has evolved full circle to the point where the question: "Is astrology a science?" becomes as meaningless now as it was then. For if we don't really know what science is, or should be, any more, how can astrology - or any other discipline for that matter - claim to be scientific?

Within the Era of Uncertainty, to be scientific is to stand at the threshold of the unknowable with humility and a certain set of imperfect tools, with no particular advantage over any other set of tools. Scientists ask different questions than astrologers but are able to feel their way into answers that are no less tentative, speculative, or open-ended than those of the best of astrologers focused on meaningful discourse with the mysteries of a human being, an historical moment in time, or the nature of the relationship between cosmos and psyche itself.

The Scientific Study of Astrology in the Era of Uncertainty

Meanwhile, although it is clear the nature of science itself is changing, the methodology employed by scientists to measure truth remains largely governed by assumptions developed in the Empirical Era. Leaving aside the question of what can actually be measured with any degree of certainty, scientists have by and large adopted an assessment of probability to be a valid substitute for an assessment of factual truth. If, in other words, something is probably true - according to certain statistical criteria - then it is considered true, although in practice this means that much of the time, it won't be true at all.

While the limitation of statistical probability continues to be a major conundrum for physical scientists, measuring what used to be considered hard, material reality, it has long been the practice in what are often euphemistically referred to as the "soft sciences" - psychology, sociology, anthropology, history, economics, or any endeavor in which human attributes, behaviors, or trends over time are measured. In general, soft sciences are considered to be less rigorous, less capable of producing testable hypotheses, less amenable to controlled experimentation and quantification, less certain in the degree of exactitude with which conclusions can be drawn, and less objective or conducive to professional consensus.

August Comte

In the nineteenth century, French philosopher August Comte, considered the father of positivism and the first modern philosopher of science, developed the idea of a hierarchy of sciences along the hard-soft spectrum, although he did not use these terms. Instead, he postulated that there were three primary stages in the quest for truth - the theological stage, the metaphysical stage and the positive stage - and that sciences that could evolve most quickly through the three stages were at the top of the hierarchy.

The theological stage was further understood as a progression from fetishism to polytheism to monotheism. The first two of these sub-stages, which are really pre-theological, can be understood as a shorthand notation for the primary approach to truth as practiced during the Mythopoetic Era – namely a kind of animistic *participation mystique* in which the polytheistic gods inhabited the natural world, including the celestial sphere, and spoke directly to humans. According to Comte, this was the lowest state of human understanding, one that eventually managed to evolve toward monotheism, still a lowly state of knowledge, but one in which there was at least some semblance of consensus. Monotheism was essentially a product of the Mystical Era, as oral tradition was gradually replaced by written scripture and the authoritative mantle it assumed, becoming the basis for the emerging religions of the Fertile Crescent, as well as in Asia.

In the metaphysical stage, the authority of this consensus was questioned by those seeking a more tangible truth, although at this point, there was little consensus and no real criteria by which to evaluate the relative validity of one speculative point of view over another. Within the context of our discussion here, we can perhaps recognize this as the general state of knowledge during the Philosophical Era. In Comte's view, metaphysical knowledge is generally considered to be more abstract, perhaps in the same way that Platonic ideals were postulated as the foundation of astronomical cycles during the Philosophical Era, rather than the more direct experimental observations that became possible during the Empirical Era.

Lastly, the Empirical Era itself can be understood to be similar to Comte's positive stage, by which he meant the possibility of hard, irrefutable knowledge of the truth – or the kind of certainty that was promised by science in the Empirical Era, but that has proven to be elusive in the Era of Uncertainty. Although his intent was to chart a pathway by which any science might gravitate to positive certainty, in retrospect within the Era of Uncertainty, his three stages can be understood as the basis for an epistemological hierarchy within which some disciplines are, in fact, considered less scientific than others.

Those sciences that passed most quickly and easily through the three stages found their way to the top or hard end of Comte's hierarchy; those that were slower to reach positive, scientific validation sank to the soft bottom. At the hard end, he put mathematics, followed by astronomy, physics, chemistry and biology. At the soft end, he put sociology, by which he meant the study of human behavior – a field that would today encompass most of the other soft sciences, including psychology and psychological astrology, at least by implication, if not by any actual recognition we could attribute to Comte himself. Although he put it at the bottom of his hierarchy, Comte is considered the father of sociology, which in his view was the study of human society, at its best, built scientifically on laws derived from the sciences toward the top of the hierarchy.

It is telling here, to see within Comte's system, the wide split between astronomy, near the top of the hierarchy, and astrology, which would presumably have been relegated to the very bottom, if he had thought to include it at all. Ironically, as pointed out by Campion:

> *While it is true that Comte . . . would (not) have accepted the term astrology, his work was undoubtedly a disguised, secularized astrology in that it projected celestial law onto human life.*[6]

That is to say, if sociology at the bottom of the hierarchy was ultimately dependent on the laws of astronomy and mathematics at the top, then this provided an opening for the kinds of correlations that astrologers routinely make. Comte, of course, would not have seen it that way, and that is not how his ideas entered into practice.

What does matter here is the emerging idea, originated with Comte, that soft sciences like sociology, psychology, anthropology, history, economics, or astrology ought to be built on scientific principles derived from biology, chemistry, physics, astronomy and ideally mathematics. This set the philosophical stage for the evaluation of astrology in the Empirical Era, and on into the Era of Uncertainty.

Probability and Statistics

In the Era of Uncertainty, however, even the very top of Comte's hierarchy becomes shaky, since very little within astronomy, physics, chemistry or biology can, in the wake of the quantum revolution, be rendered in terms of definitive mathematical laws. If this is true for the hard sciences, then the soft sciences are even less amenable to mathematical certainty. Within mathematics, especially in relation to the soft sciences, certainty gives way to statistical probability.

Although first discussed by Arab scholars Al-Khalil and Al-Kindi during the Islamic Golden Age in relation to cryptographic analysis,[7] the mathematical foundation for modern probability theory was developed in earnest, much later, during the sixteenth century through the investigations of Italian polymath and gambler Gerlamo Cardano and then during the seventeenth century through correspondence between Pierre de Fermat and Blaise Pascal – mathematicians of the Empirical Era.

The movement toward modern statistics began when de Fermat was approached by a professional gambler who wondered why, if he bet on rolling at least one 6 in four throws of a die, he won in the long term, whereas betting on throwing at least one double 6 in twenty-four throws of two dice resulted in his losing. Fermat worked out an equation showing why this was so, and probability theory was born.

Pascal further developed the theory, and then others picked up the thread, most notably Dutch mathematician, physicist and astronomer Christiaan Huygens, who wrote the first book on the subject, *On Reasoning in Games of Chance* in 1657.[8] Later contributors to the evolution of probability theory include French mathematician Abraham de Moivre, a personal friend of Newton; and nearly a century later by his compatriot Pierre-Simon LaPlace, remembered among the greatest of scientists and known as the Newton of France.[9]

Statistics, which is essentially the application of probability theory to data analysis, was first mentioned in 1663 by British haberdasher John Graunt in *Natural and Political Observations upon the Bills of Mortality*.[10] As a city councilman in London, Graunt became interested in basing city policies on demographic and economic data, which statistical analysis helped to organize in meaningful ways, and for the next two hundred years or so, analysis of political demographics was its primary application.

By the end of the nineteenth century, statistics were starting to become part of the methodology of hard sciences like astronomy, thermodynamics, statistical mechanics, medicine and epidemiology, developing alongside inductive logic as part of the emerging paradigm of the Empirical Era. Statistics was, from the beginning, an essential tool employed among the newly emerging sciences such as sociology and experimental psychology.

In the early twentieth century, English polymath Francis Galton used statistics to explore the transmission of hereditary traits from generation to generation, an interest that culminated in Galton's promotion of eugenics. Galton's work in turn fired the imagination of mathematician Karl Pearson, who emphasized the statistical foundations of scientific laws, developed statistics as a rigorous mathematical discipline, and expanded its range of application to other fields. Research design in the soft sciences was further developed by Charles S. Pierce in academic papers such as "Illustrations of the Logic of Science" (1877–1878) and "A Theory of Probable Inference" (1883), which emphasized the importance of randomization and blind experiments, an approach that became widely adopted by researchers in psychology and education. Building on the work of these predecessors, Roland Fischer wrote two textbooks, *Statistical Methods for Research Workers*, published in 1925 and *The Design of Experiments* in 1935, that became the standard for the use of statistics in scientific research in universities around the world.

By the middle of the twentieth century, statistics had permeated every branch of science, and seemingly overnight – "with a rapidity of conquest rivaled only by Attila, Mohammed, and the Colorado beetle"[11] – had become the new language of scientific uncertainty. Without going into further historical detail, statistics has continued evolving since, through the efforts of countless mathematicians and scientists, greatly aided by the development of the computer. It is now considered standard scientific methodology for measurement of psychological truth and by extension, any astrological statement that purports to have psychological implications, made by any astrologer professing to be a scientist.

Statistics in the Era of Uncertainty

Although the history of statistics largely places it as a development of the Empirical Era, it is more accurately understood as a methodology suited to scientific measurement in the Era of Uncertainty. Before the pioneering work of Karl Pearson in the nineteenth century, well before the advent of the Era of Uncertainty, scientists were aware that their measurements gave variable results, but they typically attributed this anomaly to human error, or the limits of the technology used to make measurements. Pearson was the first to suggest that:

> *Uncertainty . . . was not simply due to the limits of technology in measuring certain events – it was inherent in nature. Even the most careful and rigorous scientific investigation (or any type of investigation for that matter) could not yield an exact measurement . . . Whether it is the flight path of an arrow, the resting heart rate of an adult male, or the age of a historical artifact, measurements do not have exact values, but instead always exhibit a range of values, and that range can be quantified as uncertainty.*[12]

In the Empirical Era, statistics and other mathematical tools were used to arrive at statements of certainty about that which could be measured. In the Era of Uncertainty, the same tools were used to calculate the level of uncertainty that accompanied any statement a scientist might feel confident enough to make. This is a profound shift in emphasis that seems to have escaped the notice of working scientists in the Era of Uncertainty, proceeding as though a statement of scientific truth still carries the same level of authority that it always did.

Meanwhile, it is taken as a given that exact measurement in the Era of Uncertainty is impossible. Instead, the likelihood of any given statement being true is given in terms of statistical probability, which is generally considered sufficient proof of truth if it rises above the level predicted by chance. There are different ways of measuring statistical significance, and the mathematics involved can be complicated, which is one reason why statistics is often a dreaded required course on the way to professional accreditation in almost any field considered a science, hard or soft. Regardless of the prevailing commonsense understanding that "there are three kinds of lies: lies, damned lies, and statistics,"[13] within the scientific paradigm of both the Empirical Era and the Era of Uncertainty, statistical significance has become the best that science can do.

In a letter to Max Born in 1926, Einstein had expressed his dissatisfaction with Bohr's idea during the Copenhagen debates that the actual existence of subatomic particles depended on their observation, by famously saying, "I, at any rate, am convinced that [God] does not throw dice" or as it has since been translated, "God does not play dice with the universe."[14] This was his way of expressing dissatisfaction with the whole idea of probability as a basis for scientific knowledge. And yet, ironically, it would appear, nearly one hundred years later, that this is exactly what scientists do in the Era of Uncertainty when they want to understand what their predecessors would, in an earlier age, have called God's handiwork. They depend heavily on a tool first developed by gamblers in order to bet their empirical observations are probable enough to pass as true.

The Limitations of Statistical Analysis

As many since Einstein have pointed out, there are severe limitations to this approach. Here are just a few of the most important, especially as they can be considered applicable to the practice of psychological astrology:

1) Statistics only measure what can be quantified. Most of the essential parameters by which a life of meaning and purpose can be measured psychologically or astrologically - experiences like love, or consciousness, or creativity, or intimacy, or beauty, or fulfillment, or suffering, or grief, or joy, or countless other experiences that make up any human life - cannot be meaningfully quantified and are thus outside the range of statistical measurement.

2) Statistics only speak to averages and probabilities within the aggregate. They say nothing or very little about the actual experience of an individual within the aggregate, which can vary enough to make the average (means or median) relatively meaningless.[15]

   When discussing something as intimately personal as the soul's journey, or even the human psyche in strictly psychological terms, if not more overtly spiritual language, the individual factors that make any statement meaningful to the person hearing it cannot be rendered in statistical language.

3) The numerical value achieved through statistical manipulation of data depends upon the methodology used, and can vary widely. Not only are the various techniques for calculating means, medians, standard deviations and variance mind-numbing in their breadth and complexity, but in addition, if researchers collect data using faulty or biased procedures - through one of any number of sampling errors - then the results will not reflect the truth of whatever it is the researcher is trying to measure.

4) Statistics measure only externals. They cannot tell the story behind the numbers, which is, in fact, what matters most to anyone trying to make sense of their lives. It is out of the story, felt and integrated, that meaning emerges, not from a set of numbers that can only be understood at best, and only with proper training, as abstractions.

5) There is great temptation in statistical analysis to jump to simple conclusions to complex problems. Even if statistical correlation is found between two variables, this does not mean that there is a causal relationship between them. There may be errors in construct validity whereby what the researchers are attempting to measure is only peripherally related to the question they are asking. Researchers may not even be asking the right question.

   These errors, of course, are possible in any quest for the truth, not merely statistical science. But because of the authority given to numbers in the Empirical Era, numbers in the Era of Uncertainty continue to assume a mantle of credibility they may no longer deserve. To the extent that statistics purports to explain away or manage uncertainty, then the numbers revealed through statistical analysis can give a false impression of certainty.

6) The results given by statistical analysis must still be interpreted, and interpretation is subject to researcher bias. The meaning ascribed to statistics depends upon the agenda, often hidden, of the person quoting them.

   We all like to think of scientists as honest, ethical people, who are selflessly employed in the quest for objective truth. At their best, they are, and most of them probably at least aspire to this lofty standard, at least most of the time. But it would be naïve to assume that those who pay the salaries of scientists or provide the research grants for science to be done – most of whom are not scientists – are seeking a particular result for reasons that may or may not have anything to do with the legitimate quest for truth. Thus, statistics cannot be interpreted, even by those who understand the language, without taking into account the agendas that are driving the research effort, as well as the biases that go into research design, implementation and statistical conclusion – agendas and biases that may have nothing to do with science. When statistics are manipulated in the service of marketing decisions, corporate interests, or partisan policy decisions, for example, or to discredit astrology by those who are already convinced it isn't a valid science, for that matter, they may or may not reflect the truth.

7) Manipulation of statistical data is possible, in part, because statisticians themselves don't agree on what is statistically significant. In his comprehensive critique of astrology, based on statistical principles – *Tests of Astrology* – Dean and company dismiss many tests that do seem to validate astrology because their sample size (N) was too small. On the other hand, Dean also notes that "human data always contains microscopic correlations that a large enough N will always inflate to significant p levels." P levels, more commonly known as p-values, measure "the probability on a

scale of 0-1 that there is something in our sample size that makes it different from our control."[16]

According to this criteria, astrological studies can apparently be rejected because their sample size is either too large or too small, and should the p value prove to be significant (0.05 or less),[17] that can be attributed to a less-than optimal sample size. Combined with the scientific requirement that test results be replicated, a significant p value that can be dismissed because of sample size virtually ensures that all scientific studies of astrology, no matter how valid, can ultimately be rejected – actually for reasons that have little to do with astrology's validity and everything to do with researcher bias and skill at manipulating statistical data.

This approach to statistical analysis is commonly referred to as "p-hacking." P-hacking is a popular term for selecting the parameters of a statistical analysis so that you get the results you want. If the results don't prove what you want them to prove, then you tweak what are called "researcher degrees of freedom," changing which observations to measure, which variables to compare, which factors to combine, and which ones to control for, until the right combination gives statistical results that match your agenda.

Without mentioning p-hacking per se, Dean implies that astrological researchers do this kind of cherry-picking to arrive at conclusions favorable to astrology. And yet, it is possible, and not unlikely that those "scientists" seeking to debunk astrology, do the same at their end. Indeed, in an article ironically bemoaning the fact that the term p-hacking has entered the mainstream, an article in *Wired* concludes:

> *In a perfect world, the wider public would understand that p-hacking refers not to some lousy tendency or lazy habit particular to researchers, but one that's present everywhere. We all p-hack, to some extent, every time we set out to understand the evidence in the world around us. If there's a takeaway here, it's that science is hard and sometimes our human foibles make it even harder.*[18]

If so, then statistical p-hackers put themselves on a level playing field with the rest of us, offering no particular advantage in discerning truth from wishful thinking. This, of course, does not stop them from bluffing to maintain the same credibility that scientists held routinely in the more seemingly certain Empirical Era, gambling that those not in the know will mistake their statistical intimidation for truth.

The Evolution of Qualitative Research Methodology

While hard scientists found it relatively easy to adopt probability theory and statistical analysis as the new logic of uncertainty in the practice of science, soft scientists naturally felt more resistance, as a strictly quantitative approach to human behavior never really fit in the first place. Early psychologists like Wilhelm Wundt, Sigmund Freud and William James employed qualitative inquiries as a matter of course, simply assuming their scientific necessity to an understanding of psychological phenomena in the individual patients they were treating. Carl Jung went so far as to note that:

> *With regard to individual psychology . . . science must waive its claims. To speak of a science of individual psychology is already a contradiction in terms. It is only the collective element in the psychology of an individual that constitutes an object for science; for the individual is by definition something unique that cannot be compared with anything else.*[19]

From the beginning, it was impossible to conduct psychological research of any significance without regard to the subjective experiences of the individuals under observation. The practicing psychologist could never consider himself as a neutral observer, since his relationship with the client/patient/research subject had an obvious impact for better or worse on the outcome of the experiment – a phenomenon recognized by Freud as transference.

Statistics became the norm in all scientific research by the middle of the twentieth century while a discussion of qualitative research went underground. Psychologists became a bit more sheepish in their ongoing quest for scientific credibility, even as they continued to employ qualitative methods in their work.[20]

In 1942, Gordon Allport called for a more balanced approach to psychological research, one that did not completely ignore statistical information, but one that also took the qualitative, subjective dimensions of the individual's experience into account.

> *Only between the late 1960s and 1990 did phenomenologists, grounded theorists, discourse analysts, narrative researchers, and others articulate and assert the general scientific value, methodologies, and applicable tools of qualitative inquiry in psychology. Between the 1990s and the present, a revolutionary institutionalization of qualitative methods has taken place in publications, educational curricula, and professional organizations.*[21]

Since 1990, the limitations of statistical methods in answering important research questions in the soft sciences has led to a widespread adoption of so-called qualitative techniques. Outside of the fields in which their use has proven necessary, however, they continue to be eyed with positivist suspicion.

> *Qualitative and quantitative research methods are often juxtaposed as representing two different world views. In quantitative circles, qualitative research is commonly viewed with suspicion and considered lightweight because it involves small samples*

which may not be representative of the broader population, it is seen as not objective, and the results are assessed as biased by the researchers' own experiences or opinions.[22]

Truth be told, qualitative research is also often dismissed because it does not lead to one-size-fits all remedies for psychological ills, such as pharmaceutical interventions; and it is time-consuming, as each individual must be approached as a unique case, one that cumulative knowledge and experience of individual cases in the aggregate can serve, but one that must also be considered from a unique, intimately personal, subjective perspective, not available to quantitative researchers.

As pointed out by psychological astrologers that are intent on seeking scientific credibility, such as Glenn Perry, qualitative methods will at least do less damage to the astrological paradigm, even if they do not unequivocally prove astrology to be a science in the eyes of those scientists who are ambivalent about qualitative methods.

. . . it is of great relevance to astrologers that during the last several decades while philosophers of science were challenging the adequacy of the empirical method, various alternative systems of inquiry were proposed and have been gaining greater acceptance and systematization. These methods, known as non-numeric, qualitative, or linguistic research designs, were developed in response to the growing awareness that quantitative, experimental research is not an appropriate method for the study of human beings.[23]

It is the premise of this book that astrology itself is an alternative system of inquiry – that is to say, an epistemology unto itself. For most of astrology's history, it has evolved alongside other epistemologies, including science, in a culture with far greater latitude for intercourse between alternative systems of inquiry than we enjoy now. As science rose into dominance in the Empirical Age, it also began diverging in its focus, its methodologies, and its epistemological premises from the astrology with which it previously co-evolved, to the point where there is little room now for discourse at all.

I personally would like to believe that sometime down the road, as we enter more deeply into the Era of Uncertainty, that could change. First, however, must come the recognition that in this new era, any dogmatic assertion of the truth, or the absolute right to determine what is true and what isn't, is hopelessly antiquated, and perhaps neither scientists nor those astrologers who aspire to scientific credibility have arrived at this awareness yet.

Science's Credibility Crisis

Meanwhile, even as science struggles to hold onto its epistemological dominance in the Era of Uncertainty, it is also undergoing a credibility crisis. Aside from the inherent uncertainty of accurately measuring anything that has come to light over the last one hundred years or so, and the ongoing philosophical debates begun at the Copenhagen Conference about the rightful scope of science, public trust in the institution of science has seriously eroded since the dawn of the quantum era, and more rapidly since World War II. Within this time frame, science has been harnessed to a number of nefarious projects – the development of the Atomic bomb; the proliferation of a veritable Pandora's box of toxic and carcinogenic chemicals throughout the natural environment; the promotion of energy policies that have increased our dependence on fossil fuels and greatly exacerbated our current climate crisis; the creation of a drug-based and technology-dependent medical system that kills about a quarter million people worldwide each year;[24] economic models that favor corporate profit over the common good; and other questionable applications – that have harmed ordinary people, the culture at large, and the planet.

While science's role in these ongoing disasters has largely happened behind the scenes, away from the limelight of the media, in a supposedly neutral space, and is invisible to all but a few vocal critics of science, the recent coronavirus pandemic (of 2020-22) has exposed just how widespread this distrust in science has become within the general population. Attempting to better understand the resistance of a quarter of the US population to what seemed to them to be reasonable public health measures, such as social distancing, the wearing of masks, testing, contact tracing, and vaccines, researchers at John Hopkins Bloomberg School of Public Health conducted a survey. While the study confirmed a predictable political divide, and a slightly less obvious religious divide in the way people think about these public health measures, it also exposed a deeper more fundamental rift that cut to the core of science's credibility in the Era of Uncertainty:

> *Our survey asked: "[I]n general, would you say that you trust science a lot, some, not much, or not at all?" The public is split fairly evenly: 54% report trusting science "a lot," and 46% trust science "some," "not much," or "not at all." Simply understanding that nearly half of U.S. adults have doubts about science reveals why misinformation about the coronavirus pandemic has proliferated so easily.*[25]

Misinformation is, in and of itself, an expression of the postmodern distrust of authoritative declarations of truth, and in some cases, such as this recent pandemic, a life-threatening demonstration of the erosion of public trust in science. It can at times represent a certain laziness among those who prefer to parrot their favorite sources, rather than do the much harder parsing of informational nuances necessary to read between the lines. It can also be an honest expression of well-meaning people, who are ill-equipped to critically evaluate the overwhelming amount of nuanced information necessary to understand a bewildering world of increasing complexity.

Disinformation, on the other hand, is a more diabolical and intentional attempt to deceive. While it is generally not likely that many scientists would deliberately propagate disinformation, the success of those that do, ironically depends upon public mistrust in science. When combined with the capacity of social media platforms and alternative online media sources to facilitate a kind of mob mentality, and political leaders in the US (under Trump), Russia (under Putin), Brazil (under Bolsonaro), the Philippines (under Duterte) and other countries where a top-down attitude of anti-science has prevailed, scientists are often publicly castigated as the enemies of truth, rather than the purveyors of it.

This "infodemic," as some have called it, is not just a postmodern epistemological crisis; it also has dire consequences that go far beyond the scope of this book, and astrology's function in any potential future:

> *Mis- and disinformation can be harmful to people's physical and mental health; increase stigmatization; threaten precious health gains; and lead to poor observance of public health measures, thus reducing their effectiveness and endangering countries' ability to stop the pandemic.*
>
> *Misinformation costs lives. Without the appropriate trust and correct information, diagnostic tests go unused, immunization campaigns (or campaigns to promote effective vaccines) will not meet their targets, and the virus will continue to thrive.*
>
> *Furthermore, disinformation is polarizing public debate on topics related to COVID-19; amplifying hate speech; heightening the risk of conflict, violence and human rights violations; and threatening long-terms prospects for advancing democracy, human rights and social cohesion.*[26]

Science's Complicity in Spreading Mis- and Disinformation

While there are many factors contributing to this climate of distrust in science that have nothing to do with the earnest daily efforts of hard-working scientists to separate truth from fiction, it is also not true that scientists are entirely innocent or blameless victims. Not only does the political pressure on scientists – especially those involved in supplying a scientific rationale for the development of public policy – distort the consensus process, but so does political maneuvering within the scientific community itself. Competition for research funding is fierce, conflicts of interest are rife, and the results of research are often manipulated to ensure continued funding by those who pay. Aside from p-hacking, mentioned earlier in this chapter:

> *. . . peer-reviewed journal arrangement is known to have serious difficulties. Extreme practices include paying for authors' slots on papers written by other scientists, and buying papers from online brokers . . . false scientific papers generated by an algorithm (and) . . . predatory publishers who charge authors for publishing without providing any control or peer review.*[27]

Science is distorted, not just by political forces; media outlets with a biased agenda; and public gullibility; but by human fallibility among scientists in fields where egos, critical funding for research and public reputations are at stake, and the playing field is rigged, as it is in most human enterprises. Fully "one third of scientists in a recent poll admitted having recurred to 'questionable research practices', and in 2% of cases to have falsified research."[28]

During the recent pandemic, political and public pressure has led to a speeding up of the usual process by which rigorous studies are replicated and evaluated by peer review, effectively short-circuiting the scientific method itself and increasing the possibility that scientists could themselves be propagating misinformation.[29] Although accelerated during the pandemic, this development has been in motion now for at least three decades.

Since the 1990s, the emergence of preprint servers has allowed scientists working in a particular scientific field to share information with each other before publication, a trend generally known as the open-access movement. While ostensibly contributing to a healthy co-creative collaboration between scientists, open access has also resulted in the premature release of unvetted research, as scientists anxious to be recognized for their work send out press releases, which often then get quickly disseminated by the media to the general public, inadvertently contributing to a climate in which misinformation, or more accurately, scientific information not adequately established by science's own standards, mingles on an equal playing field with more solid scientific fact:

> *As someone who has worked for years with researchers and journalists to ensure responsible coverage of science in the media, I fear that this method of publication holds substantial risks for the broader community – risks that are not being given proper consideration by the champions of preprint. Weak work that hasn't been reviewed could get overblown in the media. Conversely, better work could be ignored.*[30]

While Sheldon's comment was specifically directed to biomedical research, the phenomenon of preprint has expanded throughout the scientific community, initiated by a relatively small number of researchers in physics and mathematics, but rapidly expanding to encompass most fields, including the social sciences.[31]

Even well-intentioned scientists, with no intent to deceive, can go bad in any number of ways.

> *Real scientists can behave as badly as anyone else. Science isn't about authority, or white coats, it's about following a method. That method is built on core principles: precision and transparency; being clear about your methods; being honest about your results; and drawing a clear line between the results, on the one hand, and your judgment calls about how those results support a hypothesis. Anyone blurring these lines is iffy.*[32]

Charting Astrology's Course In the Era of Mis- and Disinformation

Astrologers are likely to be under less outside pressure than scientists to distort or manipulate our findings, and in any case, few are waiting with bated breath for what we say, beyond our clients, or in some cases, possibly other astrologers. This does not mean we are immune to blurring the same lines that scientists do. Astrologers, no less than scientists, or players in any other field, for that matter, are subject to inflated egos, professional competition and jealousy, political infighting, emotional immaturity, unresolved psychological issues, inadequate knowledge or training, and conceptual, political or philosophical biases, all of which filter, cloud and at times distort our astrological pronouncements. Some of these issues have been partially addressed by our community; or by individual astrologers; others fester because we hesitate to be critical of each other or of our profession, when others are already so critical of us.

Aside from our credibility problem with the scientific community, we certainly have our own house-cleaning to do – which given the very broad umbrella under which astrologers from a bewildering array of persuasions gather, may or may not happen any time soon. In the meantime, it makes more sense in general for astrologers, whether working collectively or individually, to develop our own criteria for evaluating astrological truth, which is distinctly different than scientific truth. This need not be a condemnation, but can instead be a useful point of departure for exploring an entirely different order of experience than that which science is suited to measure, in ways that fail to register scientifically.

It is possible, as we shall see in Part Two of this book, that some of the qualitative tools used by cutting edge science can be useful in the development of a credible astrological epistemology – as long as we are clear that in the Era of Uncertainty, where science itself has lost its certainty, as well as some of its credibility, and with it, its claim to ultimate authority, the question, "Is astrology a science?" is no longer the right question to ask – if in fact, it ever has been.

Notes

1. The Era of Uncertainty began in the historical period leading up to the First World War, encompasses the Second World War as well (with its attendant development of nuclear weapons), along with the Great Depression, the Vietnam War, the bombing of the World Trade Towers, the subsequent War on Terror, growing awareness of climate change, loss of biodiversity, proliferation of toxic chemicals and the cancers and other fatal diseases they cause, and other impending ecological disasters, all of which have not only added to the uncertainty of the age, but have also thrown the hegemony of science itself into question. There are of course many discoveries of science that have greatly enhanced the human experience, but there is also a growing awareness of science's downside that has compromised its role as the sole arbiter of truth.
2. Tarnas, Richard. *The Passion of the Western Mind: Understanding the Ideas That Have Shaped Our World View*. Ballantine Books, 1991, 356.
3. Cohen, Barnard. "Foreword." In Bernard, Claude, *An Introduction to the Study of Experimental Medicine*, 1–4. Macmillan, 2018, v-vi. https://doi.org/10.4324/9781351320764-1.
4. Daston, Lorraine. "Scientific Error and the Ethos of Belief." *Social Research: An International Quarterly* 72, no. 1 (January 1, 2005): 18. https://doi.org/10.1353/sor.2005.0016.
5. Gribbin, John. *In Search of Schrodinger's Cat: Quantam Physics And Reality*. Bantam, 1984, 4.
6. Campion, Nicholas. *A History of Western Astrology Volume II: The Medieval and Modern Worlds*. Bloomsbury, 2009, 218.
7. Broemeling, Lyle D. "An Account of Early Statistical Inference in Arab Cryptology." *The American Statistician* 65, no. 4 (November 1, 2011): 255–57. https://doi.org/10.1198/tas.2011.10191.
8. As an astronomer, Huygens was known for his studies of the rings of Saturn and his discovery of Saturn's moon – Titan. He also improved the telescope with his invention of the Huygenian eyepiece.
9. Clerk, Agnes Mary. "1911 Encyclopædia Britannica/Laplace, Pierre Simon." Wikisource, September 24, 2020. https://en.wikisource.org/wiki/1911_Encyclop%C3%A6dia_Britannica/Laplace,_Pierre_Simon.
10. Willcox, Walter F. "The Founder of Statistics." *Revue De L'Institut International De Statistique* 5, no. 4 (January 1, 1938): 321–28. https://doi.org/10.2307/1400906.
11. English statistician Maurice Kendall, quoted in Porter, Theodore M. "Probability and Statistics | History, Examples, & Facts." Encyclopedia Britannica. September 9, 2005. https://www.britannica.com/science/probability.

12. Carpi, Anthony, PhD, and Anne E. Egger PhD. "Uncertainty, Error, and Confidence." Visionlearning, February 12, 2017. https://www.visionlearning.com/en/library/Process-of-Science/49/Uncertainty-Error-and-Confidence/157.

13. This phrase was popularized by Mark Twain, who attributed it to the British Prime Minister Benjamin Disraeli, although no corroborating evidence could be found for this assertion (Velleman, Paul F. "Truth, Damned Truth and Statistics." *Journal of Statistics* Education 16, no. 2 (2008). http://jse.amstat.org/v16n2/velleman.html.). Regardless of its source, the truth of the statement remains valid: that statistics can and often are used to make whatever case one happens to be invested in. Ethical considerations aside, it is human nature to want to find evidence to prove one's point of view, and statistics is the language of choice with which to do that, given the innate authority that numbers possess, even while knowing that what the lay public accepts as certainty is from a more accurate scientific standpoint, anything but.

14. Born, Max, and Albert Einstein. The Born-Einstein Letters, 1971. https://openlibrary.org/books/OL4913625M/The_Born-Einstein_letters.

15. As scientist Stephen Jay Gould wrote eloquently in the AMA *Journal of Ethics*, when diagnosed with mesothelioma, the statistical statement noting that those with this disease had only "a median mortality of eight months after discovery" did not mean that he would die in eight months. It did not even mean that he would probably die in eight months, as a non-scientist might assume. Why? Because the statistics did not and could not have possibly taken into account all of the individual factors – age, socioeconomic status, lifestyle, attitude, health history and a host of other factors – upon which the ultimate prognosis depends.

16. Dean, Geoffrey, Arthur Mather, David Nias, and Rudolf Smit. *Tests of Astrology: A Critical Review of Hundreds of Studies*. Amsterdam: AinO Publications, 2016, 331.

17. Statisticians are by no means in agreement about this figure. In fact, in a recent discussion of p-values (Wasserstein, Ronald L., and Nicole A. Lazar. "The ASA Statememt on p-Values: Context, Process and Purpose." *The American Statistician* 70, no. 2 (April 2, 2016): 129-133. https://doi.org/10.1080/00031305.2016.1154108), the authors put forth no less than 50 different opinions. If statistical significance depends upon opinion about what "significance" actually means, and how it ought to be measured, then the scientific community is no more unified than the astrological community it dismisses, and in no position to say with any real or definite authority what is significant and what is not.

18. Aschwanden, Christie. "We're All 'P-Hacking' Now." *Wired*, November 26, 2019. https://www.wired.com/story/were-all-p-hacking-now/.

19. Jung, Carl G. *The Collected Works of C.G. Jung, Volume 7: Two Essays on Analytical Psychology*. Princeton University Press, 1953, 289.
20. Wertz, Frederick J. "Qualitative Inquiry in the History of Psychology." *Qualitative Psychology* 1, no. 1 (February 1, 2014): 4–16. https://doi.org/10.1037/qup0000007.
21. Hammarberg, Karin, M. Sue Kirkman, and S. De Lacey. "Qualitative Research Methods: When to Use Them and How to Judge Them." *Human Reproduction* 31, no. 3 (March 1, 2016): 498–501. https://doi.org/10.1093/humrep/dev334.
22. Hammarberg, Kirkman, and De Lacey, "Qualitative Research Methods: When to Use Them and How to Judge Them."
23. Perry, Glenn. *Stealing Fire from the Gods: New Directions in Astrological Research*. East Hampton, CT: The Academy of AstroPsychology, 2006, 22.
24. Starfield, Barbara. "Is US Health Really the Best in the World?" *JAMA* 284, no. 4 (July 26, 2000): 483. https://doi.org/10.1001/jama.284.4.483.
25. Barry, Colleen, Harrie Han, and Beth McGinty. "Trust in Science and COVID-19." Johns Hopkins Bloomberg School of Public Health, August 3, 2021. https://www.jhsph.edu/covid-19/articles/trust-in-science-and-covid-19.html.
26. World Health Organization. "Managing the COVID-19 Infodemic: Promoting Healthy Behaviours and Mitigating the Harm from Misinformation and Disinformation." News, September 23, 2020. https://www.who.int/news/item/23-09-2020-managing-the-covid-19-infodemic-promoting-healthy-behaviours-and-mitigating-the-harm-from-misinformation-and-disinformation.
27. Saltelli, Andrea, and Silvio Funtowicz. "What Is Science's Crisis Really about?" *Futures* 91 (August 1, 2017): 5–11. https://doi.org/10.1016/j.futures.2017.05.010.
28. Fanelli, Daniele. "How Many Scientists Fabricate and Falsify Research? A Systematic Review and Meta-Analysis of Survey Data." *PLOS ONE* 4, no. 5 (May 29, 2009): e5738. https://doi.org/10.1371/journal.pone.0005738.
29. Mehta, Gautama. "How Scientists' Rush to Publish Covid-19 Research Fuels Disinformation." *Coda*, May 12, 2020. https://www.codastory.com/disinformation/scientists-prepublish-disinformation/.
30. Sheldon, Tom. "Preprints Could Promote Confusion and Distortion." *Nature* 559, no. 7715 (July 24, 2018): 445. https://doi.org/10.1038/d41586-018-05789-4.
31. Mehta, "How Scientists' Rush to Publish Covid-19 Research Fuels Disinformation."
32. Goldacre, Ben. "What Eight Years of Writing the Bad Science Column Have Taught Me." *The Guardian*, December 1, 2017. https://www.theguardian.com/commentisfree/2011/nov/04/bad-science-eight-years.

Chapter Seven

Knowing in the Era of Uncertainty

Before we explore how astrology might reinvent itself in a way that both honors its history and makes it more valuable in the Era of Uncertainty, let us take a moment to note some of the other emerging sensibilities that have contributed to a more level playing field on which astrology can establish its own right to exist on its own terms, apart from whatever strictures the empirical science of a bygone era might otherwise impose upon it.

Psychoanalysis

It is telling that in the early twentieth century, as quantum physicists were establishing a new standard for science in the Era of Uncertainty, early psychoanalysts like Sigmund Freud, Alfred Adler, Carl Jung, Karen Horney and Erich Fromm were working out basic psychoanalytic theory.

While quantum physics evolved through a curiosity about what was taking place at the subatomic level – largely beyond the direct possibility of observation that was the *sine qua non* for empirical science – the early psychoanalysts were fascinated by what went on below the surface of consciousness, in the unconscious realms of the psyche, as revealed to exist through the then revolutionary work of Sigmund Freud.

The term "unconscious" was coined by the eighteenth-century German philosopher Friedrich Schelling in his *System of Transcendental Idealism*, published in 1800, more than a century before Freud, and was routinely used by Freud's predecessors Gustav Fechner, Wilhelm Wundt and William James to describe peripheral psychological activity that lay outside of conscious awareness.[1] It was Freud, however, who first realized that the unconscious was not peripheral at all, but in fact essential to an understanding of the psyche, and who made its exploration central to the practice of psychotherapy.

The primacy of the unconscious created a profound conundrum for science in general, since its contents were not rational, objective or directly quantifiable, much less easily observable, and as such, did not fit the prevailing empirical paradigm. This was troubling for psychoanalysts, who perhaps like some astrologers today, wanted scientific credibility, but just didn't fit the mold. Yet, like the advent of quantum theory with which it co-evolved, psychoanalytic theory forced science to broaden its scope and relax some of its positivist strictures in order to function as a source of viable information in the Era of Uncertainty. Before Freud, the newly emerging field of psychology was largely behavioral – that is to say, focused on the measurement of the physiological dimensions of the psyche. After Freud, psychological researchers could no longer pretend or assume that the measurable dimensions of the psyche would ever tell the whole story.

With its current focus on pharmaceutical interventions, a certain segment of the psychological community has circled back to – or perhaps never left – the behaviorist fold, with its antiquated Empirical Era sensibilities. But in another parallel to the quantum revolution, those Era of Uncertainty psychologists who wished to be on the cutting edge of scientific exploration were compelled to acknowledge the limitations of the old paradigm and find ways to address the more invisible, subjective and participatory dimensions of the interface between psyche and external reality. Although psychoanalysis has become somewhat passé and fallen out of favor in the twenty-first century, at the dawning of the Era of Uncertainty, it was, like quantum physics, a point of entry into this brave new world.

Psychoanalysis postulated the existence of a hidden dimension of the psyche in which whatever we didn't know about ourselves could precipitate psychological complexes that worked against conscious agendas, producing strange behavioral patterns out of sync with our ego-based intentions. Out of these hidden complexes, in other words, came a certain, at-times profound eruption of uncertainty in an existence that otherwise would be pretty straight forward, not at all unlike the proverbial billiard ball, striking another with certain force and trajectory to yield a predictable result. As Freud and his successors made abundantly clear, the human psyche just does not work this way.

At the dawning of this realization, both quantum physicists and psychoanalysts were dealing with subterranean, chaotic dimensions of reality that defied easy explanation, much less clear-cut measurement in terms that empirical science could understand. Although psychoanalysts aspired to scientific credibility at the beginning of the Era of Uncertainty, in practice, working with actual analysands, they could not easily maintain objective distance without standing on the outside of the psychic territory they wished to enter. They had instead to engage in a participatory dialogue around dreams, early childhood memories, subjective fantasies and imaginative projections – none of which could easily be dissected or easily understood with the tools that Newtonian empiricism had to offer. As pointed out by science historian Morton Hunt:

> *The use of psychoanalytic procedures for research purposes had been much criticized as methodologically unsound. Free association leads the patient and analyst to an interpretation of a dream, but how can one prove that the interpretation is correct? In a few cases, there may be historical evidence that a trauma, reconstructed from a dream symbol, did in fact occur, but in most cases . . . there is no way to prove objectively that the interpretation has revealed the real dream content.*[2]

What does eventually confirm the validity of the dream, and the value of the psychoanalytic process in general is the patient's own response, that eureka moment when some hidden truth is revealed, and conscious awareness is suddenly thrust into a larger context where measurable external facts – as might be of interest to science – are less relevant than a more subjective understanding that rings true, whether it can be considered literally true or not. Although Freud and his successors would insist – as some astrologers do today – that their methods and procedures were, in fact, scientific, just as science itself was changing at the hands of the quantum theorists, so too was a more intuitive and imaginative way of knowing beginning to emerge, more effective at guiding individuals through the Era of Uncertainty than the science of the Empirical Era.

Surrealism

While it might seem like the wildest of *non sequiturs* to jump from science to surrealism, it is worth noting yet another parallel development. For at the same time that quantum science and psychoanalysis were co-evolving at the dawn of the Era of Uncertainty, a third group of explorers, composed of avant garde artists, painters, musicians and filmmakers such as Paul Éluard, André Breton, Louis Aragon, Luis Buñuel and Salvador Dali were birthing the surrealistic movement in art.

These artists were contemporaries of the quantum theorists and early psychoanalysts, all redefining diverse fields of endeavor for the Era of Uncertainty. Throughout the 1920s, seminal works in all three fields were being written. Four different versions of the *Surrealistic Manifesto* were published by rival factions from 1924 – 1929 in the same time frame that Louis de Broglie published *Researches on the Theory of Quanta*, establishing the dual nature of matter (1924) and Werner Heisenberg introduced his Uncertainty Principle through the publication of *On the Perceptual Content of Quantum Theoretical Kinematics and Mechanics* (1927).

Freud had been writing and publishing for some time, before he set out his basic theories of the unconscious in a 1915 paper called "The Unconscious," but then went on the elaborate his theories throughout the 1920s in such books as *Beyond the Pleasure Principle* (1920) and *The Ego and the Id* (1923). Alfred Adler published his seminal works – *The Practice and Theory of Individual Psychology* and *Understanding Human Nature* in 1927. Jung wrote *Psychology of the Unconscious* in 1912, which established his approach to the unconscious as distinctly different than Freud's, and that was revised a few years later as *Symbols of Transformation*. Like Freud, Jung went on to develop his ideas through subsequent publications in the 1920s and beyond, including *Psychological Types* in 1921 and *Two Essays on Analytical Psychology* – often considered one of the best introductions to his work – in 1928.

Although André Breton was best known as a French poet who became the principal theorist and leader of the surrealistic movement, he was trained in medicine, and used psychoanalytical techniques to treat soldiers returning shell shocked from World War I. This potential career track was interrupted when Breton was drafted, and met Alfred Jarry and Jacques Vaché, two anarchistic artists who disdained the artistic establishment of their day, at which point, he began to gravitate toward a career in renegade art. Even as he switched gears, however, Breton brought his affinity for the psychoanalytic method into the surrealistic movement where it melded with his emerging artistic sensibilities.

Surrealists in general took the psychoanalytic preoccupations with the interior, subterranean dimensions of the psyche and exteriorized it in their creative projects. While psychoanalysts explored the dream as a point of entry into the unconscious dimensions of the psyche, surrealists brought the dreamscape into waking consciousness. Although surrealism was a complex and by no means unified movement, in the end, it was an unapologetic celebration of the imagination as well as a strong reaction against positive science in the Empirical Era.

> *Under the pretense of civilization and progress, we have managed to banish from the mind everything that may rightly or wrongly be termed superstition, or fancy; forbidden is any kind of search for truth which is not in conformance with accepted practices. It was, apparently, by pure chance that a part of our mental world which we pretended not to be concerned with any longer - and, in my opinion by far the most important part - has been brought back to light. For this we must give thanks to the discoveries of Sigmund Freud. On the basis of these discoveries a current of opinion is finally forming by means of which the human explorer will be able to carry his investigation much further, authorized as he will henceforth be not to confine himself solely to the most summary realities. The imagination is perhaps on the point of reasserting itself, of reclaiming its rights.*[3]

Breton and the others were railing against the ways in which the limitations of reason had inserted themselves into everyday life and flattened the sensibilities of creative thinkers of all stripes and persuasions. Although they were on the vanguard of alternative ways of thinking at the dawning of the Era of Uncertainty, they were in fact championing an older, more primeval way of thinking and expressing rooted in the sensibilities of the Mythopoetic Era. Surrealism was, in fact, very much a radical campaign to reclaim the eighth clime of Corbin's *Mundus Imaginalis* as a legitimate realm for exploration.

By intentionally entering the same subliminal slipstream where dreams were formulated by a mind not bound by reason, surrealists hoped to liberate the mind from the fetters of rational thought, common sense and all pretensions of certainty. In this they were perhaps flirting with madness, but as intentional navigators, they were also more deliberately entering a realm of crazy wisdom beyond the reach of science, where deeper truths intrinsic to the very fabric of consciousness could be explored in the only way possible, through a deliberate exercise in *participation mystique*. As noted by Breton:

Surrealism is only trying to rejoin the most durable traditions of mankind. Among the primitive peoples, art always goes beyond what is conventionally and arbitrarily called the 'real'. The natives of the Northwest Pacific coast, the Pueblos, New Guinea, New Ireland, the Marquesas, among others, have made 'objets' . . . which Surrealists particularly appreciate.[4]

Art in general, of course, has never had any aspirations to be considered scientific, and is its own category of endeavor, largely free to go its own way without having to provide empirical evidence in order to justify its existence. This is not to say, of course, that art is not bound by its own set of aesthetic rules and standards, just that they are not expected to be scientific. Be that as it may, at the dawning of the Era of Uncertainty, art itself began to undergo a radical change.

The Changing Nature of Art in the Era of Uncertainty

While a thorough analysis of the ways in which periods of art history might parallel the various eras that we are discussing in this chapter is way beyond the scope of this book, we can note that most art in the Empirical Era was largely representational. That is to say, an artist described what he or she saw or witnessed or experienced in the world out there. There was, at times, a sense of the artist's own internal reactions to what was experienced, and a wide latitude in artistic styles of interpretation, but the focus was by and large on the external world.

Fiction, of course, was more purely an imaginative invention of the artist, and music was always perhaps the most internal of the arts, but until the Era of Uncertainty, all artists of whatever stripe or persuasion sought to communicate something about the world or the artist's experience of the world to an audience. With the surrealists, the bridge between inner experience and outer reality was far more tenuous and the interior landscape - however bizarrely it was imagined, and by whatever means it was rendered - stood on a far more equal footing with objective, consensus reality.

I believe in the future resolution of these two states, dream and reality, which are seemingly so contradictory, into a kind of absolute reality, a surreality, if one may so speak.[5]

In addition to the dream, and the psychoanalytic exploration of the unconscious, surrealists were also drawn to the occult arts, astrology, alchemy and magical traditions.[6] Among their techniques for accessing and creating directly from the unconscious, surrealists explored automatic writing and painting, and were in this endeavor, likely influenced by Madame Blavatsky and the Theosophical Society, founded in 1875 (see Chapter Eight). Indeed, artists such as Wasilly Kandinsky and Piet Mondrian were members of both circles.[7]

Breton himself studied astrology, and although he felt it too demanding for most surrealists to give it more than casual attention, also believed that it potentially provided a poetic bridge between inner and outer realities, "as long as astrologers actually go out there and scrutinize the night sky, let themselves be soaked through by the celestial emanations and then bring this brightness back to the darkness of human existence."[8] As we shall see in Part Two of this book, this is an astute prescription for how to bring back what was lost to astrology as it left the Mythopoetic and Mystical Eras, here being reiterated by a herald of the Era of Uncertainty.

Postmodernism

Arising concurrently with the surrealist movement, postmodernism was likewise a reaction to the dominance of the rational, scientific insistence on objective truth in the Empirical Era. Postmodernism recognized that what was espoused as truth by any particular thinker depended in large part upon her sociocultural conditioning, and the broader historical and cultural zeitgeist in which her perspective was rooted. Echoing the sentiments of Xenophon of the Philosophical Era, and quantum physicist Niels Bohr, postmodernists in general questioned the very possibility of knowing the Truth with objective certainty. Originally postmodernism arose as a school of literary criticism, but eventually spread to encompass every aspect of contemporary culture, especially wherever dogmatic, authoritarian or absolute truths were asserted.

Of particular interest to us here are the ways in which postmodernism has undermined scientific dominance, which began to erode within its own ranks as quantum theorists questioned its pretension to empirical certainty. As noted earlier, Thomas Kuhn's theory of shifting scientific paradigms gave credence to those who felt that competing scientific theories were little more than "outbreaks of mob psychology." Postmodernism contributed to this deconstruction of scientific hegemony by questioning the reliability of all meta-narratives, including science, that in the past provided a context in which it was possible to know something.

> *From a spiritual point of view, the horizon of meaning offered by a divine order – the "great order of Being" – is seemingly lost, while from the perspective of the postmodern subject, the world as well as life itself is not readable, understandable, or shapable anymore.*[9]

Jacques Derrida

These views were expounded and elaborated by deconstructionists such as Jacques Derrida, who is famous for his often mis-translated and misunderstood quote, declaring that "there is nothing outside context."[10] Like Francis Bacon, Derrida questioned the limits of language to explain the "thing" to which it referred, whether an idea, a scientific theory, or a work of art. Art, at least, often understood itself to be a metaphorical exploration of a reality that was elusive or ultimately unknowable. But most other attempts to explain reality failed to recognize that they were in fact dependent on a symbolic use of words, laden with metaphysical assumptions, biases born of psychological, cultural and historical conditioning, and rooted in perceptual contexts that often remained unconscious and went unacknowledged.

This is especially true, perhaps, in scientific circles, where it is tacitly forbidden to consider metaphysical assumptions at all, and great effort is expended to eliminate or negate observer bias altogether. And yet, from a postmodern perspective, the very notion that it is possible to derive an objective truth in this manner is a metaphysical assumption, one that arrogantly precludes other possibilities, as do the scientific tenets that truth is measurable; that the universe is built on causal relationships; that there are laws of nature that can be discovered; and so on. Rarely, if ever does science examine its own presuppositions, and so its biases and perceptual filters continue to limit and distort what it can and cannot know, even as it presumes to arbitrate what is true and what is not.

In the Era of Uncertainty, increased postmodern awareness of these biases has brought us full circle, back in a sense to the Philosophical Era, where the quest for truth is speculative, and yet at the same time, not quite so rational as it was then, but more self-reflective. Yes, we are all blind seekers of truth, circling a multi-faceted elephant, as the old story goes, and yet it is our willingness to explore both the limitations and the possibilities inherent in our own blindness that takes us more deeply into the heart of the mystery than any amount of groping out there for an objective or definitive truth ever could.

What this means in practice is that any idea about the nature of reality, including a well-entrenched scientific theory, is merely an attempt to explain in metaphor, within a certain perceptual context, what ultimately cannot be definitively explained. This is, according to Derrida no less true of established "facts" as of cutting edge and controversial theories. As psychoanalyst Erich Fromm was reputed to have said, for example, in parting ways from the authority of Freud:

> *The term 'the unconscious' is actually a mystification (even though one might use it for reasons of convenience, as I am guilty of doing in these pages). There is no such thing as the unconscious; there are only experiences of which we are aware, and others of which we are not aware, that is, of which we are unconscious.*[11]

It is possible to speak about the unconscious, or about sub-atomic particles, or about Saturn in a birthchart, for that matter, and find any of these explanations helpful, but there is – according to postmodern deconstructionists – no excuse for taking our explanations literally. They are, at best, an honest attempt to make sense of what appears to be real from a particular perspective, rooted in a particular context and informed by a particular set of linguistic conventions. Those conventions are radically different between astronomers, let's say, and astrologers, who ostensibly observe the same celestial panorama, but within the postmodern perspective, there is no basis for saying one is wrong and the other right. Each may be metaphorically true within its own domain or context, even if they fail to describe the same elephant.

Phenomenology

Derrida was influenced by the work of philosopher Edmund Husserl, a German philosopher who is considered the father of phenomenology. In contrast to positivism, which considers reality as an objective phenomenon – something out there – that can be observed and measured, phenomenology is concerned with our subjective experience of whatever might be out there, once we have become conscious of it.

A tree with a fragment of rope attached to it might evoke happy childhood memories of tire swings for one person, but for another, traumatic memories of ancestors lynched. So then, what is true about this fragment of rope attached to this tree? Perhaps there is a story about how the rope came to be in the tree that can be explained rationally and as a matter of objective fact. But this story will not explain the subjective reactions of those who encounter the rope in the tree.

To explore the subjective response to reality, phenomenology considers not just memory, but also sensory perception, bodily sensation, emotion, desire, intention, thought, imagination, social and cultural context, and the meaning of words that enter into an understanding of something – all with the intent of understanding the phenomena of this world, in a sense, from the inside out.

When the study of experience from a subjective point of view is combined with the importance of context, as it was by Martin Heidegger, a German phenomenologist, you have the basis for a postmodern approach to astrology, where what matters is not some external definition of astrological symbolism, but how that symbolism is experienced in a living context. Heidegger called his approach to understanding "hermeneutics."

Hermeneutics

Hermeneutics is a not entirely a new idea, having existed since the fifteenth century, where it was originally employed as a method for understanding scholarly texts. The idea behind this approach is that one needed to understand something of the subjective experience of the author and the cultural/historical context in which he or she was writing, in order to understand the text itself. Heidegger and others extended this idea to encompass the understanding of anything to which one turned one's attention, not just as a way of more organic knowing, but as a pathway to a more authentic way of being.

When the object of one's attention is oneself, then a hermeneutic approach to astrology potentially becomes a way of understanding the birthchart from within one's own experiences, rather than as something to be approached from an objective standpoint, as many astrologers attempt to do. Astrology practiced this way is less about "reading" a birthchart than allowing the birthchart to suggest a point of entry into an exploratory conversation with ourselves, or between astrologer and client, whose trajectory cannot be known in advance.

Post-Structuralism

The post-structuralist movement, which emerged in France in the 1960s, during a period of political turmoil, rebellion against societal norms, and widespread questioning of authority, takes the premise of hermeneutics one step further. Not only is the individual the ultimate arbiter of truth, but the individual self that arbitrates is itself a fictional construct. The ego that previously reigned supreme as the central organizing principle of the personality is, within the context of this emerging philosophy, but one internal voice among many, all vying for coherent expression, if not dominance. Out of this psychological cacophony comes a much more decentralized interplay of selves, each of which has its own agenda, sometimes in sync with at least some of its companions, sometimes in tension or outright conflict.

At its most extreme, the coexistence of multiple personalities within one individual has been labeled a disorder by the psychiatric profession, with evolving terminology – from "double consciousness" in the late ninetheenth century; to "dementia praecox," a term developed by German psychiatrist Emil Kraepelin in 1893; to "schizophrenia," coined by Swiss psychiatrist Eugen Blueler in 1908; to "multiple personality disorder," introduced in *DSM-III* (*Diagnostic and Statistical Manual of Mental Disorders*, 3rd Edition) in 1980; to "dissociative identity disorder" in *DSM-IV*, published in 1994, to a wider range of overlapping and more nuanced conditions in *DSM-V*, published in 2013.

To some extent, this progression of terms represents an evolution in our collective understanding of the process by which the co-existence of multiple selves within one person becomes problematic, and the mechanisms by which mental function deteriorates into autonomous alternative subpersonalities, completely dissociated from one another. Often there is a history of abuse, or repetitive trauma, and a complex web of symptoms including hallucinations, trance-like states, psychosomatic ailments with no identifiable physiological cause, dissociation, amnesia, and a failure to recognize the external world as real. There is no question but the confluence of such extreme manifestations of the post-structural awareness that we are all multi-dimensional beings is not something to be dismissed by mere linguistic sleight of hand, even if the psychiatric profession as a whole is struggling to find common footing in their understanding of it.

Yet, having said that, the post-structural argument is not about psychological extremes, but rather everyday perception. Most of us are not debilitated by dissociative identity disorders and are able to recognize ourselves as the same person from day to day. And yet, few of us are consistent throughout the day, or from one day to the next. Instead, each aspect of our life tends to demand and draw forth a different aspect of our being – the competent doer at work; the compassionate partner in relation to our spouse; the understanding disciplinarian in relation to our children. To these varied tasks, we bring our own psychological issues, our passing moods, and our shifting capacity to juggle everything we have to juggle in a complex modern life. Under stress, additional dimensions of our personality, some quite in contrast to the ways in which we normally see ourselves, may come forth to complicate the basic question, "Who am I?" Astrologers might add the shaping influences of various transits and progressions, each of which draw various aspects of our being into the foreground of consciousness, while others recede into the background. Within this shifting panoply of forces impinging on us, each of us is less a unified self than a confluence of selves, each with a different lens through which reality is filtered.

Put in psychological terms, it has long been a tradition to divide the psyche into components and discuss their relationship with each other. Freud spoke of the id, ego, and superego, each of which sees the world differently. Jung spoke of the archetypes of the unconscious – the shadow, the *anima* or *animus*, the wise old man or woman, the trickster, etc. – each of which is capable of usurping the conscious agenda and becoming the focal point of awareness. Inspired by both Freud and Jung, Roberto Assagioli postulated the existence of unconscious subpersonalities, which are relatively autonomous aspects of the psyche, each with its own characteristics, its own needs, wants and motivations, its own capacity to harness the personality in service to its agenda.

Those who have followed in Assagioli's footsteps into the era of multiple personal disorders and dissociative identity disorders (terms not used in Assagioli's lifetime), argue that:

> *. . . the difference between clients with subpersonalities and clients who suffer from DID and have 'alters' is simply a matter of degree. Alters operate much more autonomously and are harder to recognize because of an amnesic barrier. Clients with DID are unconscious of their alters as are clients with unconscious patterns called*

subpersonalities. The difference is that clients with DID ignore symptoms that point to the existence of alters and have learned to ignore the evidence that indicates they exist . . . Once a subpersonality is identified, however, clients can recognize they are captured in or acting out these patterns and can consciously work to understand and get the underlying need(s) met.[12]

Within the psychological community, there are a growing number of practitioners who see the existence of subpersonalities, even relatively unconscious and autonomous subpersonalities as not inherently problematic, but more a phenomenon called "multiplicity" that exists along a range of possibilities.

Despite this emerging sensibility designed to destigmatize those harnessed with psychiatric diagnoses and labels, in most psychotherapy, the end goal remains a working integration of the various subpersonalities, by whatever name they are called, in a sense, working toward a unified self, whose parts are seamless dimensions of a functioning whole. Until that blessed day arrives, if it ever does, each of us is a walking menagerie of selves, giving credence to the post-structural argument that the self is, ultimately like all psychological terms, a fiction, perhaps a useful fiction, but a fiction nonetheless.

The Implications of Post-Structuralism for Science

Beyond its psychological implications, the post-structural view becomes a new thorn in the side of those who would cling to scientific certainty in the Era of Uncertainty, for if it is not just the world itself that cannot be objectified, but also the observer of the world. If the subject changes perspective from year to year, season to season, sometimes moment to moment, then. "Who is there to know what exactly?" becomes a legitimate question.

The post-structuralists – including Jacques Derrida (mentioned above as a postmodern deconstructionist), Jacques Lacan, Roland Barthes, Michel Foucault and Julia Kristeva – argue that there is no fixed relationship between subject and object, or even between words and their meanings. From this perspective, all truth is contextual – a mobile alchemy between a multi-dimensional self and a world that can be seen by multiple selves in a myriad of ways – and is best described in a nuanced language that is more poetic and exploratory than literal and definitive.

Jacques Lacan

Jacques Lacan further observed that the unconscious itself was structured like a language. When physical or psychological symptoms manifest, for example, they often employ a psychosomatic metaphor that has repercussions on multiple levels that can be articulated within the larger context of a multi-dimensional life. In other words, if we are willing to listen, they speak to us about things that would otherwise escape our conscious notice. If I am carrying the weight of the world on my shoulders, for example, I may well develop an actual physical pain in my shoulders, as well as an attendant chronic sense of being depressed. All of this is part of the metaphorical language by which the unconscious makes itself known.

Similarly, when jokes, or slips of the tongue, or puns, or dreams, or other moments of unconscious spontaneity emerge, we are faced with new information, often revealed in layers foreign to the conscious mind, but ready to enter into dialogue with it. If I have a dream about drowning, then wake up to a job where I constantly feel overwhelmed by matters beyond my capacity to cope, this too is part of a language by which the unconscious gets the attention of the conscious mind, as well as an invitation to enter more deeply into a conversation with ourselves.

Lacan further postulated that this conversation between the unconscious and the conscious mind is ongoing, and at each step of the way, there is an inconclusive, open-ended possibility for meaning to emerge. Until the unconscious becomes conscious, in other words, the "sentence" being communicated is incomplete, and the words in it are "floating signifiers," whose meaning can change as additional words (basic units of information) are added. Much like Schrödinger's cat, whose status we won't know until we actually open the box, Lacan's sentence is unknowable until it is complete, or "quilted" in Lacan's terminology.

Furthermore, while sentences can certainly complete, the next sentence can also change the meaning of the first. Any sentence or paragraph taken out of context of an entire work can be misleading, as can any idea taken out of the context of an author's larger body of work, or a given author's work taken out of the context of the larger field of endeavor that contains it, as well as the general zeitgeist of the era in which it was produced.

We might even take this idea a step further to suggest that psychological truths are not complete, if parallel truths in other fields that dovetail with them – anthropology, neuroscience, sociology, history and linguistics – to name a few, are not also taken into account. The meaning to be milked through any individual perspective only emerges as the participants in the conversation perpetually reach for a broader, more inclusive context in order to understand the bits and pieces of the puzzle being ever-so-slowly assembled.

Whether we apply this way of thinking about knowledge itself to science or astrology, it suggests that we are ultimately not engaged in a quest for truth at all, if by truth, we mean a definitive statement about what is real. Instead, both science and astrology are ongoing dialogues that circle around the truth, using floating signifiers in a sentence that never definitively completes. From the post-structuralist perspective, taken to its logical conclusion, it can never be any other way, and to accept the limitations of uncertainty is to enter the conversation on an honest, more authentic footing.

This does not mean that we can never reach useful conclusions, to temporarily close a particular "sentence" in a way that brings a well-earned pause in the conversation, where we can take a breath before rushing on. It does mean that the conversation itself is one that requires humility, and must necessarily cross borders of ideology, discipline, and paradigm to enter a realm where actual data comingles with paradox, metaphor and imagination to ever broaden the scope of discourse.

The Postmodern Invitation

While postmodernism has undermined the global authority of collective meta-narratives, including the idea that science is the sole arbiter of what is real or true, the quest for truth in the Era of Uncertainty has increasingly become driven by a hunger for direct experience. No longer content to accept the pronouncements of scientists, religious authorities, political leaders, or other so-called experts as gospel truth, from the mid twentieth century on, those seeking ultimate truths have increasingly turned to a deeper source within, where the only real authority they can trust is to be found – or at least, where it makes postmodern sense to look for it.

Of course, this impulse hearkens back to the Mythopoetic and Mystical Eras, when *participation mystique* and a divinatory oral tradition allowed truth to be approached by anyone willing or able to open to it, as well as to the Gnostic tradition of the Logical Era, in which direct experience was preferable to reliance on authoritarian pronouncements. The difference now is that, as a culture, we have the benefit of everything that has come before, as well as access to various tools and awareness of their use that our ancestors could not imagine. We are also endowed with a certain self-reflective awareness, that arises looking back through our collective history with the gift of postmodern hindsight, that potentially makes our quest more sophisticated and nuanced than it could have been in an earlier era. Because of our historical perspective, we can be aware of the ways in which language conditions our perceptions. This awareness then allows us to intentionally reach for a source of knowing that arises from a deeper place within, one that transcends our capacity to clothe our experience in words. This is a possibility that was not available to our ancestors as a matter of conscious choice.

To the extent that access to this deeper source of knowing has been filtered through psychological wounding, or through the chaos of multiple fictional selves vying for dominance, it can be argued that what might be otherwise known of this deeper source is no more reliable than the discredited external sources it is replacing. And yet, as mystics, shamans, alchemists, magicians, gnostics and other seekers of direct experience have demonstrated throughout the ages, there is something beyond the noise, inner as well as outer, that is worth pursuing, even if it remains elusive. In the Era of Uncertainty, we have the benefit of prior touchstones in our collective experience, as well as the postmodern permission to find our own way into the truth, without the need for external sanction or consensual blessing.

This is both an immense opportunity and a challenge with dire responsibilities, for it is not just a matter of going our own way and doing what we damn well please. It is more fundamentally a matter of finding a synchronous interplay of all the voices, inside and out, so that as a species we can more skillfully enter an ongoing conversation with the *anima mundi* – the soul of the world itself – one that fosters abundance and co-creative synergy throughout the living cosmos. Short of that, the current era may well unfold to encompass even greater uncertainty about the future of the human species, and the planet that has so graciously hosted us until now.

The Psychedelic Revolution

For those of us who grew up in the 1960s, there was no greater point of entry to this larger conversation with the living cosmos than the psychedelic revolution that seized the collective imagination of an entire generation. The public face of this revolution was Timothy Leary, a renegade Harvard professor and his cohort, Richard Alpert, more commonly known as Ram Dass, whose book *Be Here Now* became the Bible of a new generation of seekers.

Before and behind these celebrities, who unleashed their own outburst of mob psychology, were a small, fiercely dedicated cadre of scientists, therapists, and lesser known psycho-spiritual pioneers, who were earnestly exploring the healing properties of these remarkable substances in treating addiction, depression, obsessive-compulsive disorder, schizophrenia, autism, and end-of-life anxiety, among other intractable conditions, as well inducing documented mystical experiences and life-changing epiphanies in controlled clinical settings. Between 1950 and 1965, there had been forty thousand research participants and more than a thousand clinical papers, plus six international conferences oriented around this psychedelic research.

> *But after the culture and the psychiatric establishment turned against psychedelics in the mid-1960s, an entire body of knowledge was effectively erased from the field, as if all that research and clinical experience has never happened.*[13]

In part, psychedelic research disappeared because the rampant and rapid introduction of these potent substances into the general population generated a kind of mass hysteria, fueled by mainstream mistrust of a rebellious counterculture with alternative political as well as spiritual agendas, quite in keeping with postmodern mistrust of authority figures and conventional wisdom. In part, however, psychedelic research also tested the limits of the old scientific paradigm of the Empirical Era, which despite the discoveries of scientists in the Era of Uncertainty, still prevailed within the research community.

On the one hand, the discovery of LSD in the 1950s fueled the emerging field of neuroscience, predicated on the idea that consciousness was essentially an epiphenomenon of brain function, and led to the development of SSRI antidepressants and their successors. On the other hand, psychedelic research and the more general field of consciousness research have raised many conundrums that science cannot adequately address, among them: the possibility that subjective experience will never yield to scientific inquiry; the notion that the sense of self that post-structuralists consider to be a fiction might also be the gateway to the doors of perception, beyond which lies an entire realm of consciousness not dependent on human constructs; and that consciousness itself may, like gravity and electromagnetism, may be one of the fundamental forces shaping reality.

> *How can be we certain . . . that our experience of consciousness is 'authentic?' The answer is we can't; it is beyond the reach of our science and yet who doubts its reality? In fact, the evidence for the existence of consciousness is much like the evidence for the reality of the mystical experience: we believe it exists not because science can independently verify it but because a great many people have been convinced of its reality; here, too, all we have to go on is the phenomenology – that is what people tell us about their internal experiences.*[14]

The use of psychotropic substances, of course, is not new, having been an integral part of mythopoetic and shamanic culture since the very beginnings of this narrative, as an aid to an experience of *participation mystique* and communion with the realm of the sacred. There is, in fact, a very long history of anecdotal accounts of those who have had meaningful internal experiences that are inaccessible to science, up to and including an encounter with an apparent ultimate reality out of which consciousness springs.

Consciousness and the Development of Language

Indeed, as noted in the Introduction, with reference to the work of Terrence McKenna, the evolution of consciousness itself – that is to say, the possibility of knowing anything at all – may have been closely paralleled by the use of plant medicines, particularly psilocybin mushrooms, which grew ubiquitously as a natural by-product of nomadic hunter societies and increased dramatically with the domestication of cattle.

If the quest for truth in the Era of Uncertainty can be understood to be a linguistic exploration with no ultimate completion that can be put into words, then a substance that lies at the heart of language formation and precedes it can perhaps be helpful. Although its use is still in a somewhat gray area legally, psilocybin may potentially be a vehicle that can take us as close as it is possible to get to the very origins of our capacity to know anything at all. As mystics around the world have noted, when one gets close to the Source out of which consciousness springs, language matters less and less, and in fact, dissolves in simple direct knowing of what is only described in retrospect, if it is described at all, as ultimate reality – God, Yahweh, Allah, Brahman, Wakan Tanka, Spirit, Gaia, or Great Mystery.

Astrology as a Language of Consciousness

As noted by William A. Richards, as well as many other psychedelic pioneers, "mystical experiences, which typically are extremely ephemeral and unpredictable, can actually be catalyzed in a fairly reliable and replicable way with the correct use of psychedelic substances . . .,"[15] which aside from a wide range of other uses, is no small part of their appeal. While an uninitiated non-believer might ascribe such experiences to subjective fantasy, researcher Michael Pollan, initially himself an uninitiated non-believer, or at least a skeptic, notes that:

> *. . . along with the feeling of ineffability, the conviction that some profound objective truth has been disclosed to you is a hallmark of the mystical experience, regardless of whether it has been occasioned by a drug, meditation, fasting, flagellation, or sensory deprivation. William James gave a name to this conviction: the noetic quality. People feel they have been let in on a deep secret of the universe, and they cannot be shaken from that conviction.*[16]

To the extent that our cumulative account of such experiences serves as a counterbalance to the uncertainty of our age, they open a door through which we might entertain the possibility of other, non-scientific ways of knowing. While psychedelics are not typically incorporated into standard astrological practice, for many individual astrologers, myself included, who encountered them during the general renaissance of the 1960s, the cosmological perspective behind the practice of astrology has no doubt been deepened and broadened by exposure to these substances that open a portal to the very roots of consciousness. It is at these roots, no doubt, that astrology can be understood as an attempt to put into language an understanding of the relationship between cosmos and psyche, where the split between our innermost experiences and the outer ordering of space and time maintained by the science of an earlier age is but an illusion.

At the very least, there would appear to be a correlation between the movement of planets through the cosmos and the flow of internal experience that perhaps becomes magnified by the psychedelic experience for those with the tools to map such correlations. Such has been the basis for a three-decade collaboration between pioneer consciousness and altered states researcher Stanislav Grof and archetypal psychologist, philosopher and astrologer Richard Tarnas. Initially a skeptic in the scientific mold, Grof eventually came to the conclusion that:

> *Our systematic study of the correlations between the nature and content of holotropic states and planetary transits convinced me that a combination of deep experiential*

> *therapy with archetypal psychology and transit astrology is the most promising strategy for the future development of psychiatry and depth psychology. I am aware that this is a very strong statement, particularly in view of the fact that many mainstream scientists consider astrology, as I did myself, to be in principle incompatible with the scientific world view.*[17]

Within this statement, and especially within the body of work behind it, is a strong case, not just for entertaining the possibility that astrology can provide a glimpse into the hidden dimensions of reality to which science is blind, but also that the astrological language itself may be rooted in the same preverbal possibility of knowing, out of which consciousness itself arises.

The New Age

In keeping with the postmodern emphasis on an individual, inwardly-directed quest for personal truth, and rising in parallel to the psychedelic revolution, the New Age movement opened a broad smorgasbord of avenues to self-exploration, spanning cultures around the planet, and from eras past, as well as present. The New Age drew upon a number of older esoteric traditions, including but not limited to those of pagan and indigenous cultures, shamanism, Eastern and Western mystical traditions, yogic and meditative practices, Neoplatonism, hermeticism, Western magic and Theosophy, as well as the emerging sensibilities of Jungian, humanistic and transpersonal psychologies, the human potential movement, alternative healing modalities, feminism and environmentalism.

While there is some adherence to tradition among New Agers, most spiritual seekers take an eclectic approach to their quest, gathering bits and pieces of resonant truth from a wide range of sources, synthesizing and extrapolating from them in a way that would not have been done in previous eras, but that makes good postmodern sense. The emphasis is generally not just upon passively ingesting information from external authorities, but actively seeking experiences through which a more direct gnosis, or experiential knowing, becomes possible. In practice, however, many New Age teachers have become authorities in their own right, and have developed large followings of individuals who, despite lip service to the contrary, prefer to get their truth from an external source than from within.

Like quantum theorists, early psychoanalysts, and surrealists, many New Agers are interested in exploring the hidden dimensions and the imaginal realms, which they believe to be populated by a wide variety of semi-divine non-human entities, such as angels, animal totems, ascended masters, and disincarnate beings with wisdom to share from other perspectives than the merely human, limited to bodies bound by time and space. Again, many seekers encounter these extra-dimensional beings through a select few who gain additional credibility and authority through their channeling, rather than as a direct experience of their own.

New Age Perspectives on Science

While New Agers don't generally disparage science in general, they often hold forth a vision of an integration of science and spirituality that should theoretically become possible in an Era of Uncertainty in which science is slowly changing to encompass distinctly non-scientific ideas. The fact that this integration does not actually exist is seldom a deterrent to its assumption by those who proceed as though it did. The prolific use of the word, "energy," for example, to denote a wide range of internal experiences involving strong feelings, visceral sensations, and/or spontaneously arising imagery, implies a scientific aura of authority that science itself would not bestow, because even within the quantum arena, energy means something very different to a scientist than it does in New Age contexts.

Astrologers who speak of planetary influences, for example, fall into this camp, since there is little actual scientific measurement of these influences. As a metaphor, such pseudo-scientific references might occasionally make sense within a given context, but there is a tendency in New Age and some astrological circles to take metaphors literally as a bridge to scientific validation that a *bona fide* scientist would hesitate to take.

Ken Wilbur, for example, once declared a number of the pioneers of the revolution in quantum physics – including Heisenberg, Schrödinger, Einstein, de Broglie, Jeans, Planck, Pauli, and Eddington – to be mystics, while at the same time acknowledging that "these theorists are virtually unanimous in declaring that modern physics offers no positive support whatsoever for mysticism or transcendentalism of any variety."[18]

Nor do many of the truisms to which New Age thinkers ascribe scientific validity necessarily gain any support from the scientific community whatsoever, outside of a few fringe scientists that are largely rejected by the majority of their peers. Just because quantum physicists have discovered that an observer affects the outcome of an experiment designed to measure some aspect of reality, for example, doesn't necessarily mean that a scientist would agree, "We create our own reality." This is a leap a New Ager is prepared to make, while a scientist would still, even in the Era of Uncertainty, prefer to measure whatever reality exists independent of the observer, and over which an observer can assert no influence, before drawing even a tentative conclusion. New Age thought, in general, allows for metaphorical bridges between hard reality and imagined possibilities; scientific thought does not.

This entrenched and extreme conservatism is perhaps slowly changing as scientists like Fritz Capra (*The Tao of Physics: An Exploration of the Parallels Between Modern Physics and Eastern Mysticism*, 1975), Fred Alan Wolf (*Taking the Quantum Leap*, 1981), Paul Davies (*God and the New Physics*, 1983), Nick Herbert (*Quantum Reality: Beyond the New Physics*, 1985), David Bohm (*The Undivided Universe: An Ontological Interpretation of Quantum Theory*, 1993), and Brian Josephson ("String Theory, Universal Mind and the Paranormal," 2003), among others,[19] seek to integrate their spirituality with their science. These unorthodox scientists explore the interface between ideas that would be readily embraced in New Age circles and scientific principles, but it is by no means the standard understanding.

Mainstream scientists, by contrast, are often open to a scientific exploration of new ideas; they are generally not open to a consideration of the spiritual or metaphysical implications of those ideas. As 1973 Nobel Prize winner Brian Josephson put it, "Anything goes among the physics community – just so long as it keeps its distance from anything mystical or New Age-ish" – an attitude he labels "pathological disbelief."[20] We might consider that this disconnect between physics and metaphysics is a counterbalance to the opposite extreme, often evidenced in the New Age community, of uncritically embracing the wildest of ideas with no basis in consensual reality – a stance we might label "pathological belief."

The New Age as A Postmodern Phenomenon

Meanwhile, those who observe the New Age itself find the truth of it elusive, and are uncertain how exactly to explain it, making it a quintessential postmodern phenomenon in the Era of Uncertainty:

> *One of the few things on which all scholars agree concerning New Age is that it is difficult to define. Often, the definition given actually reflects the background of the scholar giving the definition. Thus, the New Ager views New Age as a revolutionary period of history dictated by the stars; the Christian apologist has often defined New Age as a cult; the historian of ideas understands it as a manifestation of the perennial tradition; the philosopher sees New Age as a monistic or holistic worldview; the sociologist describes New Age as a new religious movement (NRM); while the psychologist describes it as a form of narcissism.*[21]

Fundamental to most New Age thinking is the idea that humanity is poised on the threshold of a monumental change that will usher in a new era of peace, global cooperation, ecological balance, and the blossoming of full human potential.[22] For those proponents of the New Age for which astrology was a *lingua franca*, the precession of the equinoxes into the sign of Aquarius was the timing mechanism by which this shift would manifest, although few could agree on when exactly this precession would take place.

For centuries before the actual New Age movement began, speculative anticipation of some kind of new age had already resulted in a widely divergent set of possible dates. In the sixteenth century, German alchemist Heinrich Khunrath declared that an "age of Saturn" (Saturn being the traditional astrological ruler of the sign Aquarius) would begin at some unspecified point in the not-too-distant future. In the eighteenth century, French Freemason Francois-Henri-Stanislas de l'Aulnaye was certain that the precession had already taken place in 1726. Alan Leo declared the Age of Aquarius would begin on the Spring Equinox 1928.

Rudolf Steiner thought a New Age began in 1899, but that the Age of Aquarius wouldn't begin until 3573.[23]

Astrologers since Alan Leo have continued to speculate, the trend more recently seeming to be that every planetary alignment of note since the Harmonic Convergence of August 16-17, 1987 (involving 8 planets in a Grand Trine, mostly in Earth) marks some seminal stage in human evolution. The latest speculation (as of this writing) swirled around the new Jupiter-Saturn conjunction at the beginning of Aquarius that took place on the Winter Solstice 2020, which marked the Great Mutation (a larger 800-year cycle) of the conjunction into air signs after a 200-year stint in earth signs.[24]

My sense about the perennial desire for a New Age, which naturally lends itself to speculation around astrological timing, is that it is part of our collective response to the uncertainty of the times. Given the history of human folly in the face of climate change; the accelerating loss of biodiversity, called by some the Sixth Mass Extinction;[25] endless wars and genocides; pandemics; and other intractable conditions seemingly getting worse, we all long for a reset, before we run out of time, if we haven't already – even though, short of extreme wishful thinking, often accompanied by willful denial of evidence to the contrary, there is no new beginning on the horizon that will mark a significant change from the collective trajectory we are already on.

At its best, the New Age has not just been idle speculation, but rather a synthesis between a metaphysical perspective and socio-political activism. In the 1960s and 1970s, New Age thinking was closely aligned with a countercultural movement that, under the influence of psychedelics and faced with the political ferment of the Civil Rights riots, the Viet Nam War, and the assassinations of Martin Luther King and the Kennedys, asserted this belief in idealistic and activist terms, gravitating to the emerging environmental movement, the anti-war movement, the rise of feminism, and other more progressive and egalitarian paradigms, as evidence that we were indeed changing the world for the better. While in retrospect, this starry-eyed idealism has proven to fall short of reality, it is gratifying to see that this activist tradition continues among new generations who are not just politically astute, but also open to new ideas about who we are and what we are doing here.

What matters most is not that we wind up, individually or collectively, in any particular place, but that we give our all to an ever-evolving path that makes sense to us. Indeed, within the Era of Uncertainty, the most sensible path forward may be what UCLA anthropology student *cum* New Age teacher Carlos Castaneda once called "a path of heart" (the parenthetical addition is mine):

> *Look at every path closely and deliberately. Then ask yourself, and yourself alone, one question . . . Does this path have a heart? If it does, the path is good; if it doesn't, it is of no use . . . All paths are the same; they lead nowhere. They are paths going*

> *through the bush, or into the bush . . . (All) paths lead nowhere, but one has a heart, the other doesn't. One makes for a joyful journey; as long as you follow it, you are one with it. The other will make you curse your life. One makes you strong; the other weakens you.*[26]

In the Era of Uncertainty, it is an act of folly to say we know anything for certain. Yet, to the extent that we can control our hubris about what we think we know, it is possible to discover a path of heart on which imagination, sensory impressions, memories, historical facts, mythopoetic sensibilities, divine revelations, rational thoughts, and astrological overlays converge in unexpectedly enlightening ways.

Scientists are welcome, if they insist, to cling to a small subset of the abundance of tools available to us in the postmodern world, and to their illusions of certainty. But in the Era of Uncertainty, the enlightened astrologer will strive to meld them all in a coherent approach to mysteries, human and sacred, that defy simple, rational, objective explanations, along a path of heart that will make our lives meaningful, regardless of what we think we know when time runs out on our very short leg of an endless journey.

The journey is meaningful, not because we will ultimately reach any kind of definitive or predictable end or arrive at any ultimate understanding of what is real or true, as might matter to a scientist, but because at each step of the way, we will enter more deeply into an endlessly fascinating dialogue with a living cosmos that perpetually reveals itself anew – and mirrors our Self to ourself anew – as we consciously and intentionally engage with it.

Even in the Era of Uncertainty, as long as we follow this path with courage, humility and the willingness to walk our talk, while learning whatever we learn along the way, our journey will be joyful.

Notes

1. Murray, Christopher John. *Encyclopedia of the Romantic Era, 1760–1850*. Routledge, 2013, 1001-02.
2. Hunt, Morton. *The Story of Psychology*. Doubleday, 1993, 180.
3. Breton, André. *Manifesto of Surrealism*, 1924. https://theanarchistlibrary.org/library/andre-breton-manifesto-of-surrealism.pdf.
4. Breton, André, and Marcel Duchamp. "First Papers of Surrealism: Hanging by André Breton, His Twine Marcel Duchamp." Internet Archive, 1942. https://archive.org/details/firstpaperssur00bret.
5. Breton. *Manifesto of Surrealism*.

6. Campion, Nicholas. "Surrealist Cosmology: André Breton and Astrology." *Culture and Cosmos* 6, no. 2 (2002): 45–56. http://cultureandcosmos.org/pdfs/6/6-2_Campion_Breton_Astrology.pdf.

7. Hughes, Robert. *The Shock of the New: Art and the Century of Change*. Thames and Hudson, 1981, 202 and 209.

8. Carteret, Jean, and Roger Knare. "An Interview with André Breton." *Culture and Cosmos* 6, no. 2 (April 1954). http://cultureandcosmos.org/pdfs/6/6-2_Campion_Breton_Astrology.pdf.

9. Stein, Murray, and Thomas Arzt. *Jung's Red Book for Our Time: Searching for Soul Under Postmodern Conditions, Vol. 1*. Asheville, NC: Chiron Publications, 2017, 17.

10. Derrida, Jacques, and Gerald Graff. "Afterword: Toward an Ethic of Discussion." In *Limited Inc*. Northwestern University Press, 1988, 136.

11. Fromm, Erich. *Beyond the Chains of Illusion: My Encounter with Marx and Freud*, 1980, 93. http://ci.nii.ac.jp/ncid/BA88825888.

12. Dummer, V., and M. Greene. "The Core Personality: Treatment Strategies for Multiple Personality Disorder." In *Readings in Psychosynthesis: Theory, Process, and Practice: Psychotherapy, Self-Care, Education, Health, Religion, Organizational Development, World Order*, edited by John Weiser and Thomas Yeomans. Department of Applied Psychology, Ontario Institute for Studies in Education, 1988.

13. Pollan, Michael. *How to Change Your Mind: What the New Science of Psychedelics Teaches Us About Consciousness, Dying, Addiction, Depression, and Transcendence*. Penguin, 2018, 141.

14. Pollan, *How to Change Your Mind*, 348-9.

15. Richards, William G. *Sacred Knowledge: Psychedelics and Religious Experiences*. Columbia University Press, 2016, xv.

16. Pollan. *How to Change Your Mind*, 41.

17. Grof, Stanislav. "Holotropic Research and Archetypal Astrology." Awaken (blog), May 18, 2020. https://awaken.com/2018/02/holotropic-research-and-archetypal/.

18. Wilber, Ken. *Quantum Questions: Mystical Writings of the World's Great Physicists*. Shambhala, 2001, 3.

19. In particular, the Fundamental Fysiks Group, founded in San Francisco in 1975 by Elizabeth Rauscher and George Weissmann, both graduate students in the Physics Department at UC Berkeley, was instrumental in exploring the philosophical implications of quantum theory. The group, which included Fritjof Capra, Fred Alan Wolf and Nick Herbert, among others, established a more open-minded attitude about the metaphysical dimensions of hard physics, which is something that physicists themselves would

typically not be prepared or willing to discuss. Critics have called the work of the group and other New Age popularizers, "pseudoscience," or worse. Murray Gell-Mann, winner of the 1969 Nobel Prize in Physics, called it "quantum flapdoodle" (on page 8 of Stenger, Victor J. *Quantum Gods: Creation, Chaos, and the Search for Cosmic Consciousness*. Buffalo, NY: Prometheus Books, 2009).

20. Josephson, Brian D. "Pathological Disbelief," June 30, 2004. https://www.repository.cam.ac.uk/handle/1810/247336.

21. Kemp, Daren. *New Age: A Guide: Alternative Spiritualities from Aquarian Conspiracy to Next Age*. Edinburgh University Press, 2004, 1.

22. York, Michael. *The Emerging Network: A Sociology of the New Age and Neo-Pagan Movements*. Rowman & Littlefield, 1995, 1-2.

23. Greene, Liz. *The Astrological Neptune and the Quest for Redemption*. Weiser Books, 2000, 55-64.

24. Davidson, Jessica. "The Jupiter Saturn Conjunction – the Start of a New Age?," February 24, 2022. https://jessicadavidson.co.uk/2020/11/16/the-jupiter-saturn-conjunction-the-start-of-a-new-age/.

25. Carrington, Damian. "Sixth Mass Extinction of Wildlife Accelerating, Scientists Warn." *The Guardian*, October 29, 2021. https://www.theguardian.com/environment/2020/jun/01/sixth-mass-extinction-of-wildlife-accelerating-scientists-warn.

26. Castaneda, Carlos. *The Teachings of Don Juan: A Yaqui Way of Knowledge*. Simon and Schuster, 1973, 121-22. Carlos Castaneda was a controversial figure, considered by some to be a fraud and castigated by many for falsely presenting a fictional account as an anthropological study. Fair enough. And yet, his books have never gone out of print, and continue to sell at a rate that most authors would envy. So clearly, fictional or not, his work contains a kernel of allegorical truth that speaks to people and strikes a collective chord. I think this is true actually, of many of those who tap into some bit of wisdom that doesn't easily lend itself to scientific or strictly academic presentation, which include many seminal thinkers who break the mold, and are then punished for it by those who prefer to walk a more linear and literal path to their truths.

Look at every path closely and deliberately. Then ask yourself, and yourself alone, one question . . . Does this path have a heart? If it does, the path is good; if it doesn't, it is of no use . . . All paths are the same; they lead nowhere. They are paths going through the bush, or into the bush . . . (All) paths lead nowhere, but one has a heart, the other doesn't. One makes for a joyful journey; as long as you follow it, you are one with it. The other will make you curse your life. One makes you strong; the other weakens you.

Carlos Castaneda, The Teachings of Don Juan, 1973

Part Two

Astrology's New Landcape In the Era of Uncertainty

The real true Astrology depended upon a man's attaining this possibility of understanding the Cosmic Intelligences . . . In the epoch during the first centuries after the rise of Christianity this ancient Astrology, that means, intercourse with the Cosmic Intelligences, was already past; but there was still some tradition of it. Men then began to calculate when the stars were in opposition or stood in conjunction, and so on. They still possessed what had come over as tradition from those times when astrologers had intercourse with the Cosmic Intelligences; but, whereas in that epoch, a few centuries after the rise of Christianity, Astrology really had passed away.

Steiner, Rudolf, "Lecture XIII - Vol. 232. Mystery Centers," December 22, 1923

Chapter Eight

The Spiritual Foundations of Psychological Astrology

We will return to a deeper exploration of this new path in Chapter Nine, which parallels the development of psychology as a distinctly postmodern discipline that necessarily moves beyond what a strictly empirical form of science has to offer, into territory that astrologers are already more intimately familiar with. Meanwhile, just as, in the words of Carl Jung, astrology could encompass the psychology of antiquity, so too was there at the beginning of the Era of Uncertainty, a movement to conserve and disseminate the spiritual teachings of antiquity. In addition to the emergence of postmodern psychology, this more overtly spiritual movement provided another kind of foundation for a more transpersonal psychological astrology, or an astrology of soul, for those ready to see it and use it that way.

This was a much larger development, affecting not just the evolution of psychological astrology, but also of the entire spiritual smorgasbord encompassed by, but also transcending New Age teachings. This would be a study worthy of a book unto itself, and is ultimately a bit outside the scope of this one. Necessarily, our focus here will be mostly on those major influences within this larger movement that have made a contribution to our field and have laid a foundation for the possibility of a meaningful soul retrieval for our profession that we will explore in Part Three.

Theosophy

Helena Blavatsky

The first, and some would say primary, stream in this revival of the spiritual teachings of antiquity converged within the theosophical movement. Theosophy was an occult movement, founded by charismatic Russian immigrant Helena Blavatsky, that wove together Western teachings from Gnosticism, Hermeticism and Neoplatonism with Eastern teachings from Hindu and Buddhist sources. Aside from the eclectic nature of the movement, which would presage the postmodern New Age, Theosophy also hearkened back to a more mystical, experiential quest for knowledge as it was practiced in the oral traditions of the Mystical Era. Blavatsky herself claimed to have gathered much of her material through extensive travels and studies with various masters in India, Tibet and the Far East, although contemporary critics and later biographers tend to consider this a fiction.[1,2,3]

In 1875, around the same time that Wilhelm Wundt was establishing the first psychological research facility, Blavatsky founded the Theosophical Society with the journalist and lawyer Henry Steel Olcott and the Irish-American mystic William Quan Judge. The term Theosophy was an amalgam of the Greek *theos* (meaning "gods") and *sophia* (meaning "wisdom"), pointing toward the kind of divine wisdom sought through mystical avenues of knowing. Blavatsky considered herself clairvoyant, clairaudient, and telepathic, learning and refining additional paranormal abilities through her studies with the adepts she met in her travels, in particular the Kashmiri Indian master, Koot Hoomi, with whom she allegedly apprenticed in Tibet.

Blavatsky was, by any measure, a controversial figure. She has been accused of fraud, charlatanism and plagiarism, freely borrowing the ideas and in some cases the verbatim quotations of others without accreditation, as well as distortion of the ideas she appropriated, misstatements, and numerous internal inconsistencies.[4] This is, of course, bad scholarship at best, and questionable duplicity at worst, but it is also very much in the spirit of the postmodern era, especially within New Age circles, in which the entire lexicon of ideas presented throughout previous eras is available, and subject to endless re-interpretation and re-invention. By many accounts, Blavatsky took enough liberties with the ideas that she appropriated that they were rendered unrecognizable by others with knowledge of her sources, although her many devotees would beg to differ.

Religious scholar Mircea Eliade once suggested that her theories about spiritual evolution contradicted the entire spirit of Eastern tradition.[5] Other religious scholars noted that she was repackaging occult tradition for the modern era, and could be forgiven the license that she took in order to do this.[6] Still others felt that despite her numerous flaws, she was "as visible today as any modern trend-setting guru, and she will most likely remain the most memorable and innovative esotericist of the 19th century."[7] She can also be credited as one of the first to turn the gaze of Western seekers to the East, a postmodern development presaging the blossoming interest of New Agers in Eastern religions, yoga and meditation that would take place nearly a century later.

Blavatsky's Attitude Toward Science

In her writings, she sought to integrate science, occult philosophy and Eastern religion, while attacking the science of her day (in the Empirical Era), which she considered too materialistic. Reading Blavatsky, however, it is clear that her defense of theosophy as a "spiritual science" staked its claim through reference to Hermeticism, which would not be considered scientific at all by the empirical standards of her genuinely scientific peers. Nor did she always seem to understand the true nature of science as it was practiced in the Empirical Era in which she lived.

> *Scientists can be fought solely with their own weapons–those of controversy and argument–an Addendum is added to every Book contrasting our respective views and showing how even great authorities may often err. We believe that this can be done effectually by showing the weak points of our opponents, and by proving their too frequent sophisms–made to pass for scientific dicta to be incorrect. We hold to Hermes and his "Wisdom"–in its universal character; they–to Aristotle as against intuition and the experience of the ages, fancying that Truth is the exclusive property of the Western world. Hence the disagreement.*[8]

It is also clear that her actual agenda was not so much to integrate occult philosophy and science, so much as it was to propose occult philosophy as a more relevant contemporary alternative to science. She argued, for example, that because scientists of different persuasions often disagree with each other about the nature of a particular phenomenon, there is room for more esoteric or occult views to exist on an equal footing with them, as science.

> *The present writer, claiming no great scientific education, but only a tolerable acquaintance with modern theories, and a better one with Occult Sciences, picks up weapons against the detractors of the esoteric teaching in the very arsenal of modern Science. The glaring contradictions, the mutually destructive hypotheses of world-renowned Scientists, their mutual accusations, denunciations and disputes, show plainly that, whether accepted or not, the Occult theories have as much right to a hearing as any of the so-called learned and academical hypotheses.*[9]

This is a case that could be more easily made in either the Philosophical Era, in which scientific theories vied and intermingled with metaphysical worldviews on a level playing field, or in the Logical Era, in which the science of Aristotle would have allowed a consideration of Occult theories, with their metaphysical underpinnings, on the basis of the logical arguments that could be made in their defense. It was not a viewpoint that would hold water in the Empirical Era in which she asserted it, although in the Era of Uncertainty, dawning just after her death – in which science is just one of many possible ways of seeing and understanding reality – it again gained some new traction among postmodern New Age seekers.

Part of her argument rested on the presumption, also popular in some New Age circles, that since occultists had access to information that scientists had not yet discovered, or were not capable of understanding, esoteric practices such as magic or the mystical tradition were, in fact, sciences in their own right – an argument that would today be dismissed as pseudo-scientific for reasons outlined in the Introduction.[10]

Taken as a whole, her arguments strike me as somewhat reminiscent of the endlessly futile debate between scientifically-minded astrologers and their biased debunkers, straddling the line between science and pseudoscience, each one arguing for the right to declare where the boundary should be drawn. Within her broader defense of spiritual science, Blavatsky gave both a green light and a challenge to would-be astrological scientific astrologers in declaring that:

> *Astrology is a science as infallible as astronomy itself, with the condition, however, that its interpreters must be equally infallible; and it is this condition, sine qua non, so very difficult of realization that has always proved a stumbling block to both . . . In astrology and psychology, one has to step beyond the visible world of matter, and enter into the domain of the transcendent spirit.*[11]

Here, Blavatsky's reference to science hearkens back to the Mystical Era, in which the clarity of the message depended upon the spiritual development of the messenger, and his capacity to receive divine instruction without distortion. This was a requirement that followed hermetic practitioners of astrological magic through the Philosophical and Logical Eras, and that to some extent, has been preserved within the New Age, in its emphasis on personal growth and self-transformation. It is an admonition largely abandoned by the science against which Blavatsky rails, despite the recognition by individual scientists from earlier eras to cutting edge "fringe scientists" in the Era of Uncertainty that the clarity of vision of the one who sees, matters. In practice, it is a possibility largely forgotten by most contemporary astrologers - no doubt, with exceptions - whether they consider themselves scientifically-minded or not.

The Theosophical Influence on the Development of Astrology

Be that as it may, Blavatsky and the Theosophical movement have had a huge, now largely forgotten influence on the development of astrology in the Era of Uncertainty, directly through individual astrologers such as Alan Leo, Alice Bailey, Charles E. O. Carter, Marc Edmund Jones, Dane Rudhyar, Alexander Ruperti and successive generations of twentieth century astrologers that were, in turn, influenced mostly by Dane Rudhyar. Astrologer Robert Hand asserts that:

> *Madame Blavatsky simply repackaged Neoplatonism in a somewhat polarized form with lots of Sanskrit terminology, but her worldview is basically Neoplatonic and most spiritual astrology is descended directly or indirectly from her.*[12]

Although there are astrological references sprinkled throughout Blavatsky's work, especially *The Secret Doctrine*, Blavatsky herself was not an astrologer,[13] nor did she provide much by way of practical information to actual astrologers, wanting to apply her esoteric principles, even if they did have the patience to wade through her weighty and often inscrutable tomes. It was primarily those that followed that took her mystical sensibilities about the possibility of knowing with the clarity of a science into the astrological realm.

Blavatsky's personal astrologer was British Theosophist Walter Gorn Old, better known as Sepharial, and dubbed by her as the "Astral Tramp."[14] Sepharial lived with Madame Blavatsky for a time and was with her when she died. He published a number of books, which are still in print, and was well respected in his day, but he did not have the impact on the astrological world that his younger contemporary Alan Leo – who was influenced by him – did, probably for the same reasons that certain astrologers rise into prominence today, while others equally worthy languish in backwater eddies: internal organizational politics, in this case, of the Theosophical Society.[15]

Alan Leo

Be that as it may, the seminal astrologer at the dawn of the Era of Uncertainty was Sepharial's contemporary, British Theosophist Alan Leo. As noted by Annie Besant in the foreword to a memorial biography written after his death by his wife:

> *His love for this ancient and much maligned science was only second to his love for Theosophy, and indeed they were so interwoven in his thought, they so permeated his life, that one can scarcely speak of first and second . . . He was one of the foremost in raising Astrology from fortune-telling to a scientific forecasting of conditions, a delineation of tendencies in a character, a map of the personal nature, and a wide outlook on coming evolution.*[16]

Leo is generally credited with popularizing astrology for the masses through an introduction via Sun signs, but beyond that with attempting to shift the astrological community as a whole away from prediction and toward what subsequently became psychological astrology – the study of "tendencies" instead of "fortunes." As quoted by astrologer Patrick Curry, at a trial for which Leo was acquitted of the crime of using astrology to tell fortunes, he was reputed to have said:

> *Let us part company with the fatalistic astrologer who prides himself on his predictions and who is ever seeking to convince the world that in the predictive side of Astrology alone shall we find its value. We need not argue the point as to its reality, but instead make a much-needed change in the word and call Astrology the science of tendencies.*[17]

Leo was tried again a few years later for the same crime and convicted, then died a few years after that as he was attempting to recover from the stress of the trial. We should note here that Leo's intent in shifting the focus of astrology in this way went deeper than the current association of sun signs with pop psychology might suggest. His interest in the Sun, rather stemmed from Blavatsky's emphasis on the Solar Logos as the source of divine reason, for which astrology was potentially, the premier language.[18] Leo also believed in a coming New Age, for which he felt an astrologically-assisted deepening of self-knowledge would help prepare us.

We can also notice here that Leo, who discovered astrology as a young man, toward the end of the Empirical Era, considered astrology a science. Presumably, as a Theosophist, he took his ideas about this, in part, from Blavatsky's insistence on moving the line of demarcation into the realm of mysticism and ancient esoteric lore, of which, in her view, astrology was part. But he also hearkened back to the Ptolemaic idea that the mechanism behind the workings of astrology was, in fact, causal, and therefore scientific, or at least what would have been considered scientific in the Philosophical and Logical Eras. According to Leo's take at the turn of the twentieth century, astrology was ". . . the science which defines the action of celestial bodies upon human character, and its expression in the physical world."[19]

This sensibility was passed on to those in the Era of Uncertainty, who continue to insist that astrology is a science, despite the fact that science and astrology have both moved on from this point, several hundred years ago, when that was still true. Meanwhile, it is also worth noting that the actual "science" to which Leo does refer, elucidated throughout theosophical writing, is in essence, an attempt to resurrect and reclaim a more direct way of knowing from the Mystical Era, and adapt it to a more contemporary culture. To call it "science" is to court confusion, but to call it forth as a counterbalance to the dominance of science is very much in line with our agenda in this book, as it will be presented in Part Three.

Alice Bailey

While the more overtly popularized theosophical teachings regarding astrology that were hinted at in the work of Madame Blavatsky were propagated by Alan Leo, the deeper esoteric teachings themselves were elaborated and extended by a younger contemporary of Leo, the British-born American Alice Bailey, particularly in Volume Three of her five-volume series, *Treatise on the Seven Rays*. In the spirit of prior mystical traditions, Bailey claimed these teachings were passed on to her telepathically by the Tibetan Master Djwhal Khul, who first appeared in Madame Blavatsky's *The Secret Doctrine*, among other Mahatmas, or ascended masters.

Bailey was eventually booted out of the Theosophical Society over political conflicts with society president Annie Besant, among them the authenticity of her supposed connection to the Tibetan Master. After that, Bailey retained her respect for Blavatsky's teachings, but formed her own organizations, the Arcane School and the Lucis Trust, to promote her elaboration of theosophical ideas, among them a form of esoteric astrology, focused on the evolution of the soul, and overcoming obstacles to that evolution, as revealed in the birthchart. Inevitably, her teachings took on their own flavor, with fundamental differences from

Blavatsky's, unnecessary to elaborate here, which in their own right, influenced both New Age and neopagan schools of thought, as well as the psychology of Roberto Assagioli.[20]

Alan Oken

The astrological teachings of Alice Bailey have been most reverently preserved in the writings of contemporary astrologer, Alan Oken, also influenced by Assagioli, Jung, and other Jungian astrologers.[21] In his work, Oken attempts to outline an astrology of the soul, as an intermediary between the realm of Spirit and everyday life on the material plane, discussing the seven rays (a cornerstone of Bailey's teachings) and how they manifest in the birthchart, as well as the more spiritual dimension of each of the signs.

> *The astrologer of the New Age must be able to distinguish not only the shades of meaning inherent in the positions of the planets by signs, houses, and geometric aspects, but to "read" the level of consciousness through which the planetary energies are operating.*[22]

The ability to "read" a chart, according to Oken, depends upon intuition, which in turn depends upon "an intimate contact with the thought-forms contained within the symbols of the twelve signs;" "an attunement to the nature of the life forces in our solar system as they work through the planets;" "a comprehension of the Ray energies, and then an attunement to their essential natures;" and lastly, "an attunement to those mutations in the collective consciousness which affect us all."[23] Within Oken's concept of attunement, it is easy to hear the call to the kind of receptivity to direct communication with the Divine that would have informed the divinatory astrology of the Mystical Era, as well as the telepathic teachings of Alice Bailey in direct communication with Djwhal Khul.

Rudolf Steiner

The Theosophical Society had a profound influence on another seminal figure in the development of ideas supporting a more direct, mystical way of knowing – Austrian esoteric philosopher Rudolf Steiner. Steiner began his career as an academic, studying and writing extensively about the work of other philosophers such as Goethe, Schopenhauer and Nietzsche. From an early age, however, Steiner had also had a number of clairvoyant experiences, out of which arose an interest in the spiritual dimension of philosophical teachings, that eventually evolved into his own more overtly spiritual philosophy called "anthroposophy."

Like theosophy, anthroposophy was essentially meant to be a path of inquiry that brought the clarity of the scientific method to spiritual experience. It sought to explore the middle ground between mysticism and science, by which he really meant the kind of rational clarity that was sought in the Logical Era, when Aristotle was the source of a more metaphysically-based science. While Blavatsky sought to reconcile her idea of a spiritual science with Eastern religions, particularly Buddhism, Steiner was an esoteric Christian working along different philosophical fault lines.

As a spokesperson for the Era of Uncertainty, although he would not have called himself that, Steiner bemoaned the intellectualization of science, which had lost all connection to the imaginative and intuitive capacities through which spiritual revelation was possible. On the other hand, he felt that mysticism lacked sufficient clarity to lead to accurate, reliable and useful knowledge. Steiner traced science's loss of soul to the rise of mathematics as its primary language, through which deeper spiritual sensibilities were reduced to calculated sums.

As noted in Chapter Four, this was largely a development in the evolution of science that became a central feature of the Empirical Era into which Steiner was born, so like Blavatsky, Steiner's idea of an "ideal" science stemmed back to an earlier age. Steiner considered science to be "a logic which educates itself by the facts of nature" and felt that "spiritual science" took this logic into a realm beyond what could be measured by empirical science in its dependence on sensory data.[24] Like Blavatsky, Steiner's spiritual science was essentially a return to the more distinct possibility of direct gnosis common in the Mystical Era, but one that also sought to illuminate mysticism with the clarity of logic that was a hallmark of Aristotelian science in the Logical Era.

Astrosophy

Like Blavatsky, Steiner was not a practicing astrologer, although he spoke in passing about astrology, mostly in connection with the precession of the equinoxes and the evolution of human consciousness in relation to the twelve zodiacal phases of the 26,000-year cycle of the Platonic Year. He believed that the planets were "the dwelling-place of a host of spiritual beings, and created only according to the needs of the spiritual beings that live on them,"[25] elsewhere considering them to be the "forsaken bodies of the gods, whose souls carry on their activities in a new manner in the world, independent of these bodies."[26] Steiner also used a knowledge of the Moon's position relative to the constellations as an integral part of his biodynamic farming methods.[27]

Steiner believed that only the most evolved beings could work with astrology as a language of communion with the divine, and that most practicing astrologers of his day did not have the requisite level of attainment.[28] The astrology of which Steiner spoke was not the astrology of his time, but rather one that, like his science, had its heyday in the Mystical Era, when it formed an important component of a spiritual practice that prepared one to receive divine guidance.

Ancient Astrology was not pursued with the abstract calculations of to-day, but with an atavistic clairvoyant power.[29]

The real true Astrology depended upon a man's attaining this possibility of understanding the Cosmic Intelligences . . . In the epoch during the first centuries after the rise of Christianity this ancient Astrology, that means, intercourse with the Cosmic Intelligences, was already past; but there was still some tradition of it. Men then began to calculate when the stars were in opposition or stood in conjunction, and so on. They still possessed what had come over as tradition from those times when astrologers had intercourse with the Cosmic Intelligences; but, whereas in that epoch, a few centuries after the rise of Christianity, Astrology really had passed away.[30]

Steiner's idea of astrology was further developed in a more fully elucidated way and reinterpreted for the Era of Uncertainty by his students, beginning with the Dutch mathematician and astronomer, Elisabeth Vreede, and later with the German astrologer Willi Sucher.

Elisabeth Vreede

Vreede's impact within the astrological world has been minimal, although her work was preserved in a book of letters written to members of the Theosophical Society from 1927 – 1930. These letters, taken as a whole, were really more of an attempt to address her seminal philosophical observation that:

Astronomical science is devoid of spirituality, but must once again be permeated with it. Astrology permeates an ancient spirituality that no longer has the same value for our own times. True astrosophy is at present not to be found outside Rudolf Steiner's spiritual science. Astrosophy is at one and the same time the goal of an anthroposophical science of the cosmos and its starting point.[31]

The letters proceed to elucidate a possible anthroposophical approach to astronomy, that is to say, one that infuses astronomical phenomena – celestial rhythms, the sun, moon and planets, eclipses, the precession of the equinoxes, meteors and comments – with a spiritual understanding absent from mainstream astronomy. She ultimately has little to say about the actual practice of astrosophy – anthroposophical astrology – other than to bemoan the loss of the sensibilities that guided astrologers in the Mystical Era. She suggests, though not showing how, that it was these same sensibilities in relation to the planetary beings and the spiritual reality of the constellations marking one's birth that held the key to it.[32]

Willi Sucher

Willi Sucher met Elizabeth Vreede at a lecture she gave in Switzerland in 1927 and was inspired by a remark she made quoting Steiner about the importance of the death chart. Over the next ten years, he became more active in Anthroposophical circles, eventually moving to England in 1937, where he started working intensively with the charts of handicapped children in Sunfield Home, a Camphill community, where anthroposophical principles were applied to their healing and rehabilitation. Until his death in 1985, in addition to his ongoing work with children, Sucher wrote a number of books and lectured extensively.

Like Vreede, Sucher bemoaned the loss of sensibilities that were the basis for astrology in the Mystical Era, as well as the absence of metaphysical considerations in modern science. Unlike Vreede, however, Sucher was a working astrologer, whose writing describes the practical application of anthroposophical principles to the birthchart. He worked with prenatal and death charts, as well as natal charts, and toward the end of his life, began to shift from geocentric to heliocentric astrology.

While there is much of value in his work, even though it would be somewhat foreign to most Western astrologers, working with natal charts, the tropical zodiac, and geocentric positions, it is mostly a sincere attempt to resurrect and apply the techniques developed by Egyptian, Chaldean and Babylonian astrologers from the Mystical Era, and the early Hellenistic astrologers of the Philosophical Era who derived their inspiration from the mystical tradition. There seems to be less of an attempt to teach interested astrologers, mostly those with an anthroposophical bent, how to directly access their own understanding through mystical communion with the source of knowledge, as it was practiced by those who "read" the divine writing in the sky.

Current anthroposophical astrologers include Brian Gray, Robert Schiappacasse and David Tresemer, who together teach a webinar in Western sidereal astrology based in anthroposophy.[33] UK astrologer Robert Powell has founded the Choreocosmos School of Cosmic and Sacred Dance, where Steiner's development of eurythmy (movement and music) serves as a point of experiential entry into the elements, the planets, and the signs of the zodiac.[34]

Perhaps the most well-known of the current anthroposophical astrologers is Ellias Lonsdale, who first studied with Marc Edmond Jones and Dane Rudhyar, but had his real epiphany after encountering the work of Rudolf Steiner and Will Sucher.[35] Lonsdale developed his own mystery school in the mountains outside of Santa Cruz, California, after a "prophetic dream took him back to the mystery temples of Atlantis, where he merged with an ancient past self and his origin in the star mysteries." He returned from the dream with a teaching he called "Star Genesis, the inner wisdom of the stars and their direct guidance from Christ and Sophia, a myriad of spirit sources and angels – all who represent the planets, the constellations, and the degree frequencies that live and speak within us." He continues to teach this work as a form of direct mystical connection with astrological truths through a series of telecourses.[36]

The Work

George Gurdjieff

Another seminal spiritual teacher at the dawn of the Era of Uncertainty was the Russian mystic George Gurdjieff. Like Madame Blavatsky, Gurdjieff was a charismatic, albeit controversial figure, called a charlatan by some, hailed by others as a master teacher, advancing our collective understanding of human nature, and our place within a mysterious cosmos. Also, like Blavatsky, Gurdjieff's teachings were claimed to have been derived from various teachers he met in his extensive travels throughout central Asia, Egypt, Iran, Tibet and Rome – travels documented in his autobiography, *Meetings with Remarkable Men.*

> *From my point of view, he can be called a remarkable man, who stands out from those around him by the resourcefulness of his mind, and who knows how to be restrained in the manifestations which proceed from his nature, at the same time conducting himself justly and tolerantly towards the weaknesses of others.*[37]

In particular, Gurdjieff was most impressed by the Sarmoun Brotherhood, "a famous esoteric school which, according to tradition, was founded in Babylon as far back as 2,500 BC, and which was known to have existed somewhere in Mesopotamia up to the sixth or seventh century AD."[38] Some scholars consider the existence of the Sarmoun Brotherhood to be a fiction, and indeed Gurdjieff's own account is often a bit of a rambling shaggy dog story, somewhat sketchy and vague.[39] An associate of contemporary Sufi teacher Idries Shah associates the Sarmouni (slightly different spelling) with the Amudaria dervishes in central Asia and Afghanistan and claims to have met nonagenarians among them with memories of "Jurjizada" (Gurdjieff).[40]

According to J. G. Bennett, one of Gurdjieff's most notable students, Sarmoun is the Persian word for "bee," "which has always been a symbol of those who collect the precious 'honey' of traditional wisdom and preserve it for further generations."[41] In particular, the Sarmoun were charged with the task of preserving the wisdom of the Zoroastrian tradition, out of which some say, Sufism first arose as a mystical path separate from Islam with which it has since become associated.[42] In another interpretation of this reference to the name, the idea of work (as in worker bees) is said to produce a "sweet essence," with work, in this case, meaning not just the work of guarding and preserving tradition, but also work on oneself – work toward a true knowledge of the self and toward the enlightenment that comes through self-knowledge.[43]

Gurdjieff taught that most humans are asleep, living their lives unconsciously, but that it is possible to awaken and cultivate a soul through the hard work of self-remembering, self-observation (akin to what Buddhists call "mindfulness" or others have called "witnessing"), and rebalancing body, mind and heart. Gurdjieff outlined a pathway to the realization of this possibility that he called "The Work," which in addition to the self-awareness practices mentioned above, included a combination of hard physical labor, lectures, music and sacred dance, but that was also individually adapted to each student's unique requirements.

Gurdjieff and Astrology

Gurdjieff was aware of the potential value of astrology, but like Blavatsky and Steiner, felt that the astrology of his day was a pale imitation of what it was during the Mystical Era, from which he, too, drew his inspiration. He argued that the focus on rational thinking that evolved among the Greeks in what I am calling the Philosophical and Logical Eras destroyed a more valuable way of knowing, "something akin to mythical thinking based on the use of images."[44]

He specifically mentions, magic, alchemy and astrology as symbolic means through which a deeper knowledge of oneself and one's connection to the cosmos can be explored, but anticipating Jung and Hillman, he warns that a symbol can never be fully understood by the rational mind, or articulated in a logical way, or taken literally without becoming rigid or lifeless, and that it can deceive as well as illuminate:

> *Pure knowledge cannot be transmitted, but by being expressed in symbols it is covered by them as by a veil, although at the same time for those who desire and who know how to look this veil becomes transparent.*[45]

As is true of the other seminal spiritual teachers at the dawn of the Era of Uncertainty, Gurdjieff himself was not an astrologer. The Irish historian of Western esotericism Sophia Wellbeloved, however, argues that his teachings were fundamentally based in astrology, rooted in ideas developed by Hellenistic astrologers in the Philosophical Era, but with sensibilities that derived from the earlier divinatory approach of the Mystical Era:

> *Gurdjieff's two primary cosmological laws, the Law of Seven and the Law of Three, have their origins in Mesopotamian astronomy/astrology, echoes of which are also found in Judaism, Christianity, Hinduism, Islam, and in Western European occult and esoteric thinking derived from Pythagoras. Gurdjieff applies a synthesis of ideas derived from Pythagoras' relation of the musical octave to the ratio of distances between the seven known planets of the ancient world to his own Law of Seven, which is also known as the Law of Octaves. All events or actions throughout the universe are the result of the interaction of three forces: the positive/active, the negative/*

passive, and the reconciling that may be either active or passive. These forces can be equated in astrological terms with the cardinal, fixed, and mutable modes.[46]

According to Wellbeloved, Gurdjieff also apparently used the zodiac as an invisible thematic structure in his writing, incorporating myths and symbols associated with the signs and their ruling planets to represent a hidden depiction both of the evolutionary solar journey of the soul, and the involutionary (backward) flow of time, as it related astrologically to the precession of the equinoxes through the Platonic Year.

Gurdjieff and Science

Like Blavatsky and Steiner, Gurdjieff sought to integrate a forgotten esoteric knowledge with modern science. Unlike Blavatsky and Steiner, Gurdjieff appeared to have some actual scientific knowledge, particularly of medicine. There are references to physical, medical and psychological experiments in each of Gurdjieff's texts, and also in the records of his group meetings during World War II, perhaps as a nod to the science of the Empirical Era. In his insistence on critical thinking skills in his students, and precise language with which to discuss his theory of cosmic levels, material density, speeds of vibrations, and the complex analysis of the digestion of food, among other occult topics, he adheres to an earlier standard of Aristotelian logic that would have informed the science of the previous Logical Era.

However, much of this apparently scientific mode of teaching belongs to 'occult science' a re-definition of the occult which arose after the Enlightenment. Where previously the teachings, unaccepted by established Christianity, had become occult religions, these now became occult sciences.[47]

Like Blavatsky and Steiner, Gurdjieff influenced many people and introduced Western culture to many ideas that became bedrock among countless New Age practitioners of all stripes and persuasions, who have largely forgotten this legacy. In his day, he also had many influential followers, most of whom were not astrologers per se, but some – like P. D. Ouspensky and J. G. Bennett, who were fluent in the language and incorporated it into their cosmological musings.

Rodney Collin

In 1954, one of Ouspensky's primary students, British author Rodney Collin, wrote an influential book called *The Theory of Celestial Influences*, which was an ambitious attempt to integrate astronomy, quantum physics, chemistry, human physiology, astrology and world history. An anonymous reviewer in Gurdjieff International Review writes:

Out of this idea there emerges a theory of human types which is an amalgam of Gurdjieff, Ouspensky, and Collin's own interpretations of astrology. The fundamental astrological idea is retained, but linked to Louis Berman's (1929) views of endocrinologically determined character patterns, on the one hand, and to the Gurdjieffian cosmology on the other. Collin attempts to synthesize these markedly different and even incompatible levels of knowledge through use of the mysterious Gurdjieffian symbol of the enneagram.[48]

Although on the surface, it appears that Collin offers a pathway into a scientific study of astrological influences, assuming Ptolemy's theory of celestial causation as a starting point, Collin offers no empirical evidence for his correlations between planets and endocrine glands, other than to suggest that "true understanding of the glands can only develop from direct study of their individual action *in oneself* (italic emphasis is mine)."[49] This a subjective form of research that would not be recognized by empirical science, but that is nonetheless possibly useful for the cultivation of astrological self-knowledge in the Era of Uncertainty. His thesis, however brilliant it might be in places, however, is essentially an argument that would have been more at home in the Logical Era than one that does or could hold scientific water in the Era of Uncertainty, where science still largely clings to empirical standards and insists on statistical validation.

Dennis Elwell

Another astrologer influenced by Gurdjieff, among many other sources, is Dennis Elwell, author of *Cosmic Loom: The New Science of Astrology*, first published in 1987. In the grand tradition of the seminal occult teachers of the late nineteenth and early twentieth century studied in this chapter, Elwell's efforts are ostensibly about presenting astrology as a science, but seem more earnestly directed at getting intelligent readers to consider the occult – that which is largely invisible and cannot be measured scientifically – as a valid source of information. His work does not provide empirical or statistical evidence for astrology's validity within the context of the current definition of science.

Like many of his peers, Elwell argues that quantum physics has opened a window into the possibility of understanding how astrology works. But like so many other astrologers who take this view, he doesn't seem to recognize that what an actual physicist sees through that window, necessarily framed by the strictures of science such as it is, would necessarily be different than what an astrologer sees. In other places, he proposes more specific mechanisms, rooted in quantum science, by which astrology might be understood – such as "backward causation"[50] – that have their own theoretical and empirical difficulties establishing themselves as scientific fact.[51] Meanwhile, he has been roundly castigated by Geoffrey Dean and company,[52] with whom he engaged, before his death in 2014, in the standard vitriolic back-and-forth that goes nowhere, as noted in the Introduction to this book.[53]

Elwell is a well-respected astrologer, an original thinker, and there is much within his work that I agree with. But as with most Era of Uncertainty thinkers who see the potential for science to one day evolve to the place where astrology can again have a place at the table, while bemoaning the loss of astrology's vitality in prior eras, when it would have had such a place, if only it hadn't gone astray, I think Elwell strains too hard to make his case. I do agree with him when he says.

> *If we accept that it is science's place to pronounce the final word on whether astrology is or is not valid (and that, I think, is a very big if) then, it seems to me, the researchers have a point. Astrology as most of us practice it today has not performed well in most scientific tests. And we need to face this fact before we can progress – whether this 'progress' consists in the formulation of more relevant tests, or in the conclusion that, whatever astrology is, it cannot be tested and measured in the same way as simple physical processes.*[54]

In the nearly 35 years since *Cosmic Loom* was written, more relevant tests have not been forthcoming. I think it is time we move on with his second possibility and begin to explore on what basis astrology might stand in its own right, not as a science, but as a very different way of knowing, of peering into the heart of the "occult," the invisible and intangible realms that elude a science that is not capable and may never be, of admitting their existence. Yes, there is a huge body of anecdotal evidence from the cumulative experience of astrologers down through the ages doing just that, that cannot be dismissed as irrelevant. But as substantial as this is, this is not what has passed for science since the days of Aristotle, so it is time to stop embarrassing ourselves by pretending that it still is or should be.

Meanwhile, we can note before moving on that Gurdjieff has not been a major influence on the development of astrology in the Era of Uncertainty, although certain of his teachings – such as the idea of awakening as a metaphor for the process of spiritual development, as well as the necessity for self-awareness and work on oneself – have become standard tenets of the New Age canon, to which most psychological astrologers probably subscribe as an *a priori* cornerstone of their craft.

Magick

Aleister Crowley

A fourth occult teacher, who contributed to astrology's metaphysical foundation in the Era of Uncertainty, was the ceremonial magician, poet, painter, novelist and mountaineer, Aleister Crowley. British historian Richard Cavendish has called Crowley, "the best-equipped magician to emerge since the seventeenth century."[55] Others associate him with the dark side of the occult,[56] or even with Satanism, which ultimately was probably more a reaction to his fairly wild and profligate life than to his actual teachings,[57] his vehement dislike of Christianity,[58] and/or his "self-confident, brash, eccentric, egotistic, highly intelligent, arrogant, witty, wealthy, and, when it suited him, cruel" personality.[59] Like Blavatsky, Steiner and Gurdjieff, Crowley was a controversial figure, whose commanding charismatic presence and strong opinions tended to elicit a polarized response.

At age 23, Crowley joined the Hermetic Order of the Golden Dawn, where he learned both ceremonial magic and astrology. The Hermetic Order was an occult society and school founded in 1887 by three Freemasons – William Robert Woodman, William Wynn Wescott and Samuel Liddell Matthews – that taught an esoteric philosophy based in part on the Kabalah of Jewish mysticism, and in part on a form of theurgic magic, stemming back to the teachings of Iamblichus. Many famous people were at one time or another associated with the order, including the Irish poet William Butler Yeats, Sir Arthur Conan Doyle (author of *Sherlock Holmes*), Bram Stoker (author of *Dracula*), and Evelyn Underhill (author of the classic *Mysticism: A Study in Nature and Development of Spiritual Consciousness*).

As with many organizations of this kind, the Hermetic Order was plagued by internal politics, rivalries and scandals, and after a battle over Crowley's initiation into the second of three levels of attainment, Crowley left the school and formed his own – called Thelema – after receiving the transmission of a sacred text called *The Book of the Law* from a disembodied entity called Alwass. Crowley also traveled through India and China, where he studied Hindu and Buddhist practices, and was eventually initiated into a second order, the German school Ordo Templi Orientis – all of which he eventually incorporated into his own teachings at Thelema.

Crowley and Science

The magic that Crowley taught was in part, an exercise in the art of causing change at will, and in part, a collaboration with beings that exist on a higher plane than ours, an approach that he understood as a kind of practical mysticism.[60] Like the other occult teachers discussed in this chapter, Crowley aspired for his magic to rise to the level of a science, envisioning an integration of the occult with the experimental method of the Empirical Era – an amalgam he called "magick."[61]

In practice, however, this meant merely encouraging magicians to keep detailed records of their "experiments" – which might have been considered good Aristotelian science in the Logical Era, but wouldn't have cut the mustard in the more rigorous Empirical Era in which he lived and taught. Science for Crowley essentially meant a careful process of learning from one's own experiences, one that is not out of line with the approach that I will suggest in Part Three, but that unlike Crowley, I would not call "science."

As seems to be the pattern here, among all occultists of the late Empirical Era, whose teachings have had their greatest influence in the Era of Uncertainty, there is a nostalgic resurrection and revival of traditions largely rooted in the Mystical Era. With the benefit of postmodern hindsight, there is also a recognition of the importance of the clarity potentially brought to mystical experiences by the analytical practices of the Logical Era, practices that once were considered scientific, but that haven't been for nearly four hundred years.

Crowley and Astrology

In astrological circles, Crowley is best known for ghost-writing two books for Evangeline Adams – *Astrology: Your Place in the Sun* (1927) and *Astrology: Your Place Among the Stars* (1930). While Adams did contribute to both books, particularly the technical chapters about casting a horoscope, the style and tone of the books, as well as their substance, steeped in magical lore and occult philosophy, were Crowley's.[62] Crowley received no credit or compensation for his effort, and the two parted company on bitter terms. His own astrological work was collated and published in 2002 as *The General Principles of Astrology*, and before that, as part of a compilation of his astrological writings called *Aleister Crowley: The Complete Astrological Writings*, including *A Treatise on Astrology (Libre 536)* – an earlier version of the material that appeared in Adams' books, along with a couple of additional essays, one of which is actually of more interest for our purposes here.

According to the editors of the compilation, Crowley's interest in astrology was incidental to his magical practice:

> *This meant that he was less concerned with astrology as a predictive science than as a means of assessing for magical ends his own relationships with people. Astrology therefore played a minor role in his activities.*[63]

Similarly, Crowley's influence on the astrological community itself is also fairly minor, although he continues to be a major influence within contemporary esoteric, magical and neopagan circles, where ceremonial astrology plays an important role, and no doubt individual astrologers within those communities likely count Crowley among their sources of astrological inspiration. Crowley's take on astrology is interesting, as it weaves together an extensive knowledge of the occult, mythology, tarot and the Kabbalah with astrological lore. Despite the fact that Crowley was not first and foremost an astrologer, his legacy also encompasses a fair amount of wisdom about the practice of astrology that can only come through extensive experience with birthcharts.

What is most relevant here, however, is taken from a much smaller work with the unlikely title of "Batrachophrenoboocosmomachia," from *A Treatise on Astrology, Liber 536*.[64] In this essay, Crowley discusses the magical practice of expanding consciousness to commune directly with stars and planets, a practice that would hearken back to the astrology of the Mystical Era. Even if it was not his primary focus, Crowley was, unlike the other seminal occultists of the day, an actual astrologer, who understood the necessity for approaching the art as more than just an intellectual exercise, and who gave a few techniques for entering into a state of astrological gnosis.

Crowley's methodology is relatively simple, and probably deceptively so, consisting of three meditations. The first involves learning to count at a glance a number of similar objects cast on a table and hastily retrieved by an assistant. The second involves constructing a complete mental image of one's surroundings with eyes closed, adding objects one at a time until the image is an exact replica of what one would see with eyes open, including objects at the farthest reaches of one's peripheral vision. And the third is to mentally construct, one planet at a time, an exact replica of the solar system, eventually adding stars, comets and other celestial objects.

How exactly this prepares a student of astrology to commune with stars and planets is presumably something to be discovered by those engaging in the practice, which is meant to take a year or more. The point is that for Crowley, astrology was not just a matter of interpretation, but of intentionally entering into an expanded state of consciousness in which a different order of knowledge would become available. It was, within the overall context of his teaching, an aspect of the spiritual training necessary to become a magical adept.

As Crowley notes, perhaps speaking of the astrologer who pursues this deeper knowledge:

> *The astrologer is more frank than the professor of other sciences. He does not endeavor to conceal his ignorance beneath an elaborately embroidered cloak of metaphysical phrases. He is content to accept the dictum of the Schoolmen,* omnia exeunt in mysterium *(everything ends in mystery), by which they meant that if you follow any idea far enough – if you keep on asking how and why and what, instead of resting contented with a superficial, half-way explanation, the result is always the same. You reach the blank wall of the inconceivable.*[65]

It is at this blank wall – the place where the mind has exhausted its resources and yet there is more to explore and understand – that the true journey begins. This is the nature of the occult, the place of hidden knowledge that all of these teachers, each in their own way, were encouraging their students to go. It was essentially the place that our mythopoetic and mystical forebearers went, because they had not yet been enchanted by the spell of reason.

Since then, reason has given rise, among other gifts, to the logical astrology we have inherited from the Hellenistic Greeks, and having received that gift, we certainly don't want to throw it away. As the occult teachers briefly surveyed in this chapter have reminded us, however, the true practice of astrology goes beyond logic, back to a time and a way of relating to the cosmos, where the rational mind was only one tool, and not necessarily the best, for entering into a deeper conversation with the reality behind the birthchart. Sorting through the *hocus pocus* surrounding occult teachings, while no doubt interesting to some, is less important for our purposes here, than taking this one teaching to heart, and finding a distinctly astrological way to achieve it. The logical astrology passed down to us from the Greeks can help us articulate what we know as we look at a birthchart, but to be truly useful to an evolving soul the knowing itself must ultimately come from a more mystical, mythopoetic communion with the divine intelligence at the heart of the cosmos.

Notes

1. Campbell, Bruce F. *Ancient Wisdom Revived: A History of the Theosophical Movement*. Berkeley: University of California Press, 1980.
2. Washington, Peter. *Madame Blavatsky's Baboon: Theosophy and the Emergence of the Western Guru*. London: Secker & Warburg, 1993.
3. Goodrick-Clarke, Nicholas. *Helena Blavatsky*. Berkeley: North Atlantic Books, 2004.
4. Coleman, William Emmette. "The Sources of Madame Blavatsky's Writings." Blavatsky Study Center. Accessed June 12, 2023. https://www.blavatskyarchives.com/colemansources1895.htm.
5. Oldmeadow, Harry. *Journeys East: 20th Century Western Encounters with Eastern Religious Traditions*. Bloomington, IN: World Wisdom, 2004, 131.
6. Ellwood, Robert. "Review of Nicholas Goodrick-Clarke's Helena Blavatsky." *Nova Religio: The Journal of Alternative and Emergent Religions* 9, no. 2 (2005), 110.
7. Santucci, James A. "Blavatsky, Helena Petrovna." In *The Dictionary of Gnosis & Western Esotericism*, edited by Wouter J. Hanegraaff. Leiden, Netherlands: Brill Academic Publishers, 2006, 184.

8. Blavatsky, Helena. *The Secret Doctrine*, 1888, 278-79. https://www.ultindia.org/books/SecretDoctrineVol1.pdf.

9. Blavatsky, *The Secret Doctrine*, 482-84.

10. Blavatsky, Helena. *Collected Writings, Vol. 1*, edited by Boris De Zirkoff. Wheaton, IL: Theosophical Publishing House, 1977, 137.

11. Blavatsky, Helena. *Isis Unveiled: Secrets of the Ancient Wisdom Tradition*. Pasadena, CA: Theosophical University Press, 1976, 259.

12. Hand, Robert. "Ep. 12 Transcript: Reconciling Modern and Traditional Astrology." Interview by Chris Brennan. The Astrology Podcast, November 7, 2021. https://theastrologypodcast.com/transcripts/ep-12-reconciling-modern-and-traditional-astrology/.

13. Campion, Nicholas. *A History of Western Astrology Volume II: The Medieval and Modern Worlds*. Bloomsbury, 2009, 230.

14. Farnell, Kim. *The Astral Tramp: A Biography of Sepharial*. London: Acella Publications, 1998.

15. Hesselink, Katinka. "Review of The Astral Tramp, A Biography of Sepharial," 2003. Accessed June 12, 2023. http://www.katinkahesselink.net/kh/rev_w_old.html.

16. Besant, Annie. "Foreword: An Appreciation." In Leo, Bessie. *The Life and Work of Alan Leo: Theosophist – Astrologer – Mason*, 1919, 8. https://archive.org/details/lifeworkofalanle00leob/page/n5/mode/2up?view=theater.

17. Leo, Alan. Quoted in Curry, Patrick. *A Confusion of Prophets: Victorian and Edwardian Astrology*. London: Collins & Brown, 1993, 149.

18. Leo, Alan. *The Art of Synthesis*. London: Modern Astrology, 1936, 30-31.

19. Leo, Alan. Quoted in Robson, Vivian, ed. *The Complete Dictionary of Astrology*. Rochester, VT: Destiny Books, 1983, 8.

20. Firman, John, and Ann Gila. *Psychosynthesis: A Psychology of the Spirit*. State University of New York Press, 2010, 16.

21. Oken, Alan. *Soul-Centered Astrology: A Key to Expanding Yourself*. Freedom, CA: Crossing Press, 1996, 11.

22. Oken, *Soul-Centered Astrology*, 44-45.

23. Oken, *Soul-Centered Astrology*, 386.

24. Steiner, Rudolf. *Approaches to Anthroposophy*. Sussex, England: Rudolf Steiner Press, 1992, 11.

25. Steiner, Rudolf. "Lecture VIII. Man's Connection with the Various Planetary Bodies - Vol. 105. Universe, Earth and Man." Rudolf Steiner Archive, August 12, 1908. https://wn.rsarchive.org/Lectures/Dates/19080812p01.html.
26. Davidson, Norman. Foreword. *Anthroposophy and Astrology: The Astronomical Letters of Elisabeth Vreede*. Great Barrington, MA: Anthroposophic Press, 2001, xiv.
27. Thun, Maria. *The Biodynamic Year: Increasing Yield, Quality and Flavour - 100 Helpful Tips for the Gardener or Smallholder*. East Sussex, England: Temple Lodge Publishing, 2010, 4.
28. Davidson, *Anthroposophy and Astrology*, xiii.
29. Steiner, Rudolf. "Lecture III. Realities Beyond Birth and Death - Vol. 180. On the Mysteries of Ancient and Modern Times." Rudolf Steiner Archive, December 29, 1917. https://wn.rsarchive.org/Lectures/GA180/English/AM1929/19171229p01.html.
30. Steiner, Rudolf. "Lecture XIII - Vol. 232. Mystery Centers." Rudolf Steiner Archive, December 22, 1923. https://wn.rsarchive.org/Lectures/GA232/English/GC1985/19231222p01.html.
31. Vreede, Elisabeth. *Anthroposophy and Astrology: The Astronomical Letters of Elizabeth Vreede*. Great Barrington, MA: Anthroposophic Press, 2001, xxii.
32. Vreede, *Anthroposophy and Astrology*, 130-151.
33. Information about the course can be found at https://www.thestarhouse.org/a-new-astrology-series2.
34. A You-Tube video of Powell's work can be found at https://www.youtube.com/watch?v=99D-MI4BmvQ.
35. By way of full disclosure, I had my very first reading with Ellias Lonsdale, over 50 years ago now, in Ashland, Oregon, when he was known as Sunny Blue Boy. It was a 5-hour reading that completely changed my life, and set me on the astrological path of calling that has led to this book. I have not had any contact with him since, and in fact, didn't really even know who he was until I did the research for this chapter.
36. "Ellis Lonsdale | Star Genesis Wisdom." Accessed June 15, 2023. https://stargenesiswisdom.com/ellis-lonsdale/.
37. Gurdjieff, G. I. *Meetings with Remarkable Men*. E. P. Dutton, 1974, 31.
38. Gurdjieff, *Meetings with Remarkable Men*, 90.
39. Sedgwick, Mark. "European Neo-Sufi Movements in the Inter-War Period." In *Inter-War Europe*, edited by Natalie Clayer and Eric Germain. Columbia University Press, 2008.

40. Burke, Omar Michael. *Among the Dervishes : An Account of Travels in Asia and Africa, and Four Years Studying the Dervishes, Sufis and Fakirs by Living among Them*. London: Octagon Press, 1973, 111.

41. Bennett, John G. *Gurdjieff: Making a New World*. HarperCollins, 1976, 56-57.

42. Hopkins, John. "Origins of Sufism & Ancient Bactria." Okar Research, October 31, 2012. https://balkhandshambhala.blogspot.com/2012/10/balkh-and-sufism.html.

43. Martin, Major Desmond R., ed. "Below the Hindu Kush." *The Lady* CLX11, no. 4210 (December 9, 1965), 870.

44. Welch, Louise. *Orage with Gurdjieff in America*. Boston: Routledge & Kegan Paul, 1982, 79.

45. Ouspensky, P. D. *In Search of the Miraculous: Fragments of an Unknown Teaching*. Houghton Mifflin Harcourt, 2001, 290-91.

46. Wellbeloved, Sophia. "Gurdjieff 'Old' or 'New Age': Aristotle or Astrology?" *JASANAS* 1 (2005). https://ccwe.wordpress.com/sophia-wellbeloveds-academic-research-page/.

47. Wellbeloved, "Gurdjieff 'Old' or 'New Age': Aristotle or Astrology?"

48. "Review of The Theory of Celestial Influences." *Gurdjieff International Review* II (3) (1999). https://www.gurdjieff.org/index.en.htm.

49. Collin, Rodney. *The Theory of Celestial Influence: Man, the Universe, and Cosmic Mystery*. Penguin, 1993, 173.

50. Elwell, Dennis. "Astrology Is a Foreign Language." Accessed June 14, 2023. http://www.skyscript.co.uk/elwell3.html.

51. Faye, Jan. "Backward Causation." Stanford Encyclopedia of Philosophy. Spring 2021 Edition, February 26, 2021. https://plato.stanford.edu/archives/spr2021/entries/causation-backwards/.

52. Dean, Geoffrey, Ivan Kelly, Arthur Mather, and Rudolf Smit. "Astrologer Attacks Researchers (Abstract+Article)." Accessed June 14, 2023. https://www.astrology-and-science.com/o-attk2.htm.

53. Elwell, Dennis. "The Researchers Researched." Accessed June 14, 2023. http://www.astrozero.co.uk/astroscience/elwell_1.htm.

54. Elwell, Dennis, and Garry Phillipson. "Astrology, Scepticism and Knowledge - A Dialogue Between Dennis Elwell and Garry Phillipson." Astrology in the Year Zero. Accessed June 14, 2023. http://www.astrozero.co.uk/astroscience/ask.htm.

55. Cavendish, Richard. *A History of Magic*. London: Sphere Books, 1977, 167.

56. Hanegraaff, Wouter J. *Western Esotericism: A Guide for the Perplexed*. London: Bloomsbury Press, 2013, 41.

57. Dyrendal, Asbjørn, James R. Lewis, and Jesper Aa Petersen. *The Invention of Satanism*. London: Oxford University Press, 2016, 39.

58. Hutton, Ronald. *The Triumph of the Moon: A History of Modern Pagan Witchcraft*. New York: Oxford University Press, 2019, 176.

59. Booth, Martin. *A Magick Life: A Biography of Aleister Crowley*. London: Coronet Books, 2000, 125.

60. Churton, Tobias. *Aleister Crowley: The Biography: Spiritual Revolutionary, Romantic Explorer, Occult Master and Spy*. London: Watkins Media Limited, 2014, 417.

61. Josephson-Storm, Jason. *The Myth of Disenchantment: Magic, Modernity, and the Birth of the Human Sciences*. University of Chicago Press, 2017, 170.

62. Campbell, Colin D. "Aleister Crowley's Contribution to Popular Astrology." Llewellyn, February 12, 2018. https://www.llewellyn.com/journal/article/2678.

63. Symonds, John, ed. *The Complete Astrological Writings of Aleister Crowley*. Gloucester, England: Duckworth, 1974, 4.

64. Crowley, Aleister. "Batrachophrenoboocosmomachia," 1917. https://astrolibrary.org/books/crowley-67/.

65. Crowley, Aleister, and Evangeline Smith Adams. *The General Principles of Astrology: Liber DXXXVI*. Red Wheel, 2002, 13.

He (the astrologer seeking deeper knowledge) is content to accept the dictum of the Schoolmen, *omnia exeunt in mysterium* (everything ends in mystery), by which they meant that if you follow any idea far enough – if you keep on asking how and why and what, instead of resting contented with a superficial, half-way explanation, the result is always the same. You reach the blank wall of the inconceivable.

Aleister Crowley, The General Principles of Astrology, 2002

Chapter Nine

Psychological Astrology in the Era of Uncertainty

Astrology currently exists in a bewildering array of forms and systems, many of which have their roots in previous eras, including the occult arts, revived in the late nineteenth century, which, as explored in Chapter Eight, served as synthesis of prior teachings from the Mystical and Logical Eras, and indirectly served as a source of spiritual context for the evolution of astrology in the Era of Uncertainty.

That being said, it seems to me that the emergence of psychological astrology, as a main branch of the sprawling tree that astrology in general has become, is endemic to the Era of Uncertainty itself and marks a new path forward – one it would have been impossible to recognize before the cultural developments of the last hundred years or so. Along this path, the possibility exists for furthering the conversation with the cosmos begun in previous eras, but with the added benefit now of being able to appreciate how the cosmos is a mirror to psychological process.

Carl Jung has called astrology "the "sum of all the psychological knowledge of antiquity."[1] But psychology itself did not exist as a modern discipline until the late nineteenth century. In 1875, the German physiologist and philosopher, Wilhelm Wundt founded the first formal laboratory for psychological research, thus distinguishing psychology as a science in its own right, separate from other fields of inquiry.[2] As noted in Chapter Seven, psychology continued to evolve as an empirical science at least until the discoveries of Freud about the primacy of the unconscious began throwing into question, science's capacity to illuminate the inner workings of the psyche.

Mainstream psychology has, of course, continued to present itself as a science beyond Freud. But through the work of Freud, and especially through the work of his successor and protégé, Carl Jung, psychology also began to travel a parallel track on which it was a more postmodern phenomena, subject to the same experimental uncertainties, limitations and possibilities as all science within the Era of Uncertainty. On this parallel track, personal experience, artistry and open-minded extemporaneous exploration have often been more productive of meaningful breakthrough discoveries than research within the strict parameters of empirical science. This was a path on which astrology – and particularly an astrology integrated with this more exploratory dimension of psychology – could once again find a meaningful foothold.

This possibility takes us at least one step beyond, "as above, so below," since it also encompasses what lies within the interior of the human psyche, an entire realm that was previously largely excluded from the conversation, because we did not know it existed, or if we did, how deeply it was rooted. Within this interior, in some mysterious way that has yet to be fully explored, we can potentially more consciously align ourselves with the same forces that have shaped the outer cosmos, and human civilizations, as well as our own psychological landscape, and direct these forces as an intentional expression of divine intelligence working through us. This is, in essence, a continuation of the path of astrological magic walked by shamans in the Mythopoetic Era, divinatory priests in the Mystical Era, theurgists in the Philosophical Era, and hermetic magicians in the Logical Era, but now with a language of deepened self-awareness that did not previously exist.

This is also a path that perhaps requires a greater level of responsibility than it did before. For in order to enter this larger, more participatory conversation with the cosmos, we must be willing to first enter the portal of our own psychological landscape and become intimately familiar with its exquisite beauty as well as its wounded minefields. This is a journey that extends far beyond the experience of learning to read a birthchart as an intellectual exercise. Astrology, of course, can always be approached on a superficial level as a source of pop psychology or character analysis. But given our hallowed history as a pathway into a deeper understanding of the cosmos itself, we now have additional tools available that our predecessors did not have, and we would be fools not to use them.

It seems to me that any serious student, who wants to use astrology as a pathway to personal growth and wisdom in the Era of Uncertainty must begin with an understanding of their own personal psychology, as revealed through the birthchart – including their core issues and the challenges associated with those issues – and then parlay that understanding into a deeper appreciation for how it opens a door to a deeper, more mystical, more mythopoetic connection to the cosmos itself, and to the divine intelligence at the heart of the cosmos. This is even more critical for anyone who aspires to be a professional astrologer, for how can you guide someone else, if you have not taken the journey yourself?

In Part Three of this book, I will demonstrate, from within my own experience, what this journey might look like, realizing of course that yours will likely be very different than mine, if no less brave in its attempt to move beyond the strictures of what has passed for astrology to this point. Before we venture into this unknown territory, it remains to continue the story of how astrology has so far become integrated with the psychological understanding that has emerged in the Era of Uncertainty.

Depth Psychology

Carl Jung

The final chapter of this story begins with Carl Jung. While Blavatsky, Steiner, Gurdjieff and Crowley were all occultists, and as such, relegated to the fringes of Western intellectual life, if not ostracized altogether, Carl Jung, their contemporary, was very much respected in his day as a psychologist, who became central to astrology's unfolding throughout the Era of Uncertainty. In his embrace of astrology, as well as alchemy and some of the other more esoteric teachings of the past, he opened a pathway for these fields to continue evolving - not through some nostalgic reference to the antiquated science of a bygone era, but in their own right, as more intuitive ways of knowing capable of speaking to postmodern sensibilities. Jung also had a far greater influence among psychological astrologers, especially those with a more spiritual bent, than any of his occult contemporaries - to the point where no currently practicing psychological astrologer worth her weight, could actually claim to be one, without paying some homage to Jung's influence on the field.

Meanwhile, although Jung considered himself a scientist throughout his career, as did most of those birthing the emerging field of psychology at the dawn of the Era of Uncertainty, he struggled with many of his ideas, which simply did not fit the scientific framework. From an early age, he was attracted not just to the empirical rigors of science, but also to the more mystical terrain - Corbin's eighth clime, to which astrology at its best could reach - a terrain that Jung called "God's world."

> *To 'God's world,' belonged everything superhuman – dazzling light, the darkness of the abyss, the cold impassivity of infinite space and time, and the uncanny grotesqueness of the irrational world of chance. 'God,' for me, was everything – and anything but 'edifying.'*[3]

To edify himself, Jung began in the relatively rational domain of comparative religion, gradually working his way through mythology, fairy tales, dreams, alchemy, and astrology. Out of this lifelong, meandering, largely intellectual voyage through God's world, came a series of unparalleled contributions to the field of psychology, and coincidentally to astrology, to name just a few: a map of the personality rooted in functions easily associated with the four elements and the four humors of both early Greek medicine and Hellenistic astrology; an understanding of archetypes that parallel and deepen our understanding of planetary processes; an elucidation of the acausal mechanism of synchronicity, which has its corollary in the daily practice of astrologers; the process of active imagination, which offers one way into a deeper understanding of astrological symbolism; and the process of individuation, which provides a brilliant overall context in which to understand the unfolding of our relationship to the birthchart, over the course of a lifetime.

Then in 1913, Jung's rational approach to God's world descended into more mystical terrain, as he began seeing visions and hearing voices. After a particular cataclysmic vision, in October of that year, in which he saw "mighty yellow waves, the floating rubble of civilization, and the drowned bodies of uncounted thousands," after which "the whole sea turned to blood," Jung at first thought he was going mad.[4] After World War I broke out nearly a year later, he realized instead that he had had a premonition of our collective experience, as we were about to take a dive into the abyss. He also realized that the advent of such visions was an unprecedented opportunity to explore the psyche, not as an intellectual exercise in armchair abstraction, but through a more direct and intimately personal experience.

This was terrifying to Jung, the rational scientist, for he could no longer rely on his intellectual constructs to orient himself. But to his credit, he groped his way through the dark, to a different, much more seasoned understanding. He realized that he could not make sense of his experiences in words; that in fact, words, particularly those that attempted prematurely to ascribe meaning to his visions, got in the way. Instead, he had to stay present with his emotions, and to work with the images that arose in connection to these emotions, without interpreting them.

> *To the extent that I managed to translate the emotions into images – that is to say, to find the images which were concealed in the emotions – I was inwardly calmed and reassured. Had I left those images hidden in the emotions, I might have been torn to pieces by them.*[5]

To calm himself in the face of these intensely treacherous emotions, Jung did yoga exercises, and then when he felt sufficiently calm, he went back to the edge, where words gave way to something more primal and more potent. This was not just an excruciating personal exercise, but ultimately an internal rewiring of Jung the scientist into a different kind of adept, perhaps one closer to the prophets of the Mystical Era, where words in the service of rational discourse had not yet entirely usurped the power of the unconscious to shape and illuminate reality.

A central component of Jung's mystical experiences was an ongoing conversation with an inner guide called Philemon. Philemon first appeared to Jung in a dream, as an old man with the horns of a bull and the wings of a kingfisher, who held in his hands a set of keys. Jung did not understand the image, but painted it, and then shortly after, in a moment of synchronicity, found a dead kingfisher (rare near Zurich) in his garden. During subsequent conversations with Philemon, and other inner figures and guides, Jung realized that "there are things in the psyche which I do not produce, but which produce themselves and have their own life."[6] Philemon, in particular, became a teacher to Jung, or "what the Indians call a guru." But more than that:

> *. . . in private comments to Cary Baynes in 1923, Jung described Philemon as something infinitely greater. He was, in multiform manifestations, an avatar of 'the Master . . . the same who inspired Buddha, Mani, Christ, Mahomet – all those who may be said to have communed with God.'*[7]

These experiences altered Jung, but he struggled with them for the remainder of his life, and ultimately was unable to fully reconcile his allegiance to science with his conviction that there was a deeper source of knowledge that was inherently non-scientific, that science in fact, could not reach. Jung recorded his mystical experiences faithfully, first in a series of black notebooks, and then in a large red leather-bound book to which he added illustrations, notes and commentaries, working and reworking the material intermittently for about sixteen years, but never actually finishing it, and never publishing it, in part for fear of ridicule by his scientifically-minded peers.

> *Regarding the significance of what the book contained, however, Jung was unequivocal. "All my works, all my creative activity," he would recall later, "has come from those initial fantasies and dreams."*[8]

Jung kept *The Red Book* locked in a cupboard, and left no instructions for its publication after death. In 1983, Jung's heirs placed the document in a safety deposit box, where it remained until 2000. In that year, there was intense discussion among the guardians of his legacy, after which it was decided to finally release the work for publication under the guidance of Sonu Shamdasani, a London-based author, lifelong student of Jung, and co-founder of the Philemon Foundation, which sought to publish all of Jung's work. The published book finally emerged in 2009.

For those who had already relegated Jung to the New Age fringe of the psychological establishment, *The Red Book* was the final evidence that he had gone off the deep-end entirely. The book, in fact, reads like a series of demented dreams, and is, in the end, like any dream, not easy to make sense of. On the other hand, and for those for whom Jung still has relevance, it was and is, a brave demonstration of what a journey into the interior of the psyche actually looks like. The point is not to marvel or roll your eyes at Jung's descent into madness, but to undergo your own journey into the interior, and write your own Red Book.

Astrology, of course, is an incredible symbolic language with which to facilitate this journey, and Jung knew that. Jung used astrology with his patients, even while decrying its lack of scientific veracity,[9] but because Jung never relinquished his desire to be scientific in his approach to the psyche, his astrological work mostly remained hidden beyond his outer role as a psychoanalyst. Nevertheless, throughout his writings, he implied that working with astrology as a language of inner life, at a deeper level, was a legitimate road to self-knowledge, and many psychological astrologers since – including Dane Rudhyar, Liz Greene, Stephen Arroyo, Karen Hamaker-Zondag, Greg Bogart, Steven Forrest and Richard Tarnas – to name a few of the most important, have taken many of Jung's ideas and translated them into various tenets of psychological astrology. This has been an invaluable service to the astrological community.

Beyond that, however, I cannot help but sense that Jung had a much deeper understanding of the spiritual dimensions of the psyche that he never could quite integrate, or articulate as a coherent pathway, despite the fact that he had gone there himself, largely because his rational mind kept getting in the way. We remember Jung today as a seminal thinker, because of the power of his intellect, and his capacity to create a conceptual bridge between ancient wisdom and postmodern culture. But he also often alluded to the deeper possibilities of symbolic language, and left us with an elaborate picture of those possibilities, without actually going through the door itself.

> *The mouth utters the word, the sign, and the symbol. If the word is a sign, it means nothing. But if the word is a symbol, it means everything . . . One can certainly gain outer freedom through powerful actions, but one creates inner freedom only through the symbol.*
>
> *The symbol is the word that goes out of the mouth, that one does not simply speak, but that rises out of the depths of the self as a word of power and great need and places itself unexpectedly on the tongue. It is an astonishing and perhaps seemingly irrational word, but one recognizes it as a symbol since it is alien to the conscious mind. If one accepts the symbol, it is as if a door opens leading into a new room whose existence one previously did not know.*[10]

Practiced in this way, astrology is potentially a pathway into a more gnostic or even mystical form of self-knowledge, rather than a mere rendering of the symbolism of the birthchart into psychological correlates – or "signs" that explain it. But this level of self-knowledge requires the kind of descent into the unconscious dimensions of the psyche that Jung himself made during his *Red Book* experiences, and few have the courage for such an undertaking.[11] Planets can easily be associated with the archetypes, and the birthchart can readily provide an archetypal map to the territory to be traversed, but the actual journey itself requires a different level of relationship to the symbolism than Jung, or the psychological astrologers who have followed in his wake, have been able to provide.

This is not so much their fault, as it is the inherent limitations of a Jungian approach to psychological astrology.

> *(Jung) set out to challenge the nineteenth-century orthodoxy in which 'psyche' has lost its associations with soul, and psychology had been reduced to the study of the brain. But Jung was far more than a psychologist . . . He was a theurgist in the style of Iamblichus, the difference being that his form of magic, the analytical session, while alive to the numinous power of symbols, eschewed the outer paraphernalia of ritual magic, and preferred the gradual, rational ascent to the divine favored by orthodox Platonism.*[12]

As I read this quote, I hear a potential that was not quite realized. In order to actually enter into the magical space that is possible in the practice of psychological astrology, one has to find a way to actually merge with and embody the numinous power of the symbols, rather than stand apart from them at a safe, rational distance. The paraphernalia of ritual magic may not be necessary, but a willingness to enter into the liminal space of the symbolism itself, where the pathway to knowledge passes through unknowing is. Or as Jung himself noted:

> *Then the spirit of the depths came to me and spoke these words:*
>
> *The highest truth is one and the same with the absurd. This statement saved me, and like rain after a long hot spell, it swept away everything in me which was too highly tensed.*
>
> *So meaning is a moment and a transition from absurdity to absurdity and absurdity only a moment and a transition from meaning to meaning.*[13]

We all want to practice astrology in a way that makes sense and that illuminates the meaning of life's most important experiences. But unless we are willing to enter into the absurdity of life, to feel the absurdity at the heart of the symbolism, absurd because it baffles the conscious mind, and then to stay with this absurdity for a while before rushing off to clutch a rational explanation, the deeper meaning of the chart will perpetually elude us, no matter how erudite we are in delineating its archetypal dimensions. More than any other seminal thinker pointing the way forward for astrology in the Era of Uncertainty, Jung has shown us the door. Now it is up to us to walk through that door into "*a new room whose existence one previously did not know.*"

James Hillman

If Jung struggled to extricate himself from the strictures of the scientific paradigm in reaching for a more immediate relationship to psyche, or soul, James Hillman had no such compunction. Hillman began his career as a Jungian therapist, studying at the C. G. Jung institute in Zurich, then becoming its Director of Studies for ten years, and was very much a part of the Jungian tradition, acknowledging his "fundamental debt" to Jung in developing his own ideas.[14] But just as Jung eventually outgrew Freud and went his own way, so did Hillman outgrow and eventually part ways with Jung. This was not a personal falling out per se, but rather a gradual realization of the limitations and pitfalls of Jungian psychology, that served as a platform for the development of his own ideas, which wound up in some ways, being both an extension of and a radical departure from Jung's teachings.

In his own way, Jung tried to make the soul central to his psychology, but as a rational scientist, his attempt was perpetually hampered by the need to anchor his conceptual understanding of the soul in language that was bound to a psycho-logical worldview. The process was one where the psyche *cum* soul was something to be analyzed and understood in psychological terms – an ego undergoing a process of individuation through a series of encounters with various archetypal aspects of the psyche, that only incidentally deepened it and made it more soulful. Hillman essentially turned this idea on its head, so that the protagonist of the psychological story was no longer the ego, but rather the soul itself.

To be sure, the soul for Hillman was not a metaphysical concept, but rather a recognition of the deep, often inscrutable mystery of the psyche that defies scientific or even psychological analysis.

> *We cannot know what exactly we are referring to because its nature remains shadowy, revealing itself mainly in hints, intuitions, whispers, and the sudden urges and oddities that disturb your life and that we continue to call symptoms.*[15]

The soul, unlike the ego, comes into being through many distinctly unheroic pathways that analytical and depth psychology labels pathological. Ego is but one voice among many, and often not the most interesting voice in the room. The true function of the psyche is, according to Hillman, not a refinement of the adaptive ego. It is soul-making itself.

Soul-making, according to Hillman – who was influenced by Corbin as well as Jung – is primarily a function of the imagination. The imagination is rooted in a polytheistic pantheon of gods and goddesses, but also in an animistic dimension of the psyche that resonates with the living essence of the world around it, in fantasies, and in pathologies of mind and body, often in ways that defy rational understanding, but that easily lend itself to a more poetic rationale. The life of the soul, according to Hillman is larger than the human who experiences it, and as deeply embedded in the world as we are able to imagine that it is – a perspective that hearkens back to the mythopoetic mindset in which everything encountered within the world was also a reflection of the inseparable relationship between cosmos and psyche and the perpetual dance between them.

Hillman also dared to suggest that understanding the life of the soul is not a scientific endeavor. Quite the contrary, science itself is a soul-making activity, albeit one that holds its fantasies too literally to be useful to the soul.

> *. . . archetypal psychology does not imagine itself or the psyche as belonging to science, even social or behavioral science . . . The science fantasy with its reliance upon objectivity, technology, verification, measurement and progress – in short, its necessary literalism – is less a means for examining the psyche than for examining science. Our interest lies not in applying the methods of science to psychology (to put it on a "sound scientific footing"), but rather in applying the archetypal method of psychologizing to science so as to discover its root metaphors and operational myths . . . For science, also, is a field for soul-making provided we do not take it literally on its own terms.*[16]

In the quote above, we could easily substitute "astrology" for "psychology" and have a statement that astrologers seeking to move beyond science's damning judgments, and Hillman himself could likely use as a supportive argument for a more imaginative approach. Hillman was as appreciative of astrology as Jung, as was Hillman's colleague Thomas Moore, but as noted by Campion:

> *The cultural zone occupied by psychologists such as Hillman and Moore places the therapeutic process first and, while respecting astrology as a means of self-understanding, avoids direct discussion of astrological technique or horoscopic examples.*[17]

A few astrologers influenced by Hillman have subsequently taken his ideas about the soul and soul-making more directly into the art and practice of astrology. Among the most important are Brad Kochunas, James' own son Laurence Hillman, and Safron Rossi, who was the curator of Opus Archives, home of James Hillman's manuscript collections. As Rossi notes:

> *James Hillman's writings provide an invaluable foundation for understanding the bridge between psychology and astrology. Yet Hillman's theoretical frame and mythopoetic perspective are rarely mentioned in astrological circles, despite the rich opportunity for cross-fertilization his work offers.*[18]

Depth Astrology

We will return to Hillman later, in Part Three, when we talk about an actual practice of astrology, rooted in an imaginal exploration of the soul. Meanwhile, as we continue the story of our gradual evolution toward a postmodern astrology oriented around an exploration of soul, we must return to one who did take Jung's ideas more directly into the heart of astrological theory and practice, and from whom all subsequent roads forward in this evolution have led. Having traced some of the most important threads of psychology and esoteric spirituality that have woven together to become the foundation for a psychological astrology of the soul, we at last come to the seminal weaver of those threads, who despite the essential contributions of other voices, must be honored as the father of psychological astrology itself – Dane Rudhyar.

Dane Rudhyar

Born in Paris as Daniel Chennevière, graduating at age 16 from the Sorbonne, and envisioning himself as a "seed man" of a new cultural revolution, Chennevière adopted the name Rudhyar – a cognate of the Hindu storm god Rudra – and migrated to Los Angeles in the 1920s, which had become the hotbed of the cultural revolution he was determined to seed.

Rudhyar, also a composer, was introduced to Theosophy when he was asked to compose music for the society's headquarters in Krotona, near Hollywood. He wound up marrying Maria Contento, who was secretary to the independent Theosophist Will Levington Comfort, who in turn, introduced Rudhyar to Marc Edmond Jones, from whom he learned astrology. At the same time, Rudhyar was immersed in a study of the teachings of Carl Jung, and began to envision a synthesis of astrology and depth psychology – a dream that came to fruition in 1936, with the publication of *The Astrology of Personality* by Alice Bailey's Lucis Trust.

Thus, began a lifelong quest to further develop astrology through integration with additional cutting-edge developments in humanistic and transpersonal psychologies that have left a lasting legacy upon which all spiritually-minded psychological astrologers stand today, whether they are directly familiar with Rudhyar's work or not. Like his teacher, Marc Edmond Jones, Rudhyar was not always an easy read, but for those of us studying psychological astrology in the 1960s, 70s, and 80s, his ideas – propagated widely in more than forty books and hundreds of articles – became the very air we necessarily had to breathe.

Like Alan Leo, the Theosophical movement in general, and Carl Jung, Rudhyar emphasized an astrology of free-will, self-knowledge and personal growth, rather than a predictive astrology focused on external events. He considered astrology to be a symbolic language, rather than an empirical science, "fundamentally the algebra of life . . . absolutely protean in its manifestation, and multifarious in the wide diversity of its approaches to particular phases of interpretation."[19] In a later work, he noted that science in the Era of Uncertainty had itself "increasingly become a symbolic language," and that cutting-edge physicists were (already in 1980):

> *. . . touching almost transcendent fields of existence and evoking though their complex mathematical symbols the feeling of the inter-relatedness of everything to everything else – a feeling that has been sung for centuries by mystical poets and interpreted in cosmic terms by great seers and occultists.*[20]

Like most proponents of New Age philosophies, Rudhyar felt that astrology could play its part, along with quantum physics, in a "re-focalization of human consciousness." Like Jung, Rudhyar felt that astrology ought to one day, theoretically prove itself scientific, provided science in the quantum era was willing to evolve beyond old outmoded ways of thinking and processing information. In the meantime, as has become the fashion in the postmodern era, Rudhyar proceeded to develop his astrology, tacitly assuming this future fusion of science and metaphysical principles to be a given.

Rudhyar's work, taken as a whole, can be seen as an effort to integrate astrology with emerging ideas in the Era of Uncertainty, primarily from Jungian, humanistic and transpersonal psychologies, but also from various occult and theosophical teachings, the philosophy of holism as presented by South African philosopher Jan Smuts, and a critical evaluation and reinterpretation of certain New Age ideas. As did his astrology teacher, Marc Edmond Jones, Rudhyar emphasized working from the perspective of the whole chart, which provided a larger context of meaning for the particulars. He also emphasized that the potentials in the birthchart evolved through the interweavings of various planetary cycles of varying durations, that unfolded over the course of a lifetime.

These personal cycles were also part of a larger, collective unfolding of cyclical evolution, marked by the precession of the equinoxes through various ages, with a New Age he expected to begin in 2062. According to Rudhyar, we were now in a transitional period that began around 1846, with the ultimate manifestation of the Age of Aquarius yet to come, dependent upon how we deal with "the 'karma' of the failures of the past."[21]

Rudhyar felt that to usher in a genuine New Age of optimal realization, not only would each person have to attain a spiritually mature state of individuation in relation to the potentials in their birthchart, but beyond that, would have to reach, individually and collectively, for a state of "more-than-individual (or 'transindividual') existence."[22] Much of his writing was oriented toward the use of astrology in order to illuminate this process for individuals striving to become self-actualized, and for civilization as a whole, striving to learn from our mistakes and become a more divinely inspired enterprise.

Rudhyar started using the word "transpersonal" in 1930, long before it became a psychological movement, to describe a "descent of transcendent spiritual power and illumination" to compliment the upward reaching individual effort to grow toward spiritual maturity. This was a kind of dispensation of grace from the divine, that in earlier eras might have been understood as mystical, although Rudhyar himself does not like that term.[23]

Nonetheless, describing the responsibility of the astrologer working transpersonally, Rudhyar suggests that, aside from cultivating a poetic approach to the language itself, a worthy practitioner must be willing to accept "being the 'agent' or 'mouthpiece' of higher powers urging the client to transform himself or herself, to open the closed center of the mandala of his or her personality to an influx of transcendent power and light."[24]

Although Rudhyar's emphasis is, like most astrologers since the Philosophical Era, on the *interpretation* of a birthchart, rather than entering into an ongoing relationship with it – as I will propose doing in Part Three – an astrologer does not attain the intuitive capacity to serve as a "mouthpiece of higher powers" without a great deal of inner work, and adequate preparation to receive a transcendent message, such as would have been recognized to be the case during the Mystical Era, when a direct transmission from the divine was the hallmark, in general, of a receptive, deeply intuitive and imaginal approach to knowledge.

There is, of course, far more that could be said about Rudhyar's work than can be elaborated here, and I would recommend to anyone reading this book that his work be an integral part of the foundation for a solid practice of psychological astrology. Many astrologers influenced by Jung, were also necessarily influenced by Rudhyar, who in addition to his profound re-conceptualization of astrology for the Era of Uncertainty, also translated Jung's ideas into practical application and a reinterpretation of the basic building blocks of the astrological language: houses, signs and planetary dynamics. Those who were more theosophically inclined were also indebted to Rudhyar, who far more successfully than Blavatsky, Bailey, Steiner, Gurdjieff or Crowley was able to create a viable bridge between the esoteric understanding of the soul's relationship to a more cosmic order and the everyday outworking of human psychology in which that order was implied, if not always consciously embraced.

Alexander Ruperti

Rudhyar's work was significantly extended by Alexander Ruperti, who wrote the classic *Cycles of Becoming*, in which every moment in time is understood to be a nexus of interlocking larger cycles, the meaning of which derives from the outworking of those cycles as an evolving opportunity for personal growth. He emphasized that what was important was not the moment itself, or the outer events that it accompanied it, but the internal response to the moment and what the individual partaking of the moment was able to learn from it and/or contribute to it.

Furthermore, Ruperti was fairly clear in asserting that astrology was a useful language, whose utility depended not on astrology's objective or scientific validity, but on the facility of the astrologer in speaking the language.[25] This was, in terms of our argument here, a step forward from both Jung and Rudhyar, who labored with far more ambivalence about whether or not astrology should measure up to scientific standards. In this way, Ruperti gave permission to subsequent generations of astrologers interested in using astrology as a path to self-knowledge, personal growth, and exploration of life's more spiritual mysteries from a uniquely individual vantage point, but who could care less whether or not their discoveries and insights were statistically sound, replicable, or objective.

Richard Tarnas

Since then, astrologers of all stripes and persuasions have taken that permission to heart and run with it. While following the various worthy threads that have unfolded from the original fabric of in which psychology and astrology have woven together would take at least another book, there is one further development that does bear mention in relation to this one: the work of Richard Tarnas and the development of archetypal astrology. After graduating from Harvard, and obtaining a Ph.D. from Saybrook Institute for a thesis on psychedelic therapy, Tarnas went to Esalen in Big Sur, California to study and teach among a celebrated faculty, including Joseph Campbell, Gregory Bateson, Huston Smith, Elizabeth Kubler-Ross, James Hillman and Stanislav Grof, with whom, as mentioned in previous chapters, he subsequently developed a pioneering collaboration integrating prenatal and perinatal psychology with psychedelic therapy and astrology.

In 1991, he published *Passion of the Western Mind: Understanding the Ideas That Have Shaped Our World View*, in which he outlines a parallel history to the one presented in this book, around the more specific thesis of how the evolution of science and monotheistic religion have led to a postmodern crisis in which the cosmos has become de-sacralized and stripped of meaning, while contemporary humans have been disenchanted and alienated from the world. As an antidote to this crisis, Tarnas proposes a participatory engagement with the world, in which human beings intentionally engage the cosmos in an ongoing conversation, out of which meaning emerges.

This is radically different from the approach to an understanding of the cosmos that has been pursued by science, in which neutral observers attempt to stand apart from the cosmos and describe it objectively. But this is also radically different than a merely subjective projection of imaginal fantasies onto the blank slate of a cosmos waiting for humans to give it meaning. The participatory approach to knowledge assumes that meaning arises as we bring imaginal attention to a living cosmos that is already teaming with spiritual significance. This was, of course, a sensibility that previously guided the shamanic astrologers of the Mythopoetic Era, and perhaps only to a slightly lesser extent, the divinatory priests of the Mystical Era.

What Tarnas is proposing is not a return to these relatively undifferentiated states, but rather a postmodern quest for meaning, in which a psychologically self-aware individual is willing to engage a living cosmos. In a back-handed sort of way, he is proposing a middle path in the Era of Uncertainty debate between Einstein and Bohr, one that requires an observer willing to enter a cosmos that is inherently meaningful. The observer is anything but neutral, and the cosmos is anything but passive, so the act of observation is a participatory act of engagement, out of which comes a collaborative exchange.

> *What ma(kes a) correlation between . . . inner and outer events intelligible (is) the presence of two factors: first, a developed capacity for thinking and perceiving symbolically, a cultivated sensitivity to metaphoric and analogical patterns that connect and thereby illuminate diverse phenomena; and second, an epistemological openness to the possibility that such meaning can be carried by the outer world as well as the inner, by all of nature and one's surrounding environment, not just by the human psyche.*[26]

Archetypal astrology bears mention because, more than any other iteration of psychological astrology, it recognizes the collaborative nature of the exercise by which the cosmos reveals its secrets to those brave enough to look. Tarnas understands the necessity for doing the individual psychological work of self-healing and self-actualization in order to participate at all in any meaningful way, integrating unconscious contents and bringing patterns hidden in the shadows into the sphere of conscious volition. But he also goes beyond that to suggest this is really only a portal to a larger possibility for knowledge.

> *. . . astrology appear(s) to possess a unique capacity for mediating a heightened level of communication and coordination between consciousness and the unconscious, with "the unconscious" now suggestive of considerably larger dimensions than originally conceived – less personal, less subjective, more cosmically embedded.*[27]

Astrology as a Postmodern Phenomenon

What I have described in this chapter, and the previous two, is an all-too-fleeting account of the most important cultural, psychological and astrological forces shaping a potential path forward for the psychological astrologer wishing to more intimately explore the interface between cosmos and psyche, soul and *anima mundi*. In concluding this chapter, and this section of the book, I would be remiss if I did not acknowledge the fact that this path snakes through a heavily traveled wilderness of ideas, worldviews and indeed, approaches to astrology, where the very idea of *a* path, never mind any pretension to anything remotely resembling *the one true* path, easily becomes meaningless. Within this wilderness, astrology in the Era of Uncertainty is a protean postmodern affair, an unwieldly proliferation of approaches, techniques and schools of thought, applied with a bewildering diversity of sensibilities, to a wide range of disparate phenomena:

> *In practice, astrology crosses the boundaries between Modernism and post-modernism precisely because it has no single identity and astrologers disagree on its fundamental nature. It speaks with radically different voices, and the astrologer plotting correlations between planetary cycles and commodity prices has no need of an astrology of the soul.*[28]

As noted earlier in this discussion, to a scientist still mired in the old paradigm of the Empirical Era, this looks like confusion, chaos, and pseudoscience. To a small subset of the astrological community, the fact that as astrologers, we agree on so little is an embarrassment they hope to rectify with sufficient research. To the vast majority of astrologers, however, the postmodern era has opened a fertile field of opportunity, where outside of a certain narrow-minded bastion of old-school thinking, the art of astrology has been liberated to find its own way beyond scientific strictures. Within this freedom, multiple paths forward are possible, and if our full potential in such a world is to be realized, each astrologer must ultimately find her own.

This, of course, does not mean that, as astrologers, we are free to go about our practice half-cocked, say anything that pops into our head and call it astrology, ignore the very long history of practice that has preceded us, or ply our trade without regard to basic professional standards of competence, ethical integrity, and commitment to learning and growth throughout our careers. It does mean we get to consider, both individually and as a community, what astrology is – or can be – on its own terms, and how we can best facilitate its efficacy doing what it, and those of us working with it, do best.

It also means that we can take it any number of directions, as a postmodern language with which to participate in an ongoing conversation with the cosmos about who we are and what we are doing here on this planet, both individually and collectively. Some astrologers may choose to shape this conversation statistically, continuing to fight what they see as the good fight in seeking scientific credibility. Others may seek refuge in astrological tradition, which most often means the Hellenistic sensibilities of the Philosophical Era, or sometimes in the divinatory practice of *katarche* during the Mystical Era that preceded it. Others might revel in some amalgamation of astrology with a school of contemporary psychology, rediscovered spiritual tradition, New Age teaching, or perennial philosophy that makes more sense to them in the Era of Uncertainty. The bravest among us might be willing to use our knowledge of astrology as the mere point of entry into a living cosmos, with its own language and its own revelations, many of which likely go beyond astrology's current reach. All of these and other hybrid expressions, made possible only within the expanded reach of a postmodern culture, proliferate today.

Personally, I think that something was gained and lost in each of the eras in which astrology has reinvented itself, and that the real opportunity within the Era of Uncertainty is, at least in part, to reclaim and integrate what we have given up in order to attain credibility according to the dominant standards – mostly scientific, but also to some extent religious and political – of each era. In Part Three of this book, I will take us backward through the history of Part One, and explore more specifically what this process – essentially of "soul retrieval," to use a shamanic term – might look and feel like at each step of the way.

Astrology's Current Renaissance

First, however, I do want to finish the history being outlined throughout Parts One and Two by talking a bit about astrology's ongoing evolution in the Era of Uncertainty, which in some ways, has been a bit of a renaissance. Astrology today does not perhaps enjoy the same prominence and respectability that it did in its former glory days – which, within the history outlined in this book, would have encompassed a period of about 3,500 years: from its influence on King Hammurabi in the Second Millennium B.C.E. of the Mystical Era through to Marsilio Ficino and the Platonic Academy at Florence in the mid Fifteenth Century, at the end of the Logical Era. Since then, astrology has nonetheless not only persisted, but in some ways, flourished, despite the efforts of positivist scientists, religious zealots and political foes to pound the final nail in our coffin.

Although the numbers of astrologers who make their living with their practice are small by professional standards, this may perhaps not be the best measure of astrology's reach.[29] A 2017 Pew Research Center poll found that about 30% of all adult Americans "believe" in astrology, with some variance across the board between those who consider themselves religious (ranging from 18% of Evangelicals to 33% of Catholics), those who consider themselves spiritual but not religious (32%), and those who consider themselves atheist (3%) or agnostic (18%). Those who subscribe to one or more New Age "beliefs" are, according to the poll, generally more likely to also "believe" in astrology, even though most astrologers would probably not consider astrology a matter of belief.[30]

However, it is conceived, with the proliferation of ideas made possible through the Internet, and especially through the rise of social media, astrology has become a second language within the New Age community, as well as among millennials and the younger generations who might not consider themselves New Age. And as the New Age has gone mainstream, and these younger generations have taken up residence in cyberspace, astrology has gone viral.

> *In its penetration into our shared lexicon, astrology is a little like psychoanalysis once was. At mid-century, you might have heard talk of id, ego, or superego at a party; now it's common to hear someone explain herself by way of sun, moon, and rising signs. It's not just that you hear it. It's who's saying it: people who aren't kooks or climate-change deniers, who see no contradiction between using astrology and believing in science . . .*[31]

We now live in an age when anyone, without knowledge of astrology, can get a chart cast online for free, download a workshop, class or webinar, and post astrologically related memes on You Tube, Facebook, Instagram or Twitter with the click of a mouse. Those coming of age today seem to simply take astrology in stride, without needing for it to be scientific to be of value. Unlike previous generations, they seem to get that astrology is not necessarily a matter of belief, nor is it something to be rigorously proven. It is, to them, mostly a matter of utility; as a language of self-reflection with the capacity to help illuminate life's challenges and manage its uncertainties, astrology is a helpful way to look at the world and think about things.

> *To understand astrology's appeal is to get comfortable with paradoxes. It feels simultaneously cosmic and personal; spiritual and logical; ineffable and concrete; real and unreal. It can be a relief, in a time of division, not to have to choose. It can be freeing, in a time that values black and white, ones and zeros, to look for answers in the gray. It can be meaningful to draw lines in the space between moments of time, or the space between pinpricks of light in the night sky, even if you know deep-down they're really light-years apart, and have no connection at all.*[32]

The Upside and Downside of Astrology's Popularity In the Era of Uncertainty

This widespread acceptance of astrology has its upside and its downside. The downside is that anything that becomes ubiquitous, tends to get watered down. Those who have read a book or taken a class suddenly feel qualified to speak on the subject, and with a ready audience a few clicks away, any reasonably intelligent, articulate and/or charismatic character can claim a presence in a much more seasoned field – one that has a long, deeply rooted history, as outlined briefly in Parts One and Two of this book and numerous other places, to which many newer practitioners might well be oblivious.

Astrology often appeals to those "who do not any longer feel that they are the self-determining subjects of their fate"[33] and are ready to resort to magical thinking as a substitute for control over their lives: "Things will get better after my next Jupiter return, or when this damn Saturn transit ends." Some find a rationale for their shortcomings and limitations: "What can you expect? I'm a Gemini." Still others will find in astrology a way to cope in an era of increasing complexity; the diminished power of most individuals to have an impact in the face of large impersonal, byzantine systems; and dire predictions about impending catastrophes, problems with no apparent solution, and situations with consequences of Biblical proportion that are met by incompetence, indifference, and/or overwhelm:

> *It's a commonplace to say that in uncertain times people crave certainty. But what astrology offers isn't certainty–it's distance. Just as a person may find it easier to accept things about herself when she decides she was born that way, astrology makes it possible to see world events from a less reactive position. It posits that history is not a linear story of upward progress but instead moves in cycles, and that historical ac-*

tors–the ones running amok all around us–are archetypes. Alarming, yes; villainous, perhaps; but familiar, legible.[34]

The upside of astrology's widespread popularity is that for those with the depth of interest and necessary spiritual maturity, astrology does provide not just a language with which to make sense of things, but a pathway to a more conscious and intentional life, one in which personal choices and actions are in line with the prevailing archetypal forces, and with the underlying intelligence that is hardwired into this universe we seek to know and join as informed participants.

Perhaps in parallel with quantum physicists, psychoanalysts, surrealists, psychedelic pioneers, consciousness researchers, deconstructionists and other explorers on the frontlines of the Era of Uncertainty, astrologers in this brave new world are, each in their own way, seeking to penetrate beneath the surface appearance of things, and feel the heartbeat of something more essential to the very existence of this place and our capacity to know it. With some form of astrology never more than a few clicks away, a potential seeker of this level of understanding might begin with a casual awareness of Sun, Moon and rising sign; go on to have a meaningful reading with a professional astrologer; be drawn to study; and potentially arrive at the portal to a much deeper possibility than might be apparent at the glittery surface of astrology's current pop meme.

Approaching Astrology as an Exploratory Language

For those that are ready for this deeper exploration, I will attempt to map out a route in the remainder of this book, beginning with a consideration of what sort of astrology might be worth pursuing in the Era of Uncertainty, given our history of evolution through previous phases. Each of these phases offers something of value to continue to pursue in the postmodern era, even as the Era of Uncertainty itself potentially opens up a new phase in our evolution - one that is not bound by the philosophical strictures of the past.

Must astrology always speak in a way that our rational minds can comprehend? Must it always be understood and practiced as a coherent system of logic? Must it provide scientific hypotheses that can be verified empirically? Or, in going back to our roots, approaching astrology as a language with which to explore the interface between cosmos and psyche, can we also perhaps find our way back to a more direct way of knowing.

As Richard Tarnas elaborates the possibility:

The many particulars of the empirical world are all endowed with symbolic, archetypal significance, and that significance flows between inner and outer, between self and world. In this relatively undifferentiated state of consciousness, human beings perceive themselves as directly – emotionally, mystically, consequentially – participat-

ing in and communicating with the interior life of the natural world and cosmos. To be more precise, this participation mystique involves a complex sense of direct inner participation not only of human beings in the world, but also of human beings in the divine powers, through ritual, and of the divine powers in the world, by virtue of their immanent and transformative presence.[35]

Since the beginning of the Era of Uncertainty, Theosophical and New Age teachings, as well as the evolution of psychological astrology, informed by Jung, Rudhyar, Ruperti, Tarnas and many other contemporary astrologers, psychologists and philosophers have all brought us to the threshold of this participatory universe, where the line between inner and outer, self and world is far more permeable, and potentially far more infused with significance than science would have us believe. At the same time, we have the tools, in a less predictive, more exploratory form of astrology, to enter into a dialogue with the cosmos in a way that science cannot or will not, and in so doing, potentially re-enchant the world with a sacred numinosity it has too long kept at the periphery of our collective experience, and largely suffered without.

My only question, as we stand at the threshold of the door into this beckoning possibility – which we will fully enter in Part Three – is, "What have we been waiting for?" Of course, those who have read to this point in this book, or who are otherwise familiar with the road we have taken to get here, will realize that our separation from science, as difficult and as painful as that has been for those who already feel themselves marginalized or ostracized from the mainstream, has been an absolutely necessary part of our growth. The path forward, in my estimation, starts with a long overdue admission that astrology is not a science, accompanied by a willingness to wonder what else it might be, and at a deeper level, a remembering of what it has been all along.

In a postmodern era, each of us gets to approach this question in a way that makes sense, without the necessity for reliance upon external authorities – whether they be scientific, religious, philosophical, psychological or astrological. Although I have taken some care, in the first part of this book, to document our collective journey, and to note the significant "authorities" who have shaped it, from this point forward, I will begin to leave those other voices behind and more fully claim my own. I will not pretend to have the definitive word about anything, but I will share with you what I have learned on my own half-century journey, and how I see the possibility of using that as a point of departure for a process that will differ from mine, and become something intimately personal to you, as you undertake it.

Notes

1. Jung, Carl G. *Collected Works of C.G. Jung, Volume 15: Spirit in Man, Art, And Literature.* London: Routledge, Kegan and Paul, 1971.

2. Hunt, Morton. *The Story of Psychology*. Doubleday, 1993, 127.
3. Jung, Carl G. *Memories, Dreams and Reflections*. New York: Vintage Books, 1965, 72.
4. Jung, *Memories, Dreams and Reflections*, 175.
5. Jung, *Memories, Dreams and Reflections*, 177.
6. Jung, *Memories, Dreams and Reflections*, 183.
7. Owen, Lance S. "C. G. Jung and the Prophet Puzzle." In *Jung's Red Book for Our Time: Searching for the Soul under Postmodern Conditions*, edited by Murray Stein and Thomas Arzt, Vol. 1. Chiron Publications, 2017, 106.
8. Corbett, Sara. "Carl Jung and the Holy Grail of the Unconscious." *The New York Times*, October 16, 2009. https://www.nytimes.com/2009/09/20/magazine/20jung-t.html.
9. Campion, Nicholas. *A History of Western Astrology Volume II: The Medieval and Modern Worlds*. Bloomsbury, 2009, 255.
10. Jung, Carl G. *The Red Book: Liber Novus*, edited by Sonu Shamdasani. W. W. Norton & Company, 2009, 391-92.
11. Jung, Carl G. *Collected Works of C.G. Jung Vol. 10: Civilization in Transition*. Princeton University Press, 1970, 59.
12. Campion, *A History of Western Astrology Volume II*, 252.
13. Jung, *The Red Book*, 161-63.
14. Hillman, James. *Re-Visioning Psychology*. HarperCollins, 1975, xvii.
15. Hillman, James. *The Soul's Code: In Search of Character and Calling*. New York: Warner Books, 1996, 10.
16. Hillman, *Re-Visioning Psychology*, 169.
17. Campion, *A History of Western Astrology Volume II*, 259.
18. Rossi, Safron. "Planetary Interiority: James Hillman & the Archetypal Psyche." Astro-Synthesis. Accessed June 16, 2023. https://www.astrosynthesis.com.au/wp-content/uploads/2020/12/Planetary-Interiority-Safron-Rossi.pdf.
19. Rudhyar, Dane. *The Astrology of Personality: A Re-Formulation of Astrological Concepts and Ideals, in Terms of Contemporary Psychology and Philosophy*, Doubleday, 1970, 18, 459.
20. Rudhyar, Dane. *The Astrology of Transformation: A Multilevel Approach*. Wheaton, IL: Theosophical Publishing House, 1980, xiii – xiv.
21. Rudhyar, Dane. "Astrological Timing: The Transition to the New Age." Rudhyar Archival Project. Accessed June 16, 2023. http://www.khaldea.com/rudhyar/at/at_c6_pp7.shtml.

22. Rudhyar, *The Astrology of Transformation*, xv.
23. Rudhyar, *The Astrology of Transformation*, x.
24. Rudhyar, *The Astrology of Transformation*, 120-21.
25. Campion, *A History of Western Astrology Volume II*, 256.
26. Tarnas, Richard. *Cosmos and Psyche: Intimations of a New World View*. Viking, 2006, 54-55.
27. Tarnas, *Cosmos and Psyche*, 68.
28. Campion, *A History of Western Astrology Volume II*, 285.
29. Campion, *A History of Western Astrology Volume II*, 278.
30. Gecewicz, Claire. "'New Age' Beliefs Common among Religious, Nonreligious Americans." Pew Research Center, October 1, 2018. https://www.pewresearch.org/fact-tank/2018/10/01/new-age-beliefs-common-among-both-religious-and-nonreligious-americans/.
31. Smallwood, Christine. "Astrology in the Age of Uncertainty." *The New Yorker*, October 21, 2019. https://www.newyorker.com/magazine/2019/10/28/astrology-in-the-age-of-uncertainty.
32. Beck, Julie. "Why Are Millennials So Into Astrology?" *The Atlantic*, June 22, 2021. https://www.theatlantic.com/health/archive/2018/01/the-new-age-of-astrology/550034/.
33. Adorno, Theodor. *The Stars Down to Earth*. New York: Routledge, 1994, 103.
34. Smallwood, "Astrology in the Age of Uncertainty."
35. Tarnas, *Cosmos and Psyche*, 17.

The mouth utters the word, the sign, and the symbol. If the word is a sign, it means nothing. But if the word is a symbol, it means everything . . . One can certainly gain outer freedom through powerful actions, but one creates inner freedom only through the symbol.

The symbol is the word that goes out of the mouth, that one does not simply speak, but that rises out of the depths of the self as a word of power and great need and places itself unexpectedly on the tongue. It is an astonishing and perhaps seemingly irrational word, but one recognizes it as a symbol since it is alien to the conscious mind. If one accepts the symbol, it is as if a door opens leading into a new room whose existence one previously did not know.

Carl Jung, The Red Book: Liber Novus, 2009

Part Three

An Astropoetic Exploration Of Psyche and Cosmos

We dream because the Earth dreams. We sing and know music because the vibrational expression we call music is inherent in this place. We have the capacity to create because the larger system from which we come has at its core the capacity to create. We express new form through dreaming because that is how all form is created in this place.

We are all of us dreamed into being. For the Earth lives im a dream. It exists in a very complex form of the state a juggler is in when he juggles, where some deeper part, some dreaming part, of himself maintains the balance point.

Stephen Harrod Buhner, Plant Intelligence and the Imaginal Realm, 2014

Chapter Ten

Basic Principles of Astropoetics

If I had to give a working definition of astrology, rooted in our history to this point, and my interest in reclaiming what was lost through that history in our collective attempt to conform to the emerging scientific paradigm, I would simply start with this:

Astrology is an attempt to understand and more consciously occupy our place in a larger, living cosmos.

One might reasonably assume that I believe that knowledge of a birthchart can be a guide to this process, and I do. But I also believe that this is ultimately a process that transcends the birthchart and its symbolic implications, and that requires us to first attend to some more fundamental questions about who it is that is looking at the chart, hoping for answers. The silent assumption throughout most of our history has been that as system of inquiry, a language, a mirror, or a map (choose your own metaphor), astrology itself is a reliable source of information. But this is really only true to the extent that the individual astrologer:

1) knows the astrological language

2) can see clearly into the heart of the symbolism; and

3) can meaningfully articulate what she sees.

Who Is it That Stands at the Astrological Threshold?

Most of our attention so far, in delineating whatever understanding of astrology we have been able to commandeer, has been on the first of these requirements. We study what other astrologers have written; we seek to apply what we learn to our own charts; and then, acquiring a certain level of confidence, we venture forth to read the charts of family, friends and eventually clients. And through this process, we undoubtedly accumulate knowledge of the astrological language, and get better at applying it. But our focus remains the chart itself, rather than the one who is looking at the chart.

So then, who is this person looking at the chart? Who are you?

Because I don't know you, and can't possibly answer this question for you, I will begin by answering it for myself, and for you, so you can get a better sense of what brings me to the threshold marked by this book.

My Astrological Story

I began my astrological quest in my early twenties, without a lot of life experience under my belt. I was actually struggling in those days, as do most young adults, trying to figure out who I was, where I belonged in this big, bad world, and how I could somehow gain a reasonable foothold. In astrology, I saw a potential aid in addressing these questions, particularly after reading Dane Rudhyar's *The Astrology of Personality*, which still sits on my bookshelf, torn and tattered and underlined on nearly every page. I am tempted to run and get it now, and quote him. But instead, I will tell you what I have learned, looking backwards from the vantage point of 50 years of practice and experience, that now makes me who I am, standing at the astrological threshold of my own journey forward. From Rudhyar, and from many other sources, converging now to form a more or less integrated stream, I have learned:

Cosmos is Self and Self is Cosmos

Astrology is essentially the study of the Self. I capitalize the word "Self" here in reference to Jung's idea, which Rudhyar shared, that there is a deeper core identity than mere personality, a core out of which one's essential nature emanates, and that informs a larger journey toward integration and wholeness. For Jung, the Self was an archetype, meaning that it was something that arose within our collective psyche, something that we all held in common, as well as something that we each individually attempted to actualize in our own way.

As an archetype, the Self is a portal to the totality of all that is, that is to say, a point of entry into a deeper, more spiritual understanding of Life, God, Goddess, Great Mystery, Cosmos or whatever other word you might want to use for an ultimate reality – one that not only encompasses the individual self, and the collective self, but really, when you come down to it, All That Is. At the end of this road, as I see it anyway, there is nothing that is not encompassed by this concept of Self.

It might appear at first blush, that what I am talking about here is a transpersonal form of psychological astrology. And to some extent, I am. But I have also come to believe that everything studied by science – whether living or believed to be inert – also partakes of this Self, and that ultimately, all knowledge, however it is derived, is knowledge of this Self. So, in this sense, whether we are studying the psyche or the stock market or black holes – from an astrological perspective, we are *attempting to understand and more consciously occupy our place in a larger, living cosmos*. Cosmos is Self and Self is Cosmos.

Or at the very least, as I personally stand at this astrological threshold, what I really want to know is this more ultimate sense of who I am, not just in the subjective world of my individual psyche, but in the larger sense in which I am a part of All That Is, and beyond that in the largest sense in which I am All That Is, temporarily being me – the mystical sense in which "I am" – is a statement of participation in the Cosmos at the deepest possible level. I'm not prepared to say, necessarily, that this is what Rudhyar or even Jung meant by an astrology as a study of the Self – although they may have – but this is where their teachings have taken me, after a lifetime of gestation and marination in my subsequent thinking and experience.

Walking the Path Between Self and Cosmos Is the Journey of the Soul

Knowing this Self is a journey that begins with the much humbler, but no less demanding task of knowing the self, small "s." Jung talks about the inflation that is possible when you identify with an archetype, and so, to simply say, "I am the Self" is a bit like claiming to be Jesus, and then drowning as you attempt to walk on water. You can't – I can't – make that leap in a single bound, even though from the ultimate standpoint, self is Self, has always been and always will be.

I see no reason not to call the quest of the self to know and ultimately evolve to reunite and merge with the Self, the journey of the soul. I have spoken at great length about soul in my first book, *The Seven Gates of Soul*, and would point the interested reader to that tome, if you are interested in a more in-depth discussion of how I think about it. For our purposes here, we can simply assume that by definition everything we do in this life, to understand and make sense of our experiences within a larger context, and with perspective, is encompassed by the journey of the soul.

It is also important to understand, in the way that the post-structuralists did, that at best the Self is a working integration of selves, any one of whom may present its face as that of the Self, at any given time, or at least try to dominate the ongoing conversation about "Who I am." Thus, a truly postmodern astrology would begin from the premise that which "self" approaches the chart at any given moment determines what the chart reveals.

As I approach a question about some aspect of my life that feels cloudy and uncertain, the chart itself will go a bit out of focus; whereas, another more confident part of my personality will approach a much clearer mirror. This is not to say that we can't lean into greater clarity, regardless of which self asks the question; this, in fact, is what the astrological language is, at its best, able to facilitate better than any other. It does this so well, in part, because the chart maps not only the psyche, but also the inter-relationship between the various selves that make up the psyche, and whose integration becomes, through a lifetime of learning and growth, a decent approximation of the kind of whole Self that Jung was talking about.

Knowing the Self and the selves is a task which psychological astrology naturally lends itself. I can easily look at my chart, and using a basic vocabulary, see my personality reflected, as well as the various sub-personalities that vie for dominance within me, the various internal conflicts and/or contradictions that complicate my life, the various issues and challenges I am likely to have to face in order to learn and grow and gradually evolve toward the place where I can entertain a more conscious sense of relationship to the Self. All of that is potentially encompassed by a knowledge of astrology, the first of our requirements, as outlined in the section above.

Having said that, however, we are also noting here that knowledge of this self, small "s," is a journey, meaning that we can't possibly know what the chart has to tell us about who we are, even on the level of personality, all at once. The journey is not ultimately an astrological journey, although a knowledge of astrology can be a useful traveling companion to it. For every step we take through life, what we see when we look at our birthchart will change.

The journey is one both of healing our core wounds, whether suffered in childhood or some other life, and a journey of self-actualization, putting our innate talents, skills and resources to use in making some contribution to the good of the larger whole of which we are part. The journey is also one of leaning into that which the mind cannot possibly understand, but which provides a compelling clue to the "meaning of it all," forming a vital relationship to the Cosmic Mystery, for lack of a better way to put it.

If we take the "right" step, that is to say, a step that moves us forward in relation to one or more of these three essential tasks, then the chart will come into clearer focus; if we take the "wrong" step, then it will go out of focus. If we take enough steps in the "right" direction, then the meaning of the chart will deepen in a fundamental way, and we will see farther into it, as though looking through a microscope or a telescope with a higher power of magnification. As we learn from the "wrong" steps we have taken, our capacity to do this will increase.

In this way, our astrological journey – particularly in relation to the second requirement of what it takes to be an astrologer, as noted in our short list above, namely, seeing clearly into the heart of the symbolism – becomes a reflection of how skillfully we learn, over time, to navigate the soul's journey. This really has nothing to do with our study of the astrological language; it has everything to do with polishing the lens through which that knowledge is applied, by becoming a better, more conscious, more integrated, more fully realized human being.

Knowledge of Astrology is an Aid to the Journey Not a Substitute For It

Everything we encounter in our life is an opportunity to move in this direction, and to polish the lens as we go. Of course, it is also an opportunity to learn astrology on a more intimately personal level, for as we correlate our experiences with our transits of natal patterns, we also deepen our study.

But really, what an astrological path to self-mastery is about is the refinement of each of our selves, so that in their domain, they make conscious and intentional choices that align with something at the core of the being they share, and so that first the smaller, personal self, and more gradually the greater, archetypal Self comes into focus.

This is not rocket science. If something in our life is out of kilter, this is our opportunity to use our birthchart as a springboard to realignment, first by understanding the cosmic pressures throwing us out of alignment, and then by deliberately using our knowledge of astrology to realign. If an opportunity presents itself that we are called to claim, then we can use our knowledge of astrology to lean into our deeper capacities. If something mysterious speaks to us from beyond the ordinary demands of everyday life, we can use our knowledge of astrology to feel our way into the heart of that mystery – not by explaining it, but by more deliberately embracing it, with our senses, our emotions, and our imaginations, as well as what we think we know about our birthcharts. As we give ourselves to these opportunities, often disguised as challenges, we learn something about our self, our selves, and the Self.

To Be Useful Astrology Must Illuminate What We Don't Already Know

Addressing the final requirement outlined above – the ability to articulate clearly what we see, like the ability to see clearly into the heart of the symbolism, depends upon more than just our knowledge or experience. It depends in part on our ability to communicate in general, which is a life skill that is useful to cultivate regardless of whether or not you want to become a worthy astrologer.

Beyond that the ability to communicate something truly interesting and useful depends upon exposing yourself to a broad multiplicity of worldviews from which to draw the language appropriate to a given astrological situation, to be able to explain it in English (or whatever your native language is), but also with reference to a larger cultural context in which something inscrutable and often ineffable can come into clearer focus. Astrology is ultimately an exploration of what we don't already know, or there would be no point in doing it. To coax what we don't already know – what is essentially unconscious – to the place where we can begin to understand it, and then put it into words, it helps to have a deep reservoir of metaphors available to bubble up at exactly the right moment.

Such metaphors can come from almost anywhere, but in addition to an ever-evolving knowledge of astrology itself, a good astrologer will at a minimum, be well versed in:

psychology

philosophy

a spiritual practice, or an eclectic exposure to multiple practices

mythology

fairy tales and folklore

astronomy and celestial mechanics

world literature and film

current events as seen through an archetypal lens

a broad palette of digested and integrated life experiences

If your aspiration is to "read" charts professionally for other people, then you will also ideally want to get some additional training in the counseling arts. Beyond that, you will want to cultivate the capacity to listen carefully, and to hear the astrological archetypes in a birthchart reveal themselves in the language of the person whose chart it is. If someone spends 20 minutes telling you how "limited" or "trapped" they feel, as you are excited about their upcoming Uranus transit, you will nonetheless be leading them astray if you cannot switch gears and recognize that they are talking about Saturn.

This is an art that does not evolve to the extent that you are enamored of your own astrological prowess. To help someone else, or yourself for that matter, "*to understand and more consciously occupy your place in a larger, living cosmos*," you must give a fair amount of attention to cultivating the kind of clarity that only becomes possible when you have used astrology to address and heal your own psychological wounds. Ideally, you have also taken some time to understand how astrology is related to other dimensions and ways of understanding the larger, ongoing conversation that human beings have been having with the cosmos, at least since human civilizations started coalescing 6,000 years ago, and if you are really brave (and as we will attempt to be in our final chapter), back before that.

Astropoetics

I call my particular approach to astrology "astropoetics" in the recognition that the "facts" of astrological interpretation are actually better understood as poetic similes and metaphors that resonate in various ways with a multi-layered truth that means different things at different times. We long to know who we are, not just in human terms, but also as souls in relation to the grand, seemingly intelligent design that permeates this vast, unfathomable cosmos. As suggested above, these two quests – which encompass a wide range of questions in between – are one and the same inquiry, which appear in various guises at various times.

Astropoetics is a useful language with which to explore our relation to the grand design, our most deeply connected sense of self, and a richly complex array of selves from a cosmic perspective within which the same quest morphs in ways that are astrological, and that transcend astrology. At the same time, astropoetics is an approach to astrology that understands everyday life to be a rich repository of meaningful images. When these images are correlated with the appropriate astrological patterns, they provide a point of entry into an intimately personal understanding of the birthchart and the life it describes, at whatever level we approach it.

Unlike traditional astrology, astropoetics does not strive toward an interpretation of the birthchart. Instead, it approaches the birthchart as an exploratory window in both time and psychic space through which the soul can be observed gradually learning how to move toward a more complete embrace of its wholeness and its rightful place within the Great Mystery of Cosmos.

The Origin of the Word

astro-

Using astrology as a primary language, the soul can be observed with uncanny clarity in relation to its movement through various cycles, which wax and wane in predictable rhythm, and are mirrored in the movement of the larger celestial patterns that routinely coalesce and disperse in the sky.

-poetics

The mystery of soul is best approached through a language that is poetic in its use of words. A poetic language conducts its quest for the truth obliquely – through simile and metaphor, image and symbol, suggestion and allusion, rather than direct, dogmatic statement of fact.

astro-poetics

When astrology is approached poetically – as an open-minded intuitive contemplation of imagery and symbolism, rather than as an interpretative system based on established definitions or preconceived ideas – it becomes a potent language of soul that allows for the possibility of deep and penetrating self-discovery.

Fate Versus Evolutionary Opportunity

Traditionally, astrology understands the birthchart to be a signature of fate. Since the advent of humanistic and transpersonal psychologies in the 1970s and 1980s, many astrologers have embraced a less fatalistic view of our creative possibilities. While fate is a complex subject with many nuanced understandings, most astrologers today accept some idea of fate, while differing in the extent to which they believe it can be mitigated.

Astropoetics understands fate – as reflected in the birthchart – to be an exquisitely designed opportunity for each individual soul to work toward healing and self-realization. This opportunity is a learning process that transcends traditional astrological judgments about good and bad placements, benefic and malefic signatures, and the relative ease or difficulty of birthcharts considered in their entirety.

Fate is not something to mitigate, but rather an elaborate opportunity for the evolution of consciousness to be understood, embraced and lived to the fullest extent possible.

Astropoetics further assumes that what becomes of the potential for good or ill that is harbored within any fate depends entirely upon you, and the consciousness that you bring to the birthchart. Whatever situation in life seems to be "fated," is at heart, an expression of divine intelligence setting you up to learn something important about yourself and about the Self.

Signs Versus Symbols

Traditional astrology – and most contemporary astrology as well – aims at an "objective" understanding of the symbolism - what this means, not just for you or I, but in general, as a statement of astrological truth. As it is routinely practiced today, astrology has become largely a matter of rationally decoding signs that have become short-hand notation for known qualities.

Astropoetics seeks instead to discover unknown sensory, emotional, psychological, imaginal, mythological and spiritual correlates to symbols, and the images that embody these correlates, along a path that is unique to the individual, even though it also navigates a field of archetypes that are common to us all.

The process is by nature an intimate journey into unfamiliar territory, and the outcome is not something that can be predetermined according to standardized definitions for astrological symbols. Astropoetics assumes that the symbolism must be referenced to both an astrological context (the birthchart considered as a whole) and a living context that is unique to the individual soul, before it can mean anything at all.

Personality Versus Evolving Sense of Self

Astrology tends to understand the birthchart as a static description of personality undergoing a series of discrete events or processes.

Astropoetics instead sees the birthchart as descriptive of a process that deepens and transmutes in cyclical time, ideally into a clearer, cleaner, more focused expression as increasing awareness is brought to the experience of embodiment it describes. The birthchart is a mirror that reflects back to you a sense of self that changes as your consciousness evolves. What you see in your birthchart depends upon how conscious you are, as well as the level of self-awareness that informs the questions and intentions you bring to the process of self-inquiry.

Causal Versus Relational Language

To the extent that an astrologer strives to be scientific, he will adopt science's insistence on causal explanations for its interpretations, even if the language that he uses emphasizes individual choice, or even if he understands Ptolemy's idea of celestial causation to be of a different order than that embraced by science. Astrologers that are sensitive to this issue might say as Paracelsus did, for example, that "*the stars incline; they do not compel.*" Actually, from the astropoetic perspective, the stars do nothing but provide an endlessly intriguing mirror to the idiosyncratic landscape of the soul – a mirror in which what you see is largely a reflection of who you are.

Instead of attempting to articulate the causal relationship between heaven and earth, however euphemistically it might be phrased, astropoetics assumes instead that everything astrological is a reflection of an interconnected web of resonant relationships, which reflect back to you who you are and where you belong within the greater whole of which you are part.

These relationships are not causal in nature, but expressions of natural metaphorical logic. Your life is reflected by your birthchart, not because the arrangement of planets in the sky at the time of our birth causes you to be who you are, but because your life and the birthchart that reflects it is part of a larger pattern in which you participate, more or less consciously, and with which you share a natural affinity. This larger pattern, in turn, is a reflection of what it appears to be, at any given time, as viewed through the lens that you bring to it by the self that is viewing.

The entire web of relationships encompassed by this pattern is suggested astrologically by the interconnected nature of the birthchart, which mirrors the coherent internal logic of your subjective soul space. Each resonant relationship within the pattern evolves cyclically through soul time, as it is reflected astrologically in the various cycles of planets that are connected by aspect in soul space.

Alleviation of Suffering Versus Empowerment Within Suffering

Lastly, while traditional astrology – at least that which is psychologically oriented – strives toward an understanding of the human predicament and an alleviation of suffering through a more enlightened perspective, astropoetics aims a bit deeper.

Astropoetics strives toward an understanding of how the human predicament is thoroughly infused by the presence of Spirit. This is true, even where the human predicament is most difficult, most painful, most intensely vulnerable, and where the seemingly intractable core issues that mark the embodied life are encountered.

Without attempting to romanticize or otherwise dismiss the pain and suffering inherent in such experiences, astropoetics aims toward a vision broad and deep enough to encompass them as the portals to a deeper, more conscious and more empowered state of being that they ultimately are.

Taken to its highest possibility, astropoetics not only describes the psychological and spiritual landscape of the soul. It also shows you how to live – how and when to apply your creative intelligence in order to play a more conscious part within the greater whole: healing yourself, actualizing your potential, making a difference in a world that needs your full presence and participation to reach its ultimate expression; leaning into a deeper, more multidimensional relationship to Mystery. Within the astropoetic worldview, suffering is merely the springboard into extreme creativity for those strong enough to make the leap – and making the leap begins with the courage to look and then to take responsibility for what you see.

A Living Example

So, what would this look like in actual practice? Let's take a real-life example from the life that I know best – my own. I do this not because I am a narcissist, although somewhere in my chart, no doubt is one, but because I only have access to the inside story of my own "wild and precious life," as Mary Oliver put it.[1] So, this is where the rubber meets the road as far as this idea that astrology is a kind of mirror, the clarity of whose reflection depends upon who is looking, and how consciously they look.

To take what I share here, and in the rest of this book, to heart, you will have to find a parallel situation in your own life, and improvise an inquiry that makes sense to you. You will not find the answers – nor the important questions, for that matter – in a cookbook. Nor for that matter, will an astrologer be able to help you. This is not to say, that from time to time, having someone else look at your chart cannot give you valuable perspective. It most certainly can. But you will get the most out of your own chart, by developing an astropoetic relationship to it. How to do that is the subject of Part Three of this book, beginning with the demonstration to follow.

To start, I will share my birthchart here. Some of you might have a field day speculating on why I indulge the particular biases that I do. But none of that really matters from an astropoetic perspective as much as what I can see in my own chart (or you in yours), approaching it with clear intention, and a willingness to perpetually polish the lens in order to enter a larger conversation about it. With that introduction as caveat, here is my chart, kept simple by including only the ten classic planets of the solar system prior to 2006 (Sun through Pluto), the four major asteroids (Ceres, Pallas, Juno and Vesta), Chiron and the Moon's Nodes. I use the Porphyry house system and the tropical, geocentric zodiac.

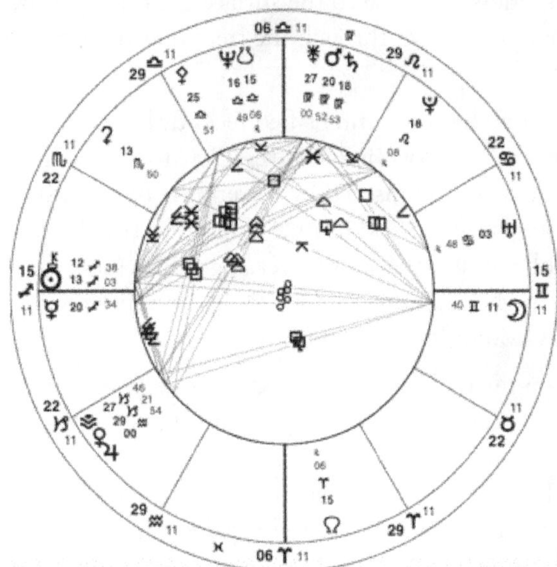

At the outset, we can acknowledge, this is a lot of information to take in all at once, which is true of any birthchart, and often why beginning astrologers feel overwhelmed at the prospect of explaining a birthchart to someone within the span of an hour. The truth is, it can't actually be done. With a bit of focus, and a willingness to start the conversation where the client wants to start it, however, a knowledge of astrology can help identify which subpersonality is asking the question and what it wants to know. Doing that, we can begin – and where we wind up at the end of a good hour of meaningful conversation will transform the birthchart from a two-dimensional abstraction into a living reflection that is both recognizable as truth, and an invitation to go deeper.

If we're honest with ourselves, it was this invitation to go deeper, and not the specific information imparted, that hooked us all. I don't remember the particulars of my first astrological reading, but I do remember the sense of a vast terrain beckoning to me in a way that I had not been beckoned before – or since. So here I am again, knocking on a door into, as Jung put it, "*a new room whose existence I previously did not know.*"

Knocking on the Door

The door opens with a question. So, as I sit in front of my chart, yet again as though for the very first time, I ask the great oracle before me, "What is it I wish to know?"

The answer to even this simple question does not come all at once, but as I sit with it now, I am aware of a sadness bubbling to the surface. It is just before sunset, and the light is growing dim, the sun about to set through the trees outside my office window. It is quiet and peaceful, and I am alone.

My sense of being alone has been intensified recently by the general sense of social isolation that has permeated the last two years of the Covid-19 pandemic, for almost everyone I know. Beyond that, it is also intensified by the ending of an intimate relationship with a woman who began to see the world and its unfolding collective drama in a radically different way than I did, and with whom I found it increasingly difficult to agree about what was real and what wasn't. This might have worked if we could have entered into a conversation across our differences. But we couldn't, and so it didn't.

As I write this, I am nearly 72 years old and, on one level, comfortable being alone. I enjoy my own company; I know how to entertain myself; and all told, I am living what I feel is a good life, feeling blessed in countless ways to be living it. I am creatively engaged with work that fulfills me; I am healthy and financially secure; I live in a beautiful forest; I have good friends, many of whom I have known for decades; I have lived and loved deeply, and I have no regrets. I see so much pain and suffering in the world, and in that context, mine is nothing. I do, however, live more intimately with my own pain and suffering, so this is where I must start my quest. It is the only place from which my quest can start.

If I had to describe this pain and suffering, what would I say? Ultimately, it is the sense of being alienated, of not belonging to the human world, of having withdrawn from the chaos and the insanity to the peace and natural balance of this woodland sanctuary, while at the same time feeling a sense of despair about our collective folly, our inability to move beyond greed, the lust for power, and our petty self-interest, to deal with the very large issues of climate crisis; loss of biodiversity and habitat, for other species, but increasingly for a growing number of human refugees; our inability to deal with increasing hordes of displaced peoples and immigrants in a compassionate and effective way; proliferation of toxic, carcinogenic chemicals that poison our food, our air, our water, and our bodies; the perpetration of racial and economic injustices; the increased atmosphere of violent tensions rising to the surface, threatening democracy here in the US and around the world; and in general, my cumulative dismay at our collective failure to live the human experiment with consciousness, compassion and any sense of wisdom born of historical perspective.

How is it that our brief moment, as a species, here on this beautiful planet has turned out so badly? And what, if anything, can we do about it now, before we dwindle and sputter toward extinction, taking numerous other species down with us? I believe the planet will go on, but will we? That is perhaps the larger question and, as far as I can tell, standing here before the oracle of my chart, the deepest root of my pain and suffering.

This, of course, is not the end of the story, because my pain and suffering also has a much more personal dimension. How could it not? I am the one feeling all this, perhaps not the only one, but the only one here, right now, in this moment, in this space, in this body, in this life. So, it is personal.

I ask myself, "What can I possibly do that will make a difference within such a world? I am writing this book, and I would not be doing that if I did not think, on some level that it matters that I write it. But assuming I could somehow parlay it into a best seller or at least rise to the top of the pile of the 2.2 million books published every year – a wildly delusional assumption at best – will it change the world? Will it make a difference? Will it matter in relation to these larger questions? Or is it just a way for me to keep myself occupied and distracted while the Titanic goes down?

I don't mean to be cynical here, but my question really is: What can be done? What can any of us do? What can I do? We all must do what we can, and yet here we are, the iceberg looming up ahead, the humungous ship too cumbersome to turn around before we hit. What can be done? And if nothing really, then where – even within this very rich and bottomless mirror that I am trying, in my own way to polish, can meaning be found?

Aside from all of that, I am lonely. It is just me, working to do what I can or what I feel I am called to do, regardless of whether or not it "saves the planet" or saves anyone but me. What does it matter to anyone, whether I do it or not? I feel this way because, at age 72, I am without a partner – that one person who gets me, and whose daily reflection of that, gives me the strength and the will to go on. Yes, I know, I must find this strength and will within myself, and I have spent a lifetime doing that, which is why I can stand here now, in front of the mirror, and say, I have lived a good life; I have loved and been loved; and I have done what I can to make the world a better place. And yet, I suffer in my aloneness – as do all sentient creatures on this planet, in one way or another, according to Buddha and everyone else who had something worth saying to say. And I wonder, "Now what? I am still here, I am still available, I am still willing to do what I can? But what would that look like? And what will it matter?"

And so, dear reader, I have rambled enough. What is my question, you still wonder? Where within all of this rambling is the key to the door that will unlock my birthchart now? At least, you can see my dilemma – which is actually not that different than the dilemma of anyone approaching a birthchart, whether on behalf of oneself or another. Like the birthchart itself, life goes around and around and everything is connected to everything else. So, where to begin becomes a worthy question, worth taking some time to feel your way into. Finding a worthy question is a quest unto itself.

As many spiritual teachers have suggested, the only place to begin is here and now. So, coming back into the here and now, as I share my tale of woe, I also notice, now that day has descended into night, that the moon is nearly full. As an astrologer, I know that this Full Moon will be a lunar eclipse at the 28th degree of Taurus, landing in my 6th house, forming the tightest aspect trine to my natal Vesta. As it happens, transiting Vesta is, at this moment, exactly opposed the eclipse degree and exactly sextile my natal Vesta.

It occurs to me to wonder, "If I were asking the question to Vesta or perhaps as Vesta, what might I say?"

> *How can I best use my vital life energy, my creativity, my sense of calling to the path that I am on now – to tend to my solitude, and my hearth – in a way that allows me to feel more deeply connected to others, to the world at large, and to the world around me – and to somehow make a difference in doing what I do, at this point in our collective history?*

* * * * *

Here I am, the following day, ready to continue this exploration, having just done a reading for a new client, who, as synchronicity would have it, was curious in particular about Vesta – which forms a couple of important patterns in her chart – with no prompting from me.

So, what did I tell her? Essentially what I wrote about Vesta in my last book, *Astrology and the Archetypal Power of Numbers, Part Two*, adapted here to suit our current context:

> *While not as striking a figure as Pallas, or as intoxicating as Venus, or as dominant in the Feminine dimensions of reality as the Moon, Vesta nonetheless plays an important role in the journey of the soul.*
>
> *As the keeper of the sacred flame – Vesta infuses the heroic soul with a sense of purpose, a relentless passion, and personal guidance from within. Guided by Vesta, the soul makes choices that are aligned with her nature, and with the cosmic function she is meant to serve in the larger scheme of things as an essential and unique individual.*

Over time, Vesta's function as a guiding daimon grows in range and power to inspire not just the individual under her sway, but the collective within the sphere of influence in which the "soul on fire" functions. Here, the inspired hero becomes the inspiration to others, a torchbearer whose legacy will carry on the work of those who came before and infuse the next generation of heroes to carry it forward.

Vesta works with Venus – in many ways, her antithesis – to facilitate sexual healing, and with Mars – her protégé and initiate – to deepen the mythopoetic roots of the hero, so she is not just serving herself, or even the collective, but the ancestors, and the gods and goddesses in who footsteps she walks. Here Vesta ups the ante, and challenges those under her tutelage to find within themselves a deeper reason for doing what they do – one rooted in increasing allegiance to and identification with the Divine Intelligence at the Heart of the One. As the personal work of healing is embraced, the transpersonal power of the One shines through unimpeded, and Vesta is an important guide to this process.

Ultimately, Vesta burns away everything non-essential within the soul to the clear and radiant embodiment of Spirit. This clear and radiant embodiment in turn becomes the source for breakthrough complex creativity capable of changing the culture in which it emerges. Among the various possibilities here, she can infuse the hero with the capacity to stand alone when he must – unpopular, vilified, castigated, excommunicated – but as a strong defender of what is right and true nonetheless, even if that means his own ultimate destruction. Along a different path, Vesta infuses a very different sort of hero with such luminescence that he becomes the invisible source of heat and light for an alchemical process that happens around him, through which Divine Intelligence is revealed.[2]

And at a different place in the book:

While the particulars seem to vary quite a bit, it appears that Vesta works as a kind of perpetual flame of inspiration, flickering brightly when activated with a new idea, or a different approach to something otherwise familiar, or a new creative exploration of some kind. In the midst of any creative life – particularly as we consider it from the perspective of our question about how I, as an individual, can contribute to the wellbeing of the whole – there are many streams and tributaries that flow into and feed the creative soul. This is not about achievement or accomplishment, but about the joys and wonders of the creative process itself.

As Stephen Buhner (303) describes it, the artistic process involves following what he calls a golden thread, which "may emerge from any ordinary thing and open a doorway into the metaphysical background of the world."

> *The initial touch of a golden thread is always attended by a specific kind of feeling. Experience will bring trust in that touch and the feeling that accompanies it, familiar recognition at its emergence. You feel the touch of the thing, it captures your attention, then, if you are a writer, you work to encapsulate it in language.*
>
> *Because the writer is in the zone, dreaming as they are writing, the lines are an expression of synesthesia, filled with feeling. The writer feels into them, tasting, savoring the feel of the words. Then they step back inside the thread and feel it. Then they compare the feeling of the thread and that of the lines they have written. They are going for congruency, for identity between the two. At the experience of any difference, they engage in tiny micromolar adjustments of the lines they are crafting, trying to get them ever closer to the thread that has touched them. Great art occurs when the lines and the golden thread become identical in feeling.*[3]

As I recognize this process, I can understand Vesta's role in the revelation of my golden thread. This revelation shows me how this is connected to that, and how both this and that interweave into a more complex and integrated picture of reality that either this or that can alone. Along this track, I have played with music and images, as well as words and ideas, and all have flown into an expression of synesthesia that I call astropoetics – the golden thread that makes any exploration of astrology an adventure in discovery, rather than a mere decoding of symbols with rote meanings. This is the improvisational art I aspire to, and in my reaching for it, Vesta becomes my guide and my muse.[4]

I wrote all this under a different set of circumstances, and in a different context, but it nonetheless still represents the thread of a conversation – one of many – that I have been having with myself for some time, and that I now pick up again. Refreshing my memory about this conversation, I can see more clearly how Vesta is an appropriate guide to the question I posed earlier, as well as a fitting muse for our exploration of the ways in which astropoetics can take us into a deeper, more specifically astro-logical way of knowing, one that engages not just our intellectual understanding, but the feelings, the sensations, the images, the memories, the visceral touchstones within our own experience that anchor the knowing in our belly and our bones.

Notes

1. Oliver, Mary. "The Summer Day." The Library of Congress. Accessed June 16, 2023. https://www.loc.gov/programs/poetry-and-literature/poet-laureate/poet-laureate-projects/poetry-180/all-poems/item/poetry-180-133/the-summer-day/.
2. Landwehr, Joe. *Astrology and the Archetypal Power of Numbers: Part Two: Arithmology in the Birthchart*. Whittier, NC: Ancient Tower Press, 2018, 453-54.
3. Buhner, Stephen Harrod. *Plant Intelligence and the Imaginal Realm: Beyond the Doors of Perception into the Dreaming of the Earth*. Bear & Company, 2014, 303.
4. Landwehr, *Astrology and the Archetypal Power of Numbers: Part Two*, 568-69.

Behind each and every interpretation of the tale is the tale. The tale provides the invisible backdrop against which all analyses parade their brilliance. Myth lies behind every account we give of it, and it gives no account of itself. Myths fall back on invisibility. They show an enchanting face, but their backing disappears under scrutiny. Nothing's there. We are lost in the woods.

James Hillman, The Soul's Code: In Search of Character and Calling, 1996

Chapter Eleven

Opening the Archetypal Eye

How do we know anything astrological? Typically, we learn astrology by reading what those who have come before us have written, or by attending classes, or conferences, and then eventually by applying what we absorb to the reading of charts, familiar and then unfamiliar. But where does what those who write about and teach astrology know come from? Presumably from their teachers, and everyone else who has influenced them, marinated in their own experiences, back and back and back to the beginning – when the early Hellenistic astrologers passed on what they had somehow absorbed from Nechepso and Petosiris. Before that, astrological knowledge was presumed to come from Hermes Trismegistus, as well as from the mystical divinatory traditions of Babylon and Egypt and before that from someone or something within a mystical fog where the true source of astrology, rooted in a more direct way of knowing, was a practice, perhaps from our contemporary point of view, a lost art.

So, what might that art look like now, resurrected in the only way possible, as a postmodern undertaking, suitable to any contemporary astrologer who wants to get his information, not second-hand, but through his own efforts to know?

Asking this question does not preclude the idea that we are a community and what we learn from each other is important. It is to suggest that before we join with others, and develop the necessary skills to separate the wheat from the chaff, in deciding what within the nearly unlimited universe of astrological offerings is worth adding to our own repertoire, there is some more fundamental process that allows us to approach any question from an astrological perspective.

Astrology as an Innate Archetypal Language

To begin, I think it is helpful to consider astrology as a language with which it is possible to have a conversation with the Self, as we discussed it in Chapter Ten. We might alternately understand this Self as Cosmos or Spirit or Mystery, which are all ways of alluding to the depth of conversation that is possible, one that takes place on the threshold between the known and the much greater Unknown, perhaps to evoke the spirit of Xenophon, a conversation that dares to lean into the Unknowable. This is a conversation that, in a postmodern world, is recognized to never complete itself, but one that if courageously pursued, can at the very least, be deeply meaningful. It is a conversation that has been going on, at least since the very beginning of the history outlined in Part One of this book, and one that will be going on, long after you and I are gone, as long as there is a cosmos to contemplate and someone to contemplate it.

Ultimately, I like to think that our ability to do this is innate. Going back to the very origins of language, as discussed in Chapter One, we might postulate, as Terrence McKenna did, that language co-evolved with visual acuity and imagination as a consequence of the rapid development of the human brain, some 100,000 years ago – whether facilitated by the ingestion of psilocybin or not – among a people who had an intimate relationship with the nighttime sky. If so, and if the theory of cognitive recapitulation embraced by Freud, Jung and modern anthropological linguists bears any credibility, then we all contain within us an innate capacity to engage the Cosmos in conversation, using the same visual, trans-linguistic language that allowed our ancestors to do so, eons ago.

We will explore this possibility more directly a little later in this book. Meanwhile, it is also not unlikely to assume that given our collective conditioning through the millennia, by a culture that has elevated the rational, linear, pragmatic, dogmatic, and scientific over the imaginal, cyclical, mystical, multi-dimensional, and yes, astrological ways of knowing, that most of us have largely forgotten how. The capacity is there, but we have to first prime the pump of our ancient memories.

We can start, it seems to me, by assuming that this language we are trying to remember is archetypal, which in fact, is another, more contemporary way of saying that it is innate. According to Jung, and actually, to Plato before him, archetypes are pre-existent patterns encoded in the human psyche itself:

> *I have often been asked where the archetypes or primordial images come from. It seems to me that their origin can be explained by assuming them to be deposits of the constantly repeated experiences of humanity. One of the commonest and at the same time most impressive experiences is the apparent movement of the sun every day. We certainly cannot discover anything of the kind in the unconscious, so far as the known physical process is concerned. What we do find, on the other hand, is the myth of the sun hero in all of its countless variations. It is this myth, and not the physical process, that forms the sun archetype. The same can be said of the phases of the moon. The archetype is a kind of readiness to produce over and over again the same or similar mythical ideas.*[1]

Here, of course, Jung alludes to a more implicit understanding of an archetypal underpinning to astrology, without actually calling it that. Might we, nonetheless, take his suggestion to heart, and begin our quest for this deeper relationship to the Cosmos by assuming that all of the planets, asteroids, centaurs, and other celestial bodies that are now part of the astrological lexicon, have this same archetypal underpinning.[2] I'm guessing that most post-modern psychological astrologers, weaned not only on Jung, but also on Rudhyar, Tarnas and other seminal thinkers moving in this direction since the dawn of the Era of Uncertainty, will not find this idea very much of a stretch.

If so, then we might further postulate that astrology is a language that describes the archetypal dimension of the cosmos. Within this language, all celestial bodies - the Sun and Moon, the planets, visible and invisible, the asteroids, centaurs and Kuiper Belt Objects - are the basic words of the astrological vocabulary, each representing a certain archetypal domain. Beyond that, I will boldly suggest that the rest of astrology - house and sign placements, aspects and harmonics, planetary patterns, transits and progressions, as well as most of the more esoteric techniques used by various segments of the astrological community - are essentially an elaborate system of astrological grammar, through which rules of syntax and semantics potentially render a birthchart understandable as an archetypal field.

Exploring Astrological Archetypes

From this perspective, the obvious question becomes, "How do we explore the meaning of an archetype?" This is by far the most important question we can ask, because if we know how to do this, then our memory of the innate ability to engage the cosmos in conversation will be rekindled, and whatever grammar we might subsequently use to frame the conversation - and yes, there can possibly be more than one - will be secondary.

To explore the meaning of an archetype, or more specifically, a "word" within the astrological language, we will want to cultivate what James Hillman has called the archetypal eye, described by Richard Tarnas as:

> *that form of imaginative intelligence, implicit and potential in all of us, that is capable of discriminating the rich multiplicity of archetypal patterns in the intimate microcosm of one's own life as well as in the great events of history and culture.*[3]

While I think there is value in this definition, it is a bit too conceptual to be of much use for our purposes here, for what Hillman is really talking about is developing the ability to see what cannot be seen. This is a paradox, a Zen koan, a pathway that goes more deeply into uncertainty, potentially a recipe for getting lost. It is also an invitation to a very intimate conversation with the cosmos that only you can have because you are who you are, having lived the life you've lived, followed the path you've followed and come to this moment in time that has prepared you to see what otherwise could not be seen. What comes out of this conversation is not something you can or will ever read in an astrology book; it is an experience that you can only have if you dare to take your imaginative astrological intelligence into the unknown.

In *The Soul's Code*, Hillman introduces the possibility of this kind of experience with a Swedish folktale about the Huldra, an enchanting siren who would appear to woodcutters in the deep forest and lure them more deeply into the woods. At a certain point, the Huldra would smile, turn her back and disappear, leaving the poor woodsman miles from nowhere, with no direction home, unable to find his way back, and likely to die.

This is perhaps a gruesome way to introduce a journey that is not for the faint of heart, and a cautionary tale for all but the most intrepid among us. For those who can get past this warning, and still feel the siren call, it is also a demonstration of where to begin. For the journey invariably follows a mythic trail, a story filled with enchanting images that speak to our imaginative intelligence and that in fact, evoke it. At a deeper level, the story is also an invitation into the deep woods, where we will be alone, and become lost, and likely undergo a death of some kind – or a transformation, if you prefer a euphemism no less cathartic for its vagueness – if only of what we thought we once knew.

Is it any wonder that humans have gravitated toward the rational, and clung to the illusion of certainty that science promises with its enforced rigor, designed to definitively separate what is true from what is not? Is it any wonder that we astrologers, following in their footsteps, while fighting for our own identity, have promised our own brand of certainty, based on the idea that a birthchart could be interpreted, and provide a reliable map to the journey of the soul? Both promises have been Huldras, for when we get to this supposed certainty, what lies behind it is always the Unknown, the deep woods, mysteries that don't resolve neatly into infallible truths, but rather smile, turn their backs, and leave us stranded in unfamiliar territory.

To use the post-structuralist Jacque Lacan's language, whatever interpretation we might give a birthchart is at best a "floating signifier," a temporary pause in the conversation, part of a larger sentence waiting for a completion that may never come:

> *Behind each and every interpretation of the tale is the tale. The tale provides the invisible backdrop against which all analyses parade their brilliance. Myth lies behind every account we give of it, and it gives no account of itself. Myths fall back on invisibility. They show an enchanting face, but their backing disappears under scrutiny. Nothing's there. We are lost in the woods.*[4]

And yet, developing an archetypal eye that has any chance at all of seeing into the mysterious depths of an astrological archetype must begin with the willingness to entertain the stories behind it and to somehow enter into them, get inside of them, let them inside of us, and then, see what happens. Maybe, instead of being entirely lost, we will remember something important, and access innate faculties that allow us to see more deeply into the darkness than we could before. Personally, I think it is a risk worth taking if all we stand to lose are the illusions that stand between us and the Unknown, for these illusions are what separate us from a more intimate conversation with the Cosmos.

In any case, as I stand on the threshold of the existential question I posed in the last chapter, I am feeling drawn to enter the known stories about Vesta, not knowing ahead of time where exactly I will wind up. Together, let us see what can be seen with eyes that may perhaps open as we dare to exercise them.

Standing at the Threshold

The name Vesta, as is true of all the names of astrological deities, now understood as archetypes, comes from the Roman pantheon. Before we enter Vesta's mythological portal itself, it can be useful to gather a few more external facts surrounding her function in Roman culture, and beyond that to her role in Greek culture as Hestia, perhaps dipping into a few additional cultures where she has had different names, and somewhat different stories.

To begin, we might note that there is some question about the etymology of the name, which different scholars attribute to different sources.[5] Ovid considered Vesta to be derived from the Latin *vi stando*, which means, "standing by power," while the Latin verb *vestio*, seemingly a closer phonological fit, means "clothe." Some scholars believe it to be an adaptation of the Greek Hestia, which derives from *hestanai dia pantos*, meaning "standing for ever;" or possibly *focus urbis*, meaning "hearth." Still others trace the name to the Indo-European root *h,eu-*, with cognates in Latin, Greek and Vedic that all mean "burning." The Gallic Celtic word *visc* also means "fire."

Certainly, the references here to hearth, fire, and burning are all in line with our astrological understanding of Vesta as the goddess of the hearth, and the tender of the sacred flame. This was the role she played in the Roman Empire, where all Roman Emperors were considered "priests of Vesta." The sacred fire that Vesta tended, was associated not just with the hearth, but with the vital force at the heart of the Roman Empire, the fertility of the land, and according to Dionysius of Halicarnassus, the celestial fires that animated the stars of the cosmos itself.[6] The hearth – which is the center of the home – is, by extension, also associated with the *omphalos*, or navel, the center of the world.[7] Every home, every village, every state, and the cosmos itself, all revolve around this center, which was also Vesta's altar.

Of course, Vesta is most often associated with the vestal virgins, sworn to thirty years (one full Saturn cycle) of chastity and charged with the serious task of tending the sacred fires in her temple. Should a virgin let the fire go out, she would be whipped; should she break her vow of chastity, she could be buried alive. In return for keeping these dire commitments, vestal virgins enjoyed privileges not available to other women, including emancipation from their father's control, and the right to own their own property. The practice of vestal virgins is believed to date back to the seventh century B.C.E. (the end of the Mystical Era) and was finally banned in 394 C.E. by Theodosius, the same Roman Emperor who banned astrology.[8]

The other enticing bit of lore from Roman times, perhaps hinting at some lost myth, was her association with liminality – or more literally, with the *limen*, or threshold to the home, of which the hearth was central. The tradition was oriented around new brides not stepping on the *limen*, which was sacred to Vesta, but the deeper implication was that a new bride was essentially entering the unknown, crossing a threshold into a new reality as a wife and likely soon-to-be mother, and beyond that into the sacred mysteries of feminine sexuality. By extension, we might assume that Vesta is an appropriate guide to the crossing of any threshold – say, in our case here, the archetypal threshold between the illusory state of certainty and the place of not knowing that awaits at the heart of the matter, somewhere in the deep woods.

Insights on the Threshold

Unfortunately, there are few surviving myths from Rome that we can enter, so at least in this incarnation, we remain somewhat stranded on the threshold – which is not to say, there isn't valuable insight to be had, as we stand here, reading the inscriptions on the portal. It is natural when approaching an archetype to gather information. As astrologers, we do this all the time, learning from each other, and from those who had come before, ideally dipping into other sources in order to broaden and deepen our knowledge of the context in which our astrological symbolism is rooted. Opening the archetypal eye, however, really means paying attention to where this information resonates on a more personal level, for it is here that we hear the call into the deep woods.

As I contemplate Vesta's association with the fire of the hearth, for example, it occurs to me that this life I am living here in my cabin in the woods, as we descend through autumn into winter, is very much about tending the hearth. I have wood heat here, and aside from whatever else I might be doing, my days are marked by tending the fire. Living on ten acres of forested land, I also cut my own wood, which means going out onto my land with my chain saw, cutting the fallen trees that are part of the ongoing attrition in any forest, and then splitting and stacking the wood for burning in my wood stove. While many people I know – friends and neighbors with wood stoves – hire others to do the hard work for them, I actually love the entire ritual, as it makes me feel more deeply connected to the land. I might even go so far as to say that it is a spiritual practice – my version, I suppose, of being a vestal virgin. In addition, Robert Graves ascribes the art of building houses to Hestia,[9] which also fits, since this house that I labor to heat is one I built myself.

I also feel myself, at this stage of my life, to be in a liminal space. Having just ended one relationship and not being ready for another is certainly one layer of the feeling. Being somewhat suspended in time with everyone else as this pandemic runs its course, is another.

Wondering what will happen to this garden planet as our climate crisis kicks into high gear, as it surely will in the foreseeable future, is a third. This layered sense of uncertainty is palpable, even as I go about my life, writing, working with clients and students, cutting and burning wood, tending the fire – both physically and metaphorically. As I think about this, it is not hard to feel Vesta's presence, as a guide, and in some ways, an embodiment of the burning questions that I carry to my birthchart at this point, as outlined in Chapter Ten.

So, feeling this presence, I am perhaps ready to enter into a deeper dialogue with Vesta, beginning as I would with anyone I wanted to get to know – by listening to her stories, the myths that are associated with her. Before I do, it occurs to me to share one more interesting tidbit, standing here on the threshold. Normally, in having a conversation with someone – anyone, even a goddess – it is natural to want to see them. Images are, in fact, as both Jung and Hillman have suggested, of more interest to one intent on opening the archetypal eye than words. Oddly, however, aside from having few myths ascribed to her, Vesta was one of the least depicted of all the deities; instead, she was often represented by the fire stick, which was an object used to start fires.[10]

Just about a month ago, I attended a men's gathering in New Mexico – a circle of trusted friends, many of whom I have known for decades – as a way of facilitating my transition through this liminal space, or at least gaining some clarity about it. There are stories I could tell about the gathering itself, but what seems more relevant here is the end of the gathering, the final ceremony of which is a giveaway. Each participant brings an object that represents something they are ready to let go of, and then chooses another object, brought by someone else, perhaps as a symbolic representation of what might be their next step.

As it happens, not thinking about Vesta at the time, the object I brought to release was a ceremonial fire stick. It was gifted to me years ago by a man, a smithy who had promised to make me a ceremonial knife in his forge in exchange for an astrological reading that I did for him but was having trouble fulfilling his end of the bargain. The fire stick was meant to be a goodwill gesture, to let me know he was still working on it. In actuality, I never heard from him again, and the fire stick – which he probably got in a gift shop somewhere for $20 or so – was all I ever got. I had long since let go of any residual anger about it, and in fact, still felt good about having been impeccable at my end of the bargain. But the transaction felt incomplete somehow, so I suppose, passing it on, was a symbolic gesture toward completion – perhaps a step, a way of moving energy, in some way, out of the liminal space in which I found myself, or so it seems in retrospect.

But the story doesn't end here, for what I picked up at the giveaway, not really knowing what it was at the time, was a Native American flute, enclosed in a handmade bag, crafted from a piece of a Navajo blanket, sewn together with elk hide. I cannot help but imagine, as I stand here on the threshold of entering this deeper conversation with Vesta, that I have recently traded one fire stick for another.

When I think of flutes, standing here on the threshold of mythic tales, I think of Kokopelli, or Pan, or Krishna – all deities associated with fertility – and I can't help but feel that the flute is, in some way that I don't yet entirely understand, a gift from Vesta, associated not just with the hearth, but also with fertility – sexual, creative and celestial.

Not coincidentally perhaps, along with myth, Hillman considers music to be another pathway into the realm of the invisibles, which is where the archetypal eye is attempting to see what cannot be seen.[11] Music has always been a passion of mine, and in another life – or so it seems now – I played the saxophone. I never could be as good as I wanted to be, however, so eventually, I gave my saxophone away, and made a conscious decision to channel my creative energies into my work with astrology and my writing instead.

Every so often, I remember my love for music and make an effort to make some. Most recently, I became enamored of hand pan drums and bought myself a baby hand pan on Amazon. As it turns out, however, I also brought this hand pan to the men's gathering, gave it away, and came home with a flute instead. It would appear that, for reasons I don't yet understand, I am not done with music, or maybe it would be more accurate to say that music is not yet done with me. Standing here on Vesta's threshold, it might just be that music, perhaps this flute in particular, is my fire stick – or somehow a talisman of it.

I don't know that literally making music is my thing, but somehow, I also feel like making music is a metaphor for keeping the sacred fire alive, or maybe that tending the fire and making music are somehow one and the same. At the very least, there is a mystery here, marked by synchronicity, related to this exploration of Vesta in ways I do not yet understand.

You see, dear reader, going through the archetypal portal, you can't know ahead of time, where you will land, or even what will come out of your mouth. We haven't even entered the stories yet, and already I can feel the archetypal eye opening, seeing connections that no one else but I could see, simply because I am the one looking. OK – enough for now; let's see what the stories have to say.

Entering the Stories

The Near Rape at Cybele's Party

Although myths about Vesta, the Roman goddess, are sparse, there is one story – written by Ovid, a Roman poet who lived during the reign of Augustus – that mentions Vesta. This is a story included in the incomplete poem, *Fasti*, describing the first six months of the Roman calendar, rich with references from Greco-Roman myths and legends. In the short tale, while discussing the Vestalia – a festival held every year on June 9, Ovid describes a wild party thrown by Cybele, during which Vesta lies down to take a nap while everyone else gets drunk; the nymphs and satyrs romp and rut; and general mayhem fills the night.[12] At one point, bad boy Priapus decides to have his way with Vesta while she sleeps but is thwarted by the braying of a mule, who awakens her just as she is about to be raped. The raucous noise draws a crowd, and red-faced Priapus is caught and banned from future parties, while Vesta's virginity remains intact. From this point forward, the mule becomes sacred to Vesta.

The Phallus in the Hearth

Although this is the only Roman myth in which Vesta appears in person, there are a couple of tales about phalluses arising mysteriously from Vesta's hearth. One, told by Plutarch in *Romulus*, is the story of Tarchetius, a king of Alba Longa.[13] When told by an oracle that a virgin must have intercourse with the phallus in the fire of his hearth, he offers his daughter, who refuses and sends a handmaiden in her place. When the king finds out, he orders his daughter executed, but Vesta appears to him in a dream and forbids it. Eventually the handmaiden gives birth to twins, and Tarchetius orders his subordinate Teratius to destroy them. Instead, he leaves them on the shore of the river Tiber, where they are raised by she-wolves. Romulus eventually kills his brother Remus, and then goes on to found the city of Rome.

The second phallus-in-the-hearth story is told by Dionysius of Halicarnassus.[14] This one appears in the fiery hearth of King Tarquinius, who doesn't know quite what to make of it. Queen Tanaquil, however, knows that it is a blessing, and that a mortal woman who has intercourse with the phallus can produce a superior child. The king chooses the handmaiden Ocresia, who had seen it first, for this honor, and she subsequently gives birth to King Servius Tullius, the legendary sixth king of Rome, who reigned from 578 – 535 B.C.E.

Hestia's Dual Birth

Vesta's counterpart in Greece was Hestia, the firstborn child of Cronus (Saturn) and Rhea (one of many goddesses we might associate with the Moon). I note briefly here that my natal Vesta is in Capricorn, forming a sesquiquadrate to the Moon, but forming no aspect to Saturn. As the firstborn child of her parents, Hestia is the first to be swallowed by her paranoid father, who fears his children will usurp his power; and then the last to be liberated by Zeus, the youngest of her siblings. I also note here than my natal Vesta is conjunct Jupiter, the ruling planet of my chart. I will speak more about these and other astrological connections within my birthchart in Chapter Fourteen.

Hestia's Oath of Virginity

The tale of Hestia's birth is told in Homer's *Hymn to Aphrodite*, where he also notes that Hestia is one of three goddesses who are not enchanted by Aphrodite's charms, the other two being Athena and Artemis. Homer tells us that Hestia is wooed by both Poseidon and Apollo, refusing both and swearing to be a virgin for the rest of her life. I note here that the Sun in my chart (referring to Apollo) is semisquare to Vesta, and that Vesta is conjunct Venus, as well as Jupiter. It is not in aspect to Neptune (referring to Poseidon). In return for her vow of chastity, and her willingness to serve both gods and humans instead, Zeus makes Hestia the foremost goddess in the Greek pantheon, the only goddess to have an altar in the temple of every other Greek deity.

> *And to her Father Zeus gave a beautiful honor, as a compensating substitute for marriage.*
>
> *She is seated in the middle of the house, getting the richest portion.*
>
> *And in all the temples of the gods she has a share in the timê.*[15]
>
> *Among all the mortals, she is the senior goddess.*[16]

Demetra George, quoting Jungian scholar Esther Harding, notes that "virgin" does not mean chaste, but rather subservient to no man.[17] Even in patriarchal Greece and Rome, Vesta and Hestia, as well as the vestal virgins tending the sacred fire, all seem to be granted special privileges, so this appears to be the subtext, even on into the Philosophical Era, where the tales of Homer and Hesiod served as the only written account of earlier oral traditions, shrouded in the fog of the Mystical Era.

The question of whether or not the vestal virgins served as "sacred harlots" in pre-Hellenic times, as both Demetra George and Esther Harding assert[18,19] – without quoting a more ancient source – is perhaps part of the inscrutable mystery surrounding the archetype of Vesta. As noted by George in her subsequent discussion of the psychology of Vesta, issues surrounding sexuality – ranging the gamut from liberated "sex outside of committed relationships" to "sexual fears, guilt and inadequacies" – are all within her domain, perhaps part of a larger question: what to do with fire, which is often one of the most difficult elements to master.[20]

This larger question would encompass the ambivalence that most people have around their sexual desires, as well as the question of how to pursue one's creative passion while maintaining one's integrity in a world where compromise is often the most efficient pathway to success, and perhaps for some, how to channel anger effectively and/or avoid unnecessary conflict. It does seem a bit odd that the goddess of fire is depicted as one of the most ordinary, non-descript, almost invisible of all the deities, male or female – as this is not generally characteristic of fire, as most astrologers well know. One cannot help but suspect there must be more to the story than we have been told, perhaps particularly by a patriarchy that feared what unleashed fire – particularly feminine sexual fire – could do.

In her rich exploration of these conundrums, *Women's Mysteries*, Harding speaks about Vesta/Hestia's association with fire being a reference to the fertilizing power of the Moon:

> *This idea of the fertilizing power of the moon being actually fire is a very common one. It is thought that this power can be hidden in wood or tree where it lies sleeping in latent form, and can be drawn out again by rubbing, the primitive way of producing fire . . . And there is another primitive myth, which states that an old woman, probably the moon herself, who is so often called the Old Woman, made the first fire by rubbing her genitals.*[21]

Controversy Surrounding Hestia's Place In the Greek Pantheon

Although there is no mention of it in any ancient source or myth, there has arisen among Greek scholars another question about Hestia's status in the Greek pantheon. Since Plato's time, it has been noted that some depictions of the pantheon – such as the altar at the Ancient Agora of Athens – included Hestia, but others – such as the east frieze of the Parthenon, had Dionysus in her place.[22] While, this mystery has not been explained, a story started circulating that Hestia, being meek and mild, willingly gave up her seat to the more powerful and assertive Dionysus, in order to avoid conflict. One scholar traces this rumor, at least in modern times, to Robert Graves,[23] who in his oft-quoted book *Greek Myths* notes:

> *Finally, having established his worship throughout the world, Dionysus ascended into Heaven, and now sits at the right hand of Zeus as one of the Twelve Great Gods. The self-effacing goddess Hestia resigned her seat at the high table in his favour; glad of any excuse to escape the jealous wranglings of her family, and knowing that she could always count on a quiet welcome in any Greek city which it might please her to visit.*[24]

Meanwhile, checking on Graves' sources – Apollodoros' *Bibliotheka* and Pausanias' *Hellados Periegesis* – Temperance notes that neither source actually mentions Hestia giving up her throne. Instead, she concludes that:

> *Graves is a storyteller; he spun stories based on facts he could find. If he could not find a fact, he made it up to fit the story. Because of this, his books are a great read, but they are not reliable as far as ancient mythology goes.*[25]

Whether or not this is true, what this controversy suggests is that the myths and stories about the divine archetypes are not always a matter of strict scholarship. As with any good story, they sometimes get embellished, or revised, depending on who is telling the story, and to whom. Keeping that in mind, when entering the stories, you want to make some effort to follow the authentic thread back as far as it goes, but mostly you want to see what resonates for you. Archetypal truth is not the same as scientific truth, nor even always the same as impeccable scholarship.

Whether or not it ever led her to give up her seat on the Dodekatheon, for example, the idea, that among all the deities in the Greek pantheon, Hestia is one of the most peaceful and diplomatic, never taking part in wars or disputes[26] – strikes me as being relevant to my inquiry now – again within the larger set of questions that Vesta poses about what to do with fire.

Obviously, conflict up to and including war – in which fiery factors such as anger, animosity, festering hatreds, fierce competition, and the destructive capacity of firepower are central issues – is where this question takes on its greatest poignancy. The fact that Vesta was able to remain neutral in what, by any account, would appear to be a rather conflicted conflagration of divine politics, suggests that aside from knowing something about how to effectively channel one's sexuality, she might also know something about this other aspect of fire.

As I contemplate this possibility, I would have to admit that I am not, by nature, very Vesta-like. For most of my life, I would not have characterized myself as peaceful and diplomatic, although this is due to other factors in my chart and other dimensions of my psyche that I have written about elsewhere and that I need not repeat here.[27] What does seem relevant, however, is that after having been engaged in many battles of one kind or another, revolving around political differences with neighbors and partners, as well as ideological differences with colleagues and peers, at this point in my life, I have no interest whatsoever in going to battle. Been there, done that. It's not that I don't think there are issues worth fighting for, just that I have come to the conclusion, through a hard, personal process of trial and mostly error, that fighting never really accomplishes much of anything. So now, like Vesta, I mostly stay out of it altogether – unless of course, I can't. And when I can't, I am more interested in dialogue, wherever possible, than I am in being right.

Brigit

Moving on to other possible iterations of Vesta/Hestia, we can note that the archetype behind the deity is not limited to the Greco-Roman culture that gives her this name. This same archetype – or any archetype – can also be seen in the mythology of other cultures. One of the perks of living in a postmodern world is that we need not limit ourselves, even as astrologers, to the Hellenistic manifestation of these archetypes.

The triune Celtic goddess Brigit comes immediately to mind, for example, as being related to Vesta/Hestia, although it would appear at first blush that Brigit is more complicated and multi-dimensional.[28] One aspect of Brigit is a goddess of poetry; the second, a goddess of healing and midwifery; and the third, a goddess of the hearth fire, with associations to the fertility of the land, as well as the creativity of the forge. Brigit is said to have kept a shrine at Kildare, Ireland, with a perpetual flame tended by nineteen virgin priestesses called Daughters of the Flame that later became a nunnery when the Christians usurped pagan sites and Brigit became a saint.

Her festival, Imbolc on the 1st of February (the midpoint between winter solstice and spring equinox), is said to harken back to Neolithic times, with a number of sacred sites, including the Hill of Tara - considered an ancient seat of power where 142 kings are said to have reigned - aligned with sunrise on that day.[29] This seems similar to the understanding in Rome that all Emperors were priests of Vesta, aligned with her cosmic function of ensuring the vitality of the state as well as the land.

Imbolc (meaning "in the belly") was an obvious reference to human fertility, as well as to the immanent return of spring, the most fertile season of the year, a time when the land bursts forth with new life. Imbolc represents the gestation of that fire within the womb, and perhaps by extension, within the liminal space that late winter often is. Brigit is said to have been born at dawn (the same time I was born), itself a liminal threshold, at which point a flame burst out of her forehead.

The Christians turned Imbolc into Candlemas, a celebration of Mary of the Candles, still a reference to fire, but one that has been largely stripped of its original transformative power.

Shakti

Many other fire goddesses exist, and some - like the Aztec Chantico, the Siberian Poza-Mama, or the Chinese Tsao-Wang - are also goddesses of the hearth. A number of others - like the Roman Aetna, the Aleut Chuginadak, the Philippino Darago, the Haida Dzalarhons, the Etruscan Feronia, the Japanese Fuji-Ainu, the Klickitat Loo-Wit, the Nicaraguan Masaya, and the Hawaiian Pele - are volcano goddesses, emphasizing a more destructive and transformative aspect of fire. Astrologically, these might be understood to be more aligned with Pluto than Vesta. Still other fire goddesses - the Japanese Amaterasu, the Egyptian Bast, the Phoenician Shapash, the Slavic Solntse, and the Cherokee Uelanuhi - are more solar in their expression. There is no shortage of mythic paths through the deep archetypal wood, which is why it pays to keep your wits about you, and follow only those threads that seem to have a personal dimension.

With this in mind, there is one other thread to the Vesta story that resonates with me. Demetra George alludes to this thread when she notes that Vesta's teachings extend to the transmutation of sexual energy to fuel spiritual attainment, a practice revolving around working with *kundalini* energy, said to be coiled like a serpent at the base of the spine. This perhaps draws upon the more volcanic aspects of the fire goddesses, one that is perhaps less obvious in Vesta, but no doubt there for those who quietly follow her path – as, in fact, I may have done without recognizing that, except right now, here in retrospect.

I say this because I spent seven years in my twenties, studying, practicing and teaching *kundalini yoga*, first under the tutelage of Yogi Bhajan and later, in a different form, with Swami Muktananda. This was not a casual interest, but rather one that I pursued while living in various *ashrams* over the course of seven years. My immersion in *kundalini yoga* coincided with my discovery of astrology, and over the course of my first decade as an astrologer, these two streams converged – along with Western psychology.

Today, googling Yogi Bhajan, you can easily find a shitstorm of allegations of sexual abuse, harassment, and the kinds of coercive, manipulative, psychologically damaging behavior associated with many spiritual cults.[30] This is happening now, almost two decades after his death because of the late 2019 publication of *Premka: White Bird in a Golden Cage* by Pamela Dawson, his former secretary of 20 years.

Some are questioning the authenticity of his teachings in retrospect, in addition to these scandals, or maybe in part because of them, and as seems to be the fate of many controversial spiritual teachers, legitimate or not, to some he was a guru while, to others he was a dangerous fraud. Perhaps I was young and naive; I certainly wasn't an attractive female; nor was I part of his inner circle. So, when I knew him, I only knew him as a teacher of *kundalini yoga*, from whom I actually learned a great deal.

Most relevant to our discussion here, I learned that in the yogic traditions in which he taught, *kundalini* was known as *kundalini shakti*, a sacred Feminine fire that was at heart, the Source of all life. If Pamela Dawson's allegations of sexual abuse are true, then he was indeed a sham. For what he taught, and what I came to believe, is that the most important part of any spiritual practice required a fundamental respect for this Feminine life force, and its transformative power, expressed in part, through conscious sexuality. He taught celibacy before marriage – an ideal I was never able to achieve; and numerous techniques for raising *kundalini*, which I did experience.

What I also learned was that raising *kundalini* was not something to be undertaken lightly, since as it rose, it brought with it all of the unresolved psychological issues that stood in the way of spiritual evolution. The nervous system had to be trained to withstand the release of *kundalini*, and to sustain the more energized states of consciousness it facilitated, one had to do one's inner psychological work. This became no small part of my incentive to study Western psychology, and I got my Master's degree while living in the ashram.

With Swami Muktananda, my experience was very different. In studying with Yogi Bhajan, I came to believe that raising *kundalini* was something that you had to achieve – through rigorous daily practice, called *sadhana*, and by consciously working toward spiritual maturity through discipline, responsibility, impeccability in one's actions, and by making a creative, constructive contribution to the spiritual community. All of this was part of ashram life. With Swami Muktananda, the experience of *kundalini shakti* was more a matter of grace and intense heat. Whenever I found myself in Muktananda's presence, I felt this intense heat in my spine, an experience I recognized as *kundalini* because I had experienced it before, usually only after hours of intense yoga.

With Muktananda, the experience did not require effort; it required opening to receive. It was essentially a much more archetypally Feminine approach to spiritual awakening. As with Yogi Bhajan's teachings, in the end, one's capacity to open depended on the inner work that one had done by way of preparation, but with Muktananda, the experience itself was one of opening to the life force, the living flame, that existed at the very origin of this manifest universe, and is still available right now, in this moment, in every moment.

I have since come to understand this living flame as a kind of immanent divine intelligence, at work in the invisible realms, orchestrating the dance of life, in all of its myriad forms, in any given moment. This understanding is depicted in the visual imagery of Shiva, through his multiple arms, doing multiple things as he dances on one foot. His partner in the dance, more invisible, but part of the lore, is Shakti, the divine embodiment of *kundalini*, and perhaps an Eastern counterpart to Vesta.

Shakti is traditionally revered in the East Indian culture, out of which yogic practice evolved, just as Vesta was revered throughout the Roman Empire as the first deity to be honored in any ritual, sacred or secular. Thousands of years of patriarchy, in both East and West have unquestionably distorted this impulse toward reverence, but as I stand here on the archetypal threshold, contemplating what I have learned so far, it seems to me, that the liminal space in which I posed my questions is sacred space. I'm guessing that this is the signal that the archetypal eye is opening, as nothing that it sees is ordinary, even if it lies beneath one or more veils of an ordinary life.

Cinderella and the Cinder Biters

The archetypal themes that we associate with gods and goddesses can also been seen in fairy tales and folklore. The theme that an ordinary exterior often reveals something exquisite that remains hidden, for example, can be seen in the common fairy tale Cinderella, in which an ordinary girl, resigned to the harsh demands of tending the hearth, defies the odds to become a princess. This tale exists in thousands of variations around the world, with the one most common – aside from the 1950 Disney movie classic – being the Brothers Grimm version, first published in 1812, five years after the discovery of Vesta.

Although the tale has several sub-plots that go beyond the mythological theme, the transition of a nondescript woman tending the hearth into a position of universal recognition and power is very much in keeping with Vesta's archetypal trajectory. There is also a subtext in the fairy tale around the idea of tending the hearth being a liminal task, out of which greatness one day emerges.

In another version of this idea, perhaps more specifically relevant to men, Robert Bly, quoting Norwegian scholar Rudolf Keyser, talks about a custom among Norwegians in Viking times, in which:

> *. . . young men sometimes would lie down in the space between the fire and the ash pile, and stay there two or three years. Such as these might constantly be seen crouching over the fire, rolling themselves in the ashes, eating ashes, and neither caring to employ themselves in anything useful, nor to keep themselves in a state of cleanliness' . . . (Such men) were called Cinder-Biters. It's clear that the young men were going through some kind of hibernation or ritual lethargy, and the older men and women allowed it.*[31]

They allowed it, according to Bly, because they had learned that after this liminal period of cinder-biting, these young men would often go on to do great things. While I am not a young man, and I am not the one to judge my own greatness, I do identify with the productivity of this liminal space, in which on the surface of things, nothing much appears to be happening, but beneath the surface, a deeper transformational magic is often afoot. This book, for whatever it may be worth, is a product of this kind of ash-time.

Calling in Vesta

So, what do I know so far? In ways that I was not aware of, before having recognized my resonance with Vesta stories, it appears I have been, in many ways, and still am, following the path of a male vestal virgin, or perhaps a cinder biter. I have been pursuing this path along the golden thread of my creative endeavors, through my study of *kundalini yoga*, perhaps through my hard-won disinterest in unnecessary conflict, and certainly through my current role as a steward of the woods and a tender of the fire of my own hearth. This fire warms the liminal space, this ash-time, in which I seek to have a deeper conversation with Vesta. At the very least, it is clear that the journey into the deep woods has begun, as I feel a sense of resonance between the archetypal stories and my musings about my own life experience.

It further occurs to me that the task before me is not so much about getting clear who or what Vesta is, so much as creating a sacred space with my intention, and with my acknowledgement of her presence in my life, and then calling her in. What exactly this means is not entirely clear as I write this, but I did decide the other day to see if I couldn't conjure a suitable image of her.

Aside from the fire stick noted earlier, where she is depicted at all – which is not often – she appears in Greek and Roman iconography as a non-descript woman, largely hidden behind a cowl that covers her face, sometimes carrying a staff, but not very visible, even when she is envisioned. These images – the few I have been able to find, don't quite do it for me. They remind me of the handmaidens in Margaret Atwood's dystopian novels, which is probably not that far off the mark to what the vestal virgins would become in such a hyper-patriarchal culture. In any case, I wanted an image that did homage to her fiery essence, and that would hopefully speak with more resonance to what she has been, and is, within my life, and my birthchart.

The Queen of Wands

Recently, I was inspired to order a new tarot deck, whose imagery resonated with me. The tarot is infused with hidden astrological references, but more importantly to our purposes here, it is a system of images – which speak more directly to the imaginal intelligence, necessary to open the archetypal eye. Astrology – at least as it has been practiced since the Logical Era – has become more cerebral and, as such, requires the cultivation of counterbalancing astropoetic sensibilities in order to become the more whole-brained art that it was when the sky itself was the canvas, rather than a computer-generated chart. More about this later. In any case, it occurred to me to see if my new tarot deck – the Light Seer deck – could provide a working image of Vesta. I set my intent, shuffled the cards, and out came the Queen of Wands.[32]

In this deck, the Queen of Wands is a joyful black woman with tightly coiled reddish hair, sitting in an illuminated circle, surrounded by lit votive candles. In her left hand, she holds a wand – or a fire stick – high above her head; in her right hand, bursting forth from her upraised palm, is a flame. I felt a chill and noted the synchronicity. I set the intention to call in Vesta, and here she was, in as good a likeness as any I might imagine.

For those of you who know tarot, you will also recognize that the suit of wands is associated with the element of fire. Wands are also, of course, a reference to magic – which can perhaps be understood as passionate desire harnessed to clear, laser-like focus. Demetra George notes that the Latin word for hearth is "focus,"[33] which of course in English means something different than it does in Latin, but which nonetheless speaks to fire's capacity for focused obsession. Focused obsession, in turn, leads to creativity, to creative breakthrough and potentially to magic, to making something happen that breaks the mold of what was previously thought possible. My sense is that this capacity also exists within Vesta's domain, although I may be going out on a limb here, since this is not overtly a part of her scant, generally more somber and contained mythological persona.

The Queen of Wands in the Light Seer tarot deck more definitely speaks to this possibility, as she gazes with joyful wonder at a flame bursting from her upraised hand, calling it forth perhaps with the wand held high in the other hand. This figure, it seems to me, has some affinity for the Yoruban goddess Oya, who in addition to being a goddess of fire, was associated with violent lightning storms, mysteries of death and rebirth, and magic, perhaps an archetypal cross between Hecate and Hestia. But here, we are no doubt going a bit too far afield, perhaps getting lost in the deep woods. For again, the Roman Vesta and the Greek Hestia had none of this drama, or violent intensity about them.

Meanwhile, taking all of these impressions in as I sift and sort through these stories, I do think it possible that *my* Vesta – the one that lives inside of me as one of my subpersonalities, as she is reflected in my chart – is closer to the Greek, but not as somber, and definitely capable of magic as an extension of *kundalini shakti* channeled through creative passion. I do not need a flash of lightning to announce this kind of magic; I just need to do what I do as an expression of it. In the Orphic *Hymn to Hestia*, she is called the "eternal, many-formed, beloved, and verdant, smiling, happy one," so that is how I will think of her, perhaps in some ways, like the Oracle in the film *The Matrix*, offering Neo a freshly baked cookie, as she tells him of the life-and-death choice he will have to make.

Opening a Dialogue with a Living Archetype

If it is not obvious by now, I will spell it out more clearly: entering into a dialogue with an archetype is not the same as doing research. Nor will the archetype that emerges through the dialogue be identical to the one presented in myth or folklore. The archetype, any archetype, is really only a portal into a more intimate conversation with some aspect of yourself, one that represents but one thread within a tapestry of threads, but that begins to glow with a light of its own as you pay attention to it. As you remember the stories and feel the resonance between the stories, your life, and who you know yourself to be, a different kind of clarity will emerge – one that is both infused with the power of the collective unconscious and with the unique individual flavor you bring to it.

If you are wondering what any of this has to do with astrology, then I assure you, in the discussion to come, I will start to more clearly associate what I see through the archetypal eye with what I see as I look at my birthchart. I would also like to suggest, at this juncture, however, that unless the archetypal eye is open, what you will see in the birthchart will tend to be exactly what you have always seen, what others have said about your chart, what you already know it to mean. It will then be just another dead letter in the dead letter file. Entering the archetypal field of a birthchart is a very different exercise than interpreting it. When you practice astrology as a living art, what you see through astrology's lens with the archetypal eye open will surprise you, challenge you, allow you to recognize yourself anew. If, in such a quest, the chart itself becomes a Huldra, smiles and disappears, this will not be a tragedy. Quite the contrary – it will be the true beginning of your astrological adventure.

Notes

1. Jung, Carl G. *The Collected Works of C.G. Jung, Volume 7: Two Essays in Analytical Psychology*. Princeton University Press, 1953, 69.
2. This is perhaps not obvious in the case of anything other than the seven visible planets of classic astrology, but given that most archetypes reside within the collective unconscious and are only coaxed into conscious awareness through our increasing experience of their presence in our lives, I believe it is possible to make this general statement. We might add the caveat that the invisible bodies must be approached differently, but given that we are reaching into the more mythopoetic dimensions of everything astrological, the process may not depend on what is visible and what isn't, so much as how well we can see into the archetypal depths.
3. Tarnas, *Richard. Cosmos and Psyche: Intimations of a New World View*. Viking, 2006, 70.
4. Hillman, James. *The Soul's Code: In Search of Character and Calling*. New York: Warner Books, 1996, 93.
5. Wikipedia. "Vesta (Mythology)." Accessed June 19, 2023. https://en.wikipedia.org/wiki/Vesta_(mythology).
6. Dionysius of Halicarnassus. *The Roman Antiquities II*, 66, 3. Accessed June 19, 2023. https://penelope.uchicago.edu/Thayer/E/Roman/Texts/Dionysius_of_Halicarnassus/home.html.
7. Graves, Robert. *The Greek Myths: 1*. New York: Penguin, 1990, 75.
8. Encyclopedia Britannica. "Vestal Virgins | Roman Religion," June 15, 2023. https://www.britannica.com/topic/Vestal-Virgins#ref185137.
9. Graves, *The Greek Myths: 1*, 75.
10. Schroeder, Jeanne Lorraine. *The Vestal and the Fasces: Hegel, Lacan, Property, and the Feminine*. Berkeley: Univ of California Press, 1998, 335-36.
11. Hillman, *The Soul's Code*, 94.
12. Ovid. *Fasti: Book I*, 192-93. Accessed June 19, 2023. https://www.poetryintranslation.com/PITBR/Latin/OvidFastiBkOne.php.

13. Plutarch. "Romulus." The Internet Classics Archive. Accessed June 19, 2023. https://classics.mit.edu/Plutarch/romulus.html.
14. Dionysius of Halicarnassus. *The Roman Antiquities IV*, 2. Accessed June 19, 2023. https://penelope.uchicago.edu/Thayer/E/Roman/Texts/Dionysius_of_Halicarnassus/home.html.
15. Timê means honor or respect, meaning in this instance, that Hestia was honored in all the temples of the gods, regardless of whose temple it was.
16. Homer. "Hymn to Aphrodite." The Center for Hellenic Studies. Accessed June 19, 2023. https://chs.harvard.edu/primary-source/homeric-hymn-to-aphrodite-sb/.
17. George, Demetra, and Douglas Bloch. *Asteroid Goddesses: The Mythology, Psychology, and Astrology of the Re-Emerging Feminine*. San Diego, CA: ACS Publications, 1986, 120-21.
18. George and Bloch, *Asteroid Goddesses*, 121.
19. Harding, M. Esther. *Woman's Mysteries, Ancient and Modern: A Psychological Interpretation of the Feminine Principle as Portrayed in Myth, Story, and Dreams*. Harper Colophon, 1971, 132.
20. George and Bloch, *Asteroid Goddesses*, 131.
21. Harding, *Woman's Mysteries, Ancient and Modern*, 129-30.
22. Dorter, Kenneth. "Imagery and Philosophy in Plato's Phaedrus." *Journal of the History of Philosophy* 9, no. 3 (January 1, 1971): 279–88. https://doi.org/10.1353/hph.2008.0975.
23. Temperance, Elani. "Hestia versus Dionysos." Accessed June 20, 2023. https://baringtheaegis.blogspot.com/2013/03/hestia-versus-dionysos.html.
24. Graves, *The Greek Myths: 1*, 106.
25. Temperance, "Hestia versus Dionysos."
26. Graves, *The Greek Myths: 1*, 74.
27. Landwehr, Joe. *Astrology and the Archetypal Power of Numbers: Part Two: Arithmology in the Birthchart*. Whittier, NC: Ancient Tower Press, 2018, 107-09, 221-23.
28. Brigit, particularly in her British incarnation as Brigantia, is more often associated with Minerva (in the Roman), and her Greek counterpart, Athena. That being said, few deities ever translate as exact equivalents from culture to culture, and within the archetypal realm, there is often a great deal of overlap, as well as significant differences that provide nuance to the archetypal exploration when taken into account. Given that Brigit is considered, among other attributes, the goddess of the hearth in Celtic mythology, I see an important overlap with Hestia's domain.
29. Murphy, Anthony. "The Hill of Tara - Teamhair." Mythical Ireland. September 14, 2022. https://mythicalireland.com/blogs/ancient-sites/the-hill-of-tara-teamhair.

30. Davis-Flynn, Jennifer. "A New Report Details Decades of Abuse at the Hands of Yogi Bhajan." *Yoga Journal*, September 2, 2021. https://www.yogajournal.com/yoga-101/abuse-in-kundalini-yoga/.

31. Bly, Robert. *Iron John: A Book about Men*. Vintage, 1990, 80.

32. Chris-Anne. "Queen of Wands." The Light Seer's Tarot. Accessed June 20, 2023. https://lightseerstarot.com/light-seers-tarot-meanings-queen-of-wands/.

33. George and Bloch, *Asteroid Goddesses*, 129.

For at least fifteen hundred years the term used for bringing images to mind was memoria . . . What today we conveniently refer to as a memory is imagining qualified by time. When we are recollecting, we are always imagining, even if what comes up is placed back in time. The sole difference between imagining and imagination on the one hand, and remembering and memory on the other, is this added element of time.

James Hillman, "Memory: Short-Term Loss, Long-Term Gain," The Sun, February 2022

Chapter Twelve

Getting Empirical

In Chapter Five, we spoke about how astrology became disenfranchised as empirical science became the standard yardstick by which truth is measured. This is not to say, however, that astrology does not have its own empirical dimension. It is merely an admission that what science means by empiricism is not conducive to good astrology, and that in order to effectively practice its own form of empirical inquiry, astrology must break unnecessary and overly restrictive scientific rules.

If, as I suggested in Chapter Five, empiricism is essentially the idea that knowledge comes primarily through the gathering of "data," in the field, so to speak, then astrologers are essentially empiricists, since we are constantly learning from our clients as they present new information (data) which correlates with the astrological symbolism of their chart or leads us to dig more deeply for a symbolic fit. If we observe that one client with Mars in Pisces is a visionary that is sometimes prone to disillusionment in dealing with the real world, while another lacks the necessary ambition or motivation to succeed in a competitive marketplace, and a third is selflessly motivated to work for the betterment of the disenfranchised, then we are gathering information about Mars in Pisces' archetypal range.

The fact that this information is somewhat inconsistent from one case to the next, at least from the standpoint of external appearances, is less important than whether it is consistent with the symbolism. As we become familiar with the full spectrum of possibilities associated with any placement, aspect or transit or whatever other factor within the astrological lexicon we are observing and refine our understanding as we learn and grow, we are essentially operating empirically.

Both astrologers and scientists are observing patterns and noting how various factors are related to each other within a pattern. But how we understand this process is fundamentally different. While a scientist is looking for data that can be quantified, statistically validated and eventually used to make an objective statement about causal correlations between variables, an astrologer is looking at the qualitative data and how it constellates around an archetypal theme in a way that is meaningful to a given client on a given day, facing a given issue. Delineation of the nature of a pattern requires empirical study, in both instances, but a scientist and an astrologer will approach this study quite differently.

Astrological Empiricism

To effectively explore a pattern astrologically, we have to first work on opening the archetypal eye, as noted in the last chapter. This gives us the capacity to identify themes, and individual expressions within a theme that are symbolically consistent with a given archetype, as well as to discern when various themes and expressions are not symbolically consistent. We develop this capacity by familiarizing ourselves with the mythological stories, by observing how these stories resonate with our own experiences and those of our clients, and I would add here, by mapping these more personal experiences to the cyclical timing that we would logically associate with them.

This last practice is not likely to be something that easily happens within the course of a consultation, but I have found, working with clients over a more extended period, that these cyclical stories are an invaluable window into how a particular client is experiencing and expressing a particular archetype. This is also of tremendous value to anyone using astrology as a language of self-reflection. The mythological stories are not just a relic of the past; they are alive within the present, as well, if we take the time to understand how they are manifesting now, within the context of an actual life, and especially if we explore the story in real time with our archetypal eye wide open. I call this process "taking a cyclical history."

If, for example, I wanted to know more about how Vesta shows up in my actual life experience, then I would track Vesta's 3.6-year sidereal cycle, using Vesta's position in my natal chart as a point of reference. Here, it stands to astro-logical reason, that Vesta's presence will be stronger during a Vesta return. As I observe my life during these windows – say within a narrow 2° orb – I can start to learn something about the range of expression within Vesta's domain that is relevant to me personally, about the various themes related to Vesta that tend to repeat themselves throughout this cyclical history, and lastly, how I personally have evolved in relation to Vesta's archetypal challenge. All of this information helps me to better understand Vesta, not in some theoretical way, but through sifting and sorting the raw data from my actual experience of her.

The same process can be applied to better understanding any aspect in your natal chart. A Saturn-Sun square, for example, will reveal itself every 7 years or so, when Saturn forms a conjunction, square or opposition to your natal Sun. A Jupiter-Moon trine might more accurately reveal itself every 4 years or so, when transiting Jupiter forms a trine (or a conjunction) to your natal Moon. You can also learn about this same aspect every 9 days or so when the transiting Moon forms a trine (or a conjunction) to natal Jupiter.

Of course, each time the aspect repeats, there are other astrological factors in play, and these will not be the same during each window of observation. The more of a sense of preliminary orientation you have created for yourself through immersing in the stories, opening your archetypal eye, and seeing where the resonance lies for you personally, the more you will be able to discern what is relevant to your observation and what isn't. This is a skill that can be cultivated with practice.

You can also use this same process to observe the passage of a planet through a house or a sign, or to learn more about eclipses, retrograde periods, or anything astrological that can be identified as a recurring astronomical event. Observation of planets past Saturn are inherently more difficult, which is why the farther out we go, the more we lean into the realm of the unknown and eventually into the unknowable. Here, the empirical basis for our knowledge necessarily becomes less empirical. We must rely instead mostly on whatever we have learned with our archetypal eye open and the application of symbolic logic as a framework for observation of work in the field, that is to say, with clients who provide the opportunity to observe a rarer astrological phenomenon in play. We can also, to some extent, observe the outworking of these larger cycles in relation to our collective history, as Richard Tarnas did so impressively in *Cosmos and Psyche*, and then extrapolate from the collective to the personal, as we move back into our natal charts.

In any case, making these kinds of observations, however we can make them, is most certainly an empirical process, even if it is not one that would be recognized as scientific. So be it. This has to be OK if we are to proceed astrologically, instead of trying to squeeze ourselves into an ill-fitting scientific understanding of empiricism.

It can be noted here that this process will work, both for professional astrologers seeking to understand an astrological dynamic within their client's chart, and for any individual seeking to better understand their own chart. The advantage, of course, of looking at your own chart is that you are less likely to be encumbered by considerations of time and money. And in any case, I would suggest here that part of the training of any professional astrologer ought to be this more intimate exploration of her own chart, and the various symbolic highways and byways through it.

This is not something that will, or can, happen all at once, but rather as an ongoing practice – one that, by the way, is greatly aided by keeping a daily journal to supplement your memory. Perhaps you are gifted with photographic recall of everything that happened the last time transiting Neptune formed a square to your natal Venus, but if not, having some written record of your experiences at that time can be invaluable. Short of that, you can feel your way into it by first noting how old you were, then where you were living at the time, in general, what your life was about in those days, and then allowing yourself to intuitively drift to specific memories. Having said that, a journal is best, and I would say necessary, for more focused empirical work.

However, you retrieve your memories, it is good to remember, as James Hillman reminds us:

> *For at least fifteen hundred years the term used for bringing images to mind was memoria . . . What today we conveniently refer to as a memory is imagining qualified by time. When we are recollecting, we are always imagining, even if what comes up is placed back in time. The sole difference between imagining and imagination on the one hand, and remembering and memory on the other, is this added element of time.*[1]

The cyclical history then is an imaginal practice of *memoria*, conducted within a temporal framework of recurring astro-logical cycles.

Exploring Vesta Empirically

Let's see how this would work in practice, continuing our exploration of Vesta in relation to the question I posed at the end of Chapter Ten. I have the advantage here of having kept a personal journal for about 45 years, while before the age of 27, like most people, I must rely on my memory. The good news here is that by the time I have worked my way back through those 45 years, my intuition will be primed to go more directly to the related memories before I started keeping a journal, and in any case, even the journal entries will be, to some extent, an imaginal reconstruction after the factual events themselves.

Actually, as a quick, perhaps relevant aside, I will admit here that I would have had over 50 years of journals to work with, but sometime around the age of 21 or 22, I had a ritual burning of all my journals to that point, along with a couple of volumes of poetry and the first draft of a novel. No doubt, this was somehow a marker on my Vestian path of learning how to work more consciously with fire, but we'll see if this shows up as a memory that I can map to the cycle.

I will note here that it is possible, if you make your windows of observation frequent enough, to fit almost any event to anything in your chart. If, for example, I were to look at not just my Vesta returns, but also to the semi-sextiles, semi-squares, sextiles, squares, trines, sesquiquadrates, quincunxes and oppositions, I could have a window of observation every 2 or 3 months, with a 2° orb, lasting 7 – 11 days each, or so, in which case, there would hardly be a moment when Vesta wasn't somehow in play.

While there is some truth to this idea, since the entire chart, including Vesta, is always present within the archetypal field of any life, we are not going to track her movement through the field quite so intensively here. When it comes to focused empirical research, less is more. Once you have a pretty good idea about the major themes and patterns related to the returns, you can if you want to go deeper, begin to look at the oppositions and then maybe the squares. Much beyond that, you run the danger of either becoming redundant, or more confused than enlightened.

In any case, having lived nearly 72 years, I now have about 20 Vesta returns to explore, at least 12 of which will be within my journaling years. This is plenty of raw data with which to undergo an astrologically empirical quest for self-knowledge.

Mapping My Vesta Returns

The first step in taking a cyclical history is to map out the relevant dates. This can be done with most astrological software, or with an ephemeris. I often find, working with both together I can get a better sense of how retrograde periods factor in to the overall cycle. I generally start with current time, and work backwards toward birth. This helps to lay a platform for better memory work, especially if you are attempting to do this without the aid of a personal journal.

In any case, using a 2° orb, the dates of my Vesta Returns to date, moving backwards in time, are as follows:

20. November 22 – December 1, 2018

19. January 20 – 28, 2015

18. March 23 – April 1, 2011

17. December 12 – 20, 2007

16. February 6 – 14, 2004

15. April 25 – May 14, 2000
    June 21 – July 11, 2000 (retrograde)
    October 15 – 28, 2000

14. December 29, 1996 – January 6, 1997

13. February 23 – March 3, 1993

12. November 15 – 24, 1989

11. January 15 – 23, 1986

10. March 17 – 26, 1982

9. December 7 – 15, 1978

8. February 1 – 9, 1975

7. April 14 – 27, 1971
   July 21 – August 8, 1971 (retrograde)
   October 1 – 18, 1971
6. December 25, 1967 – January 2, 1968
5. February 19 – 27, 1964
4. November 8 – 17, 1960
3. January 10 – 16, 1957
2. March 9 – 18, 1953
1. December 5 – 9, 1949

I will note here in passing, that periods 7 and 15, in 1971 and 2000 respectively, contain three passes, which suggests in general, according to astro-logic, that these periods might be especially important or revealing of Vesta's presence in my life. We will see. In any case, the next step is to move through these dates, with archetypal eye open, and see what within my experiences at the time, seems to fit what I know so far about Vesta.

Taking a Cyclical History of Vesta Returns

Period 20: November 22 – December 1, 2018

I was still living with my previous partner and struggling with a sense of not being seen by her for who I really was. I was working to promote a new book and got the distinct sense from her that she wasn't all that interested in what I had to say. For the most part, during this period, we got along fairly well, but this sense of not being seen, acknowledged, or appreciated for who I was, had long been a sore point in our relationship and came to the fore during this Vesta return.

This sense of invisibility, which is a theme that goes beyond this relationship, seems in keeping with Vesta/Hestia's relative invisibility within the iconography of the Greco-Roman pantheon.

Period 19: January 20 – 28, 2015

I was living here alone in my cabin between relationships, but I was more actively engaged with other people than I am now. I was working with a group of teachers and healers to create collaborative workshops, and during this period, we were gearing up to have one. We were also welcoming a new member to our Talking Council (our name for the working group) – a member whose Vesta was exactly opposed mine (within 2°).

I was also working on the book that I was promoting in Period 20, *Astrology and the Archetypal Power of Numbers, Part Two*, writing a passage about Vesta's role in Bob Dylan's chart. At the same time, I was reading a book by Stephen Buhner, called *Plant Intelligence and the Imaginal Realm*, out of which I extracted the idea of the "golden thread," which "may emerge from any ordinary thing and open a doorway into the metaphysical background of the world."[2] About this idea, I wrote (also quoted in Chapter 10):

> *I can (now) understand Vesta's role in my (chart) as the revelation of my golden thread . . . This golden thread makes any exploration of astrology an adventure in discovery, rather than a mere decoding of symbols with rote meanings. This is an improvisational art to which I aspire, and in reaching for it, Vesta becomes my guide and my muse.*[3]

Lastly, during this period, I was having my wood stove serviced by a new company I hired after a friend of mine, who was a chimney sweep, had retired. I was also contemplating taking down a large tree sitting just outside my bedroom window, but just didn't have the heart to do it. It still sits there now, towering about 60 feet above my cabin, leaning in toward it from only a few feet away. I call it my Guardian Tree.

Period 18: March 23 – April 1, 2011

I was living here in my cabin, but with a partner who was helping me market *Astrology and the Archetypal Power of Numbers, Part One*, as I was writing the Introduction to *Part Two* – with only minor moments of success that were a struggle to attain. At the time, I was engaged in an ongoing discussion with another astrologer (whose Vesta was semi-sextile mine within a 1° orb) about why I thought astrology was not a science, the subject of this current book. Lastly, in terms of Vesta's involvement in my creative life, I was reading *The Astrological Imagination: Where Psyche and Cosmos Meet* by Brad Kochunas, whom I quoted in Chapter Four.

On a more personal level, I was feeling lonely in this relationship with this partner, as our sex life was starting to disappear. In addition, I noted in my journal that I was "feeling a bit irritated at my neighbors again for not including me in the discussion about what needs to be done on the upcoming work day. Feeling alone, basically, but then again, I've been here before and I keep on keeping on anyway."[4]

This was another period of invisibility, but one in which I was diligently following my golden thread nonetheless, while continuing to tend the land on which I live.

Period 17: December 12 – 20, 2007

I was living alone in my cabin, but in anticipation of my new partner, mentioned during the previous period, joining me after the first of the year. Oddly, during this period, I noticed that there "seems to have been a shift over these past few months in my sexual energy and in my emotional response to this relationship. I still want it, and I want it to work, more than anything else I can imagine wanting now, but the hyper-romantic buzz of this summer appears to be gone, or perhaps just dormant. Seems ironic, now that she is coming here to live with me, but also seems important to just be with what is." Vesta's call to celibacy, even within the context of a new relationship? In retrospect, it didn't go that way, but the note does seem synchronistic nonetheless.

Meanwhile, I was writing *Astrology and the Archetypal Power of Numbers, Part One.*

At the beginning of this period, I was repairing my wood stove.

Period 16: February 6 – 14, 2004

I was living in Texas, buying and selling textbooks for a living, a business that required me to be on the road a fair amount. In the middle of a road trip, I found myself fantasizing about moving back to my cabin in the woods, where I live now, and longing for a simpler life. At one point, at the end of this period, over the weekend, staying at my cabin in the woods, I attended the birthday party of a friend, but I "felt oddly out of place, like I didn't belong there. So, I hung out on the sidelines and became increasingly withdrawn as the evening dragged on. I had planned to spend the night, but when the party dragged on past midnight, I began to crave my own space. I said my goodbyes and headed back to my frigid cabin to spend the night. I built a fire, put on my jumpsuit and went to bed."

Meanwhile, earlier in the week, while still on the road, in the art department of one of the colleges where I bought books, I "came across a collage hanging on the wall of the art building, depicting Urania, the Greek muse of astrology, and was inspired to want to buy it. I spoke to the professor who created it, and arranged to have a print made . . . I liked the idea of buying the muse of sacred poetry as well, but couldn't relate to the image, which was of a Holocaust victim, and didn't seem to fit my notion of what sacred poetry is about."

While Vesta (or Hestia) does not have any "formal" connection to any of the muses in Greek mythology, I have come to associate her with the creative muse, which serves as a fiery source of inspiration, and in some mysterious way, seems to guide the discovery of the golden thread. Already in this cyclical history, we can see my discovery of Stephen Buhner and Brad Kochunas, both of whom have continued to a deeper understanding of astropoetics, as I have outlined it so far in my writing. Taking these instances into account and noting the obvious reference to the muse in this period, I can empirically begin to make a symbolic connection between Vesta – as she appears during her returns – and this idea of following the muse as a process of tending creative fire.

Period 15: April 25 – May 14, 2000

This is the first of two periods, as noted above, where a retrograde pass creates an extended window in which Vesta was likely to have been active.

At the beginning of the first period, I was out on another book-buying trip. On this one, I got into a minor fender bender accident, and was given a ticket for failure to yield the right of way, even though the other driver had run a red light and hit me. Subsequently, the other driver sued me, claiming medical issues, and after a grueling 7-year ordeal with one delay after another, he finally lost his case in court when an eyewitness testified that she had seen him run the light.

Meanwhile, in addition to my book-buying business, I was teaching astrology to a number of students through a labor-intensive correspondence course called Eye of the Centaur, in which I prepared each lesson for each student individually from scratch. I was also being groomed by a local politician to lead a political campaign to keep fluoride out of the city's drinking water. At one point, "I woke up in the middle of the night, feeling too overextended with all I have taken on – two businesses, my role on the board of directors in Greenwood, our trip to Arizona, San Diego in August, and Germany in November, and my two Centaur workshops in October. I just don't see how I am going to be able to do it all. But I am concerned about the issue (the possibility of fluoride in my drinking water) and feel as though if I didn't do what I could, I would regret it later." This was a long way from a simple tending of the hearth, and I was beginning to feel the stress and strain.

June 21 – July 11, 2000 (retrograde)

During the retrograde period, I was in the middle of another book-buying trip, staying at my cabin in the woods on weekends. Previously, I had hired a contractor to build an addition onto the original cabin, and during this period, I was doing some of the interior finish work myself.

At one point, alone in my cabin, I found myself "wondering why my sexuality is so introverted. I suspect it must be some message I got from my mother about how sex was something that men imposed upon women and that they endured. If (my current partner) were here, it would be different, but even with her, I find myself holding back." It turns out this partner's Vesta was opposed mine within a 2° orb.

As in Period 17, there seems to be a theme developing of withdrawn, introverted sexual energy, which would be in keeping with at least the patriarchal stories passed down about Vesta, who by all accounts was simply not interested in sex. I would not describe myself as not interested in sex, but in each of my relationships I have come to this place where I find myself holding back and withdrawing.

My mother's Vesta was not in aspect to mine, but her Neptune was opposed my Vesta within 1° orb, perhaps echoing the story about Hestia's rebuff of Poseidon's advances, and also possibly the controversy about Dionysus (who is also part of Neptune's archetypal field)[5] replacing Hestia on the Dodekatheon, referenced in Chapter 11. Astrologically, these mythological themes potentially translate into an attitude toward sexuality when Vesta and Neptune form a hard aspect to one another, or as in this case, between one chart and another. It is possible that my mother didn't actually have the attitude that I ascribed to her, although on the few occasions where she alluded to her actual attitude toward sex, I got that impression. In any case, her Vesta was conjunct my Moon, so no doubt my attitude toward women in general was informed by her mythologically Vesta-like attitude toward sex. We never talked about it, but in retrospect, I can imagine that it was something I internalized by osmosis.

October 15 – 28, 2000

This last wave of Period 15 saw the end of my first Eye of the Centaur workshop, an annual event during which I taught a special workshop for all my students, and the beginning of the second. By this point, I had so many students that I felt a need to have two workshops, instead of one, in order to keep the numbers small enough to retain the intimate feeling of past workshops.

At one point, during the second workshop, "the discussion turned to the way in which men project sexual fantasies onto women and I realized I was guilty of that (with one of the participants). I felt embarrassed and exposed, but also grateful that we could discuss it."

At another point, toward the end of this period, while still involved with the anti-fluoride campaign, I was asked to give a 5-minute statement on a local TV station, and did. Not very Vesta-like, and a bit out of my depth, but I managed to do OK.

Period 14: December 29, 1996 – January 6, 1997

This period began with a fairly intense round of lovemaking with the same partner that I had in Period 15, a few months after we started living together, during the first New Year's Eve spent together in a shared home.

For the new year, we each drew Spirit Path cards from a deck created by Native American teachers Jamie Sams and David Carson. My partner's card was Fire Medicine. The image on the card shows a woman standing stoically in the middle of a fire. In the chapter on Fire Medicine, Sams and Carson begin by describing various forms of fire encountered in Native American tradition:

1 the fire in Grandmother Sun

2 the fire in Mother Earth's core

3 the fire that comes from lightning

4 the fire in lava that forms the Stone People

5 the fire that burns wood

6 the Fire within each of us that is the Eternal Flame of Great Mystery and is our life force and spontaneity[6]

Of these, the last two are probably most clearly aligned with the archetype of Vesta, although Vesta's cultural sisters, as discussed earlier, would cover the gamut. Since my Vesta is conjunct Jupiter/Zeus, traditionally a storm god, we might assume that "the fire that comes from lightning" is also somehow relevant to my Vesta story. My nickname in college was Lightning.

Sams and Carson conclude their section on this card by saying:

> *Fire Medicine is the reminder that all things come from and contain Great Mystery, which is Original Source. The Fire of Creation lives within us and in All of Our Relations. When we balance the Sacred Fire inside ourselves, in every form it takes, we can then perceive and become anything in Creation through melding with the Sacred Fire in all things.*[7]

Although neither the Greeks nor the Romans would have spoken this language, it would appear to me that the association of Vesta/Hestia with the *omphalos* – the center of everything – the cosmos, the culture, the community, the family hearth and the heart of the tender of the hearth, amounts to this same understanding of the central mystery of our connection to our Original Source. The card I pulled was Great Mystery. According to Sams and Carson, "the Original Source of Creation is called Great Mystery by Native Americans."[8]

It would appear in retrospect that my making sacred fire through our love-making during this Vesta Return, my previous partner and I were entering into this Great Mystery at the Source of it all. Or at least I would like to think so. This experience seems to be at the other end of the spectrum from those of previous periods in which my sexuality felt more withdrawn.

A few days later, still within the Vesta Return window, after getting back on the road with my book-buying business, I wrote in my journal, "I am feeling overwhelmed by a destiny that seems to be passing me by. I feel like I ought to be doing something of more consequence with my life, but I'm not." Looking back, I did not have the luxury then of tending the sacred fire of my passionate creativity every day, the way I do now.

Period 13: February 23 – March 3, 1993

I was living alone again in my cabin. My focus here was on making music. Having taught myself, while previously living in Santa Fe, NM, to play and compose on electronic keyboards under the tutelage of a local musician, I was now in the process of putting together my own CD of original music.

I was also in the beginning phases of developing the astrological correspondence course – Eye of Centaur – that I was teaching to a peak number of students in Period 15. At one point, I wrote that "I felt a great deal of inertia, as though the channels of information and creative intuition were rusted shut, but by day's end, the flow had begun to come more easily."

In general, aside from my creative projects, which were what kept me going, I was feeling isolated and alone. At another point during this period, I wrote, "I am feeling lonely; despairing about my life; torn between wanting to stay here and continuing to build some kind of workable logistical foundation beneath my creative endeavors and wanting to return to Santa Fe where I have friends, support resources and culture. I can't seem to resolve this agonizing dilemma. I worry about my faculties declining (although I'm only 43), feel my motivation and will to live slipping away, feel cut off from my joy, caught up in a dwindling negative spiral, desperately wanting to break out, but not sure how." The next day, finishing my Eye of the Centaur brochure, "allowed me to shift out of my despair into a more hopeful place."

In retrospect, this seems like a low point, during which tending my creative fires was what pulled me through.

Period 12: November 15 – 24, 1989

I was living temporarily in the Pacific Northwest, having decided to leave New Mexico when a job and a relationship ended all at the same time. I was staying with a friend of a friend in Eugene, Oregon, feeling lonely and isolated, trying to find work that would allow me to stay. I was taking a break from astrology, feeling as though there were more important things that I should be doing with my time and energy, although I didn't really know what. At the time, I was feeling a pull to do something to stop the rampant cutting of old growth forests, looking for a way to re-invent myself through some paid employment as an environmentalist. What I quickly discovered while I was there was that everyone there was an environmentalist, and no one got paid.

At one point, I thought about going to a meeting of Earth First! but decided not to. "I don't believe that angry, destructive approach to the very real problems we all face is my style. I believe there is a definite place for it within the overall range of responses possible, but I myself fall elsewhere in the spectrum."

This seems a Vesta-like response, but one that ultimately raised a larger question: "What do I do with my fire, including my anger and my outrage? How do I effectively channel that in a constructive way?"

At another point, I wrote that, "I was shocked at the Machiavellian plans of the lumber companies and heartened by the commitment of the activists fighting them. I want to play a larger part, although I also feel some inertia behind my life as it is. I am feeling somewhat inward at a time when I tell myself I should be directing my energies outward." Meanwhile, the meetings I did attend left me feeling intimidated and fired up with angry energy I didn't know how to channel constructively. I wanted to make a contribution, but didn't know how. "I need and want a more substantial sense of purpose to drive me. I don't know where that is going to come from, except inside of me, yet for whatever reason, I can't seem to get to it."

Period 11: January 15 – 23, 1986

I was living here in the forest, just building the cabin in which I now live. I was also doing a few readings here and there, and publishing a local quarterly called *The Cooper's Hawk Chronicles*. I was in a relationship with a woman, essentially my next-door neighbor, who wanted to move to Santa Fe, New Mexico to go to school there. I was trying to decide whether or not to go with her, feeling ambivalent. My journal entries during this period were pretty sparse, I suspect because at the end of most days, after building, I did not have the energy to wax eloquent.

Period 10: March 17 – 26, 1982

I was living in Springfield, Missouri, about two hours from the land where I live now, working in my own painting business to pay off the land and my student loans before moving there. I was living with a woman, who had a young daughter. We had the thought that if we could get her into the school associated with the land cooperative where I had bought my land, we would just move and try to make a go of it there. But my "step-daughter" was rejected, because of philosophical differences between myself and the founder of the school, and we decided to stay put, homeschooling her instead.

I was becoming disillusioned with the land cooperative – with which I would have many philosophical and political differences over the years. I was also sad to see many of the people with whom I initially felt a connection there, moving on. I was still keen on living there, however, even if it meant scrapping to save more money for a while. "Will there ever come a day when I can spend my time freely without regard to material security?" I wondered.

I don't see much of Vesta in this period, unless it would be the ongoing call to a simpler life, which was the driving force behind the more complicated life I was living at the time.

Period 9: December 7 – 15, 1978

I was living in Florida, working to save money to live somewhere in the country, at this point, without a clear idea where.

I was teaching myself piano. Within this time frame, I met with the head of the music department at a local college to see about getting into his advanced music theory class, which I did.

I was also involved with a study group in a town nearby of disciples of Swami Muktananda and was beginning to learn about *siddha yoga*, which was an alternative approach to *kundalini* from what I had previously learned with Yogi Bhajan, as mentioned in Chapter 11. At one point, during this Vesta Return, I wrote that, "I had a very moving experience as I read in *Play of Consciousness* (Muktananda's autobiography) about Baba's initiation by his own guru, Nityananda. I cried, felt warm inside, loved, blessed, and close to Baba. I felt something open up within me, perhaps the beginning of devotion; I don't know. I just know that all of a sudden I felt as though my relationship to Baba was very close and very real."

Although my experience of Muktananda was mostly one of intense heat – which would be more in keeping with Vesta's fiery domain, I suppose here, the opening of my heart was another kind of initiation into the realm of fire.

Period 8: February 1 – 9, 1975

This is now past the point where my journals go, so to feel my way into this time frame, I will have to rely on my memory. If memory serves, during this period, I would have been living and working at the Kundalini Research Institute, one of Yogi Bhajan's ashrams in southern California, and finishing my Master's Degree in Marriage, Family and Child Counseling. I was teaching kundalini yoga, working as a senior editor in the publications department, and informally studying astrology by doing birthcharts for nearly everyone who passed through the Institute. During this period, I was essentially beginning to weave the golden thread that would mark the unfolding of my creative passion over the course of the next 40+ years, a three-strand braid including astrology, Western psychology and yogic philosophy.

Period 7: April 14 – 27, 1971

I was finishing up a fairly useless undergraduate degree with a major in English and a minor in chemistry at a school designed to train scientists and engineers. I was making the best of it, but glad it would soon be over. I was discouraged to see so many of my friends line up for corporate jobs, and just couldn't bring myself to do it. I did not go to one single job interview my entire senior year and didn't really know what I was going to do next. I was making plans with a couple of friends to take a cross-country trip after graduation, in order to see the country. Beyond that, I could not imagine a future.

Somewhere around this time, I had gotten official conscientious objector status from my draft board during the Viet Nam War. This was not a matter of escaping to Canada to avoid being drafted, but rather an intensely focused effort through which I wrote out a 17-page statement of my beliefs, citing reasons from my Catholic upbringing as well as my then current practice of yoga, about why I felt it was wrong to kill. My statement was corroborated by personal references from a priest, a minister and a rabbi, as well as my next-door neighbor, who had been a Major General in the army during World War II, all attesting to the sincerity of my beliefs. The draft board simply mailed me my conscientious objector status, without insisting on a face-to-face interview, a break with procedure I later learned was most unusual, if not unheard of. Mostly, young men my age who could walk and talk were drafted, regardless of their beliefs, however convincingly presented.

I guess I had somehow made an irrefutable case, one that in the context of this empirical research, seems consistent with Vesta's policy of abstaining from the political in-fighting among her fellow deities.

July 21 – August 8, 1971 (retrograde)

This was the time frame for the road trip I took after college. There were three of us that were planning to go, but shortly before graduation, one of our gang of three got into a motorcycle accident and went into a coma. We hung around for a while, waiting to see if he was going to be OK, but eventually wound up leaving without him. After a while, the two of us wound up camping on the banks of the Applegate River in southern Oregon, eventually becoming involved with a group of local hippies who shared a dream of living on the land. My friend eventually left to go to graduate school; I stayed and got more involved with this group.

October 1 – 18, 1971

Eventually we all moved to a piece of land outside of town and started a commune called Funny Farm. Since I was the only one with money, I made the down payment, foolishly believing the others would rally to make the payments, while I kicked back and wrote my novel. It came as no surprise to anyone but me that this was not going to happen, and eventually I put the land up for sale. But at this juncture, seen in retrospect, I was getting my first taste of the dream of living a simple life on the land, tending the hearth, that I am actually living now.

Between the second and third waves of this Vesta Return, I had my first astrology reading – a 5-hour affair that left me thoroughly smitten by the astrological muse, standing at the trailhead of my golden thread. So yes, in retrospect, this period was one of the most important of my Vesta story.

Period 6: December 25, 1967 – January 2, 1968

This would have been Christmas break during my freshman year of college. Although I don't remember the exact dates when this happened, this might have been the time when I broke up with my first girlfriend, my high school sweetheart. I remember hitchhiking from my school to hers a few hours away, in the rain, thinking I would surprise her, only to be told outside the door of her dorm that she no longer wanted to be in relationship with me. I was crushed, but turned around and hitchhiked back home in the middle of the night.

Period 5: February 19 – 27, 1964

This would have been the winter of my freshman year in high school. During this phase of my life, I was in love with music, and was playing saxophone in a local rock and roll band called the Barons, as noted in Chapter Eleven. This would have been just before the advent of the Beatles changed the musical landscape and the saxophone became passé. Eventually, I was booted out of the band for this and other reasons. But for the moment, at the age of 14, I was actually working as a professional musician, making money as I wielded my musical fire stick, probably around the same time that I was also discovering my sexuality.

Period 4: November 8 – 17, 1960

I was 10 years old, in the sixth grade. I don't remember anything about this period.

Period 3: January 10 – 16, 1957

I was 7 years old, in the second grade. In the first grade, I had been getting into fights every day on the playground, and the school authorities came this close from expelling me from school. In Vesta's language, it was a hard lesson in fire-management, after which – and likely during this period – I was looking for a better way to channel my anger. From this point forward, I became a rather competitive student, vying with two other students to be the best at spelling. I eventually lost that contest but continued to excel as a student. At times, this made me more visible than I wanted to be, and I struggled with that. But for the most part, I had stepped onto a path toward personal excellence that I feel I still walk today.

Period 2: March 9 – 18, 1953

I was only 3 years old during this period, but I do have a memory of something significant that seems related to this story. Although I don't have exact dates for the incident in question, at one point, I was playing king of the mountain on a huge pile of ashes in my grandfather's back yard with the neighborhood kids, of whom I was the youngest. I somehow managed to make it to the top of the "mountain," and for a brief moment of glory, I was king. Then the other kids ganged up on me and started stuffing ashes into my mouth and up my nose. If my grandfather had not rushed out and chased the other kids away, I might not have made it to Period 3 above.

After a period of pneumonia in the hospital, I did survive, but I became very angry after that, eventually leading to the near expulsion from school that I spoke about in relation to Period 3, and the aftermath in which I sought something more constructive to do with my abundant fire energy.

I have written about this incident in other places and in other contexts.[9,10] It occurs to me here, however, that this is also a part of my Vesta story, starting with the pile of ashes itself – which was, presumably, the cumulative by-product of my grandfather's tending of his hearth – or perhaps my version of the Norwegian custom of Cinder-Biting, as mentioned in Chapter 11. In any case, the sense I have here is that this image of myself as a kind of male vestal virgin is one that I have perhaps inherited through my ancestral lineage.

This lineage does not appear to be about celibacy, nor conservation of sexual energy since I do, in fact, exist and was born the usual way – through the union of my mother and father. On the other hand, not having had children of my own, I am the last of the lineage. Nor has my sister, or any of my cousins on my father's side of the family, had any children, so we are at the end of a line, where procreativity does not seem to be on the menu. I cannot speak for my sister or my cousins, but it seems to me, in retrospect, that what happened on that day, on the ash pile, was the beginning of a Vestal journey, on which I would learn how to carry the torch of my forebearers in a different way, after an initiation in which I was literally biting cinders.

Period 1: December 5 – 9, 1949

These were the four days immediately after my birth, in which Vesta still occupied her natal position. As might be anticipated in relation to any cyclical history, I have absolutely no recollection of this time at all. Having said that, it is not out of the question that a still-living mother, other attending relative, midwife or *doula* could have a memory that would be relevant to the story. But alas, there is no one else to ask, in this case.

Memoria as a Soul-Making Empirical Quest

At this point in our process, I nonetheless have a great deal of information to work with. I have the data of my raw experience, as I remember it within the context of a cyclical history that revolves around a particular archetypal focus. Exploring the mythological stories about Vesta and elaborating beyond the raw experiences of Vesta's cyclical history itself, I have begun to gravitate toward a deeper, intuitive understanding of the symbolism that is intimately personal to me. Within this elaboration, various themes have begun to emerge that are corroborated as being relevant, not just by the mythological antecedents of the archetype itself, but through the "evidence" of my own experience, within the context of the unfolding story.

In ending this chapter, I would just like to point out, if it is not obvious, that the empirical process is very different for an astrologer than it is for a scientist. The raw data is not something that can be measured quantitatively, but rather revolves around stories – both mythological and personal – that weave certain archetypal threads together. The meaning that is derived from this data might be relevant to no one else but me, even though these archetypal themes are, in some sense, objective and collective. The exploration here moves in the opposite direction as a scientific investigation, not from the particular to the universal, but from the universal to the intimately personal.

Even at this personal end of the spectrum, the conclusions drawn from the raw data of experience itself are clouded by faulty memory, the benefit of hindsight, and other personal biases that might have more to do with my passing moods on this particular day, or a chance encounter with a passage in a book, or a fragment of conversation, or the fleeting image of a dream, than anything that could be substantially verified by an outside observer trying to make sense of the same data. This is obviously not empirical science. But it is empirical in the sense that understanding a birthchart or any aspect of a birthchart involves the gathering of data. It is a process of *memoria*, which can perhaps be understood as an empirical process infused within the soul-making power of imagination and revolving around a particular archetypal focus.

This is not the kind of astrology we normally think of practicing – largely because our current astrological sensibilities, and our practice, have been largely shaped by Hellenistic astrologers in the Logical Era and, perhaps to some extent, by more contemporary psychological astrologers, still unconsciously struggling to maintain objective, neutral distance from the symbolism, as would have been required in the Empirical Era. We will explore the logic of astrology in Chapter Fourteen. In the meantime, I would like to suggest that what we are doing here is rooting the logic of astrology in a more subjective archetypal domain, as we comb through personal experience in cyclical time, with the archetypal eye open. By doing this, when we finally do get to the logic of the birthchart itself, the astro-logical language becomes animated and revitalized by immersion in a more nuanced source of information than the logical mind can, by itself, comprehend.

This, at least is the method to my madness as I move backwards through the eras to unearth a specifically astrological epistemology, wildly different than science, but far more relevant to the quest for meaning we have embarked upon here.

Notes

1. Hillman, James. "Memory: Short-Term Loss, Long-Term Gain." *The Sun*, February 2022.
2. Buhner, Stephen Harrod. *Plant Intelligence and the Imaginal Realm: Beyond the Doors of Perception into the Dreaming of Earth*. Rochester, VT: Bear & Company, 2014, 303.
3. Landwehr, Joe. *Astrology and the Archetypal Power of Numbers: Part Two: Arithmology in the Birthchart*. Whittier, NC: Ancient Tower Press, 2018, 569.
4. Unless otherwise noted, all quotes in this chapter come from my personal journals.
5. Greene, Liz. *The Astrological Neptune and the Quest for Redemption*. Weiser Books, 2000, 77.
6. Sams, Jamie and David Carson. *Sacred Path Cards: The Discovery of Self Through Native Teachings*. HarperOne, 1990, 231.
7. Sams and Carson, *Sacred Path Cards*, 234.
8. Sams and Carson, *Sacred Path Cards*, 273.
9. Landwehr, Joe. *The Seven Gates of Soul: Reclaiming the Poetry of Everyday Life*. Abilene, TX: Ancient Tower Press, 2004, 363.

10. Landwehr, Joe. *Tracking the Soul: With an Astrology of Consciousness*. Mountain View, MO: Ancient Tower Press, 2007, 234-38.

Chapter Thirteen

Astrological Hermeneutics

In terms of our evolving astrological epistemology, we can understand this process of gathering empirical data through a cyclical history, with the archetypal eye open, as a kind of hermeneutics. It is interesting to note here that the practice of hermeneutics first arose in the Philosophical Era as an attempt to sort truth from fiction in relation to the kind of information that would have been received directly from the divine in the Mystical Era.

> *The early usage of "hermeneutics" places it within the boundaries of the sacred. A divine message must be received with implicit uncertainty regarding its truth. This ambiguity is an irrationality; it is a sort of madness that is inflicted upon the receiver of the message. Only one who possesses a rational method of interpretation (i.e., a hermeneutic) could determine the truth or falsity of the message.*[1]

The term was first used by Aristotle in his work, *On Interpretation* (c. 360 B.C.E) as part of an attempt to delineate the relationship between language - by then established in written form - and logic - soon to become the basis for science in the Logical Era. We will return to this original understanding of hermeneutics in Chapter 14. Meanwhile, in a brief history of hermeneutics, we can note an evolution from its early use in the interpretation of sacred texts to a more general theory of interpretation, applicable to any text, whether sacred or secular, and then beyond that to the understanding of a wide range of phenomena, essentially the entire realm of human experience. The application of hermeneutics to the human sciences in general - psychology, sociology, anthropology, history, political science, and so on - is generally credited to German psychologist and philosopher, Wilhelm Dilthey. Unlike hard empirical science, hermeneutics is generally an approach to information that seeks to understand the meaning and purpose of experiences, events, and the raw external "facts."[2]

In *Astrological Methods, Volume One*, Glenn Perry discussed the use of hermeneutics in astrological research,[3] citing Richard Tarnas' research into the true nature of the archetype of Uranus and his own research into the case study of an individual client.[4]

In discovering that the astrological Uranus actually behaves more like Prometheus than Ouranos, the deity after which Uranus was named, Tarnas conducted an exhaustive historical survey of several hundred figures in Western history, noting the role that Uranus played in their birthcharts, both natally and by transit, as well as key periods of history corresponding to the known themes with which Uranus is associated.[5] This work essentially began with the opening of the archetypal eye and then culminated in the gathering of massive amounts of empirical data – empirical not in a quantifiable sense, but in the more intuitive and qualitatively thematic way that we are proceeding here.

Perry's case study approach revolved around:

> *. . . the hypothesis that the astrological chart is an accurate symbolic representation of the core issues, life themes, and personality characteristics of the individual it depicts. The evidence is the client's observable behavior, his formative experiences of childhood, his current living situation, the nature and quality of his primary relationships, his difficulties and successes, career aspirations, religious beliefs, sex life, health, hopes, dreams, goals – in short, the client's entire life story.*[6]

The approach we are developing here is somewhere in between these two examples. The art of astrological hermeneutics, as I am suggesting we approach it, starts with the delineation of a specific archetype through immersion in the mythological stories, with special attention to a personal sense of resonance with those stories, or with certain aspects of them. Without then doing the kind of empirical research that Tarnas used to find extensive evidence, in the aggregate, for the correlation of these stories with an overwhelming and irrefutable confirmation of the archetypal themes being explored, we simply look at how these themes have developed since birth, within the lives of a single individual.

In this instance, our approach is like Perry's, but far less ambitious an undertaking than trying to hermeneutically understand an "entire life story" in relation to a whole birthchart. Ideally, over time, the various threads of an entire life story can be unraveled and rewoven using the same technique, but as you will see once we get into it, even restricting ourselves to one archetype – in this case, the asteroid Vesta – opens up a vast expanse of soul space, very rich in thematic material, and ripe with meaning. Since one of the principles we are working with here is that everything is connected to everything else, in a sense, it doesn't matter where we begin.

The chart ultimately provides multiple portals into the same story, which will look and feel somewhat different, depending on which one we go through. I myself have told this story, or parts of it, in relation to other astrological cycles, in other books and articles. Here, having moved through Vesta's portal into my chart, I am learning something new. The fact that such a thing is possible, fifty years after my initial discovery of astrology, is no small part of the reason that I still get a thrill from doing what I do. Astrology as a linear, rational correlation of symbols with delineated meanings doesn't interest me. Astrology as a language of exploration, facilitated by a hermeneutic approach, pivoting around living archetypes, endlessly surprising in what gets revealed about them with each fresh inquiry, does.

Elaborating Archetypal Themes

Taking this process one step further, having collected the raw data of my memories, in some cases aided by journal entries, for the twenty Vesta returns I have experienced since birth, we can sift and sort these memories for various archetypal themes related to Vesta. Here my experience becomes both confirmation of those themes, and a point of departure for further musings that make these themes more deeply meaningful to me.

Becoming a Cinder-Biter

My Vesta story begins in Period 2 with an initiation onto Vesta's path, perhaps in the Norwegian sense, as a cinder biter. For me, this was a literal experience, as it began with my mouth stuffed with ashes. This was a primal wound that had a number of reverberations, not all of which are relevant here. What does seem important to note upfront is the sense of powerlessness it unleashed in me, along with a tremendous amount of anger that had no immediate outlet. It nearly got me expelled in the first grade, and then gradually I learned to work with it more constructively. Anger, of course, can be understood as a fiery emotion, one that Vesta, for all her association with the element of fire, seems to have mastered, given her political neutrality.

In Period 3, I became a highly competitive student, determined to make it back to the top of that pile of ashes again. Alas, even in the second grade, as I started to fall behind my competitors in the race to become spelling champion, I had an inkling that this was never going to happen. But it drove me, nonetheless, through graduate school in Period 8 before this particular pathway to the transmutation of anger ran its course.

My anger re-emerged in Period 10 in a different form, as I became involved with organizational politics here in the land co-operative where I live; again, in Period 12 when I found myself railing against greedy, voracious timber companies in the Pacific Northwest, still struggling with anger I didn't know how to channel constructively; and yet again, in Wave 3 of Period 15, as I ran an anti-fluoride campaign in west Texas. Still, even now, as I contemplate how to make a difference in a world that seems to be unraveling, it begs the question, what to do with my anger and my sense of outrage about all of this.

I don't have an answer, but as a lifelong cinder-biter in training, I perhaps understand, as Vesta seems to have, as well, that engaging in conflict – Us Versus Them – is not the answer, as war – of any kind – generally ends in ashes.

In Period 2, where my training as a cinder-biter began, I made reference to the thought that this training might, in some way, be the continuation of an ancestral journey, noting here that my family name Landwehr was originally what any foot-soldier in the old Austro-

Hungarian Empire (1868 - 1918) was called, as well as what the army itself was called in Austria, Hungary, Germany, Prussia and parts of eastern Europe.[7]

So, it is not unlikely to assume that for my ancestors, the question of how to respond to the machinery of war, orchestrated by nation states, was a central issue. My paternal grandfather emigrated from Germany to the United States at the advent of World War I; my father served in the Philippines in World War II, but as a driver for the military brass; and as already noted, I myself was a conscientious objector during the Viet Nam War - not one who left the country to avoid going to war, but one who was granted this rare official status by my draft board after a serious petition.

In Period 7, I made a conscious decision not to put myself in a situation - the Viet Nam war - where I might have to kill or be killed. At the time, my anger was directed not at some abstract enemy conjured and demonized by the government, but at the government itself for fighting a war that had nothing to do with "protecting our freedoms," as we were told. I was angrier at the US government for the war itself than I would be at any potential enemy I might face in the rice paddies of a distant country - and I spent my fair share of the late 1960s, protesting the war, along with many others of my generation.

As a culture, here in the US, having fought numerous wars since, particularly most recently in Iraq and Afghanistan, it appears we have learned very little about the futility of war since those days, or perhaps we have more accurately chosen to ignore the lessons of history, for reasons that are more economic and political than humane. More to the point, I personally continue to be angry about this, as well as about all of the ways in which our culture serves the business interests of the few at the expense of the wellbeing of the many. Currently, as I write this, Russia has just invaded Ukraine, and is deliberately killing civilians and destroying the infrastructure on which human life depends, again fueling within me a dark sense of anger and despair.

This is no small part of the impetus behind the question that brings me to Vesta's door at this juncture, without offering an immediate answer. Recognizing, however, than I am in some way previously not recognized, on the path of a cinder-biter makes perfect archetypal sense, and I can see where my ancestral relationship with wars past has made me a torch-bearer, sometimes a reluctant torch-bearer, other times a clueless torchbearer, for a less conflicted way of being.

Discovering the Fire Stick

In Period 5, I discovered my first fire stick and learned that I could channel my anger, and any other emotion, for that matter, through my music. I taught myself piano and started studying music theory in Period 9. Music re-emerged as a theme during Period 13, and as noted in Chapter 11, has recently reminded me that it still exists as a potential avenue for making fire, when I received my recent synchronistic gift of the Native American flute at the giveaway ceremony at the men's gathering.

But the real discovery here, and the next step on my path as a cinder-biter was that I could, to some extent, channel my fire through an exercise of my creative passion, not necessarily just through music, but through my writing, and through my love of astrology as well. It would have been somewhere between the first and second wave of Period 7 that I discovered astrology, and Period 8 before it became the dominant focus of my creative life. In Period 13, I started developing my correspondence course, weaving together my passion for astrology with my emerging desire to teach, a creative fusion that reached a peak in Period 15, and then morphed in Period 16 into the writing of my books, which has continued through Period 20 into the present day. Through all of this history, the emergence of my creativity as a central focus, with increasing dedication seems to me to be a suitable version of Vesta's fire-tending duties - one that is far more constructive and preferable to the angry sputtering of fire energy toward conflagration and war.

Following a Golden Thread

At the heart of this path of creative self-expression lies a golden thread, a term I first encountered when reading Stephen Buhner in Period 19, but which has apparently been around for a while, and with which I have been engaged for a while without having a name to call it. Buhner traces the phrase to the poet William Stafford, who found the concept in a poem by William Blake.[8] Also referencing William Stafford, Robert Bly suggests that "mythologically, catching hold of the end of the golden thread is described as picking up a single feather from the burning breast of the Firebird."[9]

The Firebird in Slavic mythology apparently bestows a mixed blessing. "In a nutshell," claims one site devoted to Slavic mythology, "the firebird signified the beginning of a long and troubled journey" at the end of which could either be good fortune or doom.[10] Aside from noting the reference to fire, to follow the Firebird would, at this point, likely lead us too far astray, and leave us stranded in the deep woods.

What I do note here, however, is that following a golden thread - which does appear to be one of Vesta's themes, at least as I have experienced it - is a journey with no guaranteed outcome, at times a long and troubled journey, and in the end, one that can also lead one to the middle of nowhere, stranded in the deep woods. And yet, one follows it anyway, because there doesn't seem to be anything more important in life to do. This is not a quest that makes rational sense, nor is it generally considered a good career move. It is a calling that one discovers, one step at a time, with each step leading to the next.

I discovered my golden thread in Period 8, working at the Kundalini Research Institute, where I was beginning to see the connections between western psychological astrology, particularly as developed by Dane Rudhyar; Jungian, humanistic and transpersonal psychology; and yogic philosophy and practice. It wasn't until Period 13, after five Vesta cycles of marination in life experience, that I began weaving these threads together in my own way, at first through the development of my correspondence course, later through the teaching, and in greater earnest through the writing of my books from this point forward. Throughout this process, many additional sources of inspiration have joined the thread to eventually become a multi-dimensional tapestry, still very much a work in progress, but one that now has its own momentum, and for which I feel my primary job to be simply tending and facilitating that momentum, in the same way that I tend the fire in my hearth.

Moving in and out of Liminal Space

This momentum has by no means always been steady or continuous. In fact, it seems to unfold through a rhythm alternating between creative focus and liminality. Like the Huldra, the golden thread appears and then it disappears. I can, by now, remember that it exists, but I can't always feel it glowing at the center of my life. On multiple occasions, I have had to enter a period of liminality between rounds of intense creativity, so that out of a place of unknowing, the next step would reveal itself – not as part of some idealized logical progression, but more often as an unexpected flash of light illuminating the darkness.

Aside from the ash pile incident in Period 2 that initiated me as a cinder-biter, and led to a full Vesta cycle of liminality as I thrashed about in the angry emotional aftermath, my first adult experience of liminality occurred during Period 7. It was then, upon graduating from college that I realized I didn't have a clue what I wanted to do with my life. Instead, I did what most red-blooded American males did back in those days: I took a road trip. In retrospect, I can understand this road trip as movement through a liminal space in which I was slowly groping my way through the darkness, learning to trust my instincts.

On this road trip, one thing led to another, and I soon found myself literally lost in the deep woods, where I had bought land that I was in danger of losing, and rudely awakened to the hard reality of life without a clue. It was shortly after the third and final wave of this Vesta Return, however, that in desperately seeking guidance, I had my first astrological reading, and saw my first lighting flash crack open my impenetrable liminal space. It was then in Period 8 that my golden thread first began to reveal itself in the full potential of its glory.

Although this thread never really disappeared, I began losing track of it from Periods 9 through 12, where I noted that "I am feeling somewhat inward at a time when I tell myself I should be directing my energies outward . . . I need and want a more substantial sense of purpose to drive me. I don't know where that is going to come from, except inside of me, yet for whatever reason, I can't seem to get to it."[11] Lost again.

Then shortly before Period 13, I had another epiphany. On the night of the full moon after my birthday in 1992, talking to a friend, I realized that what I really wanted to do was develop and teach an astrological correspondence course. Another flash of lightning illuminated the path I took in Period 13, as I began creating the Eye of the Centaur, which I taught throughout Periods 14 and 15.

During the first wave of Period 15, however, "I woke up in the middle of the night, feeling too overextended with all I have taken on," realizing something had to give. Although, strictly speaking, it was not part of the cyclical history of Vesta Returns outlined earlier, I had a third epiphany that if I were ever going to write the books that I had talked forever about wanting to write, I would have to clear a space in my life to do that. So, I did. And in each subsequent period, to the present day, writing a series of books has been a large important piece of my creative focus.

Working at the Forge

Brigit, the equivalent of Vesta in the Celtic culture, is also known as a goddess of the forge. In that culture, the hearth and the forge are part of the same archetypal dynamic. In Greek and Roman culture, Hestia/Vesta is sometimes associated with baking, which is one kind of alchemy that takes place in this fiery place – as grain becomes bread. Working metals in the fire of the forge is another kind of alchemy in which tools and implements of various kinds, weapons, and ceremonial talisman are also fashioned. Working with words to release their magical capacities is another kind of work at the forge, perhaps more in line with my particular variety of this work – and one that was also part of Brigit's domain, as she was also known as a goddess of poetry.

A powerful creative alchemy takes place at the forge, but it is not generally one that simply revolves around a good idea, or a momentary flash of inspiration. Working at the forge requires a certain depth of commitment, a willingness to persevere despite numerous obstacles, both internal and external, and a capacity to stand in the fire of one's own creative process – a capacity that does not come without tempering in another kind of forge.

Alchemists talk about the real work not being the transformation of base metal into gold, but the inner transformation of the alchemist himself, as he works at the outer alchemical task. My sense is that to work at Vesta's forge, one must have also done, or be in the process of doing this inner work. Otherwise, the resulting creativity will lack substance, and simply be another throwaway commodity in a culture easily distracted by an endless stream of meaningless stimulation.

I experienced this more internal alchemy during Period 8, as I was living and working at the Kundalini Research Institute, studying, practicing and teaching *kundalini yoga* under the tutelage of Yogi Bhajan, and in Period 9, when I learned the more receptive style of *siddha yoga*, opening to the transformative fire generated by Swami Muktananda.

Working to raise the *kundalini* or allowing it to rise in the presence of an enlightened being is a powerful spiritual alchemy in its own right, requiring a sustained focus over time. I spent seven years working this alchemy, while it did its work on me. Every day for the 3 1/2 years I spent at the Kundalini Research Institute (essentially a full Vesta cycle), I rose every morning at 4 AM, took a cold shower, and then did 2 1/2 hours of *kundalini yoga*, meditation and chanting before the sun rose. Some mornings I had intense *kundalini* experiences, out-of-body or other experiences I can't explain; other mornings, I could barely keep my eyes open. But I rarely missed a morning, and this intense regular practice, called *sadhana* in the yogic vernacular, became my forge.

At summer and winter solstices, we would travel to tantric gatherings, spending a week doing arduous meditations with a partner, maintaining eye contact, as Yogi Bhajan, a tantric master would generate an intense field of heat, called *tapas*, a transformative fire that would accelerate the process of personal development. We would go back home after these events and find that our lives had changed in our absence, in some dramatic way. Or we made our own changes when we noticed that the old life no longer fit.

With Muktananda, my experiences were a bit more removed, as he did not maintain an ashram in the US, but only traveled here to set up temporary ashrams, usually on the East or West coast. I went to those and participated when I could. Aside from being endlessly entertaining, as Muktananda gave each student exactly what they need in a long *darshan* line of devotees, being in these temporary ashrams was like living in a sauna – always hot, and a bit uncomfortable, with nowhere to go but more deeply inside. Again, as with Yogi Bhajan's tantric courses, when you emerged from one of these sessions, you felt like you had been thoroughly cooked, and something was fundamentally different.

While I no longer actively practice *kundalini yoga* in either form, these two Vesta cycles – a period of about 7 years – was my time at another kind of forge, during which I myself was the Great Work, undergoing transformation by fire, and my life is different now because of that. As noted elsewhere, because of my need to understand the psychological dimensions of this transformation, I began studying Western psychology in Period 8 – a study that has deepened by practice of astrology, as well as given me a useful supplemental perspective from which to understand my own experiences. Working with *kundalini* also raised a number of my own issues and forced me to deal with them more consciously and intentionally. I saw, and experienced directly, the causal connection between cultivating sacred fire and accelerated, intensified growth.

Getting up every morning before sunrise to do morning *sadhana* taught me discipline, regularity, commitment and perseverance – all essential practices necessary to the tending of sacred fire, exercising creativity over the long haul in allegiance to a sense of calling. Beyond that, learning to stay focused on the reason why I was there: to fully experience a transformation by *kundalini*, amidst all of the intensified social and political melodramas within the *ashram* environment was a training unto itself. I saw both Yogi Bhajan and Swami Muktananda approach this aspect of the human zoo that swirled around them with calm, sly humor, and great compassion, and I sought to emulate them in this regard.

It is likely no small coincidence that during this same period, and on into Period 9 – I began more seriously writing, first for the publications department of the Kundalini Research Institute, and later for various other publications. I also had my first experience teaching while studying with Yogi Bhajan. While it may be nothing but coincidence, I attribute the real awakening of my creativity to the alchemy of this forge, experienced during these early years of working with *kundalini*.

Gestating Under a Cloak of Invisibility

In Period 20, I noted the theme of laboring under a kind of invisibility cloak, of doing my creative work without recognition, and in retrospect, learning to be OK with that over time. It did not always feel OK. At a certain point, I had made the conscious decision not to try to earn my livelihood as an astrologer. Aside from the fact that in the 1970s, when I was just starting out, this was not as easy to do as it might seem to be now, I also felt that I wanted to somehow maintain the purity of the amateur, doing what I did as sacred work, for the sheer love of it, not for the money.

The downside of this decision, however, was that for most of my career, I have not generally been recognized as an astrologer by very many of my peers. At times, especially through the first twelve periods of this series, my true path remained invisible, even to me.

Then there was the issue of earning a livelihood apart from the pursuit of my creative calling, which was not always easy, and time consuming at best. In Period 10, I wondered, "Will there ever come a day when I can spend my time freely without regard to material security?" In Period 14, I was "feeling overwhelmed by a destiny that seems to be passing me by" because I didn't have time to devote to it. Even as the necessity of earning a separate livelihood began to wane, during Periods 18 and 19, I struggled to promote my books, and attain any level of visibility at all for my work.

In retrospect, however, as I contemplate all of this now, I can begin to see that under Vesta's tutelage, the goal has never been to become visible or recognized for what I do; it has been to gestate something of value freely under the liberating cloak of invisibility. I am proud of what I have done, and I have grown tremendously in doing it. Whether or not the world can ever recognize my accomplishment, or value it in the same way that I do, matters less than the fact that I have done it – faithfully tended the hearth of my own creativity, and marshalled it into a body of creative work.

Building a Temple

In Vesta's mythological universe, the hearth/forge becomes the central altar of a temple. This suggests that the creative work of the forge is sacred work, the consequences of which radiate outward from hearth to household to family to community to country to cosmos. Or at least, the potential exists for this kind of radiance, depending on how deep the work of the forge actually goes. The idea of the hearth as altar at the center of a temple also implies that the work of the forge takes place in sacred space, suggesting that the creation of such space is perhaps a central dimension of the work itself.

In my case, I envision this temple being the cabin in which I now live and work, which in turn is part of a 1000-acre land cooperative, formed in the late 1970s as an effort to save a forest from being clear-cut. The land cooperative borders the Ozark Scenic Riverways, 80,000-plus acres of protected wilderness surrounding the free-flowing Jack's Fork River, a tributary of the Current River, which flows into the Black River, which flows into the White River, which flows into the Mississippi. My 10-acre parcel, in other words, has a big back yard that is mostly protected wilderness. It is sacred to me, as it was to the Osage, Delaware, Cherokee and Choctaw Indians up through the first few decades of the nineteenth century.[12]

While I didn't buy this land until sometime between Periods 9 and 10, I had my first taste of the experience of owning land during the last wave of Period 7, and dreamed about owning land again in Period 8. Since then, I have lived here in Periods 11, 13, 17, 18 and 19, and I live here now. Owning and living on a piece of land doesn't necessarily ensure that it is sacred but tending it does.

Between Periods 17 and 18, there was a huge storm here that blew down hundreds of old trees, including at least 300 mid-to-large-size oaks on my property, which I sold to a local flooring mill after hiring a mule logger to cut and skid them to a landing at the edge of my property. I now walk the skid trail around the perimeter of my property, which has become overgrown with moss and provides a peaceful daily meditation that allows me to connect with the land. In the wake of the storm, my then-partner and I worked hours every day to clean up the debris left behind by the mule loggers, a two-year *sadhana* that left me intimately acquainted with every dip and fold in the land, as I might a lover's body. We also planted countless additional trees, some of which made it and some that didn't. I built the cabin I live in now, and lived in a tipi on the land, before I built. I cut and split my own firewood, and then use it to feed my wood stove and warm the cabin for more than half the year. All of this makes the land, and this cabin, the sacred temple where I tend the hearth, and in which the forge of my creativity hums away.

Becoming a Virgin

The last theme that seems to emerge from the cyclical history of my Vesta Return has to do with Vesta's status as a virgin. As noted earlier, this does not necessarily mean sexually chaste, although it appears from the mythological stories, that Hestia at least was, in fact, celibate, rebuffing advances by Apollo and Poseidon, thwarting Priapus' attempt at rape, and taking a vow of celibacy after that. Whether or not her Roman counterpart's vestal virgins followed strictly in her footsteps, or were in fact, sacred harlots, as proposed by Demetra George and Esther Harding, is perhaps a matter of debate or speculation.

I can say with certainty that I am not, nor have I ever really been celibate. Even while living at the Kundalini Research Center during Period 8, I had a lover outside the ashram. I have never been married, but I have been through a number of serially monogamous relationships, a number of them in progress during Periods 10, 11, 14, 15, 16, 18 and 20 or about a third of the Vesta Returns in this cyclical history. For the other two thirds (eriods 1, 2, 3, 4, 5, 6, 7, 8, 9, 12, 13, 17 and 19), I was alone, and/or (in the case of Period 6), exiting a relationship.

The real story here, is what I have learned throughout this relationship history. In Period 6, I had my first major disillusionment in relationship, as the relationship with my high school sweetheart came to an abrupt end.

During the third wave of Period 7, I fell in love with the wife of my best friend at the time, as she was giving birth to their first child. It being the height of the hippy era, the three of us contemplated a kind of a *menage a trois*, which never made it past the contemplation stage and then became awkward after that.

The woman with the daughter with whom I was in relationship in Period 10 eventually left me for another man, and then moved to California.

The woman with whom I decided to move to Santa Fe, New Mexico sometime around Period 11, broke up with me a month after we landed there.

The intense love-making of Period 14 was with a partner with whom I managed to stay together through Periods 15 and 16, but by Period 15, I found myself "wondering why my sexuality is so introverted. If (my current partner) were here, it would be different, but even with her, I find myself holding back."

In Period 17, while anticipating the beginning of a new relationship, I also oddly felt this same introversion of my sexual energy, which was perhaps the ironic premonition of a relationship that ended, in part, because my partner was not all that interested in sex while I was, a development that started to unfold during Period 18.

Lastly, in Period 20, I was having a moment of rejection in a relationship that would last two more years, but end with a similar sense of despair about the possibility of a lasting, satisfying relationship that I felt at the ending of my first, in Period 6.

Taken in its entirely, this relationship history has been something of a disappointment. As I consider it now through Vesta's archetypal eye, however, I am aware that it has also been an initiation of sorts, into a place of much greater emotional and sexual autonomy. Although I still feel lonely at times, as noted in Chapter Ten, I no longer labor under the illusion that any partner could complete me, or permanently soothe the ache of anything that appears to be missing in my solitude. I know, in my belly and my bones, that I must do this for myself, and in the course of my initiation by Vesta, I have learned how.

While in a patriarchal culture, it would perhaps be disingenuous to suggest that, in the feminist understanding of virginity, I have finally gotten to the place where I am "subservient to no woman," I am no longer subservient to the romantic notion that finding my personal Cinderella could ever lead to "happily ever after." This is, as I see it here, within this exploration, ultimately a liberated state of emotional and psychological virginity, one that I can begin to understand astrologically, as a reflection of my relationship to Vesta, who is conjunct both Venus – the planet we most associate with relationship – and Jupiter, the ruling planet of my chart, and mythologically the Great Liberator.

Recognizing Archetypal Presence

Having elaborated the various themes that run through a cyclical history of Vesta Returns, I now essentially have a much more conscious awareness of Vesta's ongoing presence in my life that can serve as an experiential touchstone for her appearance during subsequent transits. For in the spirit of the deconstructionists, we must acknowledge that between those astrological moments in which Vesta is prominent, we are merely pausing between sentences, resting in the company of our latest floating signifier until new information either corroborates or modifies what we already think we know. Chances are that themes already established will accumulate additional evidence, but the possibility also exists that some previously unrecognized archetypal thread related to Vesta will reveal itself for the first time, or that existing themes will unravel to reveal a deeper layer of truth beneath what previously seemed obvious.

This, of course, is a very different approach to the birthchart than simply interpreting it, and perhaps in some ways, less satisfying because it is less definitive and perpetually incomplete. Yet, over the long haul, the natal birthchart, which follows us through life, is not just an ambidextrous oracle, waiting to give a working answer to any question we might pose to it. It is also an ongoing invitation to gain the kind of perspective that can really only come through a lifetime of experience – however long that lifetime has been in taking you into this present moment.

My sense about this is that moving into the depths of the psyche – which is what we do throughout a lifetime of experience of the various archetypal focal points in our birthchart, whether we are conscious of this or not – is a multi-layered experience. As we become conscious at one level, the layer just below it, more deeply rooted in the unconscious, may become available to us. Or not. To the extent that we do become aware of the multi-layered nature of the archetypal field, and intentionally seek the next level, whatever that might be, the meaning of our birthchart and the symbols in it, changes. In this sense, we can never finally say that "I have read my birthchart and I know what it means," as we are constantly reading and re-reading it, and discovering something new, or we see the "same old same old" from a slightly different perspective.

Taking an Awareness of Archetypal Presence Into the Present Moment

Since writing Chapter 12, for example, I have had yet another Vesta Return with which it becomes possible to test this idea. Today is March 11, 2022, and the now most recent Vesta Return in question took place from March 2 – 10. If I look to my journals for the past 9 days or so, this is what I see: not much really, unless you count efforts to reconnect with some of the people here with whom I have at times been at the opposite end of some conflict, and now have no hard feelings toward, perhaps a step or two toward transmuting anger into something more useful, on my journey toward becoming a master cinder-biter.

Or perhaps I am simply experiencing Hestia's association with liminal spaces in which nothing much happening is the norm, rather than the exception. As winter shades into spring here, the necessity for keeping the fire of the hearth going has lessened, although the humbling reminder of how difficult it was this winter, for some reason, lingers. Creative projects rumble on, as I continue working at the forge under my invisibility cloak. Loneliness permeates my days, deepened by the liminal space in which the whole world seems to be teetering on the brink of monumental change, and uncertainty hangs in the air like the pall of wood smoke from a fire slowly going out.

Or perhaps the promising Huldra who first appeared, back in Chapter Ten, has turned her back, and I am once again alone in the deep woods. We humans seem to need to make meaning out of what oftentimes seems meaningless, probably in order to otherwise avoid going mad.

I will report that since I intentionally called Vesta in, as noted in Chapter Eleven, a few months ago, I have been invited, seemingly out of the blue, but likely in response, to accompany some friends on a summer trip to Glastonbury, England. Brigit – among many other goddesses – has a presence there, especially at Bride's Mound, one of the less frequented sacred places in Glastonbury, thought to be where St. Brigid lived when she visited Glastonbury in 488 C.E.

Our trip happens to coincide with the Goddess Festival, although neither the invitation nor the trip line up astrologically with my Vesta cycle. If anything significant happens during the trip, I will report it later in this book.

Astrological Hermeneutics

Meanwhile, the important point to note here, as we conclude this chapter, is that in exploring the various archetypal themes related to Vesta, as they play out within my own experiences, and in following whatever synchronistic cues present themselves, I am entering into an ongoing conversation with myself. This conversation has certain universal touchstones, still recognizable as within the mythological domain encompassed by Vesta and her permutations in other cultures, folklore and fairy tales. But it also enters into a much more private space where perhaps the meaning extracted through this conversation pertains to no one else but me and reveals itself at times according to a timetable and in a manner that defies astrological expectation.

One gets the sense in reading about hermeneutics and its use within psychology, that the goal is still – as it is with science – to reach a place where you and I can agree about what is true. My sense is that the goal of astrological hermeneutics must necessarily be somewhat different, particularly if we are talking about its use as an aid to self-understanding. For what matters here is that I attain, through my contemplation of my own birthchart, a working articulation of whatever meaning I can extract from its symbolic depiction of my life at any given time. It matters less, if at all, that you or anyone else, come to the same conclusions that I do, or even if the same truth reverberates in a consistent way throughout the story.

Whatever sense of meaning I can derive through this exploration will necessarily be an incomplete truth for a number of reasons. In the first place, I am only considering one symbol within the entire field of factors that make my birthchart a complex symbolic statement of truth, taking it out of context as it were, and milking it for its own archetypal significance, as it relates to my experience of it. This is a necessary limitation, artificial in the sense that I am using it for purposes of demonstration, and yet at the same time, a device that makes the approach of the full and overwhelming symbolic intensity of a birthchart approachable.

In Chapter Fourteen, I will restore a bit of symbolic integrity to this exploration by placing Vesta into a more complete astrological context, primarily including its placement by house and sign, and its major aspects to other celestial bodies. Even here, however, we are dealing with one voice within a symphony of voices – trying to hear the melodic lines played by an oboe in the midst of a concerto, in which the oboe sometimes comes to the fore, and sometimes recedes into the background. Thus, even in a larger context, we are not approaching anything near a complete truth about who I am, or any kind of definitive statement that we can call an ultimate astrological truth.

Secondly, whatever sense of meaning I do attain – and I have already attained quite a bit – must be understood as a reflection of where I am now in the archetypal process encompassed by Vesta's participation in my chart and in my life. This sense is necessarily different at age 72 than it would have been at 36 or 12, or than it may be a few years from now, or even by next week. This does not make it untrue; it does make my truth provisional, a glimpse worth noting in a potential collage of glimpses, perhaps in the same way that any given photograph in an album of photos adds to a story with many faces, even as the same face is the ongoing subject of the album.

Third, even though we are not necessarily going for objective truth here, it is not out of the question to assume that others with whom I have shared these Vesta experiences – say, my previous partners who appear within the cyclical history of returns I have explored – will remember the same experiences entirely differently. In some ways, it is possible that their remembrances will be closer to some ideal of objective truth than mine are.

This does not negate the subjective truth of the meaning I ascribe to these experiences, and by extension, to Vesta's archetypal role within my birthchart taken as a whole, but it does point out the fact, that astrological hermeneutics is not, and can never be, entirely compatible with the idea of interpreting a birthchart. It is, in fact, a different approach to the birthchart altogether – one that is meant to approximate the reality of the truism that, "It ain't over until it's over." Life is an ongoing never-ending process of self-creation, and to the extent that it true, the birthchart is a moving target for any attempt at understanding. This is not a reason to abandon what might seem like an impossible quest, from a rational standpoint, but rather a call to a deepening of commitment to look and look again, as an ongoing practice of astrological self-reflection.

Two Complimentary Kinds of Hermeneutics

French critical theorist Paul Ricoeur understood the process of hermeneutic exploration as a dialectic between two contradictory, but potentially complimentary, dimensions of the process. He understood the human being to be essentially a linguistic creature, whose sense of self derives from the language that she uses to understand the life experiences that make her who she is. At the same time, Ricoeur understood language to be polysemic and symbolic, open to a diverse range of possible interpretations – a perspective very much in the spirit of our discussion above, about why the hermeneutic contemplation of any astrological symbol must be a perpetual work in progress. His view also speaks to our earlier and more superficial observation that two astrologers will not necessarily come to the same interpretative conclusions about a birthchart, or anything within it for that matter.

As already noted, this makes the result of any hermeneutic exploration of a birthchart tentative at best; it also makes the practice of astrology itself suspect from a scientific standpoint. But Ricoeur takes this observation further by noting that because language is inherently symbolic - and here we would add astrological language, although Ricoeur would not - it is, at best, a partial articulation of reality, a significant portion of which remains hidden or opaque. At the same time, "this opacity constitutes the depth of the symbol." The symbol, in other words, is "an enigma," a puzzle which challenges the interpreting intelligence to penetrate into its depth "slowly and with difficulty."[13]

As any astrologer will recognize, symbols beg for interpretation, deciphering, or exegesis, but doing so sets up a conundrum, since to interpret a symbol is to rip it up from the depths by its roots, render it lifeless, superficial, and ultimately meaningless. Through the process of interpretation, the symbol becomes a mere sign of something known, with no further capacity to illuminate the unknown, that is to say, fairly useless as a point of entry into deeper understanding of the birthchart. This paradox sets up a conundrum for the hermeneutic investigator, since to work with symbols and a symbolic language, one has to essentially follow two parallel tracks.

On the one hand, the intent of the investigation is to demystify the symbol and render it accessible to the conscious mind. On the other hand, to get to the heart of what a symbol means, it is necessary to allow the symbol to reveal itself on its own terms, over time, in ways that the conscious mind cannot anticipate, and generally doesn't have the patience to allow.

This is essentially the *yin* and *yang* of hermeneutics: *yang* being the intentional movement toward demystification, and *yin* being a receptivity to the unknown dimensions of the symbol, dimensions that only gradually rise to the surface. On the *yin* track to hermeneutic knowledge, one must live with the symbol for a while, enter into relationship with it, and let it reveal itself in its own way, and in its own time. This can ultimately take years, or perhaps in some cases, lifetimes.

The Hermeneutics of Faith

Ricoeur called the *yin* path the "hermeneutics of faith." The faith required is the belief that the symbol itself is alive, and has something to say, if we can allow it to speak, and are willing to listen. This is an art that requires a partial suspension of analytical faculties and literal thinking, and a willingness to be surprised by the spontaneous intuitive revelations of the imagination. "It is a rational faith, for it interprets; but it is a faith because it seeks, through interpretation, a second naïveté."[14]

One cannot help but strive to interpret the symbolism, and this is a process that proceeds in part by rational pathways. In the case of astrological symbolism, as we have noted in previous chapters, the rationale behind interpretation comes in part through a consideration of the mythology of the gods and goddesses represented by planets in the birthchart. This rationale allows us to say, for example, that because Vesta tended the hearth, she is an asteroid we associate with fire, in all of its metaphoric manifestations. This is not the same sort of reason that guides the astronomer, who looks at Vesta and sees only an inert planetary fragment orbiting in the asteroid belt between Mars and Jupiter. But it is rational nonetheless, a product of the symbolic logic that allowed astrology to compete with science for rational explanations of the cosmic order in the Logical Era.

Whereas the astronomer stops at the rationale of strictly factual information, however, the astrologer, with the archetypal eye open, engages in a "hermeneutics of faith" in order to make a leap from factual information to symbolic logic. What is interesting to note here is that this symbolic logic is not something conjured out of thin air, or necessarily even drawn strictly from mythology, as often the astronomical facts also corroborate the symbolic logic, provided a "second naïveté" is allowed.

When NASA's Dawn spacecraft orbited Vesta from July 2011 to September 2012, for example, it learned that Vesta was one of the earliest objects to form in our solar system,[15] a fact that correlates symbolically with the idea presented in mythology that Hestia was the firstborn of the Olympians, and the first to be swallowed by her father Saturn (Cronus).

Vesta also has one of the largest brightness ranges of any physical body in our solar system, brightness being associated with light and fire. The brightest parts of Vesta are thought to be native to Vesta herself, while scientists believe that the darkest parts of Vesta come from about 300 collisions with other asteroids crashing into Vesta, and gradually building up a blanket of material around the core, 3 – 7 feet thick. Using our second naïveté here, we see a symbolic link to the idea that Vesta is somehow related to the alchemy of anger (collisions = conflict, battle, war), transmuting it into substance, or character tempered by fire, or a kind of spiritual maturity that knows how to stand in truth without having to go to war. This would an impossible stretch for a scientist, contemplating the rationale of facts, but it is what astrologers routinely do, along the *yin* path of a hermeneutics of faith in order to make the leap from factual information to symbolic logic.

When this symbolic logic is subsequently taken into an empirical exploration of personal experience, as we have done in this chapter, it then becomes corroborated by a kind of evidence that also depends upon second naïveté. Here, the remembered "facts" of one's life become meaningful to us personally, as they are perceived and understood within the context of the symbolic logic derived through a consideration of this more collective level of information, both mythological and astronomical.

More specifically, here, for example, I remember the fact that my distant ancestors were foot soldiers in the army, while I myself, perhaps along the path of initiation laid out for me by Vesta, chose to become a conscientious objector during the Vietnam War. There is nothing within either the astronomical facts explaining Vesta's range of brightness, nor for that matter, within the standard astrological lexicon, that would allow me to make such a leap, but within the practice of a *yin* hermeneutics of faith, it becomes a meaningful association that deepens my understanding of Vesta's role in my life.

The Hermeneutics of Suspicion

Having made such leaps throughout the last three chapters, it is worth noting here – as we consider what an epistemology of astrology looks like at the empirical level – that it is possible to get carried away. Thus, within a complete elaboration of astrological hermeneutics, it becomes useful to balance the *yin* path with the *yang*, called by Ricoeur, the "hermeneutics of suspicion."

Suspicion here is warranted, because the self's ability to know itself in any kind of objective way is limited. Under the best of circumstances, each of us sees only through a filter clouded by our unresolved issues, our beliefs and patterns of conditioning, and our perceptual biases – essentially the same idols conjured by Francis Bacon during the Empirical Era in order to justify a scientific approach to truth. Science itself can be understood to proceed, in certain ways, as a *yang* hermeneutics of suspicion, and even as we develop our own epistemology independent of science, it behooves us to balance the more open-ended inquiry along the *yin* path of faith with this kind of healthy skepticism.

At best, the honest astrologer must acknowledge that the self that seeks to know itself, sitting in front of a birthchart, asking deeply meaningful questions, and ultimately attempting to articulate answers, is what is called an "unreliable narrator." The term was coined by literary critic Wayne Booth in 1961 to refer to a fictional device in which a character lacking in credibility provides the point of view from which a story unfolds. I would argue that the term also has implications for any field in which hermeneutics is a pathway to the discovery of individual truth, including psychological astrology. To the extent that we are all narrators of our own story – and Ricoeur would argue that this is the primary way in which we come to know ourselves – we are all somewhat unreliable.

This is so for a number of reasons. First, we don't remember things the way they actually happened, especially if there is any unresolved emotional charge around these memories.

Secondly, where there is emotional charge, it tends to create a gray area in which we are ambivalent toward what we remember of our experiences. Perhaps we feel guilt or shame; perhaps we harbor regrets; perhaps our disappointments and disillusionments have created perceptual limitations; perhaps we are in denial about certain things we said or did, or the consequences of our thoughts, words and deeds. There can be any number of reasons why, even with the best of intentions, unresolved emotional issues can make us unreliable narrators of our own story, and when they do, we will, as Hillman has suggested, remember what we remember as an imaginal exercise, at best taking us into a place of resolution or respite, and at worst, making us utterly delusional, usually landing us somewhere in between.

Lastly, we are unreliable because the story we are telling is incomplete, and at any point in time, we do not know how it will end, or even what the next chapter will be. As in any good story, there are plot twists and surprises, unexpected endings or new beginnings, new characters entering in mid-stream, and other developments that we can't anticipate.

Some narrators are deliberately unreliable, seeking to deceive their audience for personal gain or self-aggrandizement. These are the frauds and the fakes; some used car salesmen, lawyers, public relations personnel or journalists; criminals, telemarketers, corporate lobbyists, politicians, and so on; including all of those today who intentionally spread dis and misinformation, or who simply use the sophistry of rational argument to make a bogus or biased case.

Other narrators are more subtly evasive, perhaps because they are not being entirely honest with themselves, or they are in denial about something, or they just don't really want to talk about something that is sensitive, around which they feel too vulnerable to share. This is probably true of most of us.

Still other narrators are basically honest but lack sufficient information to tell a completely accurate story – this is basically all of us.

Few astrologers are likely to be deliberately unreliable; some will approach their interpretations through distorted filters that create biases and blind spots and will thus become evasively unreliable. All will necessarily be naively unreliable, more so than the individual contemplating his own chart, because interpreting a birthchart for others is at least one step removed from the story itself. I don't live inside of your life, so at best, even with chart in hand, I can only be an outside observer, and a naïvely unreliable narrator as I seek to decode the symbols of your chart.

The counterbalance to this potential limitation is to remain a bit skeptical about the immediate intuitive associations that we make to the symbolism. If, for example, I am ready to make a leap between Vesta and the alchemy of the forge, this may be too much of an intuitive leap from the perspective of the *yang* path. Here, sticking to a more literal interpretation of the mythology, we can make the association between Vesta and baking, but to go beyond that might be cause for suspicion. As I explore the empirical "data" of my Vesta Returns, and this theme seems to appear on a regular basis, I am perhaps more justified in making the necessary correlation on the *yin* path. But there is still room here for counterbalancing this "leap of faith" with a bit of healthy skepticism, keeping an open mind as we proceed – which means neither discounting the possibility, nor immediately embracing it as truth.

The Imbalance of Astrological Hermeneutics in Practice

In practice, most astrologers follow the *yang* path of interpretation; the *yin* path is more subtle, and I believe, less overtly or consciously entertained. As far as I can tell, few astrologers are even aware that the *yin* path exists, or perhaps they simply take it for granted without giving it a name. It is impossible to make an association between Vesta and fire, or any other aspect of her astrology, without walking the *yin* path of faith. Yet, unless we are aware we are walking it, we are not likely to understand when a scientist, strictly on a *yang* path of suspicion, calls us to task for taking too much of our astrological understanding on faith.

Of course, within the context of a professional counseling practice, unless one has ongoing clients, who return week after week for a more immersive experience, there is no time to allow the deeper *yin* revelations to unfold. One-off readings are *yang* by nature, and within this model of astrological practice, symbols quickly become mere signs, and lose their depth. This is not to say that a skilled astrologer cannot extract meaning from a birthchart through the sheer brilliance of their *yang* powers of interpretation. But to get inside a life, to feel its evolution over time along the various tracks that run through a birthchart, to cultivate an intimate relationship with the astrological archetypes that live and breathe in sync with the person who embodies them, and to feel the imaginative possibilities within the symbolism come to life, one must make time and space for the *yin* path to unfold.

It is for this reason, that I have emphasized and demonstrated the *yin* path in this chapter, and also for this reason, that my way of working here is likely to seem foreign to most astrologers, accustomed only to the *yang* path. In doing so, however, I by no means discount the necessity of balancing *yin* with *yang* and will return more overtly to the *yang* path in the next chapter. For having hopefully established the value of imaginal meandering in our understanding of the birthchart, it is time to re-consider the logic of astrology that developed under the hands of the Hellenistic astrologers in the Logical Era, and that through subsequent eras has come to define what most people, and most astrologers, understand astrology to be.

Notes

1. Grondin, Jean. *Introduction to Philosophical Hermeneutics*. Yale University Press, 1994, 21-22.

2. Polkinghorne, Donald E. *Methodology for the Human Sciences: Systems of Inquiry*. State University of New York Press, 1983, 221.
3. Perry, Glenn. "How Do We Know What We Think We Know? From *Paradigm to Method in Astrological Research." In Astrological Research Methods: An ISAR Anthology*, edited by Mark Pottenger, Vol. 1. Los Angeles, CA: International Society for Astrological Research, 1995, 43-45.
4. Perry, Glenn. "Sun Square Pluto: Aspect of the False Self." *The Journal of Astro-Psychology* 4, no. 4 (1991): 1–13.
5. Tarnas, Richard. *Prometheus the Awakener: An Essay on the Archetypal Meaning of the Planet Uranus*. Woodstock, CT: Spring Publications, 1995.
6. Perry, Glenn, "How Do We Know What We Think We Know?" 45.
7. Wikipedia. "Landwehr," April 2, 2023. https://en.wikipedia.org/wiki/Landwehr.
8. Buhner, Stephen Harrod. *Plant Intelligence and the Imaginal Realm: Beyond the Doors of Perception into the Dreaming of Earth*. Rochester, VT: Bear & Company, 2014, 299.
9. Bly, Robert. *Iron John: A Book about Men*. Vintage, 1990, 112.
10. Meet the Slavs. "Firebird: Symbolism in Slavic Folklore & Mythology," May 14, 2022. https://meettheslavs.com/firebird/.
11. Unless otherwise noted, all quotes in this section are from my personal journals.
12. National Park Service. "Ozark: A Historic Resource Study, Chapter 2: Early Native American and European Contact." Accessed June 22, 2023. https://www.nps.gov/parkhistory/online_books/ozar/hrs2.htm.
13. Ricoeur, Paul. *The Symbolism of Evil*. Boston, MA: Beacon Press, 1967, 14-15.
14. Ricoeur, Paul. *Freud and Philosophy: An Essay on Interpretation*. Yale University Press, 1970, 531.
15. NASA Solar System Exploration. "In Depth | 4 Vesta – NASA Solar System Exploration." Accessed June 22, 2023. https://solarsystem.nasa.gov/asteroids-comets-and-meteors/asteroids/4-vesta/in-depth/.

Astrology enables one to understand what role each of the gods plays in one's life, how the different gods are related to each other in one's experience, and at what times the specific mythic themes associated with certain gods or archetypes will be activated and accentuated.

If so, then archetypal astrology, by making possible just these hidden archetypal principles and themes, might restore to each individual life a sense of meaning, derived not from any religion or doctrine, nor from any philosophy or creed, but from our own personal relationship to the archetypal powers of the cosmos.

Keiron Le Grice, The Archetypal Cosmos, 2010

Chapter Fourteen

Astro-Logic

The *yang* path of the hermeneutics of suspicion returns us to the gifts of the Logical Era, in which rational argument was the primary arbiter of truth. It was during this era that mathematics became the *de facto* language of Aristotelian science, but also a period of history in which logic itself provided the legitimate scope for scientific inquiry. We saw in Chapter Six how Galileo, one of the early pioneers of the empirical revolution, was castigated by the Church because his heliocentric view "*was foolish and absurd in philosophy, and formally heretical since it explicitly contradicts in many places the sense of Holy Scripture.*"[1]

We can note here that along the *yang* path of suspicion, it was the fact that the heliocentric worldview was not logical - given the prevailing mindset at the time - that aroused suspicion in the first place. A couple more centuries into the Empirical Era, a different measure of hard truth would have allowed the evidence of stellar parallax to entertain a heliocentric explanation along a *yin* path of faith.[2] But in Galileo's time, this would have been too great a leap, and too imbalanced a statement of plausible truth.

To be sure, the emerging empirical science of Galileo's day was not an exercise in hermeneutics. I use the example only to make the point that within the scientific community, even within the strictures of empirical standards, a similar kind of balance was at work. For at the heart of the empirical revolution was the idea that any testable hypothesis that sufficiently met the challenge of replicated testing was admitted to the canon of scientific truth. Hypotheses are by nature flights of educated speculation along a *yin* path of faith until they are corroborated by a rigorous exercise in suspicion that rules out alternative flights of speculation, or at least makes them seem less plausible explanations for the raw data itself. What is less often acknowledged or considered is that the raw data is meaningless - even in scientific terms - without a *yin* flight of speculation, and even after the two come together, the perpetually tentative nature of a scientific conclusion remains a reasonable leap of faith.

The Logic of Astrology

The same is true, in a different sort of way, in the practice of astrology, although we are only now, say in the last 50 - 60 years or so, coming to the place in our evolution as a discipline, where a more balanced approach is possible. To this point, that is to say, essentially up to the emergence of psychological astrology, the practice of astrology has largely been dictated by the developments of technique, rooted in logic, that evolved at the hands of the Hellenistic astrologers of the Logical Era. This is true even for those modern astrologers who don't consider themselves to be traditional in their orientation, as most interpretive astrology, as it is currently practiced, is a *yang* exercise in analytical symbolic logic.

As Chris Brennan notes, this system of logic came together around four basic pillars of natal interpretation that coalesced in the first century C.E.: the signs of the zodiac; the houses; the known planets of the solar system; and the aspects between planets – a system that continues to form the logical basis of astrology today.[3] By the fifth century C.E., with the advent of natal astrology itself, and the increasing availability of written ephemerides, astrology became increasingly divorced from a direct observation of the sky, and a more abstract exercise in the logical interpretation of symbolism. Brennan notes this as the beginning divergence of astronomy, which remained observational, and astrology, which no longer depended on observation.[4] But it also marked the divergence of the logical astrology of the Hellenistic Era from the more observational Babylonian and Egyptian astrologies of the previous Mystical Era.

Certain concepts were borrowed from these earlier traditions, but at the hands of the Hellenistic astrologers, the birthchart became an abstracted, analytical window into an idealized cosmos, rather than a framework for an observation of discernible patterns in the sky as a reflection of divine intelligence at work. If, within the context of an earlier tradition, we include not just an observation of the sky, but the kind of *yin* hermeneutics of faith we have been exploring these past few chapters, then at the beginning of the Logical era, we witness a radical swinging of the pendulum back toward a *yang* hermeneutics of suspicion, in which the archetypally Masculine preference for rational analysis largely replaced the archetypally Feminine art of imaginal meandering through memories, both individual and collective, sifting and sorting for intuited correlations between cosmos and life on Earth.

This more rational perspective has both advantages and disadvantages, which we will consider as we proceed, but for now let us just note that one without the other is likely to make for an imbalanced astrology. *Yang* without *yin* can become way too cerebral and potentially divorced from the irrational reality of real life; while *yin* without *yang* can easily leave us stranded in the deep woods without a map, or any clear way to make practical use of what we intuit about real life. Without abandoning the *yin* path of imaginal meandering that has taken us this far, we can begin by thanking the Hellenistic Greeks for showing us the *yang* path of logical mapping.

The Logical Abstraction of the Zodiac

While a complete discussion of how the astrologers of the Logical era went about this task is beyond the scope of this book, I can at least provide a simple example around our shared understanding of the twelve signs of the zodiac. We take this basic tenet of the astrological language for granted today, identifiable by astrologers and non-astrologers alike as the very basis of astrology. And yet, in point of astronomical fact, the zodiac as used by most Western astrologers today, composed of twelve equal 30° signs, doesn't actually align with anything visible in the sky. It is a useful logical abstraction, but an abstraction nonetheless – one that essentially evolved in two steps.

The first step took place in Babylon in the fifth century B.C.E., when the framework in which celestial movements were observed was divorced from a strict alignment with the constellations, an arrangement known as the "constellational zodiac," and assigned instead to twelve equal 30° segments of the sky, an arrangement known today as the "sidereal zodiac." This step was made at a time when the signs were still more or less in alignment with the constellations to which they referred, before precession of the equinoxes became a major issue.

The second step was initiated by Ptolemy in the second century C.E., when he proposed a tropical zodiac, divorced entirely from the constellations, and measured instead from the base reference point of the vernal equinox. Ptolemy knew about the precession of the equinoxes, first introduced by Hipparchus in 127 B.C.E. about three centuries earlier, and deliberately created a logical system that would bypass this issue.[5] As noted by Brennan, it took a couple of centuries for other Hellenistic astrologers to adopt Ptolemy's tropical zodiac, during which time, the sidereal zodiac was still the primary frame of reference.[6]

Be that as it may, over the course of this seven-hundred-year transition, begun in the Philosophical Era and completed in the Logical Era, the tropical zodiac – used by the vast majority of astrologers today – was a transformation of astrology into an art of logical mapping. The signs of the zodiac today no longer reference the constellations for which they are named, none of which occupies a standardized 30° segment of arc along the ecliptic.

Nor have there ever been only twelve constellations along the ecliptic. The Babylonians originally identified eighteen in *Mul Apin* (dating from the seventh century B.C.E), the astronomical counterpart to the more overly astrological *Enuma Anu Enlil*.[7] NASA currently identifies thirteen, including Ophiuchus, which it clarified in 2016 does not obviate the tropical zodiac of astrology.[8]

The point here is not the one that would be made by scientists, which is that the zodiac is no longer based on anything that can be observed or measured and is therefore not scientific – even though that is actually true. More importantly, within our discussion here, the adoption of the tropical zodiac was essentially a mathematical abstraction that made logical sense, creating a framework in which the sky, in both its astronomical and astrological implications, could be brought from the realm of the unknown into a familiar system of rational, if somewhat artificial, order.

The standardized zodiac did parallel the 24-hour day, and the 12-month year, and thus shared in the reliable regularity of the familiar framework that this structure provided.

Twelve is furthermore what mathematicians call a "superior highly composite number," meaning it is evenly divisible by a relatively large number of factors smaller than itself – 1, 2, 3, 4, and 6 – a property that opens up many possibilities for assigning these various numbers to categories or sub-qualities. This is a logical convenience that facilitates astro-logical mapping by gender (2), modality (3), element (4) and polarity (6), as well as a parallel mathematical scheme applicable in a different way for houses, and a consideration of aspects between planets, transits and progressions, all easily divisible by whole numbers.

Twelve is also a number that carries religious, mythological and magical associations in many religious traditions, including the Greek, where twelve primary gods of the Olympian pantheon succeeded twelve primary Titans. Similarly, the twelve tribes of Judaism; the twelve apostles of Christianity; the twelve imams, or legitimate successors to Muhammad; the twelve knights of the Celtic Round Table; the twelve Jyotirlinga or devotional representations of Shiva; etc. all attest to the metaphysical significance of this number, which appears to be one that lends itself well to the archetypal delineation of whole systems.

The adoption of the 12-equal-segmented tropical zodiac brought order to what was otherwise potentially a chaotic system – one in which different people in different cultures and different ages previously saw different patterns in the sky formed by different numbers of star groupings, named differently, and associated with different stories. It was, in other words, an attempt to standardize and objectify what would otherwise be, and had been, a giant Rorschach test projected into the sky, a change that also incidentally balanced the *yin* of unbridled imagination with the *yang* of ordered logical analysis.

The Birthchart as an Archetypal Field

The twelve-sign zodiac creates a useful perceptual field in which to observe the correlations between cosmic patterns and human psychology in an archetypal sense, rather than solely as a matter of observation. That is to say, to the extent that we can understand the birthchart as an ideal template for the evolution of a soul seeking optimal expression in this life, it is helpful to have an approximation of what that ideal might be. The logical system of astrology built on the tropical zodiac provides that, in the same way that Plato's notion that the planets moved in perfectly circular orbits provided an archetypal reflection of wholeness, even if no planet actually does move in this way.

The reality of our lives may be far messier than what such an idealized system reveals, perhaps observed in actuality as something shaped more like a deflated basketball or an oblong football than a circle, but having the circle as a reference point can provide a conceptual measure of where we are in our movement toward wholeness. In the same way, surveying the abstracted birthchart, not as genuine map of the sky, but as an archetypal map of the cosmos into which we were born, can be a useful touchstone as we navigate our more complex and nuanced lives. In serving this purpose the exquisitely divisible and logically useful symbolism of the twelve speaks far more eloquently than the indivisible, irrational, sometimes feared, lunar number thirteen, or some other number. In taking advantage of the archetypal logic of the twelve in our practice of astrology, however, it behooves us to remember the messy complexity of Life itself, which without "the thirteen," becomes sterile and lifeless.

I actually think we need both sensibilities in order to deepen our practice of astrology – to make it a genuine pathway to self-knowledge. To explore the imaginal meandering path of hermeneutics by faith, we need to embrace "the thirteen," as where this path takes us will be, in a sense, off the map entirely. At the same time, having the more rational, and archetypal map at our disposal, shows us in a sense where Truth North lies. With this map in hand, we can, when we need to, find our way out of the deep woods into more familiar terrain, where it is possible to find a floating signifier that we can temporarily rely on for a healing pause in the conversation.

In this shift from observational astrology to logical astrology, the gods have morphed from the trans-human forces that previously shaped the world as well as the cosmos, to archetypal dimensions of the human psyche.[9] This has some advantage for the understanding of human psychology; and perhaps some disadvantages in understanding how humans fit into the larger cosmological scheme of things. Given that we are human beings, living on planet Earth, however, it behooves us to ground our untethered imaginal meanderings with a more analytical set of touchstones, with which we can, to some extent, grasp our human psychology in worldly, as well as cosmic terms. The logic of astrology, as developed by the Hellenistic astrologers, and as further developed by countless others since, allows us to do this:

> *Astrology enables one to understand what role each of the gods plays in one's life, how the different gods are related to each other in one's experience, and at what times the specific mythic themes associated with certain gods or archetypes will be activated and accentuated.*[10]

Entering the Archetypal Field of the Astro-Logical Map

I would add that depending on which god is front and center, the field will appear to shift – a notion that Hillman calls "polytheistic psychology,"[11] and which we might call "polytheistic astrology." As we develop our astrological epistemology then, we can look to both the *yin* path of imaginal meandering, as we explored in Chapters Ten – Thirteen, and to symbolic logic to get a more complete and balanced sense of what the field looks like from a particular deity's point of view.

Again, by "logical" here, I do not mean logical in a way that a scientist would recognize, or even necessarily in the way that an Aristotelian of the Logical Era would recognize, but rather logical in the sense of symbolically coherent, within the metaphorical logic of astrology. As Hillman notes:

> *Archetypes are semantically metaphors. They have a double existence, which Jung presented in several ways: (1) they are full of internal oppositions, positive and negative poles; (2) they are unknowable and known through images; (3) they are instinct and spirit; (4) they are congenital, yet not inherited; (5) they are purely formal structures and contents; (6) they are psychic and extrapsychic (psychoid). These doublings, and many others like them in the description of the archetypes, need not be resolved philosophically, or empirically, or even semantically. They belong to the internal self-contradiction and duplicity of mythic metaphors, so that every statement regarding the archetypes is to be taken metaphorically, prefixed with an 'as-if'.*[12]

Taking this guidance from Hillman into the astro-logical realm, we can begin to get a sense of why the pronouncement of astrologers often makes no sense to non-astrologers, even though they are archetypally coherent. Briefly translating Hillman's ideas about the six parameters of archetypal metaphors into language more meaningful to astrologers, we can note the following characteristic of astro-logic:

(1) Astrological symbolism is, like the more general category of archetypal metaphor, full of "*internal oppositions, positive and negative poles.*" Planetary archetypes are multidimensional and multivalent.[13] They can be understood mythologically, metaphysically, and psychologically, to name just a few of their most important contexts, and along each of these spectrums, they can exhibit a wide range of behavior, some of which is relatively enlightened and some of which becomes distorted by unconscious contents, and is ultimately problematic.

    This complexity is compounded when planets are placed in signs, in a different way in houses, altered in aspect to other planets, and yet again in a different way, when impacted by transit or progression, all of which – as noted in Chapter Three – contribute to an astro-logic that is synthetic and integrative, rather than extractive and analytical.

(2) To the extent that astrological indicators are treated as symbols, and not mere signs, their meaning can ultimately not be exhausted, and the birthchart will be capable of constantly generating new information. In this sense, the birthchart is unknowable in any final or definitive sense. And yet, astrologers can and routinely do extract meaning from these symbols, the best interpretations serving not as literal pronouncements, but as metaphors that reverberate on multiple levels simultaneously, in the moment that they are evoked.

(3) Entering the birthchart as an archetypal field is an exercise in practical orientation to life, in which trusting one's innate predispositions and organic instincts is a recipe for living life in alignment with one's spiritual essence. Because this is so, the same symbols provide a deep poetic description of spiritual essence at the same time that they provide a more tangible recipe for expression of that essence in the particulars of life, as it is lived day to day, month to month, year to year, transit to transit.

(4) The natal birthchart, and the symbolism it contains is, by definition congenital, and yet, it also represents an open archetypal field that is malleable to conscious choice, personal growth, and change. In this sense, it is not inherited, if by inherited we mean "fated" or destined to play out in a certain way that is set in motion before birth. The archetypal field of a birthchart is then framed by a logic that is participatory, conditioned only provisionally, depending on how we relate to it – how we meet the challenges and evolutionary opportunities it poses.

(5) The placement of planets in signs and houses, in aspect to each other, within the context of a birthchart taken as a whole, can be understood in some way to provide an archetypal structure, suggesting in a multidimensional and multivalent way, the general shape of a life in question. My sense here, is that the content of a birthchart emerges as we interact with it, and as we live our lives, all within the archetypal range of possibilities encompassed by the symbolism. In this sense, the logic of astrology comprises a structured set of symbolic relationships within which a certain range of expressions becomes possible, ultimately manifest as the particulars of a life.

(6) Given the understanding the archetypal astrology brings to the practice of psychological astrology in general, we can begin to see that the birthchart functions on a psychological level, as a kind of interior landscape of the psyche. But it also functions outside the psyche, in the cosmos, in the world, in the external environment in which a soul is seeking to manifest its potential, heal and self-actualize, connecting to a larger sense of Self that encompasses all that is.

As noted in Chapter Three, there can be more than one way to make logical sense of the birthchart, and each astrologer must ultimately approach the logic of astrology in a way that makes sense to her. Some might adopt the original Hellenistic techniques and the rationale behind them, as much as that can be known. Others will see, and have seen, the logical patterns through different eyes. What matters here is not the ultimate authority of the logical system employed, but the intent to work within a system that provides the structure of a *yang* map for the meandering exploration on the *yin* path, as we have explored it so far, one that is ideally logically consistent and coherent. This map becomes more meaningful and more useful to the extent that the logical system that is employed is flexible enough to encompass the six parameters of doubling, introduced by Hillman, adapted briefly above, in ways that are more specifically astro-logical. Any worthy astrological system will, at its best, also be capable of encompassing paradox and internal contradiction.

In the discussion that follows, in which I return to the story of my relationship with Vesta, I will make some attempt to explain my own system of astro-logic, where it might deviate from the norm (if there is such a thing). I also offer the caveat that I don't propose this system as a universal truth; merely as what has made logical sense to me.

Here, I will take each of Brennan's four pillars of the logic of astrology as developed by the Hellenistic astrologers of the Logical Era - the signs of the zodiac; the houses; the known planets of the solar system; and the aspects between planets – and add to them, a fifth pillar posed by a consideration of consciousness as outlined in my previous book, *Tracking the Soul as an Astrology of Consciousness*; and a sixth pillar oriented around a consideration of transits and progressions.

Vesta's Sign Placement

Our first astro-logical consideration as we look at Vesta's placement in my chart is the fact that she is in the sign of Capricorn, a cardinal earth sign, ruled by Saturn. What comes immediately to mind here, with my archetypal eye still open, is the mythological relationship between Vesta and Saturn. As noted in Chapter Eleven, Hestia was the firstborn child of Cronus (Saturn) and Rhea. Hestia was the first to be swallowed by her paranoid father, who feared his children would usurp his power; and then the last to be liberated by Zeus. Of all her sibling deities, she spent the longest time in Cronus' belly and presumably under his influence. This suggests to me that astrologically there is a natural relationship between Vesta and Saturn that is likely reflected by Vesta's placement in Capricorn.

This natural relationship can be seen in the seriousness of the task assigned to the vestal virgins over the course of a 30-year commitment (spanning one full Saturn cycle), entailing both a demanding discipline and dire consequences for failure. It can also be seen in the way Hestia lived a fairly monastic life, apart from the ongoing boisterous melodrama that seemed to occupy the other deities in the Greek pantheon, and to her vow of chastity, as well as the fact that she was depicted in a fairly non-descript manner, and that the stories about her were sparse. It would appear then that her long sojourn in Saturn's belly has left its mark, and that that this mark can be taken to be part of the metaphorical logic we might ascribe to Vesta in a birthchart, especially Vesta placed in Capricorn.

I can relate to this aspect of Vesta as I contemplate my solitary life, one in which continuous discipline and focused commitment to the creative forge at the center of my life has produced a certain body of work. I can also relate to Saturn's presence within Vesta's archetypal field as the sense of invisibility that surrounds my work, and movement in and out of liminal space – which astro-logically can be associated with the time spent in Saturn's belly.

At this particular time, being in between relationships, becoming virgin in the sense of moving more deeply into my solitude, outside of intimate partnership, also seems an astro-logical reflection of this association between Vesta and Saturn, emphasized with Vesta in Capricorn.

The idea of building a tangible legacy, both through a body of work, and through the construction of an earth-based temple, this cabin in the woods that I tend, on a piece of earth to which I have become rooted, all seems astro-logically indicated by Vesta's placement in an earth sign; while the cardinal nature of Capricorn makes me proactive in pursuing this path, seeking and following my golden thread regardless of the cost, and also learning hard lessons along the way through friction with others, through overcoming obstacles, through fighting my way back to the top of the pile of ashes, where I make my stand. All of this, it seems to me, is encompassed by Vesta's placement in Capricorn.

Lastly, I might note here, in a way that other astrologers might not, that Capricorn is a winter sign, a time in the annual cycle when all of life moves into a liminal space, and new life gestates beneath the visible surface of things. All of these themes, of course, have already been delineated elsewhere in this rambling exploration, but here with the additional sense that my understanding of these themes and how they interweave through Vesta's archetypal field is really only coming into focus at age 72, as I stand on the threshold of the winter of my life.

Vesta's House Placement

As I have written about elsewhere,[14] although much has been said about the houses, much has also been lost through a symbolic equation of houses with signs. Astro-logically, houses are a different frame of reference than signs, a metaphorical system that derives from the Earth's rotation around its internal axis every 24-hours – a movement in an apparent clockwise direction through the birthchart, as all planets rise at the Ascendant, culminate at the Midheaven, set at the Descendant, and anti-culminate at the Nadir. These associations, and the clockwise motion in general give rise to a different set of metaphors than those normally ascribed to houses when they are taken to be mere synonyms for signs.

This clockwise assessment starts with a consideration of the hemispheres and the quadrants, before moving into the houses themselves. Within this 24-hour scheme of clockwise motion, planets below the horizon in the northern hemisphere are invisible and internal; planets above the horizon in the southern hemisphere are external and visible, at least potentially, and of course, especially in the nighttime sky. Planets in the east are rising; planets in the west are setting. Various combinations of these references then color each quadrant with specific metaphorical implications: in the NE, planets are invisible and rising; in the SE, they are still rising, but visible; in the SW, they are still visible, but setting; and in the SW, they are still setting, but now also invisible. How this translates into meaningful correlations depends upon the living context of the life for which the birthchart is an archetypal map, but the astro-logical context of the hemispheres, quadrants and houses is determined by the symbolic logic of clockwise motion through them.

My Vesta is in the northern and eastern hemispheres, and the NE quadrant. Vesta in the north continues to underscore the theme of invisibility, while Vesta in the east suggests that despite this invisibility, something is slowly taking shape and rising toward visibility at the Ascendant. In point, of astronomical fact, Vesta would rise into visibility at the Ascendant about three hours after my birth; when and how this moment occurs in actual reference to any sense of timing in my life is perhaps open to speculation. I have, of course, had moments of visibility and recognition for my work here and there, throughout my life, but the overall sense – corroborated on a *yang* path of logical suspicion, and thus lessening the need for suspicion – is that of working quietly and diligently at the forge, slowly gestating something new.

I am reminded here as well of the association of Brigit – Hestia's Celtic counterpart (more or less) – with Imbolc, as noted in Chapter Eleven, meaning in the belly, a reference to the gestation of fire in the womb during the liminal space of mid-winter. If we can make a metaphorical correlation between the wheel of houses, considered in its clockwise motion, then the NE quadrant can be seen to represent this same liminal space of gestation, within the womb, gradually rising toward birth at the Ascendant. The association of Imbolc with mid-winter is a sign-based reference, astronomically associated with the revolution of the Earth around the Sun, as the Sun appears to move astrologically through the entire tropical zodiac. But the placement of my Vesta in a sign of winter in a quadrant associated with liminal gestation in the womb fits the symbolism especially well, and in so doing, brings the *yin* path of imaginal meandering with archetypal eye open into alignment with the *yang* path of astro-logical analysis. When this happens, we can assume that our exploration – and whatever floating signifier serves as the focal point of our interpretation – is on the right track.

It is, of course, also worth considering Vesta's placement in the 2nd house itself, which in this case, adds a new perspective and a new theme that has not yet emerged in our imaginal meandering. The 2nd house is, of course, typically associated with finances and possessions, and at times, on a deeper, more psychological level, with the issue of self-worth. Often there is a correlation with the overall sense of external abundance that graces one's life and the internal sense of worthiness to enjoy that abundance. All of this is often reflected in the astro-logic of the 2nd house.

Becoming a Comfortable Minimalist

In my case, I struggled for many years to find a balanced relationship to the whole issue of money. Until my mid 40s (when my progressed Sun was conjunct Vesta and then Venus and Jupiter as well), I was often close to the edge of not having enough to make ends meet. Understandable, this began to impact my self-esteem, especially when I was unable to find work that utilized the Master's degree in Marriage, Family and Child Counseling I had struggled to attain in my 20s during Period 8, around the same time that I was discovering my golden thread while living at one of Yogi Bhajan's ashrams in southern California.

Sometime between Periods 9 and 10, I bought the land where I live now, and worked throughout this period to pay it off, along with my student loans, saving additional money with which to build the cabin that has since become my home. By Period 11, I was living in the cabin, just freshly built. My intent in buying land, and building a cabin, was to homestead, and in general to live a life of voluntary simplicity, one in which, ideally and theoretically, it was possible to live rather well with relatively little income, and have more time to pursue creative interests.

In the 60s and 70s, this idea fueled the back-to-the-land movement, as popularized by publications such as *The Mother Earth News* and Stewart Brand's series of *Whole Earth* catalogs. With Vesta in my 2nd house, moving back to and learning how to live on the land was an attractive alternative to the more typical, often soul-deadening 9-5 existence that left only weekends to recover, and retirement to try to remember what you wanted to do with your life in the first place, before you got distracted making money.

I associate this lifestyle with Vesta for the same reason that Hestia is associated with the simple task of tending the hearth, a "lifestyle" that was the antithesis of the high melodrama, out and about in the world, that was characteristic of her divine colleagues in the wild stories that fill the canon of Greek mythology. My last partner referred to my homesteading life as that of a "minimalist," and my sense now, in retrospect, is that this is an accurate way to put it, as over the years, I have discovered that I actually don't need a lot of material things to make me happy, and not needing a lot of things means that I don't need a lot of money. I can be, and am perfectly happy to be, a minimalist in my 2nd house, thanks in no small measure to Vesta's presence there.

Having said that, what I began to realize in Period 11 was that it is not a simple thing to create a simple life, that before I could get to the place where I had enough, and could, in fact, be a minimalist, I would have to go back into the world and make more money. The trade-off here, of course, is that I had less time to follow my golden thread, less time to tend the hearth and my creative labor at the forge, less time to slowly and carefully gestate the internal alchemy of the work that has made my life meaningful and purposeful.

This began to shift in Period 13, when I was complaining to one of my astrology teachers that I was struggling to find enough time to pursue my creative interests, while also trying to earn a living doing work that wasn't actually very fulfilling. She looked at me slyly and referencing a piece of advice once apparently given by Gurdjieff to a student, astutely suggested, "Well then, I guess you'll just have to find a way to earn your livelihood with your big toe." It wasn't immediately clear what she meant, but by Period 14, I had found a lucrative part time business buying and selling college textbooks, that freed up sufficient time to begin more actively doing the work of the forge in addition to the work of making money.

Somehow, I managed to keep both going through Period 15, but after a while, the bi-polar effort wore me out, and revealed itself to be clearly unsustainable. It wasn't until sometime between Period 18 and 19, however, that I found a way to let go of the money-making path, retire, and begin more actively living the full-time life of a minimalist that I am mostly happily living now, while also slowly settling into a space psychologically where I no longer feel a compromised sense of self-worth because I have not followed a more traditional path to a more outwardly recognized form of worldly success.

In retrospect, I can see this path of a minimalist to be a solid 2nd house foundation, that allows Vesta's presence in my life through all of the other themes explored in Chapter Thirteen. This solid foundation in turn is astro-logically an expression of the 2nd house's association with the element of earth, while the intensity of focus demanded by her presence is well suited to the fact that the 2nd house is succedent, for it has been my observation that it is within the succedent houses that we are called to more fully immerse ourselves in our lives, giving 100% of our attention, our energy and our commitment. Being a minimalist is what gives me the capacity to do this.

Vesta's Aspects to Other Planets

The third pillar of logic on which an astro-logical exploration of the archetypal field rests is fashioned from the aspects that form between planets. Here, sticking for purposes of illustration with Ptolemaic aspects only, we can note most obviously Vesta's conjunction to Venus and Jupiter, all in the 2nd house. We will start by looking at these individually, and then make a few comments that go beyond the scope of astrology as it is commonly practiced.

Vesta and Venus

As noted in Chapter Eleven, Hestia was one of three goddesses mentioned in Homer's *Hymn to Aphrodite* who was not drawn into Aphrodite's erotic spell, having in fact rebuffed at least two potential suitors, escaped an attempted rape, and taken a vow of chastity. In this mythological assessment then, we can begin to speculate that in many ways, Vesta and Venus are not especially *sympatico*, making the close conjunction between them, at best, an awkward affair, since the conjunction generally involves the synthesis of archetypes into some form of composite or hybrid expression. This is necessarily more difficult when the archetypes involved are innately at odds with each other. I think this awkward alchemical task manifests in several ways, throughout several of the themes explored in Chapter Thirteen.

First, and perhaps most obviously, is the theme of becoming a virgin, in the sense of arriving at the place in my life where I no longer feel the need for a partner to complete me, emotionally, sexually, psychologically or spiritually. The evolution of this theme seems to me to be the primary expression of this juxtaposition of two goddess with seemingly antithetical perspectives on relationship. The fact that I have arrived at this place of relational autonomy after a series of intimate relationships, and not along the path of celibacy as it would appear was Hestia's preference, speaks astro-logically to the juxtaposition of Vesta and Venus in my chart.

Had I gone into the Catholic priesthood, as I now remember briefly wanting to do in Period 4, when I was ten years old; or had I followed the strict requirements imposed upon me in ashram life to remain celibate before marriage, during Period 8, I would likely have arrived at a very different place in relation to this theme, perhaps a place that would more clearly be understood as Vesta's archetypal claim on my existence. The path I did follow, however, through a series of monogamous relationships, in some of which, I felt my sexuality to be introverted or withdrawn, speaks instead to this strange amalgam of Vesta and Venus.

A second, perhaps somewhat less obvious integration seems to me to be inherent in my creative endeavors. The discovery of the fire stick (my creative passion), the following of a golden thread and the work at the forge that evolves out of this progression of themes is a perhaps less contentious collaboration between Venus and Vesta. Here Venus' creative sensibilities come into play, while Vesta's capacity to light a spark of inspiration, and tend the flame as a matter of disciplined focus all contribute to a sustained creative effort over time. I can also associate my particular work at the forge with Brigit, who in addition to being goddess of the forge, was, in one of her other triune aspects, the goddess of poetry, since my work at the forge is about exploring and elaborating the poetic underpinnings of astrology.

Within the astro-logical content of my birthchart, the collaboration of Venus and Vesta both within the cardinal earth sign of Capricorn facilitates a movement toward mastery of a creative domain, and a body of work that reflects that. Despite the likelihood that Venus (ruler of my Midheaven) would prefer more recognition for this work than Vesta needs or wants, my sense is that they have worked together to sustain a creative collaboration over time - which is, in many ways, its own pleasure and its own reward - despite the sense of invisibility that surrounds the work.

Lastly, in relation to the theme of becoming a comfortable minimalist, although it is Vesta that prefers the simple life, in tandem with Venus, mine has not been a life in which anything I've ever truly wanted has been lacking. Within the simple lifestyle I have chosen, I am surrounded by a well-loved and well-used library of books, an extensive and wildly eclectic musical collection, and a smaller collection of favorite movies, which I tend to watch over and over again. I have traveled, attended and given workshops, financed the publication of my own books, and been generous where possible with a wide variety of political causes I believe in. Just as I have not taken a vow of celibacy, I have likewise not taken a vow of poverty, instead opting for an abundant life where less has blossomed into more than enough. I see this as a collaboration between Venus and Vesta, with Venus adding the "comfort" in the life of the comfortable minimalist I have become by learning to do more with less, under Vesta's tutelage.

Vesta and Jupiter

If Hestia was the first to be swallowed by her first father Cronus, she was the last to be liberated by her youngest brother Zeus, who was the only one of her siblings not to be swallowed. He was instead whisked away by his mother Rhea from a cave at Dicte to Mount Ida, where he was raised by nymphs on goat milk and honey and hidden from his father until he was old enough to fend for himself. Instead of Zeus, Rhea gave Cronus a stone to swallow in his place, which Zeus later planted at Delphi, as "a sign thenceforth and a marvel to mortal men."[15]

Unlike Hestia, Zeus was, like his daughter Aphrodite, known for his erotic escapades, while being the head deity as well as the defeater of the old order of gods, the Titans. He was also a political animal, and a fierce warrior. This then was the mark of another awkward relationship, with the caveat here that it was also Zeus who presided over Hestia's elevation in status, empowering her as the one goddess honored in the temple of every other deity. As with the relationship between Vesta and Venus, my sense here is that there are ways in which the radical divergence between the archetypal domains of Vesta and Jupiter makes for a difficult alchemy of integration. It also potentially produces a unique synthesis that would not otherwise be possible.

The first archetypal theme articulated in Chapter Thirteen, for example, around becoming a cinder biter seems astro-logically to be an expression of the awkward dance between these two very different archetypes. This pattern revolved around my attempt to constructively channel the anger that was unleashed during the ashpile incident, which from Vesta's perspective, was my initiation onto the path of a cinder biter.

I noted in Chapter Thirteen that anger was a fiery emotion that, if present at all within Vesta's domain, had apparently been mastered and, in turn, had led to a kind of political neutrality. But we can also note here that for all her fire, Vesta is not an especially angry deity, and so anger *per se* is not necessarily part of her archetypal domain. What is perhaps a more accurate understanding of this dimension of her fiery energy, as it exists solely within her domain, would be to consider it a kind of fierce determination, coupled with focused patience – out of which gradually emerges something extraordinary. When this energy is free to operate unimpeded, it moves quietly and steadily toward its goal; when it is impeded, it remains determined and focused, but becomes patient. Conversely, the Norwegian Vikings were remarkably patient with cinder biters, who themselves were the antithesis of fierce determination, because the Vikings knew that after a period of idleness, cinder biters would often do something extraordinary.

Meanwhile, my personal path as a cinder biter was a bit atypical: angry, impatient, fiercely determined, and driven underneath it all by a sense of powerlessness for which I overcompensated by my ambition. This is not exactly how Vesta would do it. It is, in part, however, how Jupiter might do it. Like Hestia, Zeus was not especially angry either, but he was fiery. In his role as a mythological liberator, he was roused to passionate action wherever injustice was afoot, and his agenda was to free all those who had been oppressed, repressed or victimized by the Titans. As astrologers know, he is also progressive, ambitious, often competitive, and driven by a desire to excel.

My sense is that the anger I experienced at age three was, in essence, a Jupiterian response to injustice. Accessing my Jupiterian instincts, this led me first to become a competitive student, then to become involved in various political campaigns in which some sense of injustice was at issue. With Jupiter driving me, I took various stands on issues that felt important to me, such as refusing to serve in the Viet Nam war. In that refusal, I was breaking the ancestral pattern, in the same way that Zeus' ten-year war broke the ancestral pattern of the Titans and ultimately led to a changing of the divine guard, and the cosmic order of things.

On the other hand, over time, and with maturity, in retrospect, I can see that this innate impulse to right the wrongs of the world has been tempered by Vesta's capacity to more patiently sustain her determination, into a willingness to do what I can within a world that is not especially amenable to change. The anger I felt at the age of three has largely spent itself, even as my awareness of the injustices in the world has deepened. I have become better, if not completely adept yet, at living with this uneasy juxtaposition of patience and sustained determination to make what difference I can. This is my path as a cinder biter, although it was not a path that Vesta would necessarily have needed to walk; nor is it a path that Jupiter would have likely chosen. It is astro-logically, a difficult hybrid alchemy born of the conjunction of Vesta and Jupiter in my chart.

A second collaboration between Jupiter and Vesta likely takes place within the theme of following a golden thread. Vesta no doubt provides the kind of steady illumination necessary to recognize a golden thread to begin with, and the sustained focus of attention necessary to follow it. But the nature of my particular golden thread, as I look at it more closely, seems particularly Jupiterian, composed as it is of dovetailing interests in the psychology of human nature, perennial philosophy, wisdom teachings from an eclectic range of sources, and astrology, which from a Jupiterian perspective is a kind of symbolic systems theory.

Mythologically, Zeus has an association with mountains and eagles, which astrologically translates into this same kind of broad perspective that weaves together myriad details into a coherent big-picture understanding. There is also a myth about how Zeus' son Minos, a king of Crete, was reputed to travel to Mount Ida every nine years to commune with the spirit of his father, in order to bring back enlightened laws to his people. Some scholars associate Minos with the Egyptian Mane, the East Indian Manu, and the Hebrew Moses, all of whom attempted to access divine intelligence through communion with some deity on a mountain or in a mountain cave.[16]

In my own way, in following my golden thread, my sense is that it partly weaves through these unseen realms, as well as through the more obvious body of work in the wisdom traditions of the world that preceded me, and that this dimension of the process is a reflection of my Jupiterian nature. Here, the mountain cave can be seen perhaps as an astropoetic depiction of the NE quadrant, an astrological space shared by Jupiter and Vesta, as together they attempt to ferret out the divine intelligence at the heart of the sacred flame that burns in liminal space.

Lastly, the building of a temple, in my case in the middle of a forest dominated by oaks, sacred to Zeus, is also a collaboration of these two archetypes. Tending the sacred flame within this larger temple is literally a matter of managing an oak forest, and then burning oak firewood. But it is also, on a more metaphoric level, a process of finding and celebrating the sacred that permeates everyday life. In a way that Jupiter understands, this forest is but a microcosm of the entire garden planet, and the cosmic order, while the simple worship that comes through chopping wood and carrying water is Vesta's way of participating in that order.

Unlike Vesta and Venus, my Jupiter sits not in Capricorn, but in Aquarius. Traditional Hellenistic astrologers would consider these two planets to be inconjunct, while more contemporary astrologers routinely accept out-of-sign aspects. My stance is somewhere in the middle, in that I would consider an out-of-sign conjunction especially to be more difficult to integrate than an in-sign conjunction, and yet, also potentially more extraordinary in the alchemy that results.

Integrating earth and air, in this case, seems to me to be a matter of bringing down into tangible form that which cannot be easily captured, and finding a way to articulate that which lies below the apparently solid surface of what is. This, as I see it, is what I am doing here, as I try to find an astropoetic way into territory that will be somewhat familiar to practicing astrologers, and yet, at the same time, extend an invitation to move more deeply into the unknown, into the deep woods, beyond the range of our normal comfort zone.

Integrating cardinal and fixed energy is finding Vesta's patience in working at the forge, underneath a cloak of invisibility, often through periods of liminality in which the focus is temporarily lost, with unshakable determination to follow a golden thread as far as it can possibly take me. It is at the same time, moving in the opposite direction, always a matter of subjecting my most cherished and entrenched beliefs to a torrent of unstoppable forces that inevitably move them much farther downstream, and at times, leave them stranded on some unrecognizable shore.

In all of this, the unlikely alchemy of sibling deities, very different from each other, but with a deep and abiding sense of mutual respect and appreciation, produces something that probably couldn't happen any other way.

Vesta, Venus & Jupiter in the 2nd Chakra

In my second book *Tracking the Soul with an Astrology of Consciousness*, I work out my own system of astro-logic, based on an integration of astrology and the psychology of the *chakra* system, as it is implied within the yogic philosophy that I learned in my *ashram* days. This system can itself be understood as a piece of alchemy, crafted at the fiery forge of my training in *kundalini yoga*, as described in Chapter Thirteen. I was moved to do this by noting that all astrological archetypes, and the birthchart as a whole exists, essentially, as a kind of shorthand notation, encompassing a wide range of possibilities. Through my training in *kundalini yoga*, I also recognized that what determined where upon a given range a particular archetype would manifest, was the level of consciousness that was brought to the symbolism. At the same time, it was clear that the *chakras* themselves, understood as a series of psychic and psychological focal points, were an elegant way to depict this range of possibilities.

This is not to say that one cannot move up and down the range, but it seemed to me that the natal birthchart represented a clear depiction of where we start, not necessarily where we wind up. In the language I developed to talk about astrology in relation to the *chakra* system, it is what I call the "default pattern" – to some extent, a matter of preference, but also where we instinctively go when under stress, and/or when we go unconscious, or operate on automatic pilot. Any planet can function at the level of consciousness represented by any chakra, and the ultimate goal is for each planet to be able to function along the entire range as a matter of conscious choice. But in the beginning, as we contemplate the pattern of the natal chart, certain planets, especially in certain placements, will have a natural affinity for certain chakras. When three or more of those planets are all in mutual aspect to each other, we have what I call a "*chakra* pattern."

For a complete description of this system of astro-logic (as least complete at the time of publication), I would refer the reader to *Tracking the Soul*.[17] For purposes of our discussion here, I would just make the observation that Vesta, Venus and Jupiter, all in mutual conjunction with each other, placed in the birthchart in a way that supports it, all have affinity for the 2nd chakra, and in fact, form a 2nd chakra pattern in my birthchart.

The 2nd *chakra* most obviously governs sexuality, but also the transmutation or sublimation of sexuality, the exercise of creativity, and in a more general sense, the pursuit of a life marked by pleasure, enjoyment, satisfaction, abundance, and fulfillment. For those who have read this far, it should be obvious that the theme of becoming virgin, which is something that ultimately gets worked out between Vesta and Venus, encompasses the obvious 2nd chakra focus on sexuality; while discovering the fire stick, following a golden thread, working at the forge, and building a temple all involve the exercise of creativity. This is not at the sacrifice of sexuality, but to some extent in working at the forge, especially in my *kundalini* days, it is also a matter of transmuting sexual energy. Becoming a comfortable minimalist is, in the end, ultimately about creating a life that is pleasurable, enjoyable, satisfying, abundant and fulfilling, perhaps in a way that Vesta, especially, could appreciate.

Transits and Progressions to Vesta

Lastly, at least in terms of our discussion here, we can understand the astro-logic of the archetypal field in which a planet operates to be modified by transits and progressions. Transits – particularly transits of the transpersonal planets to the more personal points in a birthchart – can be indicative of outer forces that over time will change the way a particular archetype functions. At times, transits will reflect the peeling away of layers to reveal previously hidden dimensions or capacities. At other times, they will allow us to shed various skins or heal various wounds that have hampered the free and clear functioning of the archetype. Often, it will be a bit of both. Progressions can often change the archetypal field itself, altering the climate in which an archetype finds it necessary to function.

In my mid 40s, as suggested earlier, I underwent such a climate change, over the course of several years, when my progressed Sun was conjunct Vesta, Venus and Jupiter. Before that, I struggled to make ends meet, and often found the effort to do so to be a tiresome counterforce to the evolution of the various themes related to Vesta where the development of my creativity was the focus. It was hard to follow a golden thread and work at the forge in any kind of sustainable way, when I also had to make a living that seemed to have little to do with this more important work.

During this progression, however, I actually did find a way to earn my livelihood with my big toe, as my aforementioned astrology teacher put it, that freed me up in a way I hadn't quite experienced before. A few years later, toward the end of this three-planet progression, I inherited some money from my father, which further freed me, not just financially but also psychologically, took me back from the edge, and allowed me to no longer have to obsess about how I was going to keep it all together while I struggled to do what I felt I had come here to do. After that, money was no longer an overwhelming issue, and Vesta was freer to pursue the themes I have outlined in earnest, functioning in an altered climate that was much more conducive to her preferred focus.

Transiting Pluto conjunct Natal Vesta

Now, as I write this, there is a very different force at work – over the course of the last month or so, transiting Pluto has come within a 1° orb of a conjunction to natal Vesta, beginning a transit that will move through several waves, back and forth in direct and retrograde motion. Pluto will not complete its transit of Vesta until the end of 2023, while its transit of the 2nd chakra pattern noted above, involving all three planets – Vesta, Venus and Jupiter – won't be finished until the end of 2025, about 3 1/2 years from now. While it is perhaps too soon to jump to any wildly speculative conclusions – although this is what a predictive astrologer might attempt to do – we can instead begin a process of empirical observation and at the same time use our understanding of astro-logic to orient ourselves to changes likely yet to come.

As it happens, my life has most definitely intensified just in this past month, in the opening salvo of this long-range transit. The most obvious reference to Vesta, as we have explored her archetypal field so far, is in a chimney fire I had here last week, the first I have ever experienced in the 36 years I have been tending a fire in my woodstove. For those who don't know, a chimney fire happens when creosote builds up on the inner walls of a chimney flue and then catches fire. It is a rather dramatic event, sometimes with visible flames, and/or the roar of a blast furnace – one that sometimes results in a house burning to the ground. Thankfully that did not happen to me, but it was an event that shook me to my core nonetheless.

It is not hard to see here the destructive power of Pluto, making a brief appearance, reminding me that "all things must pass," and that I am, in fact, more vulnerable than my well-crafted situation might lead me to believe I am. It also seems a reminder on some level of just how precarious tending fire can be, since fire, by its very nature does not easily lend itself to tending, and can – when it is free to express itself without adequate containment – easily get out of control. Within the context of Pluto's domain, in which life and death are at times at stake, Vesta's task of tending the sacred flame becomes far more than just a domestic chore; it is, in fact, a critical task that requires both fierce determination and humility, as it is a task that must be done but, at the same time, is beyond the capacity of any mere mortal to do.

Three other experiences, just within this past month, have also alerted me to Pluto's presence. First, the stock market, reeling from the pandemic, disrupted supply chains, the war in Ukraine, a rise in gas prices, perhaps a bit of corporate gouging, and general uncertainty, has plummeted after a very good year, that despite it all, produced an unexpected tax bill from last year's capital gains that took my breath away. Thankfully, my life as a minimalist has allowed me to take it all mostly in stride, but I am well aware of just how tenuous even a simple life can be in the face of monumental forces beyond anyone's control.

Secondly, my beloved cat of 15 years, bequeathed to me shortly before Period 17, and with me ever since, died of kidney failure (perhaps an expression of Pluto conjunct Venus, associated with kidneys). It is less obvious how this dramatic event is a reflection of Pluto conjunct Vesta, other than to note that she died on June 9, which was noted in Roman times as Vestalia, the annual religious festival in honor of Vesta. On Vestalia, the Romans consecrated and sacrificed a donkey, an animal sacred to Vesta, after its bray disrupted the attempted rape by Priapus. My cat was not a donkey, but it was often quite vocal, and every bit as stubborn as a mule.

Lastly, one of my early mentors in life, whose natal Pluto happens to be opposed my Vesta, has just been diagnosed with terminal, untreatable cancer. This mentor was one who took the imaginal task of tending the sacred flame seriously, and who, along the way, earned the wisdom that only came through being burned when he let it go out. As this mentor once shared with me, anthropologists often laughed at the Lakota Sioux for their ceremony of singing the Sun up every morning. The anthropologists believed that the Lakota thought that if they didn't do the ceremony, the Sun wouldn't come up. In fact, they did it because it helped them to feel like they were participating in the cosmic rhythms shaping the world and everything in it.

In my own very different way, entering into an imaginal exploration of my birthchart, an archetypal field in which the gods and goddesses are perpetually afoot, helps me do the same. Considering the astro-logic of the birthchart, in terms of sign and house placements, aspects and transits, allows me to get a clearer sense of the archetypal field itself. It also provides analytical corroboration for many of the themes that have emerged on the *yin* path of imaginal meandering, yielding a more balanced perspective than either approach to astrological hermeneutics alone could offer. Lastly, it offers its own brand of nuanced elaboration of some of these themes, while revealing others not yet quite so obvious from an imaginal standpoint, serving as a kind of focus knob on the astrological microscope, helping us to see more clearly into the hidden heart of things.

Notes

1. Hannam, James. *The Genesis of Science: How the Christian Middle Ages Launched the Scientific Revolution*. Simon and Schuster, 2011, 329-344.
2. Stellar parallax is the apparent shift of position of a nearby star against the relatively fixed background of more distant stars.
3. Brennan, Chris. *Hellenistic Astrology: The Study of Fate and Fortune*. Denver: Amor Fati Publications, 2017, xix.
4. Brennan, *Hellenistic Astrology*, 5.

5. Jones, Alexander. *Ptolemy in Perspective: Use and Criticism of His Work from Antiquity to the Nineteenth Century*. Springer Science & Business Media, 2009, 36.

6. Brennan, *Hellenistic Astrology*, 220.

7. Campion, Nicholas. *A History of Western Astrology Volume I: The Ancient and Classical Worlds*. Bloomsbury, 2008, 70.

8. NASA. "Constellations and the Calendar." Tumblr, September 20, 2016. https://nasa.tumblr.com/post/150688852794/zodiac?linkId=94146490.

9. Hillman, James. *Re-Visioning Psychology*. HarperCollins, 1975, 36.

10. Grice, Keiron Le. *The Archetypal Cosmos: Rediscovering the Gods in Myth, Science and Astrology*. Edinburgh: Floris Books, 2010, 76.

11. Hillman, *Re-Visioning Psychology*, 26.

12. Hillman, *Re-Visioning Psychology*, 156.

13. Tarnas, Richard. *Cosmos and Psyche: Intimations of a New World View*. Viking, 2006, 87.

14. Here I would refer the reader to my article, "The Clockwise Interpretation of Houses," first published in October/November 2000 issue of *The Mountain Astrologer*, now available on my website at https://www.joelandwehr.com/clockwisehouses; and to Chapter Two of my book, *Astrology and the Archetypal Power of Numbers, Part Two*.

15. Hesiod. "Theogony 495." Greek Texts and Translations. Accessed June 23, 2023. https://anastrophe.uchicago.edu/cgi-bin/perseus/citequery3.pl?dbname=GreekNov21&query=Hes.%20Theog.%20495&getid=1.

16. Dameron, James Palatine. *Spiritism: The Origin of All Religions*, 1828. http://books.google.com/books?id=5LWEAAAAIAAJ&pg=PA91&lpg=PA91&dq=minos+moses&source=bl&ots=Q8NS3VuBAI&sig=Fs3JesIWaWIsCdCkmYfEJivSd58&hl=en&sa=X&ei=01tbUYvaDKqs2gX2zYD4Dg&ved=0CFgQ6AEwBQ#v=onepage&q=minos%20moses&f=false.

17. Landwehr, Joe. *Tracking the Soul: With an Astrology of Consciousness*. Mountain View, MO: Ancient Tower Press, 2007.

I want to beg you, as much as I can, dear sir, to be patient toward all that is unsolved in your heart and to try to love the questions themselves like locked rooms and like books that are written in a very foreign tongue. Do not now seek the answers, which cannot be given you because you would not be able to live them. And the point is, to live everything. Live the questions now. Perhaps you will then gradually, without noticing it, live along some distant day into the answer.

Rainer Maria Rilke, Letters To a Young Poet, 1954

Chapter Fifteen

Examining Philosophical Assumptions

Having explored the dual nature of astrological hermeneutics in the last two chapters, it is time to step back a bit to the awareness that behind both what seems logical, and in a perhaps somewhat less obvious way, beyond what we can imagine, is a belief system, a philosophy of life, that determines and ultimately circumscribes what we can and cannot see when we look at a birthchart.

The Belief Systems Underlying and Influencing Astrological Practice

In the Philosophical Era, emerging astrological ideas were marinated in a heady stew, including Stoicism, Hermeticism, Neoplatonism, Aristotelian science, and to some extent, Christianity, all of which contributed to the metaphysical foundation on which the logic of astrology came to rest. The familiar idea, "as above, so below," that astrologers now routinely take for granted as a pithy expression of the very essence of the astrological premise is borrowed from *The Emerald Tablet of Hermes Trismegistus*, a seminal text in the Hermetic canon. The idea that the birthchart is in some sense a depiction of fate arises from astrology's association with Stoic philosophy, while the foundational role of the four elements in delineating signs finds its origin in Aristotle's extension of the work of Empedocles and Hippocrates.

Astrologers take these and other assumptions about our craft for granted today, with little thought of their origin. But as we retrieve what has been lost by astrology's tendency to conform to the cultural *zeitgeist* of each era in order to survive, it is worth noting that a different set of philosophical assumptions might yield a very different astrology, no less valid for understanding the relationship between the cosmos and life on Earth through a very different metaphysical lens. Indeed, as we have elaborated throughout this book, without necessarily spelling it out, this has been the case, with the astrology of each era, as well as each culture, reflecting a different set of assumptions about how reality is structured.

In the Mystical Era, for example, a cultural mindset in which it was believed that the will of the gods was literally written in the heavens produced an astrology that was more observational. Meanwhile, the idea that divine guidance was available only when the seeker of guidance was able to enter a sacred *templum* within the right state of mind produced an astrology that was less analytical, and more overtly a matter of priestly training and spiritual practice. In the Mythopoetic Era, animistic sensibilities gave rise to a proto-astrology that was likely what Campion called "ecological" and participatory, in a way that modern astrologers, weaned on a different understanding of reality, can scarcely imagine. In the postmodern Era of Uncertainty, we have access to a wide range of worldviews, each of which gives rise to a somewhat different approach to astrology.

Evolutionary astrology, informed by a belief in reincarnation, finds "evidence" for previous lives in a birthchart; while psychological astrologers weaned on Jungian ideas, can see shadow, *anima* and *animus* signatures, and a persona within the same symbolism. Chinese, Mayan and Vedic astrologers all use different techniques, but beyond that, they also understand our relationship to the cosmos somewhat differently, and these differences determine not just how they work with astrology, but also what astrologers within each culture see when they look at a birthchart.

The Shaping Influence of Belief Upon Language

This is inescapable, because astrology is essentially a language, and not a belief system unto itself. Just as two people speaking English might share very different points of view in observing the same external reality, so too will astrologers holding different beliefs read a birthchart in different ways and derive a different sense of meaning from it. This is perhaps taken for granted, and immediately forgotten when a given astrologer starts speaking. But when no one else is around, and you are looking at your own chart, it is worth asking yourself what you believe, before simply taking what you see in your chart to be the gospel truth. Perhaps what you see is a reflection of those beliefs in astrological language.

It is likely that all astrologers, regardless of their worldview, share a belief that it is possible to see oneself and to some extent the life one is living reflected in celestial patterns. But how you understand what the self is, what life is, what constitutes a celestial pattern, and how you make the correlation, together determine what the birthchart can reveal to you, before you even approach it.

I shared a bit of my philosophy of astropoetics; who I consider myself to be as an astrologer; and how I have come to think about astrology in Chapter Ten. This, of course, is just the elevator speech for a much longer journey that draws its inspiration from a wide range of influences, both within the astrological community, and in the parallel fields of psychology, philosophy, mythology, evolutionary biology, anthropology, cosmology, yogic philosophy, and an eclectic sampling of the perennial wisdom teachings available to all postmodern seekers in the Era of Uncertainty. It is also rooted in no small measure, in a lifetime of experiences, each of which has its own set of astrological referents, as well as fifty-year-plus practice of astrology, working with hundreds of clients and students from around the world.

Although I do not necessarily conjure this entire history every time that I look at a birthchart, it is there, as a philosophical context in which everything I say as an astrologer is rooted. The natural tendency, within astrological circles, is to want to say, "the birthchart says this." But it is probably more accurate and more honest to say, "I say this about this particular birthchart, using astrology as my language, because of who I am, where I have been, and what I have learned along the way."

This goes back to the question I posed in Chapter Ten that is worth revisiting here in a bit more depth: "Who is it that stands at the astrological threshold?" For it is the answer to this question that will determine how you make sense of the multi-dimensional, multi-valent, sometimes paradoxical, and contradictory symbolism of a birthchart.

Whether or not you are aware of how your beliefs, your background, and your life experiences make you the astrologer that you are, they will nonetheless condition your use of the astrological language. The more aware you can be, the greater the possibility that what you say can become a useful bridge between the known and the unknown, bringing into focus that which lies just beyond your prior reach. In this way, the astrological language becomes not just descriptive of what is, but also a matter of bringing the ineffable into focus, and new, slightly more evolved possibilities within imaginal range.

Asking Key Questions as a Point of Entry Into Your Basic Philosophy of Life

For most astrologers who are not used to thinking in these terms, the question, "What is the philosophy of life that guides your use of astrology?" will feel a bit daunting, as it is too broad and unwieldly a question to consider all at once. If you have studied a particular approach to astrology, you might be inclined to simply spout the basic tenets of that school of thought, and that would be one possible response.

To some extent, this is what I did in Chapter Ten as I outlined my own approach. And yet, hopefully as my subsequent exploration of Vesta has suggested, speaking merely as a representative of a particular school only skims the surface of who it is that approaches the astrological threshold. For as you work with the approach of a particular school, and with the underlying philosophy behind it, you must find your own way to make the ideas your own, or your astrology will not go very deeply into the heart of the matter, no matter how astute you think your adopted philosophy is. So, the question here, whatever the outer trappings of your approach, is really, "Who is it that resonates with the ideas you have adopted?"

To get at a more meaningful answer to this question, it can help to start at the periphery and ask a series of questions that take us step by step into the heart of an answer. We may as well approach this task astro-logically and move conceptually from the periphery of the solar system into its core, or at least, work our way through the Chaldean order, adding the three transpersonal planets that prior to 2006 made the basic archetypal repertoire of most working astrologers.

We can begin, first stepping back a bit, by noting that in the Philosophical Era, philosophy was not primarily rooted in intellectual abstraction; it was a concerted quest for the best way to live, given the answers that one might give to certain very large and fundamental questions about the nature and purpose of life. Each school of philosophy gave somewhat different answers, and as such, prescribed a somewhat different way of life as being ideal. If we extend this idea of philosophy to the practice of astrology – which in this context, can be understood as a language with which we can talk about the meaning of a life – then as we do this, we will necessarily be measuring each archetypal parameter of this life against this idea.

If, for example, you are going to consider some planets "benefic," derived from the Greek word *agathopoios*, meaning "good-maker," while considering others "malefic," from the Greek *kakopoios*, meaning "bad-maker,"[1] then for these terms to be meaningful, you have to address a more fundamental set of philosophical questions: "What is good?" and "What is bad?" A Stoic of the Hellenistic era might have one response to these questions, while a contemporary psychological astrologer, say with a somewhat less dualistic orientation, might have another. You might have your own sense of it, but whatever answer you give to the deeper underlying philosophical question behind the concept of benefic and malefic planets will determine how you work with these astro-logical ideas, or whether you work with them at all.

Following the Chaldean order, my intent in posing the following questions will be to go beneath and beyond the particular approach to astrology you may have adopted to help you better understand why such an approach might resonate with you. With this level of awareness, you can hopefully see both the advantages of your approach, and the ways in which it might be limiting you; and ultimately, it will empower you to find more creative ways to transcend those limitations as you broaden and deepen your perspective.

Pluto's Questions

Using the birthchart to make sense of a life is predicated, first and foremost, on a very large philosophical question: "What is life?" and the corollary question, "What is death?"

Is life limited to your existence in a body, or do you believe that life begins before birth in a body and continues in some fashion after the death of the body? Do you believe in more than one life, that is to say, more than one incarnation in a body, or is this life all that we have?

What makes life worth living? Is there anything worth dying for? Or again, put a slightly different way, is there anything worth deliberately putting your life in danger or facing death for?

What is your personal experience of death? Have you ever been close to death, or been with someone as they were dying? What was that like for you, and how did the experience change you?

Is there such a thing as evil? If so, how would you define it? Have you ever encountered it, either within yourself or in others? Where do you see it in the world? What, if anything, have you learned from your exposure to it?

Neptune's Questions

Is there a spiritual dimension to life? If so, how would you describe it? That is to say, how is life a spiritual experience? If not, then what is it that gives an earthly life its meaning and purpose? Or put a slightly different way, what is the larger context in which life in a body becomes meaningful?

What is your relationship to God, the gods, Goddess, Great Mystery, the Cosmos, or whatever word you use to describe this larger context in which humans strive to make sense of their lives? Is this relationship, for you, a matter of belief or of experience?

What is reality? How do you know what is real and what is illusion? Have you ever experienced something you could not explain? How did this experience change your life?

How do you cope with loss? Have you ever lost something or someone that cracked your heart open? How willing are you to let in the pain and suffering of the world? For whom or what do you grieve?

Uranus' Questions

What excites you, inspires you, kindles your passion?

What breakthrough experiences have you had in your life that have fundamentally and irrevocably changed you?

Has your life ever broken down completely, leaving you stranded at square one? If so, how did you cope with this devastation, and what did you learn about yourself from the experience?

What is the most creative thing you have ever done? How would you describe your particular brand of genius? What makes you a unique individual, unlike anyone else?

Saturn's Questions

What is the most difficult moment you have ever faced, and how did you face it? What have you learned about yourself through rising to the occasion? What gives you whatever capacity you have to persevere through adversity and obstacles?

What are your greatest ongoing challenges in life? What are your strengths and weaknesses? What, if any, resources, attributes, or skills do you feel are lacking in your ongoing effort to cope? How willing are you to face and work on your issues, to strive to be your best self? What gets in the way of this intention?

What are you afraid of? How do you manage your fears? Do you face them head on, or do you seek to build walls of protection against them?

What are your greatest accomplishments? What are you still hoping to accomplish before you die? What do you intend your legacy to be?

Jupiter's Questions

How free are you to live an authentic life, oriented around your natural preferences, your desires, your goals and ambitions, and whatever makes life a fulfilling satisfying experience for you?

What rules do you live by? What is your bottom line, the vow to yourself that you could never break?

What gifts do you come bearing? What do you feel your greatest contribution is to the larger world in which you live?

Are there places in your life where your excesses get you into trouble, or generate imbalance? What within your life is out of control?

Mars' Questions

How would you describe your hero or heroine's journey? Where in your life have you had to be brave, to access your warrior spirit, to take a stand and/or make something happen through an act of will? What is worth fighting for?

What makes you angry? Outraged? What pushes your buttons and throws you over the line into reactivity? What do you do with these emotions, when they arise?

Have you ever had an enemy? Been attacked? Felt like a victim? How did you cope with these experiences, and what did you learn from them?

Are you a lone wolf or a team player? To what extent do you feel yourself to be in competition with others? To what extent are you able to cooperate with those who are different than you toward common goals and interests?

Venus' Questions

What are your core values? To what extent do you live by these values, and conversely, to what extent do you equivocate or fail to walk your talk?

What is your idea of beauty? What about you and the world around you is beautiful? What about you and the world around you would you consider ugly?

If life can be understood as an art, how would you describe your artistry? What special skills or talents do you possess that can help make the world a more balanced, harmonious, beautiful place?

Who and what do you love? Who are the people in your life without whom it would be greatly impoverished? Do you have a sense of community? If so, how would you describe it?

Moon's Questions

Where, within your psyche, do you feel most wounded by your past? How have you tended this wound? What have you learned from it? How do you process difficult emotions?

What is your deepest source of vulnerability? How do you protect yourself from the insensitivity of the world? How do you deal with uncertainty? How do you create safety, security and stability for yourself?

Where in this world do you belong? Are there particular places, either geographically or in relation to the natural world, where you feel a particular sense of resonance?

What, within this world, do you find most nourishing? How do you nourish and nurture yourself? How do you nourish and nurture others?

What within this world inspires a sense of awe, mystery and wonder in you? What do you do to cultivate and deepen your relationship to the Unknown and the Unknowable?

Mercury's Questions

How do you know what you know? How do you separate truth from comfortable fiction? What do you know that you would consider to be wisdom?

Where do you turn for guidance? How do you navigate unfamiliar territory? Have you ever been lost? If so, how did you find your way back again?

What is your biggest challenge in communicating with others? How well do you listen? How willing are you to share what you think, what you feel, what you believe? How willing are you to entertain points of view different than your own?

What is the biggest mistake you have ever made in your life? What is the road not taken? If you could do your life, or some part of your life, over again, or live some other life, what would that look like?

Sun's Questions

If you had to describe yourself in 25 words or less, how would you explain your essence to a complete stranger?

What is your purpose in life? How are you currently fulfilling or failing to fulfill that purpose? If you didn't serve this purpose, how would that change the world?

Why are you drawn to astrology? What have you learned being an astrologer? What has astrology taught you about your relationship with the cosmos that enlarges your sense of who you are?

Who is it that comes to the astrological mirror looking for answers? Who is that has those answers? Who is it that believes the answers are somewhere other than within?

If you could ask one question to He or She Who Knows Everything, what would it be?

Finding Your Own Seminal Questions

There may of course be other questions you could ask that would be more meaningful to you than these I have asked you, and I would be the first to encourage you to ask them. As the great nineteenth century German poet Rilke once advised in *Letters to a Young Poet*:

> *I want to beg you, as much as I can, dear sir, to be patient toward all that is unsolved in your heart and to try to love the questions themselves like locked rooms and like books that are written in a very foreign tongue. Do not now seek the answers, which cannot be given you because you would not be able to live them. And the point is, to live everything. Live the questions now. Perhaps you will then gradually, without noticing it, live along some distant day into the answer.*[2]

This is sage advice indeed for anyone seeking answers in the Era of Uncertainty, but also more specifically good advice to any astrologer, still enamored of the notion that the birthchart can provide definitive answers. It cannot. What it can do is open a window, or a series of windows, through which you can see more clearly all that is unresolved in your heart, perhaps framed as questions with no immediate answer, as though spoken in a very foreign tongue. Indeed, if the birthchart is worth the paper it is printed on, it will remain foreign until you have lived the answers pulsing at the heart of the symbolism. For it is here that the birthchart will come most alive, and you, in relation to it.

To a very great extent, what you can see in a birthchart will depend upon what you have come to believe in relation to these larger cosmological questions about who you are, how you got here, and what is this place called reality in which you have landed, as well as the smaller questions that parse the nuances and provide a more accessible point of entry into the larger questions, smaller questions that arise from within your life itself, and are no less important for their apparent size. In many ways, the more personal question, "What is this obsession around which my life seems to pivot?" although ostensibly just about you, may be a more meaningful portal to an understanding of God than the more direct question, "Who or what is God?" could ever be.

In the Philosophical Era, many great minds huffed and puffed with relatively quick answers to larger questions that, in retrospect, are still revealing secrets, slowly releasing them from what appears to be a bottomless well. Astrologers, too, were pressed for answers in order to compete with non-astrological sources of knowledge. As noted in Chapter Three, because astrology was a rational form of discourse, especially as reinvented in the logical framework of the Hellenistic astrologers, astrology held its own as a respected resource for those seeking answers. And yet, given that the answers to the deepest, most important questions are rarely a matter of straightforward logic, astrology won its place at the table at a price. Imagine what might happen, if instead of orienting itself around answers, astrologers were to use the language to ferret out the most important questions, and then advise their clients, and commit themselves, to live their way into answers.

Within this context, what you believe to be true is less important than what you wonder, and what your soul seeks to know. What you seek to know will determine where you earnestly strive to live your way into answers. And then, as the circle ultimately completes itself, what you have come to know by living your way into answers will become the source of a much more solid belief – not just an idea, however clever or convincingly argued or universally held, but a viable construction, or re-construction, of reality that you yourself orchestrated, following a path that was yours to follow.

To some extent, your birthchart will show you the path, or a plethora of paths that could be your great delight and your compelling mission impossible to follow. But what the birthchart means is ultimately something you can't know until you walk these paths and learn what they have to teach you. Then, and only then, have you earned the right to say, "I believe this is what it means to me," and even at that, with the humility of one who also knows that this is not the end of the matter, but really just the beginning.

As an astrologer, when and only when you have earned this level of belief, born of extracting genuine knowledge from your life experiences, will you enter a place where, with the archetypal eye open, you can see more clearly beyond your own biases into the essence of things. When you are able to do this, the birthchart becomes a portal to a whole new set of possibilities.

Vesta's Questions for Me

Returning to my own exploration, within this new context, peeling back yet another layer of the astrological enigma unfolding, moving beyond logic into a more fundamental relationship to the archetype I am exploring, I am compelled to think about everything I have learned – or think I know – about Vesta in a different way. Like our more theoretical exercise in ferreting out a set of possible beginning questions for each of the planets in the descending Chaldean order, Vesta's presence in my life comes with its own set of questions.

The good news here is that having opened my archetypal eye; meandered through the stories to feel the resonances within them to my own experience; sifted that experience itself, considered astro-logically in relation to Vesta's cycle; identifying the archetypal themes that emerged through this sifting, and placing these themes within an archetypal field; I am now ready to bypass the more generic questions and go more directly into a consideration of my own.

When I do, these are the questions that arise, organized in relation to the various themes I have identified in Chapters Thirteen and Fourteen:

Becoming a Cinder Biter

If anger, confrontation, conflict, war, and vanquishing "the enemy" in all of the many fiery guises this response can take is not the answer to the ongoing injustices that continue to plague this world, what is?

What, if anything, can I personally do that will help turn the evolutionary tide so that the human species can find a better way to resolve our differences, to work together to make the world a better place, to ensure the continuity of life on this planet?

Where is my power to truly make a difference at this point in my life?

How can I honor my ancestors with the extraordinary accomplishments they have tolerated my cinder biting to wait for?

Discovering the Fire Stick

After a lifetime of earnestly pursuing the cultivation of my creative talents, particularly as a writer, I must, with some embarrassment, ask: What has it all been for? Who has it served? What difference has it made? What torches have I kindled with my creative spark, and who will carry those torches?

Although music was my first love, and has always been a part of what feeds and nurtures my own spirit, I find myself wondering whether I must consider it a mere metaphor for my creativity in general, or is there something more specific to this piece of the puzzle for me to more literally and directly explore?

Following a Golden Thread

Is my golden thread taking me somewhere, or has it simply led me to the middle of nowhere, stranded in the deep woods?

Moving in and out of Liminal Space

Although my life appears to have followed a rhythm pulsing through alternate phases of creative focus and the sense of being lost in the woods, I have to wonder now, largely in retrospect, is this life itself a liminal experience?

Or to paraphrase the great Chinese sage, "Am I an astrologer who occasionally dreams he is a butterfly lost in the deep woods?" or "Am I butterfly lost in the deep woods, who keeps dreaming he is an astrologer?"

Working at the Forge

If I am the real Great Work, slowly evolving at the forge at which I work, what is it that I am becoming that I can truly call great?

Was my time working intensively to raise my *kundalini* a preliminary step on the path to the discovery of my true forge, or is it an abandoned path I failed to follow as far as I could, because I ultimately could not stand the heat?

Gestating Under a Cloak of Invisibility

Although I have learned to mostly be OK with invisibility, to hold it now as a kind of inside joke, rather than a mark of failure, I still have to wonder, "If a tree falls in the forest, and there is no one there to hear it, does it make a sound?" or in my particular version of this question, "If what I do with my life remains invisible throughout, when I fall out of this life into death, will my life have made a sound?"

Building a Temple

My relationship to this land continues to feel like life in a temple, and I continue to tend it as best I can. But I wonder, mostly what I do here, on the land, now that the transformative storm has come and gone, is to let the forest tend itself, and bear witness to that tending. Is that enough? Or is there a more active role yet for me to play?

Becoming a Virgin

Although I have learned to be comfortable alone, outside of the context of relationship, I wonder if there is anything more for me to learn in relationship, and if so, what?

How much of my "virginity" is rooted in disappointment at my cumulative failure to make a lasting relationship work, and how much is a matter of evolving beyond the need for relationship?

Becoming a Comfortable Minimalist

Now that I have arrived in my happy place as a comfortable minimalist, is it enough to know that this creates a solid foundation on which I can do my work without distraction? Or is the abundance I have managed to create for myself merely the expression of an imbalanced relationship with the world around me, where living a minimal existence is not at all comfortable? If so, then what can I do about that, short of becoming unnecessarily uncomfortable myself?

The Art of Cultivating Astrological Koans

It should not be difficult to observe that the tone and tenor of these questions is much more tentative than my previous exploration of themes. Here, my musings are permeated by a dimension of vulnerability and perhaps even in some cases, self-doubt, that wasn't there when I was generating answers, instead of asking questions.

My sense is that is the nature of this exploratory work, which is ultimately about going more deeply into a birthchart, where psyche stands on the dizzy edge of a cosmos much closer to the infinity out of which all is born, than I, the small self, am comfortable being. Questions by their very nature, perhaps especially those posed in the Era of Uncertainty, don't neatly resolve into easy bite size answers – or for that matter, into neat astrological interpretations. The really important questions may never resolve. They are, in fact, a bit like Zen *koans*, intended to tie the logical mind into knots, while the immensity of the truth that cannot be known with the mind, washes over you, and leaves you in a puddle on the floor, which is the only place the cosmos has a chance of being known by you. So, the real question here is not, "What do you know?" but, "How bravely can you face your not-knowing?"

Using Outer Planet Transits As a Catalyst to Breakthrough Questions

This state of essential vulnerability, in which logical answers fail to suffice, is greatly enhanced during an outer planet transit. This is a time during which more questions are likely to be forthcoming than answers, and as such, it is a rich and fertile time for sinking more deeply into the metaphysical soil that underlies the strictly astro-logical quest. The challenge of an outer planet transit is not something that can be met with logical or astro-logical analysis of a birthchart. Any interpretation you could possibly give on the near shore of the experience itself is destined to sound like a cliché, perhaps true as an intellectual summation of the abstract possibilities, but woefully inadequate in helping you move through the transformation at hand.

When faced with a Pluto transit, for example, it is of sadly limited utility to prattle on about life and death, or transformation, even if such discourse is informed in part by your well-educated theoretical beliefs about these very large topics. What is more relevant is the process of remembering prior Pluto transits and what it was like to go through an actual experience of life and death, an experience that may well have changed your life in irrevocable ways, and made you a different person. These memories, if in fact they are part of Pluto's archetypal mark on you, are as visceral and numinous as they are imaginal, and putting yourself back there, however you can, also puts you in the proper frame of mind to open the archetypal eye a bit wider in present time.

Standing on Pluto's Precipice

As I face this current Pluto transit to Vesta, for example, I have, in part, as my point of reference, my astrological knowledge of Pluto, both theoretical and professional, having observed how transiting Pluto functions in a variety of astrological contexts for a variety of individuals, and having read a great deal of the existing literature in the field about what a variety of other astrologers have said about Pluto. On a somewhat more deeply rooted, visceral level, however, I also have my own experience of previous Pluto transits to other planets in my chart and to Vesta itself.

Here, we can engage a similar technique to that employed in Chapter Twelve, in which I mapped a cyclical history of my Vesta returns to gain a personal sense of Vesta, through the empirical "data" of my own life experiences. The difference is that what we are seeking here is not the nature of an archetype, as it manifests through various natal themes operating in an archetypal field, but rather how a potent catalyst to transformation can plow that field, so those themes sprout like seeds out of which the questions that meaningfully frame a life can be harvested. If this sounds a bit mysterious, hopefully the nature of this part of the process will become more obvious as we enter more deeply into it.

Exploring Pluto's Function as an Agent of Transformation

The first step here is to get a general sense of what happens when Pluto triggers a major planet in my natal chart. With the understanding that any Pluto transit, whether of hard or soft aspect, will likely be a transformative event, we will focus specifically here on the conjunctions – in part, because these will tend to be more pronounced, and in part, because the current Pluto transit to my natal Vesta is a conjunction.

In my life so far, within a 2° orb, these transits will include:

TR Pluto conjunct N Saturn (October 1965 – July 1968)[3]
TR Pluto conjunct N Mars (September 1966 – July 1969)

TR Pluto conjunct N Neptune (October 1977 – October 1979)

TR Pluto conjunct N Sun (December 1999 – September 2002)

TR Pluto conjunct N Mercury (January 2003 – October 2005)

Pluto Conjunct Saturn/Mars

(October 1965 - July 1969)

Since Saturn and Mars are less than two degrees apart in my natal chart, any transit within a 1° to one of these planets will overlap a transit to the other planet. For this reason, and to conserve a bit of space, I will combine them into one set of memories.

This period marked my transition from high school to college, which was a rude awakening. I had breezed through high school near the top of my class, without a great deal of effort, but in college, amidst an entire class of fellow students who did the same, I had to hit the ground running with such intense subjects as calculus, theoretical physics and organic chemistry. We were all under immense pressure from the beginning, and not everyone made it. I had one friend who, between impossible studies and excessive partying, went absolutely mad, accused the dean of slipping LSD into his coffee, and was literally carted off in a straightjacket, ranting and raving like a lunatic.

I somehow managed to avoid going over the edge, but I was clearly out of my element, especially since after discovering the fire stick a few years earlier, I had made the "sensible" decision to put it down, in order to chart what I thought was a more practical career path in chemistry. With TR Pluto conjunct N Saturn, I managed to maintain this ultimately unsustainable course, but as Pluto moved onto Mars, I could no longer do it.

During my first LSD experience at the beginning of my sophomore year, I realized this life I was living was not mine, and I could no longer pretend it was without surrendering to a slow soul death. In the wake of that experience, I changed my major to English, and by the time this transit had run its course, I was studying world literature, philosophy and psychology, immersing myself in a world to which I more clearly belonged.

In this case, this Pluto transit precipitated a profound and absolutely necessary course correction, without which I would not likely be here writing these words today.

Pluto Conjunct Neptune

(October 1977 - October 1979)

By this point, I had made it through graduate school with a Master's degree in Marriage, Family and Child Counseling. Unfortunately, as I was graduating, the requirements for licensing in California had just been extended, rendering my degree insufficient, with no provision for grandfathering me in. So, there was no clear path forward in the career I had chosen. I had just left the ashram, moved to Florida to attend my sister's wedding, and not knowing where else to go, stayed there to try to create a life. I couldn't get a job in my field with the degree that I had, but I found a local therapist who was willing to take me under his wing and give me a shot at building a private practice. Long story short, I failed to do that, and was, after a while, rudely but deservedly booted out. I got a job as a painter and started to dream about the homesteading life.

In retrospect, I can see this period as another course correction, although at the time I felt lost and disillusioned. I considered myself a failure, and had been stripped down to the bare bones, knocked to the ground on my knees. After this death, however, eventually came rebirth and I started to find my way into a life as a comfortable minimalist, which allowed me to follow my golden thread, work at the forge, and begin to gestate something of value under a cloak of invisibility.

Again, had I not been broken down and reassembled by Pluto, I would not likely be here now, writing about it with the hard-won perspective that I have.

Pluto Conjunct Sun

(December 1999 – September 2002)

By this point in my life, I was clearly on my path, or at least so I thought. I was teaching astrology through my Eye of the Centaur correspondence course, working with as many students as I could possibly handle. At the same time, however, I was engaged in a lucrative part-time business buying and selling college textbooks, running a local political campaign to keep fluoride out of our drinking water, serving on the board of directors at the land cooperative where I was living, and remodeling my cabin in the woods.

It was just too much, and I was suffering under the strain, at a point where something was about to break. Working with a healer to recover from a bout of pneumonia during a previous and overlapping Pluto transit (TR Pluto opposed N Moon), I had realized again – that if I kept going the way I was going, I wouldn't last as long as I needed to last to do what I had, by this point, felt I had come here to do. I also realized, in the midst of all this, that I had some writing to do, and that if I was serious about doing it, I would have to clear my plate and make some space.

To honor this realization, I began letting go of various involvements. I eventually finished remodeling my cabin; I resigned from the board of directors at the land cooperative; we lost the political campaign; and I cut back on my book-buying business. By far, however, the hardest decision I had to make was to take a sabbatical from my correspondence course, since even at this reduced load, I could not focus on writing the way I would need to be able to focus.

Here, it would appear, Pluto did not issue quite so radical a course correction, but can perhaps be more accurately understood as facilitating a stripping away of non-essentials so that I could be more focused on what mattered most.

Pluto conjunct Mercury

(January 2003 – October 2005)

It was during this period that I started writing in earnest, eventually completing and self-publishing my first astrology book, *The Seven Gates of Soul*. From the beginning, I realized I had dived into the deep end of the pool, and I didn't have a clue what I was doing. I stuck with it, however, and gradually began to find my feet. In retrospect, I can see that this was Pluto taking me into my own depths and showing me what I was capable of. I have not looked back since, and here I am, four books later, still a deep-sea diver, whose breath is taken away, each time I go down.

If I had to describe Pluto's function as a transformational agent, based on my own experiences, rather than some theoretical understanding, I would have to say this: Pluto actually seems to know me better than I know myself, and is so fiercely dedicated to me, that if it needs to turn my world upside down and shake me out into a more suitable life, it will not hesitate. With my cooperation, it has, over the years, morphed into a more benign, if no less demanding *daimon*, challenging me to step into a more mature, more seasoned, wiser version of myself than I have so far been able to muster. If it continues along this trajectory, whatever the particulars of this current Pluto transit to Vesta/Venus/Jupiter might be, it will catapult me to another level of possibility. Thinking about this excites me, even as it arouses a twinge of trepidation, bordering on PTSD.

Given that we are, in this chapter, exploring questions, rather than attempting to give definitive answers about what we might expect from a given astrological event, I would translate my empirical sense of what transiting Pluto has meant to me personally, into the following question:

> *What is the more mature, more seasoned, wiser version of myself that you are challenging me to step into at this time, and how can I best cooperate with that challenge?*

Feeling Pluto's Role in Vesta's Story

To refine this question further, I will want to look more specifically at how transiting Pluto has previously challenged that part of me I might associate with Vesta, perhaps along lines related to one or more of the nine themes I have identified as related to Vesta's presence in my life.

To this point in my life, I have experienced three transits of Pluto to Vesta (considering Ptolemaic aspects only within a 2° orb):

TR Pluto trine N Vesta (October 1969 – July 1972)

TR Pluto square N Vesta (November 1981 – August 1984)

TR Pluto sextile N Vesta (November 1993 – November 1995)

Pluto Trine Vesta

(October 1969 – July 1972)

The first thing that I would observe about this period, having done the previous empirical work I did earlier in this chapter in relation to previous Pluto transits by conjunction to various planets in my natal chart, and in Chapter Twelve in relation to my Vesta Returns, is a juxtaposition of previous transits that now provide a ready-made context for further exploration. In particular, this transit of TR Pluto trine N Vesta was preceded by TR Pluto conjunct N Saturn/Mars mentioned above and contains within it the triple-pass Vesta Return of Period 7 as discussed in Chapter Twelve.

Putting this together, what I see is this: during TR Pluto conjunct N Saturn/Mars, I was, with the help of a psychoactive substance, ceremoniously booted off of a path that would not have taken me into a life that was compatible with my spirit, and catapulted to a more suitable path, where I began studying subjects that would eventually in some way, contribute to a deepening awareness of my golden thread.

The first part of this transit – more or less, the first two waves of what was a triple-pass transit – was essentially this new exploration, an exhilarating immersion. It was during this period, for example, that I first encountered Jung, was introduced to astrology, and began exploring *kundalini yoga*. In the shift between music, my first love, and astrology, I had also discovered a new fire stick, one that I could wield with more natural talent and skill.

The second part of this Pluto-Vesta transit – essentially the third pass – was a passage into a more liminal state, in which I didn't really have a clue what I could possibly do with useless undergraduate degree I had just obtained, even if the pathway to it was the beginning of a discovery of my golden thread with a shiny new fire stick in hand.

Meanwhile, during this period, I took a step along what I have been calling the path of a cinder biter, by procuring my conscientious objector status, in contrast to my lineage, along which many of my more distant ancestors were likely foot soldiers in the army.

I had my first taste of owning land, which eventually led to the land that I own and tend now, although at this earlier stage, I really wasn't settled enough to have any sense about it of building a temple.

This period also encompassed a folly of the heart, falling in love with the unattainable wife of my best friend at the time. Only in retrospect can this be understood as a step along the path of becoming a virgin, one necessarily marked by heartbreak.

Lastly, toward the end of this transit, which extends beyond the other periods that dovetail with it, I entered into a more serious phase of my relationship to *kundalini yoga*, reconnecting with my first teacher, who had in the time of my absence, started an ashram in Connecticut, into which I moved shortly after this period ended.

If I had to sum up my overall sense of this period, it would be one in which I was being introduced to many of the themes related to Vesta, and in a sense, initiated onto many of the various paths that weave through Vesta's archetypal field: becoming a cinder biter; discovering the fire stick; following a golden thread; moving through liminal space; working at the forge; building a temple; and becoming a virgin.

Pluto Square Vesta

(November 1981 – August 1984)

This period does not immediately precede or follow any of the previous Pluto transits explored earlier in this chapter, but it does encompass the Vesta Return of Period 10, in which I was working to pay off my debts, so that I could move onto the land where I live now. As I wrote in Chapter Twelve, "I don't see much of Vesta in this period, unless it would be the ongoing call to a simpler life, which was the driving force behind the more complicated life I was living at the time." I wondered, "Will there ever come a day when I can spend my time freely without regard to material security?"

In retrospect, I could call this a serious immersion in liminal space, as I struggled to find my way onto the path of a comfortable minimalist. But this Pluto transit to Vesta did eventually see me moving on to my land and beginning to tend it – not just a significant movement toward a simpler life, but also a more serious step along the path of building a temple than I had taken before, and also perhaps, an early warning of just how serious a commitment this was.

In the early days, I had a romantic notion, fueled by my reading of *The Mother Earth News* and *The Whole Earth Catalog* of what it meant to homestead. I had decided, as part of this romantic notion, that I wanted to live my first year on the land in a tipi, so that I could observe the natural patterns of sun, wind and water, before building a more permanent structure.

By winter of 1983-1984, I had erected my tipi over a platform floor, on which I had installed a woodstove with a free-standing stove pipe that went up toward the smoke hole. The woodstove was a "modern" convenience, but the idea of building a fire in the center of a tipi and letting the smoke go out the smoke hole was the common indigenous practice. It was also most definitely a Hestian exercise in tending the hearth, although the indigenous peoples would obviously not have called it that.

In any case, on Christmas Eve, 1983, I had my first rude awakening about what tending a fire actually meant. That day was extremely cold and I had the woodstove cranked up as high as it could go. As it happened, an ember caught up in the ropes wrapped around the intersection of the tipi poles and started burning. I climbed up on a ladder with a fire extinguisher, and attempted to put the fire out, but as fate – or maybe Pluto, in his destructive mode – would have it, the wind picked up just at that moment, and fanned the ember back into flame. After that, the tipi burned to the ground, providing an obvious lesson in the previously unrecognized dangers involved in working with fire.

After the fire, I was "homeless," but wound up moving in with a woman with whom I was pursuing an intimate relationship, taking another (largely unconscious) step on my path of becoming a virgin.

Lastly, it was during this period that I became, for a brief time, president of the land cooperative of which my 10-acre parcel is part. In terms of the themes that I have identified as belonging to Vesta, this would have been another step on my path as a cinder biter, one in which I got burned through my political naiveté, essentially becoming the target of other community members' unresolved authority issues, even though I did not consider myself an authority by any stretch. Most of my time as president, in fact, was spent trying to mediate various conflicts among community members, most of the time, getting caught in the middle and making matters worse. Toward the end of this Pluto transit, I resigned in what felt like disgrace and failure.

In retrospect – often a more useful perspective than what arises in the heat of the moment – I can see this Pluto transit to Vesta being an initiation onto the more difficult, challenging, and potentially hazardous dimensions of being a tender of the sacred flame, which is as capable of burning something down as it is of illuminating it. As I see it, Vesta's path is one that teaches humility, and during this period, I was at the receiving end of this fundamental lesson.

Pluto Sextile Vesta

(November 1993 – November 1995)

This period neither dovetails with any of the Pluto transits conjunct to natal planets explored above, nor encompasses any previous Vesta Returns.

There were, however, several significant developments during this period that relate to my nine identified themes. I was developing my first astrological correspondence course *The Eye of the Centaur*, and at the same time, studying medical astrology with a teacher from Santa Fe, New Mexico. I was beginning to think about astrology in a somewhat different way – a period in other words, when I was, essentially, sharpening my fire stick, and working more intently at the forge. I had a difficult relationship with the teacher, but wanted to learn what she had to teach, so I hunkered down, kept my focus, and finished the three-year course she was offering.

This was the teacher that had suggested that I figure out a way to earn my livelihood with my big toe, in order to free up more time to pursue my creative interests, and shortly after this period began, I launched my book-buying business. Although it would be another twenty years before I could actually become comfortable as a minimalist, this was a significant step on that path.

Lastly, during this period, I was in a long-distance relationship with a woman who was ambivalent about whether she wanted to be in a relationship at all, another relationship that ultimately wound up a source of disillusionment, and another step on my path of becoming virgin.

Formulating Questions for This Pluto Transit to Vesta

Having considered this short cyclical history, as I stand on the edge of this new Pluto transit to Vesta, I am now prepared to refine my earlier question, formulated thus far as:

> *What is the more mature, more seasoned, wiser version of myself that you are challenging me to step into at this time, and how can I best cooperate with that challenge?*

To start, I am drawn to the parallel between the recent chimney fire I had, just as this new Pluto transit began, and the burning down of my tipi during TR Pluto square N Vesta, when I first moved onto my land, nearly 40 years ago. In retrospect, I can see this seemingly destructive aspect of fire as an intensification of the process of working at the forge, in which the real object of the work is purification – burning away the dross, so that a clearer, revitalized essence might reveal itself. This was the nature of my involvement with *kundalini yoga*, for example, and in a more benign way, the nature of my work with the whole process of tending the land, cutting and splitting my own firewood, and keeping a fire going in my woodstove through the winter.

When I think about the previous transit – TR Pluto square N Vesta – I remember a profound sense of disillusionment about the precarious nature of life, and about the difficulty in facilitating any kind of outer change at all. In the wake of my fire, and beyond that, in the wake of my resignation as president of the land cooperative, I became much more inward, much more focused on working to change the only thing I really had the power to change – myself. I have since let go of much of the bitterness, and the sense of resentment about the fact that the world, approached politically, is the way it is, and am no longer trying to fight my way to the top of the ash pile.

But my sense, in facing this new transit, is that there is perhaps more left to burn away, that I am not done yet, not that the work at the forge is ever entirely done, but that during the next few years in particular, there may be more purification, more burning away of dross, more refinement required of me. In considering this possibility then, my question to Vesta, under Pluto's charge, now becomes:

> *What must I let go of in order to more fully claim my essence as a dedicated keeper of the hearth, in all of the ways that manifests for me?*

Secondly, in considering the impending death of a mentor noted as a significant development in Chapter Fourteen, I can also note parallel relationship with teachers in previous Pluto transits to Vesta – one during TR Pluto trine N Vesta with my first *kundalini yoga* teacher, who took me more deeply into the first manifestation of my work at the forge; and one during TR Pluto sextile N Vesta with my medical astrology teacher, who helped me step more clearly onto the path of a comfortable minimalist and who provided me with several hints along the path of my golden thread that have informed my work with astrology.

All three of these teachers have been difficult relationships, challenging me both to stand in my truth, and at the same time, be humble in that stance. All three have also empowered me in some ways, perhaps mirroring Pluto's process through an outer relationship of significance.

At age 72, having become a teacher myself, I have long stopped thinking of the possibility or the necessity of having yet another teacher, although I have often said that my students are my teachers, and this is true. All that aside, however, in remembering my original question to Vesta, first posed in Chapter Ten,

> *How can I best use my vital life energy, my creativity, my sense of calling to the path that I am on now – to tend to my solitude, and my hearth – in a way that allows me to feel more deeply connected to others, to the world at large, and to the world around me – and to somehow make a difference in doing what I do, at this point in our collective history?*

I am left wondering how to do this. Within my own small sphere, I do make a difference, but in the face of the very large dilemmas facing us as a culture, and as a species on this planet, which we have largely trashed, I don't have a clue how to begin to make a more significant contribution. Is there anyone out there who does? If so, I would like to learn from that person, in light of which, my second question to Vesta, under Pluto's charge, might be this:

> *Who is out there, or perhaps within me, who can teach me what I need to know in order to rise to a more significant level of possibility in making a contribution to this*

> *suffering world? How can I more consciously tend not just my own hearth, but the sacred flame that burns at the heart of the anima mundi?*

These are the questions that emerge as I stand on the threshold of this major activation of Vesta's presence within my archetypal field. Other questions may join them as I move more deeply into the transit. Meanwhile, in bringing this chapter full circle, we would note that although all these questions are informed by a consideration of the astrology involved, they are more accurately understood as arising from within the philosophical bedrock on which my life and my practice of astrology are rooted. A different astrologer, faced with the same symbolism, might well ask an entirely different set of questions.

I would further note that as I lean into these questions, as I cannot help but do when entering the living reality behind this major Pluto transit to Vesta, the philosophical bedrock of my life will deepen and broaden, and in some cases, perhaps shift to reflect what I learn, how I grow, how life itself becomes the sacred space in which I work on myself.

In our next chapter, we will look more closely at this possibility, which is, to take another step backward into a more mystical relationship to the birthchart, ultimately where all truly useful questions are born.

Notes

1. Brennan, Chris. *Hellenistic Astrology: The Study of Fate and Fortune*. Denver: Amor Fati Publications, 2017, 185.
2. Rilke, Rainer Maria. *Letters To a Young Poet*. Norton & Company, 1954, 34-35.
3. From this point forward, I will use TR as an abbreviation for transiting, and N as an abbreviation for natal.

In the beginning, before language and complex thinking, hominins pushed air up the trachea, shaping meaningful and comprehensible alarm calls and breeding calls. And then came something else, something that conveyed the meaning that melody can carry but which words can't. These were tones strung together around emotions and thought, runs of sound like the trills and vibrato in birdsong. Hominins came to know one another as individuals in a new way. The level of cooperation possible between hominins expanded by an order of magnitude.

With his fingertips on the cranium of an australopithecine skull not much larger than a grapefruit, on the forward part of the vault where one day frontal lobes would rise up in Homo, he (a colleague in Africa) says, 'Barry, I can't prove this, but I believe we sang before we spoke.'

Barry Lopez, Horizon, 2019

Chapter Sixteen

Entering the Archetypal Field as a Spiritual Practice

The more conscious you can become of the important questions that you carry with you through your life, the more relevant the birthchart will become as an archetypal field in which these questions resonate. Your work with the birthchart, within the context of these questions that never completely resolve, and the life that revolves around that work, will then become a quest. This is ultimately not a goal-oriented quest, but rather one that over time takes you into a deeper relationship with the archetypes that shape your existence, and that infuse your life with meaning and purpose.

Approaching Astrology as a Spiritual Discipline

Embarking on this quest takes us back to possibilities that were largely abandoned as astrologers moved on from the Mystical Era – possibilities that essentially revolved around the idea that developing the capacity to read what was written in the sky was a matter of spiritual attainment, that is to say, clear receptivity to and alignment with the divine.

I realize in saying this that there was also a strong political component in the practice of divinatory astrology, which sometimes, maybe even often, corrupted the practice. There was, within this era, great political pressure brought to bear upon astrologers, whose livelihood and at times, very existence depended upon the ability to accurately predict in ways that were useful to the rulers of the cosmocracy in which they operated.

But having said this, the very fact that astrologers of the era were also priests suggests that beyond the politics of religion was a spiritual practice that preceded the written word, out of which the early observations that eventually got codified on the tablets of the *Enuma Anu Enlil* were rooted. To reclaim what was lost as we moved into the Philosophical Era then, we can think in terms of restoring the astrological priesthood, not in the sense of starting or resurrecting a religion, but in reconsidering the practice of astrology itself to be a spiritual discipline. This is a very different kind of astrology than is usually practiced – not just a matter of decoding symbols on a piece of paper or a computer screen, but a much deeper process of communion with the sacred intent that reverberates at the heart of the celestial patterns depicted in the birthchart.

Although we could perhaps get a glimpse of what such a discipline might have looked like in the Mystical Era by more carefully researching the fragments of the ancient texts that are available, scholarship can only take us so far, as our reach backwards recedes into the oral tradition out of which what was only later written down emerged. From what we have been able to reconstruct, it appears that the *Enuma Anu Enlil* was mostly a compilation of omens related to various celestial phenomena, as well as weather patterns and earthquakes. The earlier *Mul Apin* provides an astronomical framework for observation and is less overtly astrological. There is little in either text about a possible spiritual discipline that might accompany such observation.

As Campion notes, most of what we know about Mesopotamian cosmology and the astrological practices that arose within that context derive from "intelligent reconstruction" and is, like most such scholarly endeavours, subject to polarized debate.[1] Within that debate, it is generally noted that throughout the fifth century B. C. E., astrology was geared primarily toward ensuring the wellbeing of the state and the ruler of the state through alignment with divine will, as reflected by the cosmological order. Prediction, though most often associated with the astrology of the era, was a secondary goal.[2]

Namburbi, Magic and the Ongoing Work of Self-Transformation

This use of astrology to ensure the wellbeing of the state generally entailed three processes: first, an observation of the cosmological order; second, an interpretation of what the observed patterns in the sky might mean, based on observed correlations between celestial and terrestrial phenomena in the past; and third, a more priestly practice of rituals, known as *namburbi*, whose intent was partly to appease the appropriate deities and partly to mitigate what was written in the sky through magical and practical interventions. "*Namburbi* means 'loosing,' so we have a sense of a future fate being loosened."[3]

After the fifth century B.C.E., and especially as the individual natal horoscope increasingly became the focus of astrology, eventually eclipsing concern about the wellbeing of the state and its rulers, this same trifold approach to astrology presumably became the basis for a more personal practice of *namburbi*. In terms of our purposes here – reclaiming whatever spiritual practice might lie at the secret heart of astrological practice in the Mystical Era – and readapting it to life within the Era of Uncertainty, it is primarily this process of *namburbi* that seems most promising.

Such a discipline can perhaps be considered to have been rooted in the same impulse that was evidenced in the influence of Hermeticism and Neoplatonism in the Philosophical Era, and that resulted in a form of astrological magic based on electional timing, talismanic resonances, and formalized ritual. The same impulse also shows up in numerous subsequent incarnations: from the theurgy of Iamblichus; to Alfonso the Wise, the *Picatrix* and the astrologer-magicians of the medieval era; to the Renaissance magic of Marsilio Ficino; to the occult magick of Aleister Crowley, the Hermetic Order of the Golden Dawn and its various competitive permutations; to the renewed interest in astrological magic being pursued by a new generation of astrologers today, such as Benjamin Dykes, Austin Coppock, Christopher Warnock and others.

Having said that, what I am proposing is not necessarily magical in this more explicit sense of the word. *Namburbi*, however, does share magic's interest in mitigating fate, as well as the notion that astrology is not merely descriptive, but also prescriptive in its call to conscious action. Conscious action, conducted within what Cornelius has called the *templum*,[4] or what magicians might call the ritual space of the pentagram, or what we might more generally simply understand as sacred space – marked by intention, attention and purposeful activity – is necessary, within this approach, to mitigate fate. The birthchart, in other words, is not something to be interpreted or decoded, so much as it is a set of instructions for a meaningful pursuit of *namburbi*, a loosening of that which is written in the sky in a way that turns life itself into a sacred, participatory, and at times, magical act.

This kind of astrological magic happens, according to my sense of it, when psyche and cosmos are aligned within sacred space, not so much within the context of ritual action, as with a clear intention to consecrate one's every action, day in and day out, through an intentional alignment with divine intelligence, manifest according to various cyclical planetary rhythms and within the context of various emerging archetypal themes that can be mapped astrologically. There is no reason why more formal ritual action cannot be a part of this process, but it is, in my opinion, secondary to and dependent upon a fundamental attitude toward life in which an ongoing refinement and clarification of your relationship to the Self – as discussed in Chapter Ten – is a prerequisite to practicing the kind of astrology that harbours the magical power to change lives, beginning with your own. Within this context, all action and life itself, is charged with ritual significance because it takes place in a sacred space.

The Work of Self-Transformation That Precedes Astrological Wisdom

In the Era of Uncertainty, it seems to me that the most fruitful approach to this ongoing work of self-transformation will be within the context of the further evolution of psychological astrology, particularly as it has melded with humanistic and transpersonal schools of thought, through the work of Carl Jung, Dane Rudhyar, Richard Tarnas, and the various legions of psychological astrologers that have furthered the theory and practice since. This approach, however, cannot be merely theoretical if it is to bear edible fruit. It must revolve instead around the use of psychological astrology as a basis for a spiritual practice, specifically designed to foster the kind of clarity that allows the astrologer, whoever he or she might be, to more skilfully read the divine intelligence that is written in the sky, and then to embody it in living a conscious life.

What this looks like in practice will take different shapes at different times. In the post-modern era, we have a broad range of tools and resources, beyond the birthchart, that can potentially facilitate this work, as well as many possible approaches to the birthchart itself that fall within this broad umbrella. Whatever the outer particulars of the specific approach you adopt and the tools and resources to which you will gravitate, however, an astrologically-based spiritual practice must, as I see it, essentially encompass three dimensions:

1) **Healing and becoming whole.** Having entered a separate body from the realm of Spirit, each of us is born essentially whole, pure and innocent, with traces of that blessed state typically lingering for a few years after birth. Inevitably, however, we are wounded in childhood, either through outright neglect or abuse by wounded parents, teachers in school, religious authorities, or other early sources of exposure to a wounded world, or more typically in a subtler way, just by not being fully understood, accepted, or appreciated for who we are. These core wounds, as I call them, then become our initiation onto the soul's journey, which entails a lifetime of learning and growth as we reach in various ways, by trial and error, for the wholeness that we once knew, and that can now potentially know at a deeper level of intimacy for having done the work on ourselves necessary to embrace it.

   This work of healing inevitably involves learning to love self and others, and the world, unconditionally and without holding anything back – a long road and complex arena for most of us.

2) **Self-actualization.** Each of us is endowed with certain natural talents, innate skills and abilities, and ultimately a unique personal genius that can potentially form the basis for a meaningful contribution to the greater whole of which we are part. At the heart of this personal genius is the spark of the divine, a sacred flame to use Vesta's language, that is our task in life to tend, and to cultivate as a light unto the world, a gift that makes this world a better place when we depart than when we arrive, for our having been here, participating at our full capacity.

3) **Opening to the sacred.** The third dimension of self-transformation is a matter of entering into a deeper relationship with the cosmos, one in which we feel ourselves to be part of something that both encompasses and transcends our individual existence, something that extends our limited sense of self to merge with the Self. This can take any number of forms, and potentially encompass a number of dimensions: understanding our place within an ancestral lineage; feeling the interconnectedness of all life with the biosphere of a living planet; embracing our humanity without regard to secondary divisions of gender, race, ethnicity, or political affiliation; cultivating a spiritual life rooted not just in belief, but in communion with the divine; and for astrologers, being able to experience the birthchart, not just as a set of ideas,

but as a portal into an actual relationship with the celestial pantheon of numinous, living archetypes that dwell there.

The relative importance of these three tasks will shift throughout a lifetime, in part, as a reflection of transits and progressions that draw our attention to areas of the birthchart where these tasks are emphasized. At a deeper level, we might begin to observe that all three tasks are entailed in every challenge or opportunity that will arise in the course of our lives, regardless of the transits or progressions that reflect them astrologically.

Self-Transformation and the Saturn Cycle

In part, I think it is also true in a general way, that the relative emphasis of these three tasks will shift in relation to the three Saturn cycles that archetypally frame a complete life. The parameters of the first task - that of healing and becoming whole, as well as the particular wounds that serve as the catalyst to this process - will be emphasized and brought to light during the first Saturn cycle, up to age 29 or 30. I have found that the core wound - which serves as a pivot point of healing and growth and that initiates us onto our soul's journey - often occurs between the ages of 3 and 4, around the time of TR Saturn's first waxing semi-square to its natal position; or sometimes around the age of 7, TR Saturn's first waxing square. In my case, for example, I experienced the ash-pile incident that served as my initiation onto the path of a cinder biter at about age 3 1/2.

During the first Saturn cycle, we will also begin the second task of self-actualization, and perhaps begin to cultivate our unique expression of genius, although for most of us, this preliminary foray into the second task will take place within the culturally conditioned range of options for employment, and in primary allegiance to the more practical task of earning a livelihood, paying the bills, and learning how to navigate the world of mundane reality, such as it is. It is also not out of the question that we will have early experiences of an opening to the sacred, but at this stage, generally without the benefit of a larger context of meaning, rooted in the kind of perspective that only becomes possible later in life.

During the second Saturn cycle, through age 58 or 59, the work of healing will continue, but the second task of self-actualization will begin to take precedence, as we attain a certain level of success in relation to our careers, and with that success, ideally increasing latitude to pursue a more autonomous path of creative nuance. As with the first Saturn cycle, the second Saturn cycle can also bring experiences of opening to the sacred, but these will generally be subsumed within the larger agenda of living - pursuing a career, raising a family, staying busy.

Lastly, during the third Saturn cycle, or however much of it we experience before death, we get to reap the harvest of the work of healing we have done, as well as of the creative contribution we have made, and can begin to shift our focus increasingly toward the third task.

This is, of course, by no means a given, although in more indigenous cultures, this was often encouraged in a way that it is generally not, in the contemporary Western world. Because most of us are slow learners, the third Saturn cycle will inevitably be complicated by the unfinished business of the first two Saturn cycles. On the other hand, for many of us who are in our third Saturn cycles now, and who have spent a lifetime valuing whatever experiences of opening to the sacred we have had during the first two Saturn cycles, this is our time for opening to the deeper mythopoetic dimensions of the archetypal field, and experiencing the larger context that ties these experiences together.

Obviously, the particulars of this generalized assignment of soul tasks to Saturn cycles will vary considerably from individual to individual. In general, however, an awareness of these three soul tasks, and the shifting balance of their relative importance that shapes any life over time, will give you a conceptual framework in which to understand what you are dealing with, at any level, at any particular time, as the basis for using your birthchart as the point of entry into a spiritual practice that revolves around one or more of these tasks.

In a more detailed way, the tasks specific to each stage will revolve around additional transits and progressions, which call our attention to various natal signatures that contain more specific instructions for healing, learning and growing. As noted in the last chapter, for example, this current Pluto transit to natal Vesta in my natal chart is drawing my attention to the possibility of deepening my relationship to this archetype, as well as to the possibility for self-actualization at a deeper level of realization at the forge, and to healing old wounds related to one or more of Vesta's themes, still in need of my attention. Transits and progressions come and go, but with an attitude that understands the birthchart to be an ongoing invitation to spiritual work on oneself, the astrological priestess will approach each moment as an opportunity to polish the lens through which she more clearly sees the divine intent that is being written in the sky.

Self-Transformation Understood as an Archetypal Quest

From within the context of the astrological perspective being developed in this book, the work will revolve around the questions that have become the pivot point of your quest, and the various themes you have identified around which these questions revolve – and these will appear differently in each phase, and from the perspective of each soul task. The archetypal field in which these themes and questions reverberate will change from time to time, as various planetary forces come to the fore and others recede into the background, and as various soul tasks demand your attention at various phases of your life. But whatever phase you find yourself in, whatever shape your questions take, and however you articulate the various themes around which these questions pivot, as you hold the intention to use your birthchart as a platform for an ongoing spiritual practice, the path into the work will become clear.

Approaching My Work with Vesta as a Spiritual Practice

Having laid the foundation for this work in relation to Vesta in preceding chapters, I can now enter each theme and consider the pivotal questions around which the theme endlessly perambulates from a slightly different, and more prescriptive perspective, a recipe, as it were, for self-transformation and magical mitigation of fate. Or put another way, if I am brave enough to move to this level of engagement with my birthchart, considered in this case as Vesta's archetypal field, I can know what she is asking of me, and what I must ask of myself if I am to connect with her in a meaningful way. Following this path, then, under her tutelage, I can gradually become a better, more empowered, more consciously enlightened version of myself in deeper relationship to the Self.

Becoming a Cinder-Biter

When I speak of becoming a cinder biter, for example, this already implies a process that unfolds over time – a process that I can now recognize as an important component of what astrology, considered as a spiritual discipline, might look like for me. Using verbs like "becoming" a cinder biter or "discovering" the fire stick to describe the themes associated with a given archetypal field is helpful, as it provides a natural context for doing with conscious intent. Mapping these themes to specific memories unfolding in cyclical time reveals what I have done so far, probably mostly unconsciously, but obviously moving toward sufficient awareness to elucidate a pattern unfolding. Formulating questions about what I still most earnestly want to know, in relation to these themes, considered in light of my history around these various themes, in turn shows where the learning curve lies in relation to each pattern. It is at this learning curve, that the greatest opportunity for self-transformation and magical mitigation of my fate currently exists. Lastly, as I willingly lean into this learning curve, I enter a sacred space where my life becomes a spiritual practice inviting me toward a deeper communion with the archetype I am currently working with – in this case Vesta.

So, what is it that Vesta is asking of me as I walk this path? Revisiting the personal questions of Chapter Fifteen, now understood within this new ever-deepening context brings me to another level of understanding.

> *If anger, confrontation, conflict, war, and vanquishing "the enemy" in all of the many fiery guises this response can take is not the answer to the ongoing injustices that continue to plague this world, what is?*

As noted in Chapter Thirteen, this thread of my journey through Vesta's archetypal field began with what I call the ash pile incident during my first Vesta Return. During this traumatic soul initiation, I had my mouth stuffed with ashes by the neighborhood kids, who might here be understood in their unwitting role as a microcosm of the world, which at the time, and for a long time afterward, I was angry – and ready to fight whoever or whatever threatened to knock me down again.

My anger, in this case, arose within the context of powerlessness, and as an expression of it. I was blindsided on that day by people who I thought were my friends, and left gasping for air. For a few short minutes, I had the illusion of power, having made it to the top of the pile of ashes, but I had that power taken away, just like that. It made me angry, and it put me in a driven state of mind, determined to take it back.

At first, my anger was directed toward a few other students in my class, other boys who were ready and willing to fight. I got into fights every day on the playground, and generally held my own, but derived no sense of power at all from these fights, nor even much satisfaction or release, and at the end of the first grade, nearly got expelled for my all effort – another moment, actually, in which whatever power I might otherwise have had, was stripped away. Over the years, as outlined in Chapter Thirteen, I subsequently channeled this anger into fighting my fellow students for academic achievement; fighting my neighbors here in the land cooperative where I live over various issues; fighting timber barons in the Pacific Northwest; fighting the city of Abilene, Texas to keep fluoride out of the local drinking water; fighting for a short time against all the forces impinging upon the rainforests of Ecuador; and in many other arenas, throughout my life, some in ways that line up with Vesta transits, and some that do not.

With all of this fighting, in retrospect, I feel I lost more than I gained. For whatever momentary victories I might have won, I paid a huge price in terms of isolation, loss of friendship, loss of time, money and focus, loss of innocence, loss of faith in the human species and increasing alienation from the dysfunctional culture we have created. In retrospect, I can honestly say that it has not been worth it. This is not to say there are not certain ideals or causes worth fighting for, but what this path has taught me is that fighting is simply not my thing, not a productive path to power, not constructive or useful in making any kind of meaningful contribution with my life, nor is it, in my experience, an effective strategy for changing the world.

I did feel powerful, actually, when I was granted my conscientious objector status by my draft board during the Viet Nam war, which as noted in Chapter Thirteen, was not just a personal act, but also a matter of breaking the family pattern, in which my more distant ancestors had all been foot soldiers in the army. So, it would appear there is more power in simply standing on principle, without fighting, and yet in some ways, this feels like a quaint position to hold in a world wracked by increasingly vociferous conflict, with many important principles on the line. It almost feels irresponsible within such a climate not to fight for something, and yet, it is clear – at least from Vesta's point of view, filtered of course through my own perception of it – that this is not the way to go, not a path that will lead to a place of power, or any place at all that I, or we as a culture and a species, would really want to go.

One thing I do notice here, as I write this, is that through all of the fighting I have done, and through all of the experiences that have colluded to show me the futility of fighting, my anger has dissipated and morphed into something else. This is not to say that I can't still feel anger, or even outrage, about certain things. But the predominant feeling seems to be one of sadness. This sadness is at times tinged with despair, but also tempered by an increasingly steady determination to do what I can, where I can, even if that doesn't seem like it amounts to much.

Here, I have learned to operate within what effectiveness guru Stephen Covey once called my "circle of influence."[5] My circle of influence – the range within which I can actually do something that will make a difference – will always be much smaller than my "circle of concern" – the full gamut of all those things that make me sad, angry, or fill me with despair. So, even if it's only a small thing I can do, I have learned it is somehow more empowering to do that, than to rage impotently at all those injustices I can do nothing about.

> *What can I personally do that will help turn the evolutionary tide so that the human species can find a better way to resolve our differences, to work together to make the world a better place, to ensure the continuity of life on this planet?*

A month or so ago, shortly after transiting Pluto was first conjunct natal Vesta within a 1° orb, I had such an opportunity, when one of my neighbors asked for volunteers to help build a trail through the common land of this land cooperative where I live. As noted elsewhere, I have not always had the most harmonious relationships with my neighbors, often being on opposite ends of various political battles that have plagued our shared history for the past forty years. This, in fact, is one primary arena in which I have realized the futility of fighting, and have largely backed off, except where it does still seem important for me to speak up and take a stand. Meanwhile, I have felt myself shift toward trying to offer something positive, wherever I can.

So, this opportunity to help build a trail was one such moment. I showed up, ready to fully participate, and for my effort, I gained a new appreciation for my neighbors, and I believe they for me. We had an experience of camaraderie around our common love of this forest and helped create something that will benefit us all. Along this learning curve as a cinder biter, it doesn't get much better than that.

> *Where is my power to truly make a difference at this point in my life?*

I am not naïve enough to believe that all the world's problems can be solved this way. But I do believe that for me, at this point in my life, whatever I can do with an open-heart, a willing spirit, and the steady intention to help, will be enough. To some of you, this might seem like a retreat into New Age idealism and magical thinking, but given my 72-year history of fighting on multiple fronts, sweating the small stuff as well as the incomprehensible, and paying too steep a price for too many inconsequential victories, the idea that I can make more of a difference doing less with more heart is a hard-won piece of wisdom that I can recognize as a next step on my endless path of learning and growth.

> *How can I honor my ancestors with the extraordinary accomplishments they have tolerated my cinder biting to wait for?*

I seriously doubt that any of my more distant ancestors, the Landwehr foot-soldiers in the armies of the Austro-Hungarian Empire, who largely served as cannon fodder for enclaves of the wealthy whose walled cities they were guarding, ever benefitted much from going to battle. If it is true – and I like to think it is – that everything we do to heal our ancestral wounds benefits not only us, but them as well, then starting with my grandfather and my father, the old patterns were being broken by men who were not interested in fighting. I believe I have continued that more recent track of pattern-breaking, not just by becoming a conscientious objector, but by facing that same conundrum in countless forms, on countless less obvious fronts, and having seen through the seductive instinctual knee-jerk call to war, however it manifests.

Does this mean that I am free and can simply walk away from any further lessons that might be in the offing? Probably not. But I can be clear that wherever possible, however the call to battle presents itself, part of my learning curve and my spiritual path from this point forward will be to, as much as possible, step back from the impending conflagration and tend a much smaller, but no less vital sacred flame. This flame lives in my heart, and it is also the center of the cosmos, and when it is burning brightly, it seems plausible to assume it will illuminate a path along which, instead of fighting, I can contribute something positive into the mix. There is a great mystery here to be explored that I can thankfully sense is the key to making a difference, even if my mind can't fully comprehend it.

Discovering the Fire Stick

> *After a lifetime of earnestly pursuing the cultivation of my creative talents, particularly as a writer, I must, with some embarrassment, ask, what has it all been for? Who has it served? What difference has it made? What torches have I kindled with my creative spark, and who will carry those torches?*

Again, the answer to this question may not be one my mind can comprehend. Indeed, as hinted in Chapter Fifteen, that is the nature of these seminal questions that I carry with me. And yet, from time to time, I have glimpses of a possible answer. Every so often, someone will come forward and say something like this: that reading that you did for me 20 years ago is still meaningful and continues to guide me today. Just the other day, I did a reading for a young 18-year-old man, wondering what path he might best follow as he enters college. My answers surprised him, and in fact, surprised me, but there was the fire of conviction behind them and I could feel them sparking a slowly dawning recognition at the other end of the Zoom call.

Who knows what will come of this reading and this young man 20 years from now? In this case, I may not live long enough to get the kind of feedback that in the past has let me know that, even if it is not obvious in the moment, I have made a difference and will continue to do so as long as I draw breath. What occurs to me now as I write this is that in honing my awareness further around this theme, the next step might be to pay more attention to the sparks flying from my fire stick than trying to see where they land. If the stick is sparking, the chances are something worthy is happening beyond the reach of what, in that moment, can probably be known. If I can remember that, less of me will be drawn into this place of doubt, which in and of itself, may well dampen the flame.

> *Although music was my first love, and has always been a part of what feeds and nurtures my own spirit, I find myself wondering whether I must consider it a mere metaphor for my creativity in general, or is there something more specific to this piece of the puzzle for me to more literally and directly explore?*

Just this morning, unbeknownst to me, I was reading a passage in a book – *Horizon* by Barry Lopez – that, in retrospect, seems to provide the hint of an answer to this question:

> *In the beginning, before language and complex thinking, hominins pushed air up the trachea, shaping meaningful and comprehensible alarm calls and breeding calls. And then came something else, something that conveyed the meaning that melody can carry but which words can't. These were tones strung together around emotions and thought, runs of sound like the trills and vibrato in birdsong. Hominins came to know one another as individuals in a new way. The level of cooperation possible between hominins expanded by an order of magnitude.*
>
> *With his fingertips on the cranium of an australopithecine skull not much larger than a grapefruit, on the forward part of the vault where one day frontal lobes would rise up in Homo, he (a colleague in Africa) says, 'Barry, I can't prove this, but I believe we sang before we spoke.'*[6]

I don't know yet what exactly to do with this idea. But the purpose of this exercise is not to answer these rascally questions that have eluded answers for the better part of a lifetime. It is rather to open them up to the idea that beyond what we already know is an open space where something new can happen, if we are willing to go there with everything we have and everything we think we know now. This is where life becomes a sacred space, and a journey more deeply into a mystery that keeps on giving long after less intrepid souls have explained it all away. That is where I want to live, and that is where I go now with this idea that behind rational thoughts are words that haven't quite lost their poetic numinosity, and then, behind the words is music.

I can feel the sparks flying here, even if I can't yet know where they will land.

Following a Golden Thread

Is my golden thread taking me somewhere, or has it simply led me to the middle of nowhere, stranded in the deep woods?

Contemplating this question in the wake of the unexpected revelation I have just had in relation to the last one, it occurs to me that maybe the whole point of following a golden thread is to wind up in the deep woods. Metaphorically or not, as I sit here in these woods around my cabin, I realize I also sit in the middle of a symphony of birdsong.

Maybe the golden thread is not just a visual metaphor, but an auditory one, as well. Thinking back to Terrence McKenna's idea, introduced in Chapter One that language may have originally been a kind of synesthesia, in which sight and sound merged into a trans-linguistic experience of communion with the Transcendent Other, or the cosmos, or an archetypal field, together with Barry Lopez' insight in Africa about the music within or behind the words, then I am left with the sense that the next step along this path of following a golden thread might well involve learning to listen more deeply and engage the archetypal field with my ears, as well as my eyes, wide open. If, along this golden thread, these ideas merge with Kepler's interest in the harmony of the spheres, then perhaps there is more to explore here than mere ideas.

Moving in and out of Liminal Space

Although my life appears to have followed a rhythm pulsing through alternate phases of creative focus and the sense of being lost in the woods, I have to wonder now, largely in retrospect, if life itself is not a liminal experience?

Or to paraphrase the great Chinese sage, "Am I an astrologer who occasionally dreams he is a butterfly lost in the deep woods?" or "Am I a butterfly lost in the deep woods, who keeps dreaming he is an astrologer?"

I am, of course, long familiar with the time-worn metaphor that reminds us that "life is but a dream," and yet, working with my own dreams, I have gravitated to the work of people like Stephen Aizenstat (*Dream Tending*), Robert Bosnak (*Tracks in the Wilderness of Dreaming*), and Edward Tick (*The Practice of Dream Healing*). All three of them build on the work of Jung and Hillman, moving away from an interpretive approach to dreams, and toward a more exploratory strategy, such as I am suggesting here for work with astrology. Within the context of this paradigm shift, the suggestion that "life is but a dream" actually opens it up to a deeper, more richly meaningful experience.

I have the same attitude now toward liminal space, which is not just a hiatus or a lull between chapters of a life, but a pregnant void within which life reinvents itself. The key to experiencing liminal space this way, as with so many other aspects of the spiritual journey, is to pay attention and try not to miss a thing. Earlier in my life, liminal space was disconcerting, and my attention was invariably either drawn backwards to a past that had proven disappointing, or toward a future I could not quite touch, nor at times, even imagine. Now, at this point in my life, having been through many such rites of passage, they are not quite so intimidating. In fact, I feel a kind of open expectancy of nothing in particular, curious to see what comes next, not in any hurry to get there.

I feel my task, at this phase of my journey along this thread of Vesta's path, to be to simply pay more attention, be here now, come more fully into the present moment and observe what might otherwise escape my attention because my consciousness is elsewhere. If I can do this with the awareness that "life is but a dream," the dream itself may become more lucid as I awaken within it. If the dream is of being lost in the deep woods, then I can take solace in the fact that the deep woods is alive with presence to be soaked in through every pore and embodied.

Working at the Forge

> *If I am the real Great Work, slowly evolving at the forge at which I work, what is it that I am becoming that I can truly call great?*

I honestly don't know, but then again, if I did know, this would not be a worthy question to carry in my medicine bag. I don't think of myself as great, but maybe that is a good thing, as it means that whatever "great" might mean, for me it has little to do with ego. That kind of "great" is probably mostly an assessment by others, and yet others do not see the Great Work that unfolds at the forge, so how can they possibly know what they are talking about. It is, of course, human to want to be recognized for what we contribute with our best effort, but true greatness, it seems to me is merely a horizon that only we can see and that keeps receding the closer we get to it. It also has more to do with the integrity of my relationship with myself than to anything the world has to offer.

For me, the Great Work has been a lifetime effort of groping toward my best self, often unconsciously in darkness, and often in the invisible chambers of my own heart. At the beginning, I carried the baggage of self-judgment, internalized when others did not see or recognize me for who I felt myself to be, great or not. But over the years, as I have become more comfortable with myself, these judgments have mostly fallen away, to be replaced by a deepening self-acceptance. This self-acceptance is not a matter of complacency, as I am always reaching toward a clearer, more vibrant, more authentic, more fully integrated expression of who I am. But it is no longer about proving myself worthy to be myself. That I take as a given, not really knowing any other way to do it.

So, how would I describe this Great Work now? It seems to me that over the past few years, what I have been most earnestly working on is learning how not to take it personally, or shut down, or withdraw, when what I have to offer is not being received. Back in the days when I was far angrier than I am now, and at the same time, far more convinced that I was right, I was fully invested in asserting myself into the conversation and fighting for my place.

On one level, of course, this goes back to the ash pile incident, and the learning curve associated with my role in breaking the pattern set by my warring ancestors. But on a deeper level still it is more simply about occupying my place in the cosmos often without an agenda – it occurs to me now, like the oak trees that surround me. Oak trees offer themselves freely at all times, whether anyone else is paying attention or reaping the benefit of that, or not. In my relationship to the Great Work now, I aspire to be like an oak tree. Whatever greatness I attain doing that will not be for me to claim; and yet, along this path, there is always greatness in saying yes to essence, without strings, without needing anything in return. It is for this kind of greatness that I am reaching.

> *Was my time working intensively to raise my kundalini a preliminary step on the path to the discovery of my true forge, or is it an abandoned path I failed to follow as far as I could, because I ultimately could not stand the heat?*

If I am honest with myself, I will admit that over the years I have backed away from this heat, not just in terms of my exposure to my teachers who taught me how to raise it (Yogi Bhajan) or exposed me unrelentingly to it (Swami Muktananda), but also to those situations in my life that would otherwise tend to run hot. Learning to back away from anger, becoming increasingly apolitical – not just in terms of my response to the daily news, but in terms of my participation in life – retreating in this forest sanctuary apart from the hustle and bustle of the world, being retired from my "day job," no longer aspiring to climb to the top of the ash pile, or the mountain, any mountain, has all cooled me down, and made working at the forge a more tolerable and more sustainable experience.

I don't think this is necessarily a bad thing. On the other hand, given that the world itself is heating up – through climate change, through increasing tensions between white supremacists bent on hierarchical autocracy and progressive social democrats working toward a more egalitarian society, through mounting uncertainty in the face of large, intractable problems with no easy answers, seemingly getting worse – perhaps there is some way that I could bring more of my cooling presence, what I have learned and am learning as I align myself with Vesta, to the world.

What this would look like, at this point, I don't know. But in terms of this pattern of working at the forge and this question about the purifying fires of *kundalini*, it probably means walking more deliberately at the edge of my comfort zone, testing my resolve to be a neutral source and a steady, cooling flame amidst the chaotic turmoil of a world on fire. If I think in terms of working at the forge – not just in terms of my creative output, but in terms of my capacity to face the heat without burning – it occurs to me that learning how to intentionally cool things down is what this particular component of my spiritual work on myself might look like at this juncture.

On the other hand, I have also learned over the years that it is hardly necessary to go looking for a point of entry into the fire that burns all around us now. It is only necessary to be present and willing to respond, when the fire licks up against the door as it will do if and when there is another piece of work to be done. I see nothing on the horizon now, but would be a fool not to expect that a Pluto transit would not bring something.

Gestating Under a Cloak of Invisibility

> *Although I have learned to mostly be OK with invisibility, to hold it now as a kind of inside joke, rather than a mark of failure, I still have to wonder, "if a tree falls in the forest, and there is no one there to hear it, does it make a sound?" or in my particular version of this metaphysical version of a question about Schopenhauer's cat, "If what I do with my life remains invisible throughout, when I fall out of this life into death, will my life have made a sound?"*

On one level, I already know it has made a sound. It has mattered to many people – students, clients, readers, friends, lovers, everyone whose lives I have touched with my own. I haven't made a sound loud enough to gain me any kind of notoriety or fame or even very much recognition, but from Vesta's perspective, this is as it should be. This kind of sound would, in her domain, be way too loud.

Having said that, I do feel that to the extent I have been gestating something of value, I also have some responsibility for putting it out into the world. Lately, for example, I have begun to feel the dead weight of the 2,000+ copies of my first self-published book, *The Seven Gates of Soul*, languishing in my storage shed and am inclined to make it a focus to give the majority of those books away, perhaps to libraries, at least to start. Looking back to what I tried to do, along these same lines, in 2011, around Period 18, I recognize now a capacity I didn't have back then, to do the same with far less attachment. The goal is not suddenly to become more visible, but rather to be a little less complacent in my invisibility, and a little more proactive in affirming the value of what I have been gestating. Perhaps, as a step on my spiritual path in allegiance to this theme, I will start there, and see where it takes me.

Building a Temple

My relationship to this land continues to feel like life in a temple, and I continue to tend it as best I can. But I wonder, mostly what I do here, on the land, now that the transformative storm has come and gone, is to let the forest tend itself, and bear witness to that tending. Is that enough? Or is there a more active role yet for me to play?

If I get more specific about what I have actually done to tend the land, it has been mostly an extension of what I did in the aftermath of the storm – clearing away dead trees and making space for new growth, which within an oak forest is a process that doesn't actually require much human intervention. A friend, who also happens to be a professional forester, once described what I do as a Zen style of forest management – basically a minimalist approach. If a tree falls somewhere on my land, I cut it up for firewood, and then, if I happen to have a bit of gas left in my chain saw, I might do some judicious thinning of smaller, crowded trees (sometimes called "dog hair" in the joking vernacular of forest managers), or otherwise allow myself to consider what minor bit of pruning might improve the health of the forest at this particular spot. But otherwise, my tending of the forest is mostly hands-off, as opposed to the more typical active style of management.

The interesting thing about this approach is that it seems to create the tangible sense of being in a temple, of being in a self-regulating ecosystem where it is possible to feel the spaciousness of a forest that is free to be itself. In many cultures around the world, before there were churches or temples, indigenous peoples worshipped in groves of trees, including the sacred oak grove at Dordona in Greece, where priestesses and priests considered the rustling of the leaves in the trees to be an oracle.[7] Most of these sacred groves were probably old growth, the mighty oak being a towering presence that easily commands respect and awe.

This is not an old growth forest by any stretch, but it is a forest that has had almost half a century to do its own thing. I have friends comment on how much they appreciate the park-like nature of my land, and I just smile, for I have done nothing to create a park. Writing this now, my sense is that they are able to recognize the fact that they have entered a temple, a sacred grove of oaks, without using those words to describe their experience.

This tells me that, along this thread of my spiritual journey, I am on the right path. Having been away for the last three years, however, I have some catching up to do, as there are several downed trees I have not gotten to yet. Summer is coming now – not the best time to be out in the forest working – but as part of my spiritual path, along the tributary of this theme, this type of Zen forest management continues to be what calls me forward.

Becoming a Virgin

Although I have learned to be comfortable alone, outside of the context of relationship, I wonder if there is anything more for me to learn in relationship, and if so, what?

It occurs to me, as I follow the natural progression of these questions, that my current approach to relationship is very much like my approach to forest management. I don't really have a plan, but I am aware of being in relationship with a number of people, who for one reason or another, have adopted me, expressed an interest in my life, and who have opened a space for me to participate vicariously in theirs. I am continuing to cultivate these relationships, without very many preconceived ideas about where they might go. Some of these relationships are with women, who given the right conditions, could become more than friends. I am not actively seeking this, but I am also available, should a given relationship evolve in that direction.

This feels like a good place to be – a place where I don't necessarily need someone to complete me, but I can still enjoy interacting with others who bring something new or different or interesting into the space where I am becoming a virgin. I don't think there is anything in particular for me to do in this space, other than be open and receptive, and honest about my feelings and my vulnerabilities as they arise.

How much of my virginity is rooted in disappointment at my cumulative failure to make a lasting relationship work, and how much is a matter of evolving beyond the need for relationship?

From a philosophical perspective, I am of the mindset not to consider anything to be a failure that teaches me valuable lessons, and most certainly, each of my intimate relationships has done that. Over the years, I have learned much from various partners: the importance of letting the other person be who they are, and not who I think I need or want them to be; the necessity of being true to myself and not sacrificing anything essential in order to merge with another; a recognition that the art of sharing space only really works when the other person's space, physical and psychic, feels like home; the critical importance of good communication taken into the depths of shared vulnerability and what can happen when that fundamental resource is not a part of relationship; and my preference to be with someone who gets me, on every possible level, just as I get her – to name a few. All of this I take with me into every relationship, but especially those with whom I sense a potential for deepening intimacy.

I don't actually think it is possible to outgrow the need for relationship, but perhaps I have outgrown certain kinds of relationship that I have learned the hard way, simply don't work. At least, I like to think I have, without diminishing the ever-reverberating truth of the old cliché that love is blind. Yes, it is. I, however, am grateful for being able to see with the relative non-attachment that not being in love with anyone in particular affords me. My plan – if I have one at all – is to slow the whole process of relationship down, so that I can maintain this relative clarity of the heart, even as I keep my heart open to more, should more be in the offing.

Becoming a Comfortable Minimalist

Now that I have arrived in my happy place as a comfortable minimalist, is it enough to know that this creates a solid foundation on which I can do my work without distraction? Or is the abundance I have managed to create for myself merely the expression of an imbalanced relationship with the world around me, where living a minimal existence is not at all comfortable? If so, then what can I do about that, short of becoming unnecessarily uncomfortable myself?

Just recently, it has occurred to me that the life of a minimalist is not a passive venture, but rather one that requires a constant attention to the superfluous and the excess that, without such vigilance, can accumulate in any life. To be a minimalist is to continually ask myself where can the forest of my life benefit from pruning? Which of my possessions that I no longer use can I give away to someone else? Where can I use what I have to help someone else's life become better? My earlier thought, for example, that I might give away the spare copies of *The Seven Gates of Soul* currently collecting dust in my storage shed, for example, also represents this kind of step forward on the path of a minimalist.

At the other end, being a comfortable minimalist requires me to acknowledge where, if anywhere I am uncomfortable – as I did, for example, this past winter in recognizing that there might be times when wood heat is simply not enough to keep me warm, and took the additional step of installing a back-up mini-split system.

Translating this awareness into a component of my spiritual practice on this particular by-way through Vesta's archetypal field, I would be more vigilant about opportunities to create more circulation in the flow of goods and services through my space. Is this something that Vesta would do? Perhaps not directly, except with the understanding that the sacred flame she tends lies at the heart, not just of the hearth, but of the entire realm in which commerce and human enterprise swirl around a largely invisible center. The sacred flame itself sets up the movement of air around it, in which this pattern of circulation becomes a natural consequence. As I open myself to this possibility then, I find a new way – among many others likely yet to be discovered – to honor this goddess, who for whatever reason, is choosing to make herself known to me.

Opening to this Current Pluto Transit

Lastly, if I contemplate the questions that arise at the threshold of this current Pluto transit to Vesta, I can perhaps put this entire exercise in fleshing out the various dimensions of a spiritual path in allegiance to Vesta, into a more overarching context:

> *What is the more mature, more seasoned, wiser version of myself that you are challenging me to step into at this time, and how can I best cooperate with that challenge?*
>
> *What must I let go of in order to more fully claim my essence as a dedicated keeper of the hearth in all of the ways that manifests for me?*
>
> *How can I best use my vital life energy, my creativity, my sense of calling to the path that I am on now – to tend to my solitude, and my hearth – in a way that allows me to feel more deeply connected to others, to the world at large, and to the world around me – and to somehow make a difference in doing what I do, at this point in our collective history?*
>
> *Who is out there, or perhaps within me, who can teach me what I need to know in order to rise to a more significant level of possibility in making a contribution to this suffering world? How can I tend not just my own hearth but the sacred flame that burns at the heart of the anima mundi?*

To be honest, these questions are a bit daunting in their intensity, as I might expect when faced with a Pluto transit, even when a review of my previous history of Pluto transits brings with it as much exhilaration as trepidation. What becomes clear as I contemplate these questions, taken together, is that as I stand on the cusp of this three-and-a-half-year transformational experience, whatever that turns out to be for me, I am clearly reaching for something. I am seeking to embody

> *. . . a more mature, more seasoned, wiser version of myself . . . to more fully claim my essence . . . to feel more deeply connected to others, to the world at large, and to the world around me . . . to rise to a more significant level of possibility in making a contribution to this suffering world."*

I won't attempt to predict what this might look and feel like on the near shore of this Pluto transit. I will simply assume that as I walk the spiritual path Vesta has revealed to me, it will all naturally unfold.

Articulating My Spiritual Path in Allegiance to Vesta

Summarizing then, this is what this foray into self-reflection around the idea that something more is being asked of me, has yielded:

1) Look for opportunities to contribute something positive to the world, in alignment with my own internal sacred flame, burning clear and bright.
2) Be more aware of what ignites my fire stick and causes it to spark; then put more of my energy into that.
3) Listen to birdsong; and for the song humming at the heart of the *anima mundi.*
4) Be more willing to be; without an agenda just to see what shows up, what draws my attention.
5) Like an oak tree, learn how to simply offer my cooling presence to a world grown too hot, while spreading my branches beyond the reach of my comfort zone.
6) Turn my first self-published book *The Seven Gates of Soul* into a giveaway.
7) Continue actively practicing the Zen of forest management.
8) Be open and receptive; be honest about my feelings and my vulnerabilities to myself and others; practice clarity of the open heart.
9) Be aware of opportunities to create more circulation in the flow of goods and services through my space.

If you, dear reader, are wondering at this point, what this spiritual practice has to do with my birthchart, or with astrology as it is usually practiced, the honest answer is: not much. And yet, if we can consider the birthchart to be a portal into a more conscious participatory relationship with the cosmos, then it should be possible to also see that these practices are a prescription for exactly that, arrived at through a process of self-reflection that is rooted in a distinctly astrological way of knowing. From this perspective, the birthchart and your astrological understanding of it is not the end of the journey, but just the beginning.

Where this process will take you is not written in your chart or in the sky until you write it through the choices that you make. If you write with humility, knowing this life to be nothing more than an elaborate invitation to commune with the sacred pulsing at the heart of all the archetypes, then what you create with your life will matter more than what you can merely read in your chart.

Notes

1. Campion, Nicholas. *A History of Western Astrology Volume I: The Ancient and Classical Worlds*. Bloomsbury, 2008, 36.
2. Campion, *A History of Western Astrology Volume I*, 42.
3. Campion, *A History of Western Astrology Volume I*, 62.
4. Cornelius, Geoffrey. *The Moment of Astrology: Origins in Divination*. Wessex Astrologer Limited, 2002, 132.
5. Covey, Stephen R. *The 7 Habits of Highly Effective People: Powerful Lessons in Personal Change*. Simon and Schuster, 1989, 83.
6. Lopez, Barry. *Horizon*. Vintage, 2019, 342-43.
7. Ludwig Preller quoted in Frazer, James George. *The Golden Bough: The Roots of Religion and Folklore*. New York: Crown, 1981, 291.

The ground principles, the *archai*, of the unconscious are indescribable because of their wealth of reference, although in themselves recognizable. The discriminating intellect naturally keeps on trying to establish their singleness of meaning and thus misses the essential point. For what we can above all establish as the one thing consistent with their nature is their manifold meaning, their almost limitless wealth of reference, which makes any unilateral formulation impossible.

Carl Jung, Archetypes of the Collective Unconscious, 1934

Chapter Seventeen

Getting Intimate with the Cosmos

If it is not obvious by now, in outlining an astrological epistemology in Part Two of this book, I have been essentially working backwards through the various eras of our history, as outlined in Part One. I am attempting to reclaim as I go, what has been lost along the way, in part, because astrologers of the day made the compromises that they did in order to fit within the overall cultural zeitgeist of each era. This is a perspective that is possible now, in no small measure, because within the Era of Uncertainty, as a global culture, we better understand the relativity of each perspective, as well as the value of entertaining multiple perspectives in relation to anything we wish to know. Within such a climate, we astrologers are free at last to claim our own identity, as a postmodern language with which to parse the meaning of life, rooted in a participatory relationship between cosmos and psyche - one that was once as natural to us as breathing, and one that we can know again.

As I have pointed out throughout this book, what this freedom means, first and foremost, is that we need not try to couch any postmodern definition of astrology in scientific terms, even if we could. I have also tried to point a way beyond a pretension to scientific credibility in pursuing an approach to psychological astrology that potentially opens a portal to a deeper, more intimate relationship between psyche and cosmos, demonstrating as I go, how one might actually move through this portal.

The Method to My Madness

The caveat here is that this is by no means the only possible path forward. But hopefully by now, the attentive reader can begin to see some method to my madness, which revolves around the idea that what the birthchart actually reveals at any given time depends upon who is observing it, how clearly they can see into it, and ultimately how well they can embody what they see.

Opening the Archetypal Eye

We began in Chapter Eleven, by opening the archetypal eye. If you can accept the premise that the birthchart describes the interplay of planetary archetypes within both cosmos and psyche, then it helps to have a frame of reference and a methodology with which to explore this interplay. The frame of reference is the global canon of mythological stories, fairy tales, and folklore that has served as a reservoir of perennial wisdom, out of which one generation has passed to the next its cultural pearls, since the beginning of time – most of which have astrological correlates. Within this frame of reference, the archetypal stories often parallel and mirror our personal stories, which is where we begin our quest into territory that is at once universal and deeply personal to each of us.

While this is potentially a complex, multi-dimensional exploration, given the presence of between seven and an almost infinite number of celestial bodies within a birthchart, depending on which kind of astrology you practice, you can greatly simplify the task by focusing on one archetype at a time. Here, you can lean into the idea that each planetary archetype represents a holographic facet of the self, or a subpersonality, with its own somewhat unique perspective. Within the entire archetypal field and the life that takes place within that field, each planetary archetype will appear differently, feel differently, and yield a different sense of meaning than the others – and yet, at the same time, it is also, in its own way, representative of the whole.

With training, it is possible to develop the archetypal eye to be able to see and understand the birthchart from multiple perspectives, including all of the hybrids made possible through aspects, patterns of rulership, and planetary patterns. But just as interpreting a birthchart is rarely a matter of grasping everything everywhere all at once, so too is opening the archetypal eye best approached as a matter of noticing which archetype seems to be coming into the foreground at any given time, and focusing there.

Sometimes this is a matter of activation by transit; sometimes it is just an intuition. In my case, choosing Vesta was initially an intuition spawned by observing what was happening in the sky at the time, perhaps in the way an astrologer from the Mystical Era might do, but then this choice morphed into a deeper awareness of an activation by transit that hadn't previously registered. In any case, it helps at this stage of the process to find a single focal point, with the broader awareness that everything is ultimately connected to everything else, and regardless of where you start, with the right intention, you can find your way into the heart of your birthchart.

Once you have your focus, opening the archetypal eye begins as you familiarize yourself with the myths and stories associated with the archetype you are seeking to understand. Because Western astrology is rooted in the Greco-Roman tradition, it is natural to begin with the deities for whom the planets are named. This exploration, however, need not stop there, as other associations to the relevant myths, fairy tales, bits of folklore, and teaching stories of other cultures from around the world, are all available points of reference within a postmodern reach, as are pieces of world literature, films, poems, paintings, photographs, and other cultural expressions.

The goal here is not to compose a scholarly dissertation offering a global, multi-dimensional perspective on the nature of the archetype being explored, but to see where the resonance lies for you. This resonance will derive, in part, through a broad reference to your own life experience, within a context of freeform association. In my case, for example, I was able to make a connection between Vesta, a Native American flute, *kundalini shakti*, the cinder biters of Norwegian Viking culture, and the Queen of Wands – references that another astrologer with a different set of experiences and a different sense of resonance to the same archetype would not likely make.

Thus, what you are doing in opening the archetypal eye is not a matter of gaining objective perspective, in the way that a scientist, or even a strictly logical astrologer might aspire to do, but rather a matter of entering into a more personal relationship to the archetype and seeing what arises naturally as that relationship unfolds. This is not something you could necessarily predict ahead of time, even if you had read everything that was previously written about the archetype you are exploring. This is so because as the quantum physicists discovered over one hundred years ago now, you can't observe anything without changing the nature of what you observe. The act of observation itself is entering into an experiment in which your participation is as much a factor in the outcome as what it is you observe.

In opening the archetypal eye, then, what you see is not necessarily the archetype itself, but a facet of the archetype that reflects your relationship to it. From a scientific standpoint, this is contamination by observer bias. From the perspective we are exploring in this book, however, this is where astrology starts to get interesting. This is where you get to throw your cookbooks away, and begin cooking; where the symbolism comes alive, because you have fully invested it with your imaginative, associative, and creative attention.

Opening the archetypal eye, in the way that I have described it, is something that we can only do now because of all that has come before. In the Era of Uncertainty, we have the postmodern freedom to be eclectic in how we seek our personal truth, which has become more a matter of personal resonance than an allegiance to tradition, authority, or dogma. We inherently understand, at least potentially, the relativity of our perceptions, beliefs and opinions in a way that would not have been possible in previous eras. We also have the historical global perspective to reach across time and space in our choice of sources, living as we do in a much broader field of influences, resources and possibilities than at any other time in history – not just astrological, psychological, or even mythological, but archeological, anthropological, biological, historical, cultural and spiritual.

The more exposure you have to this broader field, and the more open-minded and eclectic you can be, the deeper your exploration of archetypes can go. While astrologers can be just as attached to their understanding as any human being, with the archetypal eye open, there is also the opportunity to attain a level of understanding that is fluid, alive within a living field of endlessly fresh information, and capable of evolving into a vibrant embodiment of archetypal wisdom. This depends less upon what you think you know, and more upon how open and receptive within the archetypal field you can be. Opening the archetypal eye, in the way I have described it, is a good first step.

Astrological Hermeneutics

The next step is to enter more deeply into your personal experiences with the archetypal eye open. Allow ample room for free association to memories of personal experiences that, outside any kind of astrological frame of reference, seem to be part of the overall resonance with the archetype you have chosen to explore. This helps to establish an intuitive relationship to the archetype in the broadest possible way as you enter a more specific astrological framework that derives from the orbital motion of the associated celestial body. In my case, asteroid Vesta's 3.6-year cycle creates an extended framework for a more empirical observation of Vesta's archetypal presence in my life.

I call this process taking a cyclical history, which is in essence, a method of gathering data. As noted in Chapter Thirteen, this kind of astrological empiricism is distinctly different than scientific empiricism in that it is entirely anecdotal, based on the inherently unreliable and James Hillman would add *imaginal* exercise of memory, and not subject to or in need of outside replication, or any kind of objective validation by consensus.

What matters in taking a cyclical history is that you find those memories that seem most relevant to the broad sense of the archetype you have developed this far, with your archetypal eye open, for these are the memories that will make your general sense of resonance with the archetype more specific. In this step, you are, in a sense, gathering data that establishes this relationship, not just as a vague abstraction, but through an actual history of your interaction with the archetype.

With sufficient data, you can then begin to identify various themes that are consistent with your sense of the archetype as you have experienced it so far. Some of these themes may be confirmed by what has been written about these archetypes by other astrologers or mythologists, but some of them may evolve as a matter of discovery that has limited precedence.

In my case, for example, the theme of becoming a cinder biter revolves around my family name and an ancestral history of a relationship to war. This is a trail through Vesta's archetypal field that is mostly personal to me and that would probably not show up in a generic survey of Vesta's archetypal domain. I can associate this theme with Hestia's apolitical stance in a highly charged political field, but this is not something that to my knowledge has been written about elsewhere, except perhaps as a minor footnote to Vesta's already meager mythological canon. It is certainly not something on the radar screen of most astrologers, even though, in a far more general way, the symbolic association of fire and anger is well established.

The same is true of many of the other themes I have identified – from following a golden thread to gestating something under a cloak of invisibility to becoming a comfortable minimalist. Hopefully, the reader can see how all these themes are consistent with the field in which Vesta takes archetypal shape and derives meaning, but the elaboration of these themes and the particular experiences that constitute the history of their evolution in my life are fairly unique to me. Even within a more easily recognizable theme, such as what I am calling becoming a virgin, revolving around the universal association of Vesta with the Vestal virgins of Roman lore, the empirical elucidation of that theme as it plays out within my life still makes it uniquely my own.

The important thing here is not to derive a set of themes with universal recognition and applicability, but to more clearly delineate your relationship to an archetype along multiple tracks that together weave a richer tapestry than a more monolithic understanding could ever do. Within the context of the idea that this is an astrological form of empiricism, this step would then be the equivalent of looking at the same pattern through a microscope or telescope with higher powers of magnification and seeing more clearly into the intricacies of the pattern.

I have called this step astrological hermeneutics, which is distinct from hermeneutics practiced as a technique of qualitative research. Here, we are not necessarily attempting to bring rational order to the irrational chaos of a multi-dimensional life, so much as we are focusing our archetypal imagination within a personal history of experiences. A sense of order does emerge through this process, but it is one that might not make sense to anyone else but you.

We are not, as Richard Tarnas did in exploring Uranus, conducting an exhaustive survey in order to arrive at some objective sense of an archetype. In this context, Tarnas' exploration is useful in adding to the field of possibilities that might be surveyed in relation to Uranus with the archetypal eye, but where the goal is self-understanding, it is the excavation of this field for shards of personal relevance that is more to the point and closer to what we are doing here.

Nor are we, as Glenn Perry did in his exhaustive case study of a particular birthchart, attempting to demonstrate astrology's utility in illuminating the various themes that run through a life using a hermeneutic approach, although we are illuminating themes in a more focused way. Our point of departure merely assumes astrology's utility for this purpose and then attempts to fine tune that utility in a way that allows it to take on a life of its own, largely outside of preconceived ideas about what astrology, as it is more traditionally practiced, might tell us.

When I explore the theme of following a golden thread, for example, this theme emerges not from any identifiable astrological reference to Vesta or anything else in the birthchart, but rather from my observation of the resonance between my introduction to this idea during a Vesta return, and the sense of Vesta that I have developed in opening my archetypal eye. There is nothing here that would corroborate astrology's utility to an outside non-astrological observer, or even to another astrologer, although this is an awareness meaningful to me that evolved out of an archetypal exploration conducted within an astro-logical framework. The window of observation was astrologically determined, but what I observed, and the connections that I made to the archetype I am exploring were personal to me and transcend astrology.

Astrological hermeneutics in this sense is not about using qualitative techniques to validate astrology, but rather of using astrology as a framework within which meaningful, though highly idiosyncratic observations can be made and organized in a way that makes sense to the observer. At this point, there is really no limit to what can be noticed or what conclusions might be drawn about what you see with the archetypal eye open, although your previous investigation of the mythological stories will potentially put you in a state of mind where what you observe resonates within the larger field of possibilities that the archetype encompasses. This, at least, is our goal – one that is far less ambitious than proving astrology's worth, while at the same time, already taking us farther and more deeply into the subjective nuances of the birthchart than a more rational and objective form of hermeneutic analysis ever could.

Orienting Within an Archetypal Field

This kind of exploration can sometimes be as overwhelming as it is exciting, and it can also lead into the deep woods, where getting lost is a distinct possibility. Sometimes the path dead-ends. Sometimes you get to a place that merely seems impenetrable, largely because you are not yet emotionally, psychologically or spiritually ready to see what lies beyond. Sometimes you come to a fork in the road, with no clear sense of which way to turn. If you are successful in your exploration of the birthchart, in the way that I am describing, whichever way you turn, it will take you somewhere you have never been before, somewhere off the map.

This is precisely where the astrological birthchart can become useful as a map – not in any kind of literal way, dictating where you must go, but in showing you the lay of the land, including the particular astro-logical song lines that weave through the archetypal field into which you were born. This is true in the same way that the rational mind can seem like more solid ground than a free flight of intuition or a foray into the imaginal realms, into Corbin's eighth clime. It is also true, I believe, in a larger context, in which humans have insisted on rational underpinnings for all statements of truth, and eschewed or denigrated the more imaginal meanderings of poets, sybils and madmen for most of our cultural history. Sometimes the *yin* path of imaginal meandering can be a slippery slope, at which point, it becomes useful to re-engage the logical mind.

Ideally, we want to find a sweet spot of integration or at least peaceful co-existence between logic and imagination, and the birthchart – considered astropoetically – offers us that possibility. I'm sure every practicing astrologer has come to the place in their practice where logical analysis of the birthchart leads to a boring and meaningless flatland. This is always a danger when the birthchart is merely interpreted as an exercise in rational deciphering of symbolism. On the other hand, to approach the birthchart psychically – that is to say, as a merely imaginal exercise, can also lead to some pretty strange places, where imagination easily becomes contaminated by undigested emotions, unresolved psychological patterns, and belief systems that filter and distort the message. My sense is that to make best use of a birthchart, we need both the *yin* of imaginal meandering through an uncharted archetypal field, and the *yang* of a symbolic logic that preserves a certain archetypal integrity and cohesion within the same field.

In this sense, knowing that Vesta in my chart sits in the 2nd house in the sign of Capricorn, conjunct Venus and Jupiter, and is currently being transited by Pluto provides an astro-logical context for my meandering that keeps me from straying too far afield. While not preventing me from getting lost, it will at least offer a compass with which I can find my way back to more familiar ground. If, for example, being in liminal space or laboring for too long under my cloak of invisibility leads to a diminishment of my sense of self-worth, at any given part of my journey, I can understand this to be a reflection of the astro-logical fact that Vesta is in my 2nd house, where the task is to cultivate a more solid sense of self-worth that is not dependent on external validation.

If, along the path of a cinder biter, I should encounter someone or a situation that arouses my anger, I can remember that my Vesta is in a cardinal sign, where I can expect to be provoked and to sometimes provoke others, in order to learn something about myself.

With Vesta in an earth sign, I know that my job is to provide a solid container for the sacred flame, so that in part, it does not flare out of control, and burn down the house. Knowing the logic of this placement then allows me to appreciate the cosmic humor behind the set-up, in which Vesta's function in my psyche is to test my capacity to successfully contain fire without putting it out, and will, if I can stay with this test long enough, lead me to mastery. Remembering this allows me to maintain my bearings, and keeps me from straying too far into the deep woods, where anything goes, but ultimately where meaning dissipates.

In proposing that symbolic logic can be a useful guidance system for navigating the imaginal realm, we must also recognize that logic is largely in the eye of the beholder, and relative to the one for whom it makes rational sense. In the Philosophical Era, there were many schools of thought, each of which considered itself rational, and yet, each of which drew different conclusions about the nature of reality, and the relationship between human beings and the cosmos. Within astrological circles there are multiple systems of logic, that were worked out by the Hellenistic astrologers (which in and of itself, was not uniform), differing considerably from that employed, let's say, by Vedic astrologers, Mayan astrologers or Chinese astrologers, or even within the Western traditions, from that employed by cosmobiologists, siderealists or Uranian astrologers.

In my previous books, *Tracking the Soul* and *Astrology and the Archetypal Power of Numbers, Part Two*, I worked out additional systems of astro-logic based on a correlation of planetary patterns and *chakras*, and planetary patterns and tenets of Pythagorean number theory, respectively. Although I would be the first to suggest that these systems are not to be employed in any kind of dogmatic way, once inside the system, I would also suggest they are useful in their own right. I suspect the same is true for most astrologers, each of whom has adopted their system of choice, or in some cases, their hybrid system of choice, because it makes rational sense to them, and because it does, then it also works for them.

The point here, however, is that presented with a birthchart, there is no one system of astro-logic that holds a definitive answer. In many respects, my experience as an astrologer has taught me that each birthchart has its own logic, which is inherent in its structure, but that also derives in part from how the native of the chart has chosen to navigate it. The chart itself is an ongoing invitation to a participatory exercise, out of which a certain organic logic begins to emerge.

To the extent, for example, that my experience of Vesta in the 2nd house requires me to learn how to do more with less, which at times, it has, then it makes sense to consider this placement in light of the usual counterclockwise consideration of houses in parallel to their correspondent signs. That is to say, in this case, the 2nd house becomes an earth house that correlates with the fixed sign of Taurus, and Vesta in the 2nd house becomes a matter of consolidating resources and doing more with less. When, however, I begin to understand and experience the freedom that becoming a comfortable minimalist affords me, then it actually makes more sense to consider the 2nd house in terms of daily rotation of the Earth about its axis, within which Vesta is moving clockwise and is still invisible but rising.

The archetypal field, in this case, remains the same, but the astro-logic with which we approach it shifts the way we see it. Conversely, how we see it, and experience it, and live it, will dictate how best to approach the archetypal field as an exercise in logic. In a postmodern era, the freedom to move from one logical system to another when it better fits need no longer be the taboo it would have been in the Logical Era, when we were compelled to defend our system of choice and argue its merits within a crowded, competitive field of alternatives. Of course, many still do that now, both within and outside of the astrological community, but if the goal of exploring a birthchart is to trigger insights and yield perspective, then rigid adherence to any one system is a liability, or at best, a temporary aid to the beginner's false sense of security.

Finding A Worthy Quest

In the end, we all choose a logical framework that makes sense to us, and a great deal can be discovered within any framework that is mastered by the one who uses it. But as long as the choice is unconsciously made, the framework itself will limit what we can see and what we cannot. This is why the next step in my proposed path of astrological epistemology is to become clearer about who it is that chooses the system and about what you believe dictates your choices.

Beliefs, of course, are often invisible and, at times unconscious, so in order to take this step, it is necessary to ask yourself some fundamental questions. In Chapter Fifteen, I outlined what might be considered a starter set of questions, derived through the astro-logic of the Chaldean order, moving from the outermost planet in the solar system to the Sun at its core, the metaphor being that where we are ultimately going with these questions is into the very interior of your psyche, where you are most you, but at the same time, where you are most likely to be most invisible to yourself.

At first, your beliefs may initially appear to be a matter of resonance with certain ideas to which you were exposed, perhaps in childhood as a matter of conditioning by a family worldview, or religion, or the educational system, or the culture of the era into which you were born. Some of these beliefs will derive or become modified by what you subsequently read, watch, hear, learn or most importantly, what you experience as you move through your adult life.

As you become more aware that what you believe is, at least in part, dictated by what you have experienced, you can begin to more specifically map these experiences to the relevant astrological cycles in which they arise, which in turn will color how you think about the various factors in your birthchart and the logic you bring to your understanding of what makes sense as you look at your birthchart.

The most important beliefs, however, will be those that only take you so far, before they seem to unravel in a set of questions that are not that easy to answer. Logicians, beginning with the Cretan poet Epimenides in the sixth century B.C.E., found this impasse in the idea of paradox – questions that cannot be answered, such as:

If all astrologers are liars, and I am an astrologer, is this statement true?

Which came first, the chicken or the egg?

or statements that contradict themselves, such as:

All that I know is that I know nothing.

The opposite of a great truth is another great truth.

The Eastern version of paradox is the Zen *koan:*

What is the sound of one hand clapping?

What was your name before your mother was born?

These are questions that defy and transcend logic. In terms of our exploration here, they are questions that arise where belief ends, where in fact, we don't know what to believe, where, if we are honest with ourselves, we must inevitably declare, "I don't know."

Consider, for example, the question, "What happens when we die?" While I could conjure many possible answers drawn from religion, philosophy and spiritual teachings, the most honest answer I could give is, "I don't know. Ask me again when I am dead."

The process is one, in fact, where you start at the surface, with more generic questions, and gradually move into a place where the questions that arise are far more personal to you. You can, at this point in the process, use the various themes you have identified in the hermeneutics phase as the springboard for questions that take you to the cutting edge of your knowing. This is the place where a deeper relationship to the archetype you are exploring becomes possible, one that begins to bypass your preconceived ideas about what it means. In this place, questions are far more powerful than answers, even though the conscious mind, the one who thinks it is in charge, is likely to balk at this suggestion.

When you have arrived at your most relevant set of questions for you, you are likely to recognize them as those you have carried with you for a lifetime, questions more like paradoxes or Zen *koans* with no easy or final answer the logical mind can recognize, and that in some way have served as a pivot point of learning and growth as you circle around them. In my own exploration, for example, I ask, "Where is my power to truly make a difference at this point in my life?" This is a question I have asked at many times in my life, and that I expect to keep on asking. It doesn't ever fully resolve, although from day to day, it often allows a working answer to guide my actions.

Cultivating a Spiritual Practice

As these questions come more consciously to the fore, and you pay more deliberate attention to them, they naturally begin to constellate as a spiritual practice that is fairly unique to you. You are finding your way through an archetypal field and the archetypes are a collective resource. But this does not mean that the issues that you wrestle with and the lessons that you are learning have never been encountered before. The more deeply you enter into a relationship with these worthy questions, the more nuanced the specific practices become, infused as they are with divine intelligence that knows you as well, if not better, than you think you know yourself.

This intelligence, which necessarily filters itself through your imperfect understanding, and is colored by the emotional residues and the imaginal embellishments that you bring to your memory of the journey to this point, nonetheless takes you most directly to where you need to go next in order to take another step toward a deeper embrace of the full radiance of the Self that you are.

Some of these next steps will be to heal what remains broken, fragmented, wounded within you, so that you can function more seamlessly as a whole being, in which all the selves come more together in a magnificent symphony of expression.

Some of these next steps will be toward a more fully realized actualization of this symphony, toward honing the exquisite gifts you have been given, so that your contribution to the wellbeing of the larger Self that we share will continue giving, even after your body falls away.

Some of these next steps, and often the most mysterious, the ones that make the least rational sense, will entice you toward a horizon somewhere in the eighth clime, where your life is but one breath in the larger life of the divine, and as you participate in that breath, you are filled with presence. This is that ineffable place where the small self dissolves into the Self, and yet loses nothing as you surrender what was never yours to begin with in order to partake more fully of All That Is.

Some of these steps, as I outlined mine in Chapter Sixteen, are fairly sensible: "Look for opportunities to contribute something positive to the world, in alignment with my own internal sacred flame, burning clear and bright." This makes fairly rational sense as a spiritual practice that will take me forward in my ongoing attempt to "be all I can be."

Other steps are a bit less easily understood in terms I can identify with an ordinary life in progress: "Listen to birdsong; and for the song humming at the heart of the *anima mundi*." What does this even mean? Can I possibly know until I somehow find a way to actually do it? And is doing it even possible without leaving this world behind? If I lean into this possibility, I find myself peering through a veil, not unlike the famous woodcut by nineteenth century French artist Camille Flammarion – *L'atmosphère Météorologie Populaire*.

Participating More Fully in a Living Cosmos

Peering through this veil takes us to our last step in this process of astrological epistemology, which I will remind the faithful reader here, is ultimately about knowing what it only becomes possible to know when we ease the artificial barriers between self and other - ultimately, I would argue between self and Self - and enter into a more intimate relationship with whatever lies, or appears to lie, on the other side of that barrier. We are at this point, essentially going back to the experience of *participation mystique* that lay at the heart of knowing in the Mythopoetic Era, and deliberately evoking what may have been a more unconscious choice for our distant ancestors.

It has been the premise of this book that astrology is potentially a language that allows us to explore this possibility. In order to take us to the threshold, however, it has been necessary first to go backward into our history, to take stock of what has been lost, as astrologers have attempted to conform and take their place within each era, paying homage in particular to the science of the day. It has also been necessary to make some attempt to reclaim what was lost in paying the price for this adaptation, in much the same way, that each of us must individually assess our conditioning by society and reassess what is more innately true for us personally, before we can claim a more authentic self.

In doing this, we have likely arrived at a place that is somewhat unfamiliar to most astrologers, a place where the reasonable among us would be expected to ask: Is this still astrology that we are doing here? The answer to that question will depend upon how willing you are to honor our history, but at the same time, take a broader, deeper and older view of that history, circling back to our origins, not just in theory, but also in practice, all the way back to a time before astrology had a name.

If you are willing to do this, then you will enter a time and a sacred space when Vesta, for example, is no longer just an abstract concept that gave her name to a particular glyph in a birthchart, but a living presence that both challenges us and completes us. This is possible only to the extent that you enter into a *hieros gamos* with her, a mystical communion that breeches the safe, but limiting boundaries of your separate self.

If you'd rather just think about your chart, and what it means as an intellectual construct through a more pedestrian interpretation that the mind can grasp, that is always an option. That is, in fact, mostly what astrologers have done for the last two thousand years.

If, on the other hand, you can recognize the chart as a mere portal to an exploration of an archetypal field, where actual communion with the gods and goddesses that dwell within the field is on offer, then perhaps you can appreciate how the process I have outlined in this book has taken you to the edge of that possibility. The last step is a bit more intimidating, even for me, since I have not actually taken it yet myself, even though I feel myself yearning to bravely feel my way into it and describe what that might be like, even as I realize that for you, it might be quite different.

Courting Vesta

When I read the language that I have been using as I edge toward the possibility of *hieros gamos*, of mystical union with Vesta, I can easily imagine myself courting her in the way that I might a potential lover. Of course, in this case, the irony is not lost on me that Vesta, or at least Hestia, the Greek goddess, was quite firm in her vow of chastity, and not especially open to being courted. Having said that, and recognizing at the same time, that in my chart, Vesta dwells in tandem with Venus and Jupiter (Aphrodite and Zeus), I cannot help but be drawn nonetheless to this possibility, despite the fact that from a strictly mythological perspective, courting Hestia/Vesta is at best an oxymoron, at worst a fool's errand, not likely to be met with success.

I think, at this point, to cross the threshold of this final step, governed by *participation mystique*, however, one has to be a Fool, that is to say, endowed with a healthy dose of beginner's mind, and open to imaginal possibilities that don't exist until we conjure them. So then, it is in this spirit, that I persist.

Leaving aside for the moment that sometimes, in this imperfect world, people court other people for all sorts of secondary agendas, approaching this exercise as a Fool, any courting I might do can only begin with love. Only a Fool in Love can cross the threshold. It is no coincidence that Christian mystics, Sufi poets, and pagan bards all used the language of love to cross the threshold in which union with the divine became possible. Although it is not the only way, this is probably the most potent as well as the most commonly familiar opening we contemporary seekers in the Era of Uncertainty have to the experience of *participation mystique*, where the barriers break down and we get to speak about knowing an archetype, not in the abstract but in an almost Biblical sense of "having had intercourse with."

What this means in practice is that to court Vesta, to know her, not as an outside observer but through my union with her, I must first "count the ways" in which I love her, not just in the abstract but in which I actually feel that love.

Of all the themes I have outlined that describe my relationship with her, sitting here in this moment, the one that seems to evoke this deepest sense of love is the idea that in tending this forest sanctuary that is my home, I am building her a temple. As I write this, a mourning dove coos in the background of a simmering summer day. I am surrounded by the healing green energy of trees, basking in late afternoon light that penetrates the canopy in dappled patterns. This place exists in stark contrast to the world "out there" in which dark forces of willful ignorance serve toxic patterns that undermine the very fabric of life in which this forest sanctuary exists. And yet, here at the heart of the temple, the sacred flame burns with quiet, steady reassurance that is a palpable antidote to anything that might otherwise disquiet the mind, unsettle the heart, and cast a shadow on the hungry soul that sits here, soaking it all in with immense gratitude.

* * * * *

As I sit on my deck the following day with my morning cup of coffee, I catch a glimpse of a bright red northern cardinal darting through the canopy of healing green, its unlikely contrast with its surroundings a call to attention. It is not unusual to see a cardinal here, as they are ubiquitous and do not migrate in winter. And yet, despite their omnipresence, I do not see that many. When I do, I always get a bit of a lift, as to me, they represent hope for the kind of future that increasingly seems out of reach.

Cardinals are hardy survivors. Unlike other birds that either live here or pass through from time to time – Whip-poorwills, Red-headed Woodpeckers, Eastern Towee, and ten other species that are considered highly vulnerable; and Canadian Geese, American Robins, House Wrens, American Goldfinches; Yellow Warblers, and twenty-two other species that are considered moderately vulnerable to climate change, northern cardinals are considered species of low concern.[1] As climate changes, they appear to be expanding their territory and adapting.

I am tempted to call the cardinal Vesta's bird, although there are certain ways the epithet would not fit. Cardinals are sometimes known as "angry birds," because while fiercely defending their territory, especially during mating season, they will attack anyone who comes near the nest. They have even been known to fight their own reflection in a window for hours, and several cardinals have banged into my windows here, from time to time.

This attribute does not fit well with my Vestal aspiration to become a cinder biter, one who is more Hestia-like in her apolitical refusal to get caught up in the fitful thrashings of a world, where most territory – geographical, political, religious, professional and cultural – is routinely defended with irrational and sometimes violent intensity. The cardinal would seem to be a more typical reflection of this world, and yet, its defense of its territory somehow seems more understandable and more justifiable than most of what humans fight over in their hubris and willful ignorance. I myself have fought for the integrity of this forest sanctuary when I thought it was threatened, whether it actually was, or not. I like to think that the cardinal and I share a love for this forest, which we are both willing to defend in order to keep its sacred flame alive – although I am sure that is just a projection on my part.

On the other hand, the fact that I am making such a projection suggests that I am possibly entering a state of *participation mystique* in which what I think I see becomes a reflection of who I am. This cardinal was apparently not alarmed by my presence; in fact, it seemed to hop closer, as though curious about me, in order to better watch me from its safe perch above. Similarly, the white-tailed deer who graze across landscape often stop to wonder, as do

I, when we encounter each other on the path. Even the shyest of creatures – the box turtle who lives here too – seems to keep its head poked out of its shell during our encounters until I move. The trees, of course, do not move, or at least they do not run away as I approach. But they too, seem not just to tolerate me being here, but welcome me, curious two-legged alien that I am.

In any case, all of these creatures, animal, plant and lichen-covered rocks, all seem to belong here, as do I. We are neighbors in this sacred temple, this sanctuary in which the sacred flame at the heart of it all, is keeping us all alive – but more than that, at least in my case, is giving me a reason to live. Just to be able to appreciate this place daily, off the beaten path, in regular conversation with my more-than-human neighbors, is more than enough reason to be alive, curious and engaged, steeped in tangible mystery, available to the constant movement of life all around and through me.

I cannot help but feel this life is Vesta's gift to me, and I love her deeply for freely giving it. I have lived in other places, had and still have other reasons to live, but at the end of the day, and at the end of each chapter of my life, I have returned to this stillness, where the hum of the hearth makes itself known through birdsong, the rustling of the wind in the trees, and comforting silence.

I am reminded now of the poem I wrote, returning to this place, shortly after transiting Pluto began the first wave of its current conjunction to natal Vesta:

Going Home

I've got hoot owls outside my window,
mooning with earnest concern,
skittish deer, drawn despite themselves by careful curiosity,
the occasional wild coyote,
ravishing some hapless creature caught in the wrong ravine,
and trees that think I am one of them, all around me.

I am not alone,
but my fellow humans keep their distance.

Perhaps it is the green phosphorescence slowly engulfing me
as I become a part of this forest community,
a clueless upstart newcomer,
but welcome nonetheless
as is all of life in the deep woods.

If I could track myself through the oak leaf litter,
perhaps I would note the place
where my human foot left the ground for the last time,
and something else emerged with a grunt or a sigh of relief,
something with fleet-footed fur,
fluted wing or gnarled bark-like skin,
something committed
to photosynthesize and compost and
feed the myriad creatures
that call this place home
with the one and only life
that I had to give,

a life that was not mine to give,
but that I gave anyway
gladly

to those who would receive it.

I love Vesta for putting these words into my mouth, the succulent fruit of the forge at which I labor to give birth to the best of everything that gestates within me, invisible to the world, but eminently shareable, nonetheless. As my t-shirt notes, "*I live in my own little world. But it's OK. They know me here.*" Within my own little world, I am blessed to have had many friends and lovers, clients and students, even a sister, who have known me well. Like my more-than-human neighbors, these members of my tribe and I are bound by love. Most of them, it seems, also know what it means to live in relative obscurity, yet find purpose and meaning in life while taking delight in its small, endearing gestures.

They know I can be wordy, and they forgive me for that. Many of them appreciate my words, and whatever hard won wisdom forges them, even if they can't quite see the golden thread that snakes invisibly through the underbrush of the deep woods in which I occasionally get lost. I love this golden thread, another gift from Vesta, and have even learned to love being lost in the liminal space that sometimes seems necessary for the golden thread to glow with a light that can be seen.

In a sense, the writing of this chapter is about feeling my way through liminal space. I just spent the last several minutes looking for a juicy quote by David Abram about the joys of being lost, of deliberately getting lost, in order to discover something new, but I could not find it. This tells me I am, in fact, lost, on my own, and yet at the same time, never entirely on my own, as long as I feel this connection to the forest temple in which I live, the small tribe of kindred spirits that feel the illuminating heat of the forge at which I ply my craft, and the golden thread that no one else but I can see.

All of this is Vesta's gift to me, a reflection of her love for me, and my love for her. As I feel the healing power of these gifts, and steep myself in it, we naturally court each other, and out of our love, there is a kind of magic that emerges that opens the heart and the senses to a deeper experience of *participation mystique*.

Entering the Defenseless Heart

Opening the heart in love is, of course, also a matter of opening the door to extreme vulnerability, to all those feelings we would rather not feel, to the overwhelming feelings we believe we cannot feel without being annihilated by them. And yet, there is no true communion with the gods without this annihilation.

If we are to take our astrology to the place where it can change the way we see the world – and why else would we do it, if not for that? – we ourselves must be willing not just to be ravished by the gods, but to be dismembered and reassembled by them. It is the capacity to feel deeply that allows this to happen. Erudition won't take us there at all really; and loving appreciation will take us only halfway there. The other half – the underworld of dark, troubled feelings, hidden in the shadows, understandably kept at bay as long as possible, is the only place that love is able to transmute into the trembling cauldron of awe, and it is only in our trembling that we truly know we are in the presence of a god.

Most recently, I am being taken to this place by the death of my beloved cat, Marigold, who, as noted in Chapter Fourteen, died of kidney failure on Vestalia, the Roman holiday dedicated to Vesta. I've also been affected by the sudden death of a friend, and the impending death of my mentor – these more personal losses taking place with the context of an ongoing pandemic, a horrific war, the possible impending death of democracy in this country and in many places around the world, endless mass shootings, the ongoing Sixth Mass Extinction affecting the local birds listed above and thousands of other species, and the impending point of no-return in our relentless slide toward climate crisis.

To open my heart completely to these losses and impending losses seems, quite honestly, beyond my capacity. Having said that, however, I am also aware that I ultimately have no choice if I am to tend the sacred flame that burns at the heart of the *anima mundi*, where our small lives come and go, but Life Itself continues. I can't possibly know from within this limited human perspective, whether this is guaranteed for all time, or whether as the Mahabharata says, every 4.32 billion years, Brahma will die, and be reborn, taking with him, the entire manifest universe – including everything we can possibly know, assuming that there is anyone to know anything.

These questions take me too far into my head and make me tired. What seems more relevant now, as I struggle to keep my heart open, is that whatever I can do, in the here and now, to mitigate the pain and suffering of the world, whether that be holding a dying cat in my arms, encouraging a young woman coming to me for astrological advice to reach toward the shining potential on her horizon, or just appreciating the opportunity to commune with the cardinals, the whip-poor-wills, and the bard owls in my own backyard, is helping to keep the sacred flame alive.

The great paradox here is that I can only do these things well to the extent that I feel how precious they are, in the face of monumental forces, beyond my control, that can, in a heartbeat, sweep them all away. Beneath the particulars of the path laid out for me in my exploration of Vesta's role in my birthchart and presence in my life, is this simple, though not necessarily easy to resolve conundrum: life itself is a liminal space, a passage through unknown territory, at the center of which lies a forge where the possibility exists of tending a creative spark capable of illuminating the darkness.

If this is all I do with this one wild and precious life that is given me, I will have honored my love for Vesta. Everything else, including this book, is just fuel for the perpetual flame.

Taking Astrology Back to Its Mythopoetic Roots

Hearing a distant cough in the back of the room, after an awkward moment of respectful silence, I remember that I am writing the final chapter of this book, which is ostensibly about using astrology as a language with which to move into a more intimate relationship with the cosmos. The intimacy that is possible here depends, first and foremost, not upon an intellectual understanding of astrology's intricacies, but rather upon a willingness to approach the language with an open, deeply honest, heartfelt vulnerability that allows the gods and goddesses that dwell within the archetypal field of the birthchart to have their way with us and irrevocably change us.

In the last seven chapters, I have outlined a methodology for taking the willing astrologer to this threshold, reviewing the method behind my madness at the beginning of this chapter. I have further hinted that crossing the threshold into the last step – into the place where there is no longer any conceptual distance between the symbolism of the chart and your direct understanding of it – is a matter of falling in love with the god or goddess you are exploring archetypally, and at the same time, being willing to enter that state of numinosity, kneeling before the deity, where the only possible response is trembling, wordless awe.

I have attempted to describe the barebones outer process as it has recently manifested for me, but ultimately, I cannot tell you how to get there. The process will necessarily be unique for each of us. Chances are, if you have been paying attention, life itself has been nudging you toward that final step, and you are already aware, on some level of your being that beckons you with the panicky excitement of whitewater ahead. Most of us spend a great deal of our time, pedaling furiously away from this whitewater until, at some point, we can't any more. When that moment comes, you can use your birthchart, and the process that I have outlined here, as a paddle of sorts, for a ride I guarantee you won't soon forget.

* * * * *

Having said all that, if you are still back-pedaling, but curious, there are some additional steps that can be taken that can help you past your fear and resistance:

Carl Jung talked about the use of active imagination to evoke images that can serve as a bridge between the conscious self and the unconscious realm, in which the many selves and the particular deities that resonate with those selves intermingle. Some of these images might appear spontaneously in dreams; others can be evoked through various techniques of waking meditations, visualization, or self-hypnosis.

In the 1950s, Mary Stark Whitehouse – a student of both Carl Jung and modern dance choreographer Martha Graham – extended the idea of active imagination to "authentic movement," directed not by the mind, but by the body, which is already in a largely unconscious state of communion with its environment, and knows how to bring the rest of you into communion as well. Other forms of movement, including Gabrielle Roth's Five Rhythms and Contact Improv, can be useful in getting out of your head and intentionally exploring an archetype in a more embodied way.

In the early twenty-first century, Jung's ideas were further extended by clinical psychologist Stephen Aizenstat and a small band of dream-tending pioneers at Pacific Graduate Institute to encompass the idea of animism, in which the images spontaneously arising in dreams, as well as in moments of synchronicity in waking life, are allowed to live and breathe with a reality of their own, outside of our rational interpretation of them – through dream re-entry, through holding a mental space in which an image can reveal itself on its own terms, through artistic rendering of images, through dance and movement, through cultivating the art of dialogue and council with images.

I believe such techniques can be applied to astrological symbols as well, once you have gone through the necessary preliminary steps as outlined in this book to discover what these symbols mean to you, personally, instead of just in the abstract. Once you have a more personal sense of an archetype like Vesta, let's say, you can draw her, paint her, dance her, make a ceremonial mask with her face on it, talk to her, walk with her, invite her into your space and your life as you would a friend, and let her slowly reveal herself to you on her own terms.

You don't need to interpret what Vesta means in your birthchart; you can instead, experience her presence in a more immediate way, with the understanding that she already lives within you and permeates the same space you inhabit. Here, some of the techniques of experiential astrology developed by Barbara Schermer can be helpful points of entry into a more emotional and embodied connection with an astrological archetype.[2]

As will be attested by multiple generations of astrologers who also study and practice magic, going back to the astrologer-priests of the Mythopoetic Era, the use of ceremony and ritual can be a powerful tool for evoking the presence of an archetype, otherwise understood as a spirit or a deity. Rituals have the power and authority of tradition behind them, and contemporary schools of magic, most of which are also steeped in astrological understanding, can provide a solid foundation for this kind of work.

Ultimately more powerful, in my opinion, however, are the development of ceremonies that arise out of the specific personal work you are doing in relation to the archetypes, perhaps with this book as a source of guidance. No one can tell you what these ceremonies are, nor can you know what they are yourself until you reach a certain level of intimacy with the archetype that you are tracking. When you have reached this point, you will be given further instruction about how to proceed. Other ceremonies may arise spontaneously in the moment, when you are in the proper frame of mind. It can be helpful in preparing yourself for this kind of work by familiarizing yourself about the kinds of plants, animals, gemstones, foods, music, incense, colors, textures, and other talismans that are sacred to your archetype, and to pay special attention to those attributes and preferences you learn about through your own experiences.

If, for example, in working with the tarot, the Queen of Wands makes an appearance, this could be my Vesta trying to get my attention. If I associate cardinals with Vesta – which may be an association unique to me, probably not written down in any book – then the appearance of a cardinal can be signal that Vesta is present and available to be honored with ceremony. This kind of work can only be done in the deep woods, where there are no trails other than those you discover as you walk them.

Some techniques along these lines have been developed by people like eco-psychologist Bill Plotkin and the Animas Valley Institute. His approach involves taking the images that are speaking to you into the natural world, where they also resonate as primal forces that continuously shape that world and everything in it. This sense of the archetypal power of the gods and goddesses is intensely powerful in nature, especially the farther out into wilderness you go.

Again, there is no reason why you can't literally follow the astrological archetypes that beckon you out into the deep woods, where getting lost or not, they will reveal themselves to you in a way that transcends the feeble efforts of your rational mind to understand them. If you yourself are not skilled at navigating the wilderness, I would highly recommend working with guides, such as those available at the Animas Valley Institute, or perhaps the School of Lost Borders, the original teachers of vision questing in this country, and still one of the best resources for this kind of exploration.

At times, a pilgrimage to some sacred site associated with a particular deity or to a place off the beaten path that, for whatever reason, you associate with the archetype you are exploring can be an excellent way to immerse yourself in its archetypal field. From time to time, especially pre-pandemic, astrologers like Daniel Giamario, Anyaa McAndrew, and Demetra George, have led astrologically-based journeys to places where the mythological and mythopoetic underpinnings of the sacred archetypes resonate with special intensity. Or you can create your own, as you are called to a particular place. Shortly after I started working with Vesta, for example, I was invited to accompany some friends to Glastonbury, where Vesta's Celtic sister Brigit has a history and an ongoing presence. I will approach this journey as a pilgrimage in my courtship of Vesta and see what I can learn through my full presence and participation in her field.

For those who are brave enough to go this route, I would not hesitate to recommend an astrological experience of *participation mystique*, facilitated by a guided use of psychedelics. As noted in Chapters Seven and Nine, the pioneering work of Richard Tarnas and Stanislav Grof in the use of psilocybin to assist a powerful process of psychological catharsis, timed astrologically, opens the door to more of this kind of work. This is perhaps especially true now that the overall climate has shifted to once again accommodate the idea that psychoactive substances can be useful, not only in treating various psychological disorders, but in exploring the nature of consciousness itself. Here, the work of people like Christopher Bache, professor emeritus in the Department of Philosophy and Religion at Youngstown State University, as well as a student of Grof and Tarnas, can also be a guide, as documented in his fascinating account – *LSD and the Mind of the Universe: Diamonds from Heaven*.[3]

While the laws are still a bit of a patchwork minefield in this country, in other places around the world like Amsterdam and Portugal, where a more liberal atmosphere prevails, I have no doubt that in the years ahead, a new generation of psychedelic guides will emerge who have familiarity with the astrological language and who can perhaps take any willing participant back to the place where there is no separation between the symbolism of a birthchart and the sacred reality of which it ultimately speaks.

Lastly, as astrologers, we can always take our heads out of the charts we study with such passion and simply look up into the night sky, preferably in a place of minimal light pollution. Ever since Copernicus and the displacement of Earth from the center of the universe, science has made us feel small and insignificant as we live our meaningless lives on a tiny speck orbiting a minor star in an endless sea of billions of stars. And yet, as astrologers, we know better. Just the fact that we can marvel, wonder, and be open to the awe of such an endless sea of light allows us to swim in that sea the way a scientist keeping her distance never could. I encourage you, standing on the threshold of your own archetypal investigation to do this as often as possible.

A Final Word

However you get there, it is important to understand that the final step in this process is not understanding but embodiment. We are here not just to make analytical sense of the sacred order, dimly reflected in the birthchart as an archetypal map of the interface between cosmos and psyche, but to consciously embody the divine intelligence already pulsing in every molecule of this place.

The birthchart is a useful guide for teaching you what you need to know to be able to do this, but only if you find a way to enter into it and to let it enter into you, seep into your pores, fill your lungs with air, pulse through you like the lifeblood of a mighty river.

Forget what you think you know about your birthchart through your study of astrology, however honestly you have come by it, or however deep you think it goes. Forget what the mind, conditioned by science and religion and politics, and astrological tradition itself, tells you it ought to say, and just listen to its roar. Become one with it. Don't be shy. Merge.

With the roar of the divine in your ears, close your eyes and find the sacred flame within. Using the sacred flame as your only light, learn how to see in the dark. When you are ready, open your eyes and gaze anew upon your birthchart. Let your birthchart become a portal through which you and the gods find common ground.

Walking this common ground as a spiritual practice, awaken to the living cosmos all around you. With or without your map in hand, when your archetypal eye is lit by sacred flame, your hungry heart is open and willing to tremble, all shall be revealed as the illusory barrier between psyche and cosmos dissolves in boundless love.

Notes

1. Audubon. "How Climate Change Will Affect Birds in Missouri." Accessed June 27, 2023. https://www.audubon.org/climate/survivalbydegrees/state/us/mo.
2. Schermer, Barbara. *Astrology Alive!: Experiential Astrology, Astrodrama, and the Healing Arts*. HarperCollins, 1989.
3. Bache, Christopher Martin. *LSD and the Mind of the Universe: Diamonds from Heaven*. Rochester, VT: Park Street Press, 2019.

Postscript

My Pilgrimage to Bride's Mound

As noted in Chapter Thirteen, I was invited by some friends on a trip to Glastonbury, England, where Brigit is historically believed to have had a presence, at last since 488 C.E., if not before, when her Christian counterpart St. Brigid is said to have visited, and briefly taken up residence at Bride's Mound. Having just returned from that trip, I thought I would write a short note about my experiences there.

My Experience of Brigit in Glastonbury

As a friend and respected scholar has suggested in private conversation, St. Brigid was thought to have traveled far and wide through half the known world at the time, and her association with Glastonbury is, by no means, unique. Be that as it may, as far as I could tell, the local community in Glastonbury has fervently adopted her, in both her Christian form, and in her wilder, older, more pagan manifestation. As noted in Chapter Eleven, Brigit is a more complex archetype than Vesta or Hestia, and I felt that complexity in Glastonbury, mostly as a detour a bit too far into the deep woods.

Brigit, not only shares Hestia's function as keeper of the sacred flame. She is also the goddess of poetry and the patron deity of bards, who understood the magical power of words and a goddess of healing and midwifery, with a special affinity for the healing power of water. In Glastonbury, while all these functions are honored and available to be explored for serious adepts and spiritual tourists alike, it seems to be Brigit's association with the healing power of water that is most publicly celebrated there, primarily at the Chalice Well.

Currently maintained by the Chalice Well Trust, founded by Wellesley Tudor Pole in 1959, the history of the well is associated with Joseph of Arimathea, who ostensibly placed the Holy Grail there shortly after the death of Christ. Sometimes called the Red Well, because of the iron oxide content of the water, Christians associate the waters of the well with the blood of Christ, still present in the Grail that caught his blood at his crucifixion. The well itself, however, according to archeological records, likely goes back much farther than Christ to Paleolithic times, where it would have most certainly been sacred to a goddess like Brigit, who was said to preside over sacred wells throughout the Celtic world. The Grail is associated not just with Christ but also with Brigit through its link to the Cauldron of Inspiration which was given to the Dagda by Brigit's father.

Regardless of whether these mythic stories are historically accurate or not, modern day devotees of Brigit can be seen to congregate at the Chalice Well, honoring the sacred healing waters, alongside devout Christians and the unaffiliated clueless, who appreciate the meditative peace of the well-kept gardens surrounding the wells, some oblivious to how the history is parsed. Devotees of Brigit are even more noticeable at the less formal White Well, just across a narrow road to the east, where during the time I was there, ceremonies and rituals honoring the goddess went on frequently, sometimes into the wee hours of the night. The B & B where we stayed in Glastonbury was a two-minute walk from the White Well, and more than once I was awoken by drumming, chanting and the occasional wild keening howl.

On the day my friends and I arrived in Glastonbury, the White Well happened to be open, so after settling into our Air B and B, we wandered over. The White Well is housed in a stone grotto that immediately had a more ancient, primal feeling than the manicured Red Well, and walking into the grotto was like stepping back in time. We happened to be there during an impromptu ceremony to the goddess, attended by a couple dozen priestess sisters in varying degrees of undress, bathing in the well itself, and gyrating meditatively to a trance beat kept by drummers.

Although this ceremony did not necessarily belong exclusively to Brigit, the congregation of women who had come to this place to worship and embody the goddess seemed to revolve around an alchemy of fire and water that can easily be associated with the Celtic goddess. As I witnessed it there, Brigit's worship seemed to be mostly about women claiming their feminine power, both as healers and as fierce, passionate, uninhibited warrior spirits, ready to assert themselves and be themselves without apology or self-censure.

Differentiating Brigit and Hestia

While this is an admirable goal and I fully support it, somehow it did not feel particularly Hestia-like in the way that I have gotten to know the Greek goddess who has been the subject of the exploration in this book. Keeping the sacred flame, in Hestia's domain, feels like a much more private affair, as does following a golden thread, moving in and out of liminal space, gestating something of value under a cloak of invisibility, becoming virgin, and most of the other themes that have evolved out of my work with her.

While Brigit is celebrated in Glastonbury, at least, as an activist who takes her fire bravely onto whatever field of battle serves to right the wrongs of the world, becoming a cinder biter on a path laid out before me in exploration of Hestia feels less overtly political and more a matter of quiet strength and of being rooted like a tree, whose source remains invisible.

Within the neopagan community that celebrates Brigit in Glastonbury and elsewhere, all of the intrigue, melodrama and pageantry that characterized the mythology of the Greek pantheon, swirls in full color and intensity, and my sense is that had Hestia been born in the Celtic lands, instead of Greece, she would have stepped away and sought a quieter refuge beyond the sacred hustle and bustle. It would not have been her scene.

Bride's Mound and Well

While in Glastonbury, we also made a pilgrimage to Bride's Mound, which actually did feel like it could be a bit more hospitable to the Hestia I have come to know and love. Bride's Mound is thought by some, including William of Malmesbury, writing circa 1135 CE, and the monk John of Glastonbury, writing circa 1400 CE, to have briefly been St. Brigid's residence before she set up a more permanent home in Kildare, Ireland. The area, more generally known as Beckery, a papal charter dating back to the twelfth century CE, is also known as Little Ireland, a pilgrimage site for many Irish visitors traveling to honor St. Brigid.

An archeological dig in 2016 unearthed evidence of a chapel and human remains dating back to the fifth century, predating the nearby Glastonbury Abbey built in the seventh century. Today, Bride's Mound, which lies a bit outside of Glastonbury, is one of the least frequented sacred sites in the area. Finding it was not easy, as there were no obvious markings that would direct a spiritual tourist to it, although the locals seemed to know where it was. After asking directions from several travelers, modern-day itinerant gypsies living in caravans, also on the edge of town, we found it past what felt like a semi-abandoned industrial afterthought, in a field of brambles, nettles and thistles, intuitively following a nondescript footpath that could easily have been used by wildlife as humans. A flock of ravens scattered upon our approach.

The site was marked only by a small plaque and a number of makeshift Celtic crosses hand woven from river grass and flowers. In 2005, the land on which the Mound rests was purchased by a local group called Friends of Brides Mound to save it from being paved over as a parking lot, but who apparently were not interested in turning it into another tourist attraction. It appeared some effort was made to weed whack the area immediately around the plaque itself.

Finding Brides Well, another quietly celebrated feature of the site, proved to be even more difficult, as it is marked only by a small stone, overgrown by weeds, near the river Brue, which is, for all intents and purposes, little more than an irrigation ditch feeding the nearby fields. I was able to find it, in fact, only by gravitating toward two people who seemed to be sitting near the irrigation ditch. I made my way there slowly, aware as I approached that some kind of ceremony was in progress. On our way there, we passed a couple of tents in the field, which I gathered belonged to homeless people, as they seemed to be semi-permanent installations, complete with solar lights and shower facilities. Perhaps the people doing the ceremony lived there.

In any case, the two men engaged in ceremony seemed to appreciate my respectful approach, and after initially being surprised by our presence there, graciously stepped back in silence to allow the three of us some space to connect with Brigit on our own. I felt, or imagined I felt, a warm flush, not unlike what I remembered from my ashram days, but I was too intimidated by the presence of these witnesses to linger long. I said a silent prayer, thanked my "hosts," and then we made our way back to Bride's Mound.

At the time, the pilgrimage felt a bit anti-climactic. Then again, as I reflected on it in the days that followed, it felt perfect. I had, after all, come here as part of a larger, ongoing attempt to connect more deeply with Hestia, and not with Brigit. While Brigit was the life of the party in Glastonbury proper, it seemed to me that Hestia would have felt more at home in this field. This was perhaps the kind of place where homeless people could tend a flame that would not otherwise exist were they not acutely aware of its importance, somehow made more poignant in the absence of a more permanent home.

This, of course, is all projection on my part, but what I took away from that field was something that could not be taken away from me, and it is easy to speculate that this is why those who go there go. In the wake of my own experiences, I was easily able to imagine that the purpose of a pilgrimage to Bride's Mound is so that returning back home to tend the hearth around which everyday life revolves, all pilgrims could do so with a more unshakeable confidence that the sacred flame they carry inside is all they really need.

This is something I felt Hestia would want us all to know.

Bibliography

Abbott & Costello Fan Club. "Abbott and Costello's Classic 'Who's on First?' Routine | Abbott & Costello Fan Club," July 16, 2021. https://www.abbottandcostellofanclub.com/whos-on-first/.

Adorno, Theodor. *The Stars Down to Earth*. New York: Routledge, 1994.

Aschwanden, Christie. "We're All 'P-Hacking' Now." *Wired*, November 26, 2019. https://www.wired.com/story/were-all-p-hacking-now/.

Audubon. "How Climate Change Will Affect Birds in Missouri." Accessed June 27, 2023. https://www.audubon.org/climate/survivalbydegrees/state/us/mo.

Aurata, Aquila. "Welcome to the Network for Objective Research in Astrology (NORA)." Objective Astrology.net - Home. Accessed April 28, 2023. http://www.objectiveastrology.net/.

Aveni, Anthony. *Conversing with the Planets: How Science and Myth Invented the Cosmos*. TImes Books, 1992.

Bache, Christopher Martin. *LSD and the Mind of the Universe: Diamonds from Heaven*. Rochester, VT: Park Street Press, 2019.

Barnstone, Willis, and Marvin Meyer. *The Gnostic Bible: Revised and Expanded Edition*. Shambhala Publications, 2009.

Barry, Colleen, Harrie Han, and Beth McGinty. "Trust in Science and COVID-19." Johns Hopkins Bloomberg School of Public Health, August 3, 2021. https://www.jhsph.edu/covid-19/articles/trust-in-science-and-covid-19.html.

Beck, Julie. "Why Are Millennials So Into Astrology?" *The Atlantic*, June 22, 2021. https://www.theatlantic.com/health/archive/2018/01/the-new-age-of-astrology/550034/.

Bennett, John G. *Gurdjieff: Making a New World*. HarperCollins, 1976.

Bergstralh, Jay T., Ellis D. Miner, and Mildred Shapley Matthews. *Uranus*. University of Arizona Press, 1991.

Besant, Annie. "Foreword: An Appreciation." In Leo, Bessie, *The Life and Work of Alan Leo: Theosophist – Astrologer – Mason*, 1919. https://archive.org/details/lifeworkofalanle00leob/page/n5/mode/2up?view=theater.

Blavatsky, Helena. *Collected Writings, Vol. 1*, edited by Boris De Zirkoff. Wheaton, IL: Theosophical Publishing House, 1977.

——. *Isis Unveiled: Secrets of the Ancient Wisdom Tradition*. Pasadena, CA: Theosophical University Press, 1976.

——. *The Secret Doctrine*, 1888. https://www.ultindia.org/books/SecretDoctrineVol1.pdf.

Bly, Robert. *Iron John: A Book about Men*. Vintage, 1990.

Booth, Martin. *A Magick Life: A Biography of Aleister Crowley*. London: Coronet Books, 2000.

Born, Max, and Albert Einstein. *The Born-Einstein Letters*, 1971. https://openlibrary.org/books/OL4913625M/The_Born-Einstein_letters.

Brennan, Chris. *Hellenistic Astrology: The Study of Fate and Fortune*. Denver: Amor Fati Publications, 2017.

Breton, André. *Manifesto of Surrealism*, 1924. https://theanarchistlibrary.org/library/andre-breton-manifesto-of-surrealism.pdf.

Breton, Andre, and Marcel Duchamp. "First Papers of Surrealism: Hanging by André Breton, His Twine Marcel Duchamp." Internet Archive, 1942. https://archive.org/details/firstpaperssur00bret.

Brewster, David. *Memoirs of the Life, Writings, and Discoveries of Sir Isaac Newton. Vol. 1*. Cambridge University Press, 2010.

Broemeling, Lyle D. "An Account of Early Statistical Inference in Arab Cryptology." *The American Statistician* 65, no. 4 (November 1, 2011): 255–57. https://doi.org/10.1198/tas.2011.10191.

Brown, David. *Mesopotamian Planetary Astronomy-Astrology*. Vol. 18 of Cuneform monographs. University of Virginia Press, 2000.

Buhner, Stephen Harrod. *Plant Intelligence and the Imaginal Realm: Beyond the Doors of Perception into the Dreaming of Earth*. Rochester, VT: Bear & Company, 2014.

Burke, Omar Michael. *Among the Dervishes : An Account of Travels in Asia and Africa, and Four Years Studying the Dervishes, Sufis and Fakirs by Living among Them*. London: Octagon Press, 1973.

Burtt, E. A. *The Metaphysical Foundations of Modern Science*. Atlantic Heights, NJ: Humanities Press International, 1952.

Cambridge Centre for the Study of Western Esotericism. "Sophia Wellbeloved's Academic Research Page," October 14, 2014. https://ccwe.wordpress.com/sophia-wellbeloveds-academic-research-page/.

Campbell, Bruce F. *Ancient Wisdom Revived: A History of the Theosophical Movement*. Berkeley: University of California Press, 1980.

Campbell, Colin D. "Aleister Crowley's Contribution to Popular Astrology." Llewellyn, February 12, 2018. https://www.llewellyn.com/journal/article/2678.

Campion, Nicholas. *A History of Western Astrology Volume I: The Ancient and Classical Worlds.* Bloomsbury, 2008.

——. *A History of Western Astrology Volume II: The Medieval and Modern Worlds.* Bloomsbury, 2009.

——. "Surrealist Cosmology: André Breton and Astrology." *Culture and Cosmos* 6, no. 2 (2002): 45–56. http://cultureandcosmos.org/pdfs/6/6-2_Campion_Breton_Astrology.pdf.

Carlson, Shawn. "A Double-Blind Test of Astrology." *Nature* 318, no. 6045 (December 5, 1985): 419–25. https://doi.org/10.1038/318419a0.

Carpi, Anthony, PhD, and Anne E. Egger PhD. "Uncertainty, Error, and Confidence." Visionlearning, February 12, 2017. https://www.visionlearning.com/en/library/Process-of-Science/49/Uncertainty-Error-and-Confidence/157.

Carrington, Damian. "Sixth Mass Extinction of Wildlife Accelerating, Scientists Warn." *The Guardian*, October 29, 2021. https://www.theguardian.com/environment/2020/jun/01/sixth-mass-extinction-of-wildlife-accelerating-scientists-warn.

Carteret, Jean, and Roger Knare. "An Interview with André Breton." *Culture and Cosmos* 6, no. 2 (April 1954). http://cultureandcosmos.org/pdfs/6/6-2_Campion_Breton_Astrology.pdf.

Cashford, Jules. *The Moon: Myth and Image*. New York: Four Walls Eight Windows, 2003.

Castaneda, Carlos. *The Teachings of Don Juan: A Yaqui Way of Knowledge*. Simon and Schuster, 1973.

Cavendish, Richard. *A History of Magic*. London: Sphere Books, 1977.

Celâyir, Sirman A. "Astrology, Reality & Common Sense by Sirman A. Celâyir," n.d. http://cura.free.fr/xx/17sirman.html.

Chris-Anne. "Queen of Wands." The Light Seer's Tarot. Accessed June 20, 2023. https://lightseerstarot.com/light-seers-tarot-meanings-queen-of-wands/.

Churton, Tobias. *Aleister Crowley: The Biography: Spiritual Revolutionary, Romantic Explorer, Occult Master and Spy*. London: Watkins Media Limited, 2014.

Clerk, Agnes Mary. "1911 Encyclopædia Britannica/Laplace, Pierre Simon." Wikisource, September 24, 2020. https://en.wikisource.org/wiki/1911_Encyclop%C3%A6dia_Britannica/Laplace,_Pierre_Simon.

Cohen, Barnard. "Foreword." In Bernard, Claude. *An Introduction to the Study of Experimental Medicine, 1–4*. Macmillan & Co., 2018. https://doi.org/10.4324/9781351320764-1.

Cohen, S. Marc. "Aristotle's Metaphysics." Stanford Encyclopedia of Philosophy. November 21, 2020. https://plato.stanford.edu/entries/aristotle-metaphysics/.

Coleman, William Emmette. "The Sources of Madame Blavatsky's Writings." Blavatsky Study Center. Accessed June 12, 2023. https://www.blavatskyarchives.com/colemansources1895.htm.

Collin, Rodney. *The Theory of Celestial Influence: Man, the Universe, and Cosmic Mystery*. Penguin, 1993.

Corbett, Sara. "Carl Jung and the Holy Grail of the Unconscious." *The New York Times*, October 16, 2009. https://www.nytimes.com/2009/09/20/magazine/20jung-t.html.

Corbin, Henry. Alone with the Alone: Creative Imagination in the Sufism of Ibn 'Arabî. Princeton University Press, 1998.

——. "Mundus Imaginalis or the Imaginary and the Imaginal." *Cahiers Internationaux De Symbolisme* 6 (1964): 3–26. http://www.bahaistudies.net/asma/mundus_imaginalis.pdf.

Cornelius, Geoffrey. "Divination, Participation and the Cognitive Continuum." Field of Omens | Astrodivination. Accessed May 12, 2023. https://www.astrodivination.com/field-of-omens/.

——. *The Moment of Astrology: Origins in Divination*. Wessex Astrologer Limited, 2002.

Covey, Stephen R. *The 7 Habits of Highly Effective People: Powerful Lessons in Personal Change*. Simon and Schuster, 1989.

Crowley, Aleister. "Batrachophrenoboocosmomachia," 1917. https://astrolibrary.org/books/crowley-67/.

Crowley, Aleister, and Evangeline Smith Adams. *The General Principles of Astrology: Liber DXXXVI*. Red Wheel, 2002.

Culver, Roger B., and Philip A. Ianna. *Astrology: True Or False?: A Scientific Evaluation*. Prometheus, 1988.

Cumont, Franz. "Astrology and Religion Among the Greeks and Romans." Sacred Texts. Accessed April 28, 2023. https://www.sacred-texts.com/astro/argr/argr03.htm.

Curry, Patrick. *A Confusion of Prophets: Victorian and Edwardian Astrology*. London: Collins & Brown, 1993.

Curry, Robert. "Why It Is Unacceptable to Dismiss Astrology as Rubbish." Accessed May 6, 2023. http://www.astrology.co.uk/tests/basisofastrology.htm.

Dameron, James Palatine. *Spiritism: The Origin of All Religions*, 1828. http://books.google.com/books?id=5LWEAAAAIAAJ&pg=PA91&lpg=PA91&dq=minos+moses&source=bl&ots=Q8NS3VuBAI&sig=Fs3JesIWaWIsCdCkmYfEJivSd58&hl=en&sa=X&e

i=01tbUYvaDKqs2gX2zYD4Dg&ved=0CFgQ6AEwBQ#v=onepage&q=minos%20 moses&f=false.

Daston, Lorraine. "Scientific Error and the Ethos of Belief." *Social Research: An International Quarterly* 72, no. 1 (January 1, 2005): 1–28. https://doi.org/10.1353/sor.2005.0016.

Davidson, Jessica. "The Jupiter Saturn Conjunction – the Start of a New Age?," February 24, 2022. https://jessicadavidson.co.uk/2020/11/16/the-jupiter-saturn-conjunction-the-start-of-a-new-age/.

Davidson, Norman. Foreword. *Anthroposophy and Astrology: The Astronomical Letters of Elisabeth Vreede*. Great Barrington, MA: Anthroposophic Press, 2001.

Davis-Flynn, Jennifer. "A New Report Details Decades of Abuse at the Hands of Yogi Bhajan." *Yoga Journal*, September 2, 2021. https://www.yogajournal.com/yoga-101/abuse-in-kundalini-yoga/.

Dean, Geoffrey, Ivan Kelly, Arthur Mather, and Rudolf Smit. "Astrologer Attacks Researchers (Abstract+Article)." Accessed June 14, 2023. https://www.astrology-and-science.com/o-attk2.htm.

Dean, Geoffrey, and Arthur Mather. *Recent Advances in Natal Astrology: A Critical Review 1900-1976*. Bromley, England: The Astrological Association, 1977.

Dean, Geoffrey, Arthur Mather, David Nias, and Rudolf Smit. *Tests of Astrology: A Critical Review of Hundreds of Studies*. Amsterdam: AinO Publications, 2016.

Derrida, Jacques, and Gerald Graff. "Afterword: Toward an Ethic of Discussion." In *Limited Inc*. Northwestern University Press, 1988.

Dionysius of Halicarnassus. *The Roman Antiquities*. Accessed June 19, 2023. https://penelope.uchicago.edu/Thayer/E/Roman/Texts/Dionysius_of_Halicarnassus/home.html.

Donner, Fred. "The Historical Context." In The Cambridge Companion to the Qur'ān, edited by Jane Dammen McAuliffe. Cambridge University Press, 2006.

Dorter, Kenneth. "Imagery and Philosophy in Plato's Phaedrus." *Journal of the History of Philosophy* 9, no. 3 (January 1, 1971): 279–88. https://doi.org/10.1353/hph.2008.0975.

Dummer, V., and M. Greene. "The Core Personality: Treatment Strategies for Multiple Personality Disorder." In *Readings in Psychosynthesis: Theory, Process, and Practice: Psychotherapy, Self-Care, Education, Health, Religion, Organizational Development, World Order*, edited by John Weiser and Thomas Yeomans. Department of Applied Psychology, Ontario Institute for Studies in Education, 1988.

Dyrendal, Asbjørn, James R. Lewis, and Jesper Aa Petersen. *The Invention of Satanism*. London: Oxford University Press, 2016.

Eisler, Riane. *The Chalice and the Blade*, 1987. https://openlibrary.org/books/OL2740056M/The_chalice_and_the_blade.

"Ellis Lonsdale | Star Genesis Wisdom." Accessed June 15, 2023. https://stargenesiswisdom.com/ellis-lonsdale/.

Ellwood, Robert. "Review of Nicholas Goodrick-Clarke's Helena Blavatsky." *Nova Religio: The Journal of Alternative and Emergent Religions* 9, no. 2 (2005).

Elwell, Dennis. "Astrology Is a Foreign Language." Accessed June 14, 2023. http://www.skyscript.co.uk/elwell3.html.

——. "The Researchers Researched." Accessed June 14, 2023. http://www.astrozero.co.uk/astroscience/elwell_1.htm.

Elwell, Dennis, and Garry Phillipson. "Astrology, Scepticism and Knowledge - A Dialogue Between Dennis Elwell and Garry Phillipson." Astrology in the Year Zero. Accessed June 14, 2023. http://www.astrozero.co.uk/astroscience/ask.htm.

Encyclopedia Britannica. "Vestal Virgins | Roman Religion," June 15, 2023. https://www.britannica.com/topic/Vestal-Virgins#ref185137.

Ertel, Suitbert. "Appraisal of Shawn Carlson's Renowned Astrology Tests." *Journal of Scientific Exploration* 23, no. 2 (January 1, 2009): 125–37. https://journalofscientificexploration.org/index.php/jse/article/download/99/37.

Eysenck, Hans. "Michel Gauquelin. [1928-1991] Obituary. *The Independent*. 20 June 1991." Accessed May 6, 2023. http://www.astrology.co.uk/bio/gauquelin.htm.

Fanelli, Daniele. "How Many Scientists Fabricate and Falsify Research? A Systematic Review and Meta-Analysis of Survey Data." *PLOS ONE* 4, no. 5 (May 29, 2009): e5738. https://doi.org/10.1371/journal.pone.0005738.

Farnell, Kim. *The Astral Tramp: A Biography of Sepharial*. London: Acella Publications, 1998.

Faye, Jan. "Backward Causation." Stanford Encyclopedia of Philosophy/Spring 2021 Edition. February 26, 2021. https://plato.stanford.edu/archives/spr2021/entries/causation-backwards/.

Ferguson, John. "Hellenistic Age | History, Characteristics, Art, Philosophy, Religion, & Facts." Encyclopedia Britannica, March 17, 2023. https://www.britannica.com/event/Hellenistic-Age.

Finocchiaro, Maurice A. "Book Review – The Person of the Millennium: The Unique Impact of Galileo on World History." *The Historian* 69, no. 3 (2007).

Firman, John, and Ann Gila. *Psychosynthesis: A Psychology of the Spirit*. State University of New York Press, 2010.

Fowler, Michael. "Early Greek Science." Accessed May 12, 2023. http://galileoandeinstein.physics.virginia.edu/lectures/thales.html.

Frank, Adam, and Marcelo Gleiser. "Opinion | A Crisis at the Edge of Physics." *The New York Times*, June 5, 2015. https://www.nytimes.com/2015/06/07/opinion/a-crisis-at-the-edge-of-physics.html.

Frazer, James George. *The Golden Bough: The Roots of Religion and Folklore*. New York: Crown, 1981.

Fromm, Erich. *Beyond the Chains of Illusion: My Encounter with Marx and Freud*. Touchstone Books, 1980.

Gauquelin, Michel. *Birthtimes: A Scientific Investigation of the Secrets of Astrology*. Hill & Wang, 1983.

——. *Dreams and Illusions of Astrology*. Amherst, NY: Prometheus Books, 1979.

——. *Les Hommes et Les Astres*. FeniXX, 1959.

——. *L'influence Des Astres: Étude Critique et Expérimentale*. Edition du Dauphin., 1955.

——. *Neo-Astrology: A Copernican Revolution*. Penguin, 1991.

Gecewicz, Claire. "'New Age' Beliefs Common among Religious, Nonreligious Americans." Pew Research Center, October 1, 2018. https://www.pewresearch.org/fact-tank/2018/10/01/new-age-beliefs-common-among-both-religious-and-nonreligious-americans/.

George, Demetra, and Douglas Bloch. *Asteroid Goddesses: The Mythology, Psychology, and Astrology of the Re-Emerging Feminine*. San Diego, CA: ACS Publications, 1986.

Gieryn, Thomas F. "Boundary-Work and the Demarcation of Science from Non-Science: Strains and Interests in Professional Ideologies of Scientists." *American Sociological Review* 48, no. 6 (December 1, 1983): 781. https://doi.org/10.2307/2095325.

Gilbert, Robert Andrew, and David E. Pingree. "Astrology | Definition, History, Symbols, Signs, & Facts." Encyclopedia Britannica, April 27, 2023. https://www.britannica.com/topic/astrology.

Gimbutas, Marija. *The Language of the Goddess*. Thames and Hudson, 1989.

Golb, Norman. *The Jews in Medieval Normandy: A Social and Intellectual History*. Cambridge University Press, 1998.

Goldacre, Ben. "What Eight Years of Writing the Bad Science Column Have Taught Me." *The Guardian*, December 1, 2017. https://www.theguardian.com/commentisfree/2011/nov/04/bad-science-eight-years.

Goodrick-Clarke, Nicholas. *Helena Blavatsky*. Berkeley, CA: North Atlantic Books, 2004.

Graves, Robert. *The Greek Myths: 1*. New York: Penguin, 1990.

Greene, Liz. *The Astrological Neptune and the Quest for Redemption*. Weiser Books, 2000.

Greer, John Michael, and Christopher Warnock, trans. *The Complete Picatrix: The Occult Classic of Astrological Magic Liber Atratus Edition: The Classic Medieval Handbook of Astrological Magic*. Adocentyn Press, 2011.

Gribbin, John. *In Search of Schrödinger's Cat: Quantam Physics And Reality*. Bantam, 1984.

Grice, Keiron Le. *The Archetypal Cosmos: Rediscovering the Gods in Myth, Science and Astrology*. Edinburgh: Floris Books, 2010.

Grof, Stanislav. "Holotropic Research and Archetypal Astrology." Awaken (blog), May 18, 2020. https://awaken.com/2018/02/holotropic-research-and-archetypal/.

——. *The Adventure of Self-Discovery: Dimensions of Consciousness and New Perspectives in Psychotherapy and Inner Exploration*. SUNY Press, 1988.

Grondin, Jean. *Introduction to Philosophical Hermeneutics*. Yale University Press, 1994.

Grove, J. W. "Rationality at Risk: Science against Pseudoscience." *Minerva* 23, no. 2 (January 1, 1985): 216–40. https://doi.org/10.1007/bf01099943.

Gurdjieff, G. I. *Meetings with Remarkable Men*. E. P. Dutton, 1974.

Haeckel, Ernst. *The Riddle of the Universe at the Close of the Nineteenth Century*. Harper & Brothers EBooks, 1900. https://doi.org/10.1037/13290-000.

Halsall, Guy. "The Sources and Their Interpretation." In *The New Cambridge Medieval History: Volume 1*, c.500-c.700, edited by Paul Fouracre. Cambridge University Press, 2015.

Hammarberg, Karin, M. Sue Kirkman, and S. De Lacey. "Qualitative Research Methods: When to Use Them and How to Judge Them." *Human Reproduction* 31, no. 3 (March 1, 2016): 498–501. https://doi.org/10.1093/humrep/dev334.

Hand, Rob. "Arhat Media | Books, Articles and Information on the History of Astrology." Accessed May 15, 2023. https://www.arhatmedia.com/Matter&FormArticle.htm.

Hand, Robert. "Ep. 12 Transcript: Reconciling Modern and Traditional Astrology." Interview by Chris Brennan. The Astrology Podcast, November 7, 2021. https://theastrologypodcast.com/transcripts/ep-12-reconciling-modern-and-traditional-astrology/.

Hanegraaff, Wouter J. *Western Esotericism: A Guide for the Perplexed*. London: Bloomsbury Press, 2013.

Hannam, James. *The Genesis of Science: How the Christian Middle Ages Launched the Scientific Revolution*. Simon and Schuster, 2011.

Hansson, Sven Ove. "Defining Pseudoscience and Science." In University of Chicago Press EBooks, 61–78, 2015. https://doi.org/10.7208/chicago/9780226051826.003.0005.

——. "Science and Pseudo-Science." Stanford Encyclopedia of Philosophy/Summer 2021 Edition. May 20, 2021. https://plato.stanford.edu/archives/sum2021/entries/pseudo-science/.

Harding, M. Esther. *Woman's Mysteries, Ancient and Modern: A Psychological Interpretation of the Feminine Principle as Portrayed in Myth, Story, and Dreams*. Harper Colophon, 1971.

Harte, Erin. "How Your Brain Processes Language." *Brain World*, September 13, 2021. https://brainworldmagazine.com/how-your-brain-processes-language/.

Hesiod. "Theogony." Greek Texts and Translations. Accessed June 23, 2023. https://anastrophe.uchicago.edu/cgi-bin/perseus/citequery3.pl?dbname=GreekNov21&query=Hes.%20Theog.%20495&getid=1.

Hesselink, Katinka. "Review of The Astral Tramp, A Biography of Sepharial," 2003. Accessed June 12, 2023. http://www.katinkahesselink.net/kh/rev_w_old.html.

Hilliam, Rachel. *Galileo Galilei: Father of Modern Science*. New York: The Rosen Publishing Group, 2004.

Hillman, James. "Memory: Short-Term Loss, Long-Term Gain." *The Sun*, February 2022.

——. *Re-Visioning Psychology*. HarperCollins, 1975.

——. *The Soul's Code: In Search of Character and Calling*. New York: Warner Books, 1996.

Homer. "Hymn to Aphrodite." The Center for Hellenic Studies. Accessed June 19, 2023. https://chs.harvard.edu/primary-source/homeric-hymn-to-aphrodite-sb/.

Hopkins, John. "Origins of Sufism & Ancient Bactria." Okar Research, October 31, 2012. https://balkhandshambhala.blogspot.com/2012/10/balkh-and-sufism.html.

Hughes, Robert. *The Shock of the New: Art and the Century of Change*. Thames and Hudson, 1981.

Hunger, Hermann. *Astrological Reports to Assyrian Kings*. Vol. 8. Helsinki University Press, 1992.

Hunt, Morton. *The Story of Psychology*. Doubleday, 1993.

Hutton, Ronald. *Shamans: Siberian Spirituality and the Western Imagination*. A&C Black, 2007.

——. *The Triumph of the Moon: A History of Modern Pagan Witchcraft*. New York: Oxford University Press, 2019.

Iamblichus. *On the Mysteries of the Egyptians, Chaldeans, and Assyrians: The Complete Text*, translated by Thomas Taylor. Columbia, SC: Adansonia, 2019.

NASA Solar System Exploration. "In Depth | 4 Vesta – NASA Solar System Exploration." Accessed June 22, 2023. https://solarsystem.nasa.gov/asteroids-comets-and-meteors/asteroids/4-vesta/in-depth/.

Jones, Alexander. *Ptolemy in Perspective: Use and Criticism of His Work from Antiquity to the Nineteenth Century*. Springer Science & Business Media, 2009.

——, ed. *The Jerusalem Bible*. Doubleday, 1968.

Josephson, Brian D. "Pathological Disbelief," June 30, 2004. https://www.repository.cam.ac.uk/handle/1810/247336.

Josephson-Storm, Jason. *The Myth of Disenchantment: Magic, Modernity, and the Birth of the Human Sciences*. University of Chicago Press, 2017.

Jung, Carl G. *The Collected Works of C.G. Jung, Volume 3: Psychogenesis of Mental Disease*. Princeton University Press, 1960.

——. *The Collected Works of C.G. Jung, Volume 7: Two Essays in Analytical Psychology*. Princeton University Press, 1953.

——. *The Collected Works of C.G. Jung, Volume 9 (Part 1): Archetypes and the Collective Unconscious*. Princeton University Press, 1980.

——. *The Collected Works of C.G. Jung Vol. 10: Civilization in Transition*. Princeton University Press, 1970.

——. *The Collected Works of C.G. Jung, Volume 15: Spirit in Man, Art, And Literature*. London: Routledge, Kegan and Paul, 1971.

——. *Memories, Dreams and Reflections*. New York: Vintage Books, 1965.

——. *The Red Book: Liber Novus*, edited by Sonu Shamdasani. W. W. Norton & Company, 2009.

——. *Synchronicity: An Acausal Connecting Principle*. Princeton University Press, 1960.

——. "Transformation Symbolism in the Mass." In *The Mysteries: Papers from the Eranos Yearbooks*. Princeton University Press, 1955.

Kemp, Daren. *New Age: A Guide: Alternative Spiritualities from Aquarian Conspiracy to Next Age*. Edinburgh University Press, 2004.

King, Preston. *Thomas Hobbes: Critical Assessments*. Routledge EBooks, 1993. http://ci.nii.ac.jp/ncid/BA18891323.

Kochunas, Brad Hiljanen. *The Astrological Imagination: Where Psyche and Cosmos Meet*. iUniverse, 2008.

Koch-Westenholz, Ulla. *Mesopotamian Astrology: An Introduction to Babylonian and Assyrian Celestial Divination*. Copenhagen: Museum Tusculanum Press, 1994.

Kolisko, Lili. "Working With the Stars In Earthly Substance." Rex Research, 1928. http://rexresearch.com/kolisko2/koliskoworking.html.

Kollerstrom, Nick. "Galileo's Astrology." Accessed May 18, 2023. http://www.skyscript.co.uk/galast.html.

Kuhn, Thomas. "Logic of Discovery or Psychology of Research?" In *The Philosophy of Karl Popper*, edited by Paul Arthur Schilpp, 798–819. La Salle, IL: Open Court, 1974.

Landwehr, Joe. *Astrology and the Archetypal Power of Numbers: Part Two: Arithmology in the Birthchart*. Whittier, NC: Ancient Tower Press, 2018.

——. *The Seven Gates of Soul: Reclaiming the Poetry of Everyday Life*. Abilene, TX: Ancient Tower Press, 2004.

——. *Tracking the Soul with an Astrology of Consciousness*. Mountain View, MO: Ancient Tower Press, 2007.

——. "Why Astrology Is Not a Science." Accessed May 6, 2023. https://www.joelandwehr.com/blog-posts-2/why-astrology-is-not-a-science.

Laufer, Berthold. "Origin of the Word Shaman." *American Anthropologist*, July 9, 1917. https://doi.org/10.1525/aa.1917.19.3.02a00020.

LeCron Foster, Mary. "Symbolism: The Foundation of Culture." In *Companion Encyclopaedia of Anthropology*, edited by Tim Ingold. Routledge, 1994.

Leo, Alan. *The Art of Synthesis*. London: Modern Astrology, 1936.

Leo, Bessie. *The Life and Work of Alan Leo, Theosophist, Astrologer, Mason*, 1919. Internet Archive. https://archive.org/details/lifeworkofalanle00leob/page/n5/mode/2up?view=theater.

Levy-Bruhl, Lucien. *How Natives Think*, translated by Lillian A. Claire. Martino Fine Books, 2015.

Lewis-Williams, David, and David Pearce. *Inside the Neolithic Mind: Consciousness, Cosmos and the Realm of the Gods*. Thames and Hudson, 2018.

Limar, Igor V. "C. G. Jung's Synchronicity and Quantum Entanglement: Schrödinger's Cat 'Wanders' Between Chromosomes." *NeuroQuantology* 9, no. 2 (2011): 313–21.

Lopez, Barry. *Horizon*. Vintage, 2019.

Machamer, Peter. "Galileo Galilei." Stanford Encyclopedia of Philosophy/Summer 2017 Edition. May 10, 2017. https://plato.stanford.edu/archives/sum2017/entries/galileo/.

Mahner, Martin. "Demarcating Science from Non-Science." In Elsevier EBooks, 515–75, 2007. https://doi.org/10.1016/b978-044451548-3/50011-2.

Martin, Major Desmond R., ed. "Below the Hindu Kush." *The Lady* CLX11, no. 4210 (December 9, 1965).

McDonough, Richard. "Karl Popper's Critical Rationalism And The Notion Of An 'Open Society.'" *The Postil Magazine*, March 1, 2021. https://www.thepostil.com/karl-poppers-critical-rationalism-and-the-notion-of-an-open-society/.

McKenna, Terence. *Food of the Gods: The Search for the Original Tree of Knowledge A Radical History of Plants, Drugs, and Human Evolution*. Bantam, 1992.

McRitchie, Kenneth. "Commentary of Geoffrey Dean and Ivan Kelly's Article, 'Is Astrology Relevant to Consciousness and Psi?" Astrological Reviews and Essays. Accessed April 28, 2023. https://www.astrologicalreviewletters.org/.

Meet the Slavs. "Firebird: Symbolism in Slavic Folklore & Mythology," May 14, 2022. https://meettheslavs.com/firebird/.

Mehta, Gautama. "How Scientists' Rush to Publish Covid-19 Research Fuels Disinformation." *Coda*, May 12, 2020. https://www.codastory.com/disinformation/scientists-pre-publish-disinformation/.

Mendelson, Michael. "Saint Augustine," November 12, 2010. https://plato.stanford.edu/archives/win2012/entries/augustine/.

Metzner, Ralph. *Well of Remembrance: Rediscovering the Earth Wisdom Myths of Northern Europe*. Shambala, 1994.

Meyer, Marvin W., and James M. Robinson. *The Nag Hammadi Scriptures: The International Edition*. HarperOne, 2007.

Murphy, Anthony. "The Hill of Tara - Teamhair." *Mythical Ireland*, September 14, 2022. https://mythicalireland.com/blogs/ancient-sites/the-hill-of-tara-teamhair.

Murray, Christopher John. *Encyclopedia of the Romantic Era, 1760–1850*. Routledge, 2013.

Murray, Gilbert. "The Stoic Philosophy; Conway Memorial Lecture Delivered at South Place Institute on March 16, 1915." Internet Archive, 1915. https://archive.org/details/thestoicphilosop00murruoft.

Narby, Jeremy. *The Cosmic Serpent: DNA and the Origins of Knowledge*. Tarcher, 1998.

NASA. "Constellations and the Calendar." Tumblr, September 20, 2016. https://nasa.tumblr.com/post/150688852794/zodiac?linkId=94146490.

Nasser, Rafael, Steven Forrest, and Robert Hand. *Under One Sky*. Borrego Springs, CA: Seven Paws Press, 2004.

Naughton, John. "Thomas Kuhn: The Man Who Changed the Way the World Looked at Science." *The Guardian*, March 22, 2018. https://www.theguardian.com/science/2012/aug/19/thomas-kuhn-structure-scientific-revolutions.

Needham, Joseph. *Science and Civilisation in China: Volume 3, Mathematics and the Sciences of the Heavens and the Earth*. Cambridge University Press, 1959.

Nelson, John. "Shortwave Radio Propagation Correlation with Planetary Positions." *RCA Review* XII, no. 1 (March 1951).

Neumann, Erich. "Mystical Man." In *The Mystic Vision: Papers from the Eranos Yearbooks*, Bolligen Series XXX 6:375–415. Princeton University Press, 1968.

——. *The Origins and History of Consciousness*. Bollingen Series. Vol. XLII. Princeton University Press, 1970.

O'Grady, Patricia. "Thales of Miletus | Internet Encyclopedia of Philosophy." Accessed May 12, 2023. https://iep.utm.edu/thales/.

Oken, Alan. *Soul-Centered Astrology: A Key to Expanding Yourself*. Freedom, CA: Crossing Press, 1996.

Oldmeadow, Harry. *Journeys East: 20th Century Western Encounters with Eastern Religious Traditions*. Bloomington, IN: World Wisdom, 2004.

Oliver, Mary. "The Summer Day." The Library of Congress. Accessed June 16, 2023. https://www.loc.gov/programs/poetry-and-literature/poet-laureate/poet-laureate-projects/poetry-180/all-poems/item/poetry-180-133/the-summer-day/.

Ouspensky, P. D. *In Search of the Miraculous: Fragments of an Unknown Teaching*. Houghton Mifflin Harcourt, 2001.

Ovid. *Fasti: Book I*. Accessed June 19, 2023. https://www.poetryintranslation.com/PITBR/Latin/OvidFastiBkOne.php.

Owen, Lance S. "C. G. Jung and the Prophet Puzzle." In *Jung's Red Book for Our Time: Searching for the Soul under Postmodern Conditions*, edited by Murray Stein and Thomas Arzt, Vol. 1. Chiron Publications, 2017.

National Park Service. "Ozark: A Historic Resource Study, Chapter 2: Early Native American and European Contact." Accessed June 22, 2023. https://www.nps.gov/parkhistory/online_books/ozar/hrs2.htm.

Paulsson, B. Schulz. "Radiocarbon Dates and Bayesian Modeling Support Maritime Diffusion Model for Megaliths in Europe." *Proceedings of the National Academy of Sciences of the United States of America* 116, no. 9 (February 26, 2019): 3460–65. https://doi.org/10.1073/pnas.1813268116.

Perry, Glenn. "Astrological Research: From Paradigm To Method." Accessed April 28, 2023. https://aaperry.com/astrological-research/.

——. "How Do We Know What We Think We Know? From Paradigm to Method in Astrological Research." In *Astrological Research Methods: An ISAR Anthology*, edited by Mark Pottenger, Vol. 1. Los Angeles: International Society for Astrological Research, 1995.

——. *Stealing Fire from the Gods: New Directions in Astrological Research*. East Hampton, CT: The Academy of AstroPsychology, 2006.

——. "Sun Square Pluto: Aspect of the False Self." *The Journal of Astro-Psychology* 4, no. 4 (1991): 1–13.

Plese, Zlatko. "Fate, Providence and Astrology in Gnosticism (1): The Apocryphon of John." Unc, June 3, 2014. https://www.academia.edu/3063711/Fate_Providence_and_Astrology_in_Gnosticism_1_The_Apocryphon_of_John.

Plutarch. "Romulus." The Internet Classics Archive. Accessed June 19, 2023. https://classics.mit.edu/Plutarch/romulus.html.

Polkinghorne, Donald E. *Methodology for the Human Sciences: Systems of Inquiry*. State University of New York Press, 1983.

Pollan, Michael. *How to Change Your Mind: What the New Science of Psychedelics Teaches Us About Consciousness, Dying, Addiction, Depression, and Transcendence*. Penguin, 2018.

Pollock, Sheldon. "The Revelation of Tradition: Sruti, Smriti, and the Sanskrit Discourse of Power." In *Boundaries, Dynamics and Construction of Traditions in South Asia*, edited by Federico Squarcini. London: Anthem Press, 2011.

Popper, Karl Raimund. *Conjectures and Refutations: The Growth of Scientific Knowledge*, Routledge, 2014.

Porter, Theodore M. "Probability and Statistics | History, Examples, & Facts." Encyclopedia Britannica, September 9, 2005. https://www.britannica.com/science/probability.

Prine Pauls, Elizabeth. "Matriarchy | Social System." Encyclopedia Britannica, July 20, 1998. https://www.britannica.com/topic/matriarchy.

"Review of The Theory of Celestial Influences." *Gurdjieff International Review* II (3) (1999). https://www.gurdjieff.org/index.en.htm.

Richards, William G. *Sacred Knowledge: Psychedelics and Religious Experiences*. Columbia University Press, 2016.

Ricoeur, Paul. *Freud and Philosophy: An Essay on Interpretation*. Yale University Press, 1970.

——. *The Symbolism of Evil*. Boston, MA: Beacon Press, 1967.

Rifkin, Jeremy. *The Empathic Civilization: The Race to Global Consciousness in a World in Crisis*. Penguin, 2009.

Rilke, Rainer Maria. *Letters To a Young Poet*. Norton & Company, 1954.

Rincon, Paul. "BBC NEWS | Science/Nature | 'Earliest Writing' Found in China." Accessed May 12, 2023. http://news.bbc.co.uk/2/hi/science/nature/2956925.stm.

Roberts, Courtney. "Christian Astrology, the Dark Ages, and the Celtic Church." Accessed May 16, 2023. http://cura.free.fr/xxx/29robts.html.

Robson, Vivian, ed. *The Complete Dictionary of Astrology*. Rochester, VT: Destiny Books, 1983.

Rossi, Safron. "Planetary Interiority: James Hillman & the Archetypal Psyche." AstroSynthesis. Accessed June 16, 2023. https://www.astrosynthesis.com.au/wp-content/uploads/2020/12/Planetary-Interiority-Safron-Rossi.pdf.

Rudhyar, Dane. "Astrological Timing: The Transition to the New Age." Rudhyar Archival Project. Accessed June 16, 2023. http://www.khaldea.com/rudhyar/at/at_c6_pp7.shtml.

——. *The Astrology of Personality: A Re-Formulation of Astrological Concepts and Ideals, in Terms of Contemporary Psychology and Philosophy*. Doubleday, 1970.

——. *The Astrology of Transformation: A Multilevel Approach*. Wheaton, IL: Theosophical Publishing House, 1980.

Rutkin, H. Darrel. "The Use and Abuse of Ptolemy's Tetrabiblos in Renaissance and Early Modern Europe." In *Ptolemy in Perspective: Use and Criticism of His Work from Antiquity to the Nineteenth Century*, edited by Alexander Jones. Springer, 2010. http://ci.nii.ac.jp/ncid/BB00470708.

Saltelli, Andrea, and Silvio Funtowicz. "What Is Science's Crisis Really about?" *Futures* 91 (August 1, 2017): 5–11. https://doi.org/10.1016/j.futures.2017.05.010.

Sams, Jamie, and David Carson. *Sacred Path Cards: The Discovery of Self Through Native Teachings*. HarperOne, 1990.

Santucci, James A. "Blavatsky, Helena Petrovna." In *Dictionary of Gnosis & Western Esotericism*, edited by Wouter J. Hanegraaff. Leiden, Netherlands: Brill Academic Publishers, 2006.

Schermer, Barbara. *Astrology Alive!: Experiential Astrology, Astrodrama, and the Healing Arts*. HarperCollins, 1989.

——. "Experiential Astrology." In TheFreeDictionary.Com. Accessed May 19, 2023. https://encyclopedia2.thefreedictionary.com/Experiential+Astrology.

Schniedewind, William. "Origins of the Written Bible." NOVA | PBS, November 18, 2008. https://www.pbs.org/wgbh/nova/article/origins-written-bible/.

Schroeder, Jeanne Lorraine. *The Vestal and the Fasces: Hegel, Lacan, Property, and the Feminine*. Berkeley: Univ of California Press, 1998.

Scofield, Bruce. "Were They Astrologers? – Big League Scientists and Astrology." *The Mountain Astrologer* 80: August/September (1998).

Sedgwick, Mark. "European Neo-Sufi Movements in the Inter-War Period." In *Inter-War Europe*, edited by Natalie Clayer and Eric Germain. Columbia University Press, 2008.

Seymour, Percy. *Astrology: The Evidence of Science*, 1991. https://openlibrary.org/books/OL15306678M/Astrology.

Sheldon, Tom. "Preprints Could Promote Confusion and Distortion." *Nature* 559, no. 7715 (July 24, 2018): 445. https://doi.org/10.1038/d41586-018-05789-4.

Shlain, Leonard. *The Alphabet Versus the Goddess: The Conflict Between Word and Image*. Penguin, 1999.

Singer, Charles. *A Short History of Science to the Nineteenth Century*. Oxford: Clarendon Press, 1941.

Smallwood, Christine. "Astrology in the Age of Uncertainty." *The New Yorker*, October 21, 2019. https://www.newyorker.com/magazine/2019/10/28/astrology-in-the-age-of-uncertainty.

Smit, Rudolf. "Grand Summary." Accessed April 28, 2023. https://www.astrology-and-science.com/u-gran2.htm.

Smith, Robin. "Aristotle's Logic." Stanford Encyclopedia of Philosophy. November 22, 2022. https://plato.stanford.edu/entries/aristotle-logic/#AriLogWorOrg.

Snow, Edward. "New Study Confirms Gauquelin 'Plus Zones.'" The Friends of Astrology Inc. Accessed May 6, 2023. http://www.friendsofastrology.org/featured-articles/new-study-confirms-gauquelin-plus-zones-may-2016.

Starfield, Barbara. "Is US Health Really the Best in the World?" *JAMA* 284, no. 4 (July 26, 2000): 483. https://doi.org/10.1001/jama.284.4.483.

Stausberg, Michael, Yuhan Sohrab-Dinshaw Vevaina, and Anna Tessmann. "The Wiley Blackwell Companion to Zoroastrianism." In Wiley EBooks, 2015. https://doi.org/10.1002/9781118785539.

Stein, Murray, and Thomas Arzt. *Jung's Red Book for Our Time: Searching for Soul Under Postmodern Conditions. Vol. 1*. Asheville, NC: Chiron Publications, 2017.

Steiner, Rudolf. *Approaches to Anthroposophy*. Sussex, England: Rudolf Steiner Press, 1992.

——. "Lecture III. Realities Beyond Birth and Death - Vol. 180. On the Mysteries of Ancient and Modern Times." Rudolf Steiner Archive, December 29, 1917. https://wn.rsarchive.org/Lectures/GA180/English/AM1929/19171229p01.html.

——. "Lecture VIII. Man's Connection with the Various Planetary Bodies - Vol. 105. Universe, Earth and Man." Rudolf Steiner Archive, August 12, 1908. https://wn.rsarchive.org/Lectures/Dates/19080812p01.html.

——. "Lecture XIII - Vol. 232. Mystery Centers." Rudolf Steiner Archive, December 22, 1923. https://wn.rsarchive.org/Lectures/GA232/English/GC1985/19231222p01.html.

Stenger, Victor J. *Quantum Gods: Creation, Chaos, and the Search for Cosmic Consciousness*. Buffalo, NY: Prometheus Books, 2009.

Symonds, John, ed. *The Complete Astrological Writings of Aleister Crowley*. Gloucester, England: Duckworth, 1974.

Tarnas, Richard. *Cosmos and Psyche: Intimations of a New World View*. Viking, 2006.

——. *Prometheus the Awakener: An Essay on the Archetypal Meaning of the Planet Uranus*. Woodstock, CT: Spring Publications, 1995.

——. *The Passion of the Western Mind: Understanding the Ideas That Have Shaped Our World View*. Ballantine Books, 1991.

Temperance, Elani. "Hestia versus Dionysos." Accessed June 20, 2023. https://baringtheaegis.blogspot.com/2013/03/hestia-versus-dionysos.html.

Tester, Jim. *A History of Western Astrology*. Ballentine Books, 1987.

Thagard, Paul. "Why Astrology Is a Pseudoscience." *PSA*, 1978, no. 1 (January 1, 1978): 223–34. https://doi.org/10.1086/psaprocbienmeetp.1978.1.192639.

Theodosiou, Efstratios, Vassilios N. Manimanis, and Milan S. Dimitrijevic. "Astrology in the Early Byzantine Empire and the Anti-Astrology Stance of the Church Fathers." ResearchGate, June 1, 2012. https://www.researchgate.net/publication/248386545_Astrology_in_the_early_byzantine_empire_and_the_anti-astrology_stance_of_the_church_fathers.

Thun, Maria. *The Biodynamic Year: Increasing Yield, Quality and Flavour - 100 Helpful Tips for the Gardener Or Smallholder*. East Sussex, England: Temple Lodge Publishing, 2010.

Trismegistus, Hermes. *The Emerald Tablet of Hermes*. Createspace, 2017.

Van Gent, R.H. "Isaac Newton and Astrology." Accessed May 19, 2023. http://www.staff.science.uu.nl/~gent0113/astrology/newton.htm.

Velleman, Paul F. "Truth, Damned Truth and Statistics." *Journal of Statistics Education* 16, no. 2 (2008). http://jse.amstat.org/v16n2/velleman.html.

Voss, Angela. "Astrology: The Astrology of Marsilio Ficino: Divination or Science?" Accessed May 17, 2023. http://cura.free.fr/decem/10voss.html.

Vreede, Elisabeth. *Anthroposophy and Astrology: The Astronomical Letters of Elizabeth Vreede*. Great Barrington, MA: Anthroposophic Press, 2001.

Washington, Peter. *Madame Blavatsky's Baboon: Theosophy and the Emergence of the Western Guru*. London: Secker & Warburg, 1993.

Wasserstein, Ronald L., and Nicole A. Lazar. "The ASA Statement on p-Values: Context, Process, and Purpose." *The American Statistician* 70, no. 2 (April 2, 2016): 129–33. https://doi.org/10.1080/00031305.2016.1154108.

Welch, Louise. *Orage with Gurdjieff in America*. Boston: Routledge & Kegan Paul, 1982.

Wellbeloved, Sophia. "Gurdjieff 'Old' or 'New Age': Aristotle or Astrology?" *JASANAS* 1 (2005). https://ccwe.wordpress.com/sophia-wellbeloveds-academic-research-page/.

Wertz, Frederick J. "Qualitative Inquiry in the History of Psychology." *Qualitative Psychology* 1, no. 1 (February 1, 2014): 4–16. https://doi.org/10.1037/qup0000007.

West, Anthony. "The Gauquelin Controversy April, 2016." The Friends of Astrology Inc. Accessed May 6, 2023. http://www.friendsofastrology.org/featured-articles/the-gauquelin-controversy-april-2016.

Westran, Paul. "Replicated Study Enhances Astrological Claims." Astrology News Service, June 11, 2021. https://astrologynewsservice.com/research/replicated-study-enhances-astrological-claims/.

Wheeler, Brannon M. *Prophets in the Quran: An Introduction to the Quran and Muslim Exegesis*. A&C Black, 2002.

Whitehouse, David. *Renaissance Genius: Galileo Galilei & His Legacy to Modern Science*. New York: Sterling, 2009.

Whitfield, Peter. *Astrology: A History*. New York: Harry N. Abrams, 2001.

Wikipedia. "History of Scientific Method." Accessed May 8, 2023. https://en.wikipedia.org/wiki/History_of_scientific_method.

——. "Landwehr," April 2, 2023. https://en.wikipedia.org/wiki/Landwehr.

——. "Vesta (Mythology)." Accessed June 19, 2023. https://en.wikipedia.org/wiki/Vesta_(mythology).

Wilber, Ken. *Quantum Questions: Mystical Writings of the World's Great Physicists*. Shambhala, 2001.

Willcox, Walter F. "The Founder of Statistics." *Revue De L'Institut International De Statistique* 5, no. 4 (January 1, 1938): 321–28. https://doi.org/10.2307/1400906.

Williams, Matt. "Who Was Galileo Galilei?" Universe Today, October 8, 2019. https://www.universetoday.com/48756/galileo-facts/.

Winborn, Mark, ed. *Shared Realities: Participation Mystique and Beyond.* Skiatook, OK: Fisher King Press, 2014.

Wolff, Robert. *Original Wisdom: Stories of an Ancient Way of Knowing.* Inner Traditions, 2001.

World Health Organization. "Managing the COVID-19 Infodemic: Promoting Healthy Behaviours and Mitigating the Harm from Misinformation and Disinformation." News, September 23, 2020. https://www.who.int/news/item/23-09-2020-managing-the-covid-19-infodemic-promoting-healthy-behaviours-and-mitigating-the-harm-from-misinformation-and-disinformation.

World Wildlife Fund. "Amazon | Places | WWF." Accessed May 11, 2023. https://www.worldwildlife.org/places/amazon.

Wray, David. "Astrology in Ancient Rome: Poetry, Prophecy and Power." Accessed May 16, 2023. http://fathom.lib.uchicago.edu/1/777777122543/.

Yates, Frances. *Giordano Bruno and the Hermetic Tradition.* Routledge, 2014.

York, Michael. *The Emerging Network: A Sociology of the New Age and Neo-Pagan Movements.* Rowman & Littlefield, 1995.

Zimecki, M. "The Lunar Cycle: Effects on Human and Animal Behavior and Physiology." PubMed, 2006. https://pubmed.ncbi.nlm.nih.gov/16407788/.

The range of the human mind, the scale and depth of the metaphors the mind is capable of manufacturing as it grapples with the universe, stand in stunning contrast to the belief that there is only one reality . . .

To allow mystery, which to say to yourself, "There could be more, there could be things we don't understand," is not to damn knowledge. It is to take a wider view. It is to permit yourself an extraordinary freedom; someone else does not have to be wrong in order that you may be right.

Reality is a mystery and bound to remain so. And it may be as good an idea to live within the mystery as it is to stand outside, possessed of the notion that it can be explained.

Barry Lopez, Of Wolves and Men, 1978

Irrespective of how much we work at it, we will never understand all there is to know about the universe or this planet. We are children counting grains of sand at the seashore - and we will never be anything else. The impact of that realization forces a great humility.

Stephen Harrod Buhner, Plant Intelligence and the Imaginal Realm, 2014

Index

A

B

C

D

E

F

G

H

I

J

K

L

M

N

O

P

Q

R

S

T

U

V

W

X

Y

Z

Astrology and the Archetypal Power of Numbers
Part Two: Arithmology in the Birthchart

by Joe Landwehr

ISBN: 978-0-9747626-3-0
LCCN: 2010913875
LOC: BF1711.L362 2017 DD: 133.5

652 pages (including appendices, bibliography and index)

$39.95 retail price plus shipping and handling

Which system holds the key to understanding the universe, astrology or mathematics? Planets or numbers? Probably the best answer is "Yes." And in *Astrology and the Archetypal Power of Numbers*, Joe Landwehr masterfully brings the two systems together in a kind of divinatory United Field Theory. His book is an impresive intellectual *tour de force*, with all the principles backed up with copious chart examples. I heartily recommend it! - **Steven Forrest**, master teacher, author of *The Inner Sky*

Astrology and the Archetypal Power of Numbers (both parts) is the work of a wise, hardworking, and resourceful person who has put much of his life-energy into using astrology to understand and guide others. I especially appreciated his determination to go beyond self-actualization and look at how we as individuals participate in a larger world, and that the astrological chart can give indications how this can happen. Daunting and difficult as it may be, Joe Landwehr's work deserves respecct for its strong positive motivation and its great originality. - **Joseph Crane**, Director of the Astrology Institute

Referencing many birthcharts and attendant life stories, Landwehr writes about individual souls as well as the collective memories that influence the movment of history and specific world events. These examples are gratifying to read, since he tells these stories with many quotations from biographical and autobiographical sources, and he places these world events into substantive historical context. - **Mary Plumb**, review in the February/March issue of *The Mountain Astrologer*

In this book, Master Astrologer Joe Landwehr weaves togetehr systems of knowledge gained through decades of deep exploration and practice of astrology and numerology. Though I'm not well-educated in numerology, Landwehr's discussion of planetary themes in the realm of numbers 1-9, engaged me at a new level, offering new insights on the astrology front as well. Landwehr's evocative phraseology reveals stimulating and useful insights on a variety of topics. This is one I keep handy to open up for inspiration, often ending up following a new trail - perhaps Pluto's resonance with Five or its aspects with Pallas - made easy using his excellent, suggestive index, one of my favorite parts of the book. Somehow *Astrology and the Archetypal Power of Numbers* tailors itself to the reader in a rare and special way. I recommend you give it a read and find out for yourself. - **M. Kelley Hunter**, author of *Dark Moon Lilith*

Astrology and the Archetypal Power of Numbers
Part One: Contemporary Reformulation
of Pythagorean Number Theory

by Joe Landwehr

ISBN: 978-0-9747626-2-3
LCCN: 2010913875
LOC: BF1711.L36 2011 DD: 133.5

361 pages (including appendices, bibliography and index)

$19.95 retail price plus shipping and handling

As astrologers, we make extensive use of numbers for everything from chart calculaton to aspect theory. Yet very little has been written on the relationship between astrology and numbers and much of what has been written is very sketchy. Joe Landwehr has set out remedy this with the first of a two-volume set that will ulitmately allow you to use this system of Pythagorean number theory with your chart and add to the system of spiritual astro-psychology elucidated in Landwehr's previous books. Heartily recommended to astromythologists, psychospiritual astrologers, and those interested in Pythagorean theory in relation to astrology. - **Donna Van Toen**, *NCGR Newsletter*, May-June 2011

How can you take a tour of the counting numbers, each in turn, and yet have the sense that you have been exploring the very nonlinear reaches of a fractal galaxy? Yes we begin at 0, and yes, we progress linearly through 9, but this book is a framework for a very nonlinear, enlightening and sometimes breathtaking journey through the landscape of humanness. – **Dr. Mark Arnold**, Associate Professor of Mathematical Sciences, University of Arkansas – Fayetteville

Astrology and the Archetypal Power of Numbers, Part One is to be read as an epic poem that moves into unknown realms below, above and beyond our usual daily lives. This impressive work of scholarship is not an easy read, but then whoever said that deep knowledge is undemanding? The book offers a new language for living everyday in a deeper and more meaningful spiritual context within the cosmos. Like a long slow thermal mineral bath, this is the type of experience each reader will want to come back to, again and again. – **Dr. Jonathan de Vierville**, Professor of Humanities, History and Interdisciplinary Studies at St. Philips College, San Antonio, TX

The book's author is one of the few who has the intelligence and commitment to rescue the invaluable *kerygmas* of the Great Wisdom Traditions that modernist and post-modernist perspectives have all but have erased from contemporary minds. He legitimizes the core ideas in astrology and numbers as archetypes by interfacing them with his profound knowledge of several schools of psychology, Eastern religions, mythology, awareness of environmental issues and courageous self-exploration. Landwehr not only displays a wide range of speculation, he is a superb discursive writer. – **Dr. Rockey Robbins**, Assistant Professor of Counseling Psychology, University of Oklahoma – Norman

Tracking the Soul with an Astrology of Consciousness

by Joe Landwehr

ISBN: 978-0-9747626-1-6

LCCN: 2006909996

LOC: BD421.L363 2007 DD: 128'.1

498 pages (including appendices, bibliography and index)

$24.95 retail price plus shipping and handling

This book is a marvelously imagined integration between western astrology and Indian metaphysic. Joe Landwehr displays a wide-ranging mastery of the material and communicates it crisply and clearly to his audience. Readers interested in deepening their understanding of chakra theory in its application to astrology would do well to open this treasure house of ancient knowledge written from a modern psychological perspective. – **Brad Kochunas**, author of *The Astrological Imagination*

This excellent book describes the relationship of astrological symbols to the psychology of the chakra system. Joe Landwehr shows how the natal chart and transits become a basis for inner work and transformative yoga, helping us work through the emotional issues and energetic blocks associated with each chakra, to become progressively liberated on every level. Joe writes with heart and humor, focus and fire, drawing the reader into a deeper personal experience of astrology as a living spiritual philosophy and a tool for consciousness growth, This book is inspiring reading for astrologers of all levels. Highly recommended. – **Greg Bogart**, author of *Astrology and Meditation: The Fearless Contemplation of Change*

Joe Landwehr's *Tracking the Soul* is a fascinating and eloquent look the spiritual dimensions of astrology. His take on the relationship between astrology and the chakras is original, and bound to stimulate further discussion on this important topic. Highly recommended. – **Ray Grasse**, author of *The Waking Dream* and *Signs of the Times*

Joe Landwehr's ability to communicate is so extraordinary it took me several chapters to comprehend the scope of his scope and relax into reading his work. It's the difference between listening to a guy plucking on his guitar in the corner of a coffee shop and being in the room with a full-blown symphony orchestra, you have to adjust. But as I grew used to being stimulated on multiple levels simultaneously I became more and more appreciative of the author who manages to teach while being both spiritual and sober. He is also high-minded and deep. He is humble and confident and I was thrilled when midway through this ride (half-way through the book) he included his own chart like some kind of present that explained it all and I had to laugh. You can get your copy direct from him at Ancient Tower Press and if you do you are bound to be enriched in the same way a trip to the symphony feeds the soul. – **Elsa Panizzon**, ElsaElsa.com

The Seven Gates of Soul:
Reclaiming the Poetry of Everyday Life

by Joe Landwehr

ISBN: 978-0-9747626-0-9

LCCN: 2004091983

LOC: BD421.1.L36 2004 DD: 128'.1

472 pages (including appendices, bibliography and index)

$29.95 retail price plus shipping and handling

Here you will find an ingenious, carefully laid out path not only to a deep practice of astrology, but also to the wisdom of the ages. This book is nothing less than an imaginative course in the Western imagination, culminating in astropoetics, itself an ancient idea now brought to life by Joe Landwehr. It's about time astrology was given its place in the history of thought. ~ **Thomas Moore**, author of *Care of the Soul* and *Dark Nights of the Soul*

Joe Landwehr is a creative and imaginative thinker and has given us a rich treatment of a complex subject. . . . *The Seven Gates of Soul* is . . . a welcome addition to the growing body of work in recent years that aims to question assumptions held by contemporary astrologers and to inspire us to consider astrology in the wider cultural and spiritual context. ~ **Mary Plumb**, *The Mountain Astrologer* (July, August, 2005)

This is a huge book. . . vast, encompassing and a complete philosophy in itself. . . . Mr. Landwehr clearly has been thinking for a very long time about astrology, philosophy and the moral and theological issues that have vexed humanity from the beginning of intellectual time. Not only that, he also concerns himself with the issues that went before intellectual time; times when there was no Cartesian divide, no chasm between nature and culture, body and soul. . . . His work in this book is extensive, and in the reading, expansive. From "participation mystique" – the time of total involvement between human and its environment – through post-Newtonian science, Landwehr explores the vast realm of the historical and practical aspects of astrology and philosophy. ~ **Erin Sullivan**, *The international Astrologer* (Winter/Spring, 2005)

A well written, extensively researched and thought-provoking book... a brave attempt to fill a massive gap in basic astrological theory . . . His attempt is . . . of immense value and it will surely stimulate others to think long and deep about the essential foundation of our subject.~ **Ken Gillman**, *Considerations* (November, 2004)

I think the book is quite special. . . It may be the kind of book that doesn't create a sudden excitement, but will become a classic, growing slowly in popularity over the next decades. ~ **Brita Adkinson**, *New Age Retailer*

Imaginal Meandering

Not all who wander are lost

Gandalf

Beyond the symbolism of the birthchart is a story. The story might appear to be about your life, but that is really only the outer layer of a vast epic, part fairy tale, part myth, part movie script being written in real time. In many ways, the birthchart is merely a point of entry to this larger story, and an opportunity for you to meander through the imaginal landscape of your own pscyhe in search of archetypal adventure. The process begins with a pattern that seems ripe for illumination and perhaps transformation to a higher level of possibility. But then, over the source of six (or more) sessions, we will follow a trail that reveals itself only as we walk it, into the heart of something unexpected and magical.

I met Joe when I was exploring whether and how to reshape my psychotherapy practice following the forced stuckness of Covid. Since then, I've found working with him to be so worthwhile. He's extremely challenging and also highly supportive. He's funny and kind, also sharp and pointed. He's learned and wise which so are not the same thing. We never quite know how a session is going to go, and that's exciting. He's real and doesn't hide, which is encouraging me to do the same both with him and in my practice. – **S. W.**, a client from Epsom, Surrey, UK

I reached out to Joe for astrological guidance on navigating a confusing, transitional phase in my life. But there was no way I could have anticipated the profoundly insightful, spiritually-rich adventure I was signing up for. Less than a year later, I'm forging a new path in my career; my sense of identity feels expanded and more dynamic; and my everyday life is imbued with a newfound sense of meaning, excitement, and an indescribable reverence for the mystery of life and my place within it. Working with Joe isn't for the faint of heart. He's wiser than Yoda and Gandalf combined, and what you'll learn about yourself on this journey can (and will!) call you to adventure. I suspect it's nearly impossible to embark on this exploration together with Joe, and not create unbelievable magic in your life. – **J. B.**, a client from Red Bank, New Jersey

Learn more at www.joelandwehr.com/consultations

Printed in the USA
CPSIA information can be obtained
at www.ICGtesting.com
CBHW080045010424
6154CB00001B/1